RANDY TURNE

5:41

Stories from the Joplin Tornado

**10-YEAR
ANNIVERSARY
EDITION**

To the people of Joplin and those who came to help

Table of Contents

Table of Contents

Table of Contents

Table of Contents

Introduction

By Randy Turner

For those of us who live in Joplin, it seems impossible to believe that nearly 10 years have passed since the tornado obliterated much of our landscape.

Everywhere we turn, we see a reminder of May 22, 2011, whether it be in the new school buildings that replaced those that were lost, new construction that is still happening in the areas that were in the tornado's path and in the places where we look and remember what used to be- the stores where we shopped, the homes where we lived, structures that had stood the test of time, but within a few deadly moments, were consigned to memory.

The tornado that hit our town was the deadliest to touch down in the United States in six decades and the reporting began on it almost immediately.

Many of us listened to KZRG, which immediately dropped its regular programming and spent the next nine days serving as a lifeline to the community and as a voice to the world.

Editor Carol Stark and the staff at the Joplin Globe threw themselves into coverage of an event that not only affected much of their readership, but which had also cost many of them their homes

Barbara Bryant is shown with some of the few possessions she was able to salvage after her home was destroyed. Photo by Jace Anderson, FEMA

and cost one staff member, page designer Bruce Baillie, his life.

Regional, state and national media descended upon Joplin to tell the world what was happening here.

Thanks to social media, the story of the Joplin Tornado began to spread almost immediately. Within minutes of the tornado, people began posting their stories and photos.

It was those stories that inspired the first edition of this book when it was published in August 2011. Thanks to social media and particularly, in this case, to Facebook, we began collecting these stories and received permission to publish them.

The idea was to allow survivors to tell their stories, without the filter of the media, simply their thoughts and emotions laid bare within minutes or days of the disaster.

At the time of the tornado, my co-author John Hacker was managing editor of the Carthage Press, holding a job that I held through much of the 1990s. John collected even more tornado stories, as well as offering coverage of the recovery period and especially chronicling the work of local hospitals and charities and the volunteers who came from across the United States and the world to lend a hand to a community in need.

In 2011, I was working as an eighth-grade English teacher at East Middle School, one of the schools that was destroyed in the tornado. I began to write the stories of that school, as well as a district that immediately set a goal of starting school on time in August- less than three months after the tornado.

In addition to those stories and others we contributed to the book, as well as stories told by the numerous photos that were featured, Hacker and I decided to print documents, as well as transcripts of speeches that told Joplin's story to the world, some made by local officials, others from ministers, celebrities and officials from Joplin, the state, Congress and all the way up to the president.

This edition features more stories, more photos and transcripts and documents.

The transcripts begin with the addresses delivered by Pastor Aaron Brown, Gov. Jay Nixon and President Barack Obama at the Joplin Tornado Memorial Service May 29, 2011, and continue on to then Vice President Joe Biden's speech at the dedication of the new Joplin High School October 3, 2014.

The final section of this book features the stories of those who lost their lives as a result of the tornado.

Our hope is that the story of the bravery and spirit of the people of Joplin and how the people of the nation rallied around them will offer a valuable lesson in these polarizing times.

When the volunteers came to Joplin after May 22, 2011, no one asked people in need whether they were Democrats or Republicans.

The only question they asked was "How can we help?"

Randy Turner | John Hacker

Surviving

By John Hacker

Moments after a category EF-4 tornado turned the heart of Joplin's residential district into a post-apocalyptic wasteland, bloodied, wet and tired survivors began to emerge from the wreckage and take stock of a new reality.

Many who emerged from the rubble of homes around 20th Street and Wisconsin Avenue bore some kind of injury, but they rushed to help others who were trapped in the rubble of churches and apartments in the area.

This remarkable storm's sound, a powerful roar that permeated everything for a few brief moments, was a theme that ran through most residents' tales of survival.

Larry Thomas emerged from the rubble that was the Missouri Place Apartments remarkably uninjured, but he knew his neighbors were not so lucky.

"There's some fatalities back there," Thomas said. "I suspect that the woman across the hall from me stayed in her apartment thinking she was going to be safe and it's gone, too."

Thomas said the roar was the first thing that got his attention.

"I opened my bedroom window and looked in this direction and heard the freight train coming," Thomas said. "I was in the hallway

A husband receives help removing his wife and 82-year-old mother from a car in the area south of 20th Street. Photo by John Hacker

and we've got glass doors on both ends and it just busted the windows out. The wind shoved me into a vacant apartment. It forced the door open into a vacant apartment and I got into the kitchen which is a narrow little place and I hunkered down. I've lost a lot of property in there, but I came out of it — let me see, do I have any scrapes? Not really. I have mud on me. I'm alive."

As he walked on Wisconsin Avenue, looking for the home of one of his professors, Thomas, who is also vice chair of the Homeless Coalition for Jasper and Newton counties, wondered about his future.

"My desktop and my laptop are gone and I'm due to start school in two weeks," Thomas said.

"At Pitt State, I have one summer class, and this fall I have my practicum and then I've got my bachelor's degree. I don't have transportation to get there now, it's trashed."

Edward Allen pulled himself from the rubble of his home at 2308 Indiana Ave. after the tornado passed. Photo by John Hacker

VICTIMS TO RESCUERS

All over the neighborhood south of 20th Street and east of the shattered Joplin High School, victims became rescuers as they struggled to deal with the loss of homes and loved ones.

Several people took crowbars and their bare hands, anything, they could find to rip into a small white car on the side of Wisconsin Avenue and pull two older women out of it.

A man covered in blood and with a swollen face watched and tried to help the rescuers get his wife and her mother out of the car.

The man said the three were headed for their home in the 2900 block of Wisconsin Avenue, but they didn't make it and rode out the EF-4 tornado in their small white Toyota.

"I got hit in the face by a two-by-four, or that's what it felt like," the man said. "I lifted my head up for a second when the wind started pushing the car and something hit me."

Larry Thomas was uninjured, but he knew some of his neighbors in the Missouri Place Apartments were not so lucky. Photo by John Hacker

With the doors jammed, the man's wife and her 82-year-old mother were trapped in the car. Both were covered in blood from cuts and scrapes. Debris covered the car; some had come through the windows and pummeled the three occupants.

Finally, rescuers were able to pry open the driver's side door.

As that was happening, others were yelling for anyone who could to run to the nearby Mormon Church on Indiana Street to help pull trapped people out of that flattened building.

Edward Allen was one of many survivors who dove for their bathroom and rode out Sunday's storm that tore his home at 2308 Illinois Ave. to pieces.

"The last I saw on the TV, it was going off and on, and they said you hit cover," Allen said. "If you can still hear us, take cover. So I ran in the bathroom and all I had in there was one of those mats, the big fuzzy one, and I put over my head. There are some two-bys

A home burns west of Joplin High School in the wake of the tornado. Countless natural gas leaks fed some flames in the rubble. Photo by John Hacker

fell right there beside me."

Allen said the storm seemed to last a lifetime.

"I knew that it was a tornado, and it was a-coming, and I was just wondering when it was going to stop," he said. "The bathroom was kind of in the middle of the house, that's what they recommend. It did work because these other places and my place are just gone."

Once the winds died down, Allen, who lived by himself, faced another challenge — hail the size of golf balls started falling on his suddenly-exposed bathroom.

"After it hit, the top of my bathroom was gone," he said. "I went to another room because it began to hail real bad, so I got in the other bathroom and other closet and that area still had kind of a cover over it, so I got in there. I'm not hurt, I don't know why."

As he walked around with shirts tied around his neck, Allen was in shock, but he was also thankful.

"I look up and say God I'm thankful I'm still alive," he said. "That's what you can do."

Ron Smith's pickup was battered, likely beyond repair, but for a while on Sunday it served as shelter for him and his wife, Ellen and their two dogs, Buddy and Buffy after the tornado shattered their home at 2402 Illinois Ave.

Ron and Ellen Smith took cover with their two dogs in their bathroom as the winds of up to 195 miles per hour ripped their home apart.

"There was a big roar," Ellen Smith said. "We were in the dining room and the TV went out and I heard that roar toward the west and there was some kind of banging all of a sudden. We grabbed the dogs and headed to the bathroom."

At first, Ron dismissed the warnings on television, but he soon changed his mind.

"I was sitting in the dining room watching TV thinking, oh, it's just another damn storm," Ron Smith said. "She came in and said did you hear that roar, and I started to hear it. We barely made it to the bathroom in the hall with the dogs."

"The way that roar sounded and the shaking of the doors and the walls, you don't know what's going to happen," Ellen Smith continued. "I've been through tornados, but they were small ones in Wisconsin."

The destruction of their home and its contents was dire, but their situation was made even more serious because of a decision the two made just a few weeks ago out of economic necessity.

"I lost my job a few months ago and we had to cancel the insurance on the house last month," Ron Smith said. "I couldn't afford it; it was $400 a month. We've got probably a good $50,000 or $60,000 worth of furniture in there and it's all ruined."

The two were upbeat about their situation as they looked around at the devastation that surrounded them.

As they sat, their daughter, Joanna, and granddaughter, Hannah, fought their way through the rubble-strewn streets to reach them.

Daughter and granddaughter broke down emotionally as they held Ron and Ellen.

"We didn't hear about this until 30 minutes after, and they said the Joplin school is gone," Joanna said. "We had to get over here, we had to. I didn't care how long it took us. It took us an hour to get here from the mall. We went down one road and had to turn around, down another road and they said it was blocked. The closer I got here, the more damage you could see.

"We're getting the hell out of here. We've got to get out of here. Now where are you going to stay, you all are going to have to come to my place now."

Randy Turner | John Hacker

the Stories

Randy Turner | John Hacker

forty-five Seconds That Changed Everything

By Kelly Maddy

It started much like any other Sunday. Getting up around 9ish, mowing a few lawns, and Adriel bustling around the house cleaning up before we started our work week. It is always our day to get the house looking good for the week, so it doesn't stress us out through the busy days where we don't have time to mess with it.

Later on, it would all seem so funny. Washing the dishes, putting clothes away, storing my lawn mower nice and snug by my garage with weed-eater. We had no idea this would all be for naught.

3:40 P.M.

I was finishing my last lawn and started heading back on East 32nd toward my house on 20th and Kentucky. I watched the development of a supercell storm on my phone's radar app near Parsons, Kansas and started to take notice.

Through the years, I have been very interested in meteorology, plotting storm tracks by making my own maps and jumping up and down from my childhood home's roof to make sure I caught all the "Local on the 8's" via the Weather Channel.

I knew the May 22 storm was going to most likely produce a tornado, I just didn't realize the scale of what was about to happen.

That was a bad idea.

The shear was strong, and it was a towering, independent cumulonimbus cloud that would be relatively easy to navigate around the south side of...so I thought. I sent my wife Adriel a text message asking her if she wanted to go chase the storm and try to catch a glimpse of some rotation.

4:30 P.M.

After putting up my lawn equipment, we went in our Ford Focus down 7th Street and then to Stateline Road. We stopped at the gas station near the Stateline Road and 7th Street intersection, got a tea to drink and then gauged where to go next.

I was observing the storm was still on an east-northeast track, bringing the southern portion of the cell, in my estimates, to cross around Stone's Corner (Main Street and Airport Drive intersection north of Joplin). We dipped around the Galena area for a moment through some country roads and observed the transpiring rotation on the southern flank of the storm. The rotation looked robust and we were experiencing dime size hail at the time.

4:55 P.M.

We got out of that area and took Stateline Road to SE 110 in Kansas all the way up to Fir Road and started heading toward Stone's Corner.

We pulled into Snak Atak and waited with our vehicle watching the storm come in. I don't know how to explain it, but I KNEW something wasn't right. Nothing to do with the storm data, reports on the radio, etc. I just somehow knew this wasn't like other storms.

Not sure if it was the purple and black, bubbling mammatus clouds, or the obvious shift in the winds, but I tried to remain calm because I didn't want to worry Adriel.

Things that didn't have much scientific meaning started racing through my brain and veins and I became very nervous. I noticed the body of the storm was a lot farther south, not the earlier east-northeastern trek I envisioned. So I took myself about a half mile south hoping to get out of the bulk of precipitation and back to a good vantage point for the southern end of the storm.

5:11 P.M.

The first sirens sounded with spotters indicating a strengthening rotation via doppler radar just west of Joplin. We were at the Community Bank and Trust on North Main St. (across from Black Cat Fireworks) under their ATM roof to avoid precipitation and the sky was the most ominous thing I have ever seen in my life, except for what was 35 minutes away.

Thinking we needed to get out of the way and back to the house, we started in that direction. Driving down Main Street and onto Murphy Boulevard, we pulled behind the Landreth Park stage.

It is about 5:35 and the air had dried up considerably, but the darkness had begun to wrap the city. I should have noticed the rear flank of the storm pulling in all the precipitation, but I didn't.

I saw what appeared to be a large area of precipitation and thought I should just get inside and somewhere safe if something were to happen, still thinking it wouldn't.

5:41 P.M.

The second sirens sounded, and I knew this was what appeared to be a last-ditch effort to warn of what was most likely a tornado on the ground near Joplin. I could no longer contain how nervous and panicked I was to my wife.

We accelerated quickly, racing across Joplin going down Pennsylvania Avenue all the way from 4th Street. I was going as fast as I can when I started to notice something far out of the ordinary. I looked ahead near the chain link surrounded playground and I saw a misty, gray edge defined, area of rain that was swirling.

I continued to advance about half a block to about two houses before Orient Express on 20th Street. I threw the car in park and just waited on the side of the street. As I looked to my left, I noticed there was much more than rain in these clouds as the first large branch struck our vehicle and more were in the air about to rain down with other debris. Then it all started.

5:50 P.M.

Trees, fences, utility poles, anything moderately exposed and sticking vertically out of the ground started to break and be blown around. As the strength of the winds grew, I look and not only see debris and branches out of my driver side window, I started to see sections of roofs and houses hundreds of feet in the air.

I will never forget the imagery as it is burned into my brain as sure as anything I could ever recall. Then our windows started going...both driver's side windows first.

I pushed Adriel into the floorboard of the front seat and leaned over her to shield her from anything that might fly in while trying to protect the back of my neck and head. I held her tight and exchanged "I love yous" over and over again. It was all I could say that offered any sense.

I couldn't describe the storm, yell obscenities, or breathe like I was panicked. I could only say, and in turn receive, the only thing that made sense at the time...to exchange the very simple phrase "I love you."

We continued to yell this to each other as the storm lifted my driver's side up in the air, buffeting the underbelly of the vehicle with the most unsettling force I have ever felt in my life. The car was only probably up on the passenger side wheels for 15-20 seconds, but it seemed like an eternity as I am sure many have said. It was like 1,000 golf clubs beating apart the vehicle and trying to toss it at the same time.

A large piece of debris came and shattered the back glass and I wondered, "Will it ever end?"

It finally did but the rain kept coming down.

6:05 P.M.

Shocked, the radio still blaring "Take cover Joplin," we lifted our heads to see what had happened. My wife, sobbing, said, "Kelly our house...Kyle's house.... where is our roof? There isn't a garage."

Kyle, my brother, lived right next to us and his house was severely damaged as well, and his fiancée Kelsi, were inside with their animals as far as we knew. We had to get to them to make sure they were OK along with our neighbors.

My roof crashed into Kyle and Kelsi's house and car.

The car was still running, and I attempted to pull onto 20th, but my path was blocked by debris, trees, and power lines. I reversed and managed to make it to 19th and over a block to my street of Kentucky Avenue.

Again, it was blocked with power lines, but these were up off the ground enough for us to sneak under...not a great idea but we had to. I ran with Adriel hand in hand across 20th Street as fast as I could to my brother's house.

His home was caved in and none of the doors would open, so we kicked ourselves in to find them and their animals OK, but very disoriented and stunned.

We still had standing walls at our house, so we collected all animals and our thoughts for a brief moment and charted a plan of action. I was going to check on neighbors while Kyle stayed with the animals and girls.

6:15 P.M.

My block. War zone.

Walking down Kentucky Avenue that night was the most heartbreaking and gut-wrenching thing I have ever experienced. While I was battered and bruised, making my way through the block, my neighbors appeared to be all safe.

At the end of our block was another story. I don't want to elaborate on any of that in this note, as these people were brothers, sisters, sons, daughters, wives and husbands of my neighbors. I will say a little bit of me changed that day with what I had seen. Some people deal well with trauma, but I am not one of those. I nearly became physically ill on the curb and had to go back to check on my family.

Before I did, a house fire broke out in the 2100 block of Kentucky Avenue and people were walking the streets with severe injuries, carrying what they could, heading to somewhere.... but I don't think anyone really knew where we all were going.

Just about that time, a large great Dane came running up on our property.... he looked really familiar. It was the dog of my brother's friend Nick Dagget, who lived behind Dillon's. Seeing that dog alone made our hearts drop. Kyle could barely contain the thoughts of what might have happened to his best friend and we all kept him calm as we could, promising we were going to put the dog up and head towards Nick's house.

My family across town made their way to our house by this time and we saw them running across 20th toward us. We got the car out of the street and into the parking lot of Brandon's Gun Shop on 20th and start to head the only way we can, west on 20th.

We filled up the car, not knowing how long traffic out of town would be stuck. We circled around and made it to I-44 so that we could come into Joplin off Range Line and got to Nick's house that way.

We approached Nick's house from 26th and Connecticut and found a route there unobstructed after trying multiple streets. When we reached his neighborhood and I looked toward the west, I soon realized what had taken place. Like the lawn mower I pushed on an overgrown lot hours before, I could see a path all the way to St. John's Hospital, a path that is still viewable all the way from the former Walmart until this day, bare of trees and structures.

This was a war zone.

We searched frantically for Nick in the rubble of his house; nothing indicated he was there. His cell phone and a small amount of blood were in the tub, but no Nick. We couldn't do anything else as dark was approaching and we were without flashlights and rescue crews haven't made it to this area yet.

We reassured Kyle that he probably made it out, like his dog, but was at a local hospital with modest injuries. Thankfully, that was exactly what happened, and we received information later that night that Nick was o.k.

We made it back to my brother's house in Webb City and attempted to sleep, but as for me, and I am sure the others in the basement....no one got a wink of sleep. It would stay that way for about a week.

AFTER MAY 22

Starting that night and continuing until this day my friends, people I never met, and more took to the streets to do what we could. We loaded trucks, sharpened chain saw blades, offered help and rescue, doing what we could.

Everyone is still doing what they are able to do, but it is no surprise that we will need help for years to come.

Our city has been bent, but not broken, and in turn has become a more solidified tight knit community that can rise from a storm like this and we impatiently ask, "What is next? What can I do? How can

I help?"

Hearing those questions and those in turn being answered by groups of regular people is the most heartwarming thing I have ever seen.

Through cleanup I was approached by churches, local businesses, people from all of the country...putting their hand on our backs and asking, "Can I do anything? Are you ok?" while handing out food, supplies, tetanus shots, and tools to aid the cleanup effort.

A month of this has impacted my life and motivated me to live for others, not just in times of tragedy, but throughout the rest of my life.

None of us are going to have all the answers about how to deal with this or other hard situations in life, but I came away knowing it does get better and that the astounding momentum of the human spirit is something a horrible EF5 tornado can't stop. Life isn't over, it is just different after the 45 seconds that changed everything.

Armageddon At the Hospital

By Dr. Kevin Kikta

One of the lasting memories of the tornado was provided by Dr. Kevin Kikta, an emergency room doctor at St. John's Regional Medical Center and is shared courtesy of Mercy Medical.

I was one of two emergency room doctors who were on duty at St. John's Regional Medical Center in Joplin, MO on Sunday, May 22, 2011.

You never know that it will be the most important day of your life until the day is over.

The day started like any other day for me: waking up, eating, going to the gym, showering, and going to my 4:00 pm ER shift. As I drove to the hospital I mentally prepared for my shift as I always do, but nothing could ever have prepared me for what was going to happen on this shift.

Things were normal for the first hour and half. At approximately 5:30 p.m., we received a warning that a tornado had been spotted.

A shattered St. John's Regional Medical Center became the backdrop for countless press briefings from held at Cunningham Park, across 26th Street from the hospital. John Hacker. Photo by John Hacker

Although I work in Joplin and went to medical school in Oklahoma, I live in New Jersey, and I have never seen or been in a tornado. I learned that a "code gray" was being called. We were to start bringing patients to safer spots within the ED and hospital.

At 5:42 p.m. a security guard yelled to everyone, "Take cover! We are about to get hit by a tornado!"

I ran with a pregnant RN, Shilo Cook, while others scattered to various places, to the only place that I was familiar with in the hospital without windows, a small doctor's office in the ED.

Together, Shilo and I trembled and huddled under a desk. We heard a loud horrifying sound like a large locomotive ripping through the hospital. The whole hospital shook and vibrated as we heard glass shattering, light bulbs popping, walls collapsing, people screaming, the ceiling caving in above us, and water pipes breaking, showering water down on everything.

The Medflight Helicopter sits mangled among vehicles and other debris on the north side of St. John's Regional Medical Center on May 23, 2011.
Photo by John Hacker

We suffered this in complete darkness, unaware of anyone else's status, worried, scared. We could feel a tight pressure in our heads as the tornado annihilated the hospital and the surrounding area. The whole process took about 45 seconds, but it seemed like an eternity. The hospital had just taken a direct hit from a category EF5 tornado.

Then it was over. Just 45 seconds. 45 long seconds. We looked at each other, terrified, and thanked God that we were alive. We didn't know but hoped that it was safe enough to go back out to the ED, find the rest of the staff and patients, and assess our losses.

"Like a bomb went off."

That's the only way that I can describe what we saw next. Patients were coming into the ED in droves. It was absolute, utter chaos. They were limping, bleeding, crying, terrified, with debris and glass sticking out of them, just thankful to be alive.

The floor was covered with about three inches of water. There was no power, not even backup generators, rendering it completely dark and eerie in the ED. The frightening aroma of methane gas leaking from the broken gas lines permeated the air; we knew, but did not dare mention aloud, what that meant. I redoubled my pace.

We had to use flashlights to direct ourselves to the crying and wounded. Where did all the flashlights come from? I'll never know, but immediately, and thankfully, my years of training in emergency procedures kicked in.

There was no power, but our mental generators were up and running, and on high test adrenaline. We had no cell phone service in the first hour, so we were not even able to call for help and backup in the ED.

I remember a patient in his early 20's gasping for breath, telling me that he was going to die.

After a quick exam, I removed the large shard of glass from his back, made the clinical diagnosis of a pneumothorax (collapsed lung) and gathered supplies from wherever I could locate them to insert a thoracostomy tube in him. He was a trooper.

I'll never forget his courage. He allowed me to do this without any local anesthetic since none could be found. With his life-threatening injuries, I knew he was running out of time, and it had to be done. Quickly.

Imagine my relief when I heard a big rush of air, and breath sounds again; fortunately, I was able to get him transported out. I immediately moved on to the next patient, an asthmatic in status asthmaticus. We didn't even have the option of trying a nebulizer treatment or steroids, but I was able to get him intubated using a flashlight that I held in my mouth.

A small child of approximately 3-4 years of age was crying; he had a large avulsion of skin to his neck and spine. The gaping wound revealed his cervical spine and upper thoracic spine bones. I could actually count his vertebrae with my fingers. This was a child, his whole life ahead of him, suffering life threatening wounds in front of me, his eyes pleading me to help him.

We could not find any pediatric C collars in the darkness, and water from the shattered main pipes was once again showering down upon all of us. Fortunately, we were able to get him immobilized with towels, and start an IV with fluids and pain meds before shipping him out.

We felt paralyzed and helpless ourselves. I didn't even know a lot of the RNs I was working with. They were from departments scattered all over the hospital. It didn't matter. We worked as a team, determined to save lives.

There were no specialists available -- my orthopedist was trapped in the OR. We were it, and we knew we had to get patients out of the hospital as quickly as possible. As we were shuffling them out, the fire department showed up and helped us to evacuate. Together we worked furiously, motivated by the knowledge and fear that the methane leaks to cause the hospital could blow up at any minute.

Things were no better outside of the ED. I saw a man crushed under a large SUV, still alive, begging for help; another one was dead, impaled by a street sign through his chest.

Wounded people were walking, staggering, all over, dazed and shocked. All around us was chaos, reminding me of scenes in a war movie, or newsreels from bombings in Bagdad. Except this was right in front of me and it had happened in just 45 seconds.

My own car was blown away. Gone. Seemingly evaporated. We searched within a half mile radius later that night, but never found the car, only the littered, crumpled remains of former cars. And a John Deere tractor that had blown in from miles away.

Tragedy has a way of revealing human goodness. As I worked, surrounded by devastation and suffering, I realized I was not alone. The people of the community of Joplin were absolutely incredible.

Within minutes of the horrific event, local residents showed up in pickups and sport utility vehicles, all offering to help transport the wounded to other facilities, including Freeman, the trauma center literally across the street. Ironically, it had sustained only minimal damage and was functioning (although I'm sure it was overwhelmed). I carried on, grateful for the help of the community.

Within hours I estimated that over 100 EMS units showed up from various towns, counties and four different states. Considering the circumstances, their response time was miraculous. Roads were blocked with downed utility lines, smashed up cars in piles, and they still made it through.

We continued to carry patients out of the hospital on anything that we could find- sheets, stretchers, broken doors, mattresses, wheelchairs—anything that could be used as a transport mechanism.

As I finished up what I could do at St John's, I walked with two RN's, Shilo Cook and Julie VanDorn, to a makeshift MASH center that was being set up miles away at Memorial Hall. We walked where flourishing neighborhoods once stood, astonished to see only the disastrous remains of flattened homes, body parts, and dead people everywhere.

I saw a small dog just whimpering in circles over his master who was dead, unaware that his master would not ever play with him again.

At one point we tended to a young woman who just stood crying over her dead mother who was crushed by her own home. The young woman covered her mother up with a blanket and then asked all of us, "What should I do?" We had no answer for her, but silence and tears.

By this time news crews and photographers were starting to swarm around, and we were able to get a ride to Memorial Hall from another RN. The chaos was slightly more controlled at Memorial Hall. I was relieved to see many of my colleagues, doctors from every specialty, helping out. It was amazing to be able to see life again. It was also amazing to see how fast workers mobilized to set up this MASH unit under the circumstances.

Supplies, food, drink, generators, exam tables, all were there—except pharmaceutical pain meds. I sutured multiple lacerations, and splinted many fractures, including some open with bone exposed, and then intubated another patient with severe COPD, slightly better controlled conditions this time, but still less than optimal.

But we really needed pain meds. I managed to go back to the St John's with another physician, pharmacist, and a sheriff's officer. Luckily, security let us in to a highly guarded pharmacy to bring back a garbage bucket sized supply of pain meds.

At about midnight I walked around the parking lot of St. John's with local law enforcement officers looking for anyone who might be alive or trapped in crushed cars.

They spray-painted X's on the fortunate vehicles that had been searched without finding anyone inside. The unfortunate vehicles wore "X's" and sprayed-on numerals, indicating the number of dead inside, crushed in their cars, cars which now resembled flattened recycled aluminum cans the tornado had crumpled in her iron hands, an EF5 tornado, one of the worst in history, whipping through this quiet town with demonic strength.

I continued back to Memorial Hall into the early morning hours until my ER colleagues told me it was time for me to go home. I was completely exhausted. I had seen enough of my first tornado.

How can one describe these indescribable scenes of destruction?

The next day I saw news coverage of this horrible, deadly tornado. It was excellent coverage, and Mike Bettes from the Weather Channel did a great job, but there is nothing that pictures and video can depict compared to seeing it in person. That video will play forever in my mind.

I would like to express my sincerest gratitude to everyone involved in helping during this nightmarish disaster. My fellow doctors, RN's,

Volunteers and St. John's Medical Center employees take in the scene at the shattered hospital two days after the tornado on May 24, 2011.
Photo by John Hacker

techs, and all of the staff from St. John's. I have worked at St John's for approximately 2 years, and I have always been proud to say that I was a physician at St John's in Joplin, MO. The smart, selfless and immediate response of the professionals and the community during this catastrophe proves to me that St John's and the surrounding community are special. I am beyond proud.

To the members of this community, the health care workers from states away, and especially Freeman Medical Center, I commend everyone, giving 110% the way that you all did, even in your own time of need.

St John's Regional Medical Center is gone, but her spirit and goodness live on in each of you.

EMS, you should be proud of yourselves. You were all excellent and did a great job despite incredible difficulties and against all odds.

For all of the injured who I treated, although I do not remember your names (nor would I expect you to remember mine) I will never forget your faces. I'm glad that I was able to make a difference and help in the best way that I knew how, and hopefully give some of you a chance at rebuilding your lives again. For those whom I was not able to get to or treat, I apologize whole heartedly.

Last, but not least, thank you, and God bless you, Mercy/St John's for providing incredible care in good times and even more so, in times of the unthinkable, and for all the training that enabled us to be a team and treat the people and save lives.

Sincerely,

Kevin J. Kikta, DO Department of Emergency Medicine Mercy/St John's Regional Medical Center, Joplin, MO

Death, Destruction Hit Joplin, Missouri

By Randy Turner

Note: This column was written the day following the tornado and was originally published May 23, 2011, on the Huffington Post.

Each year, my eighth graders at Joplin East Middle School look forward to their first official visit to Joplin High School. They have heard the horror stories about the school, how they, as freshmen the next year, will need to stay clear of the seniors who have worked their way up to the top of the food chain.

They speak in hushed whispers of Eagle Alley, a near mythical hallway that one almost needs a guide to navigate.

That first trip, which was scheduled for Wednesday, will never happen.

Eagle Alley is a thing of the past. After the devastating killer tornado that ripped through the heart of my city Sunday night, Joplin High School, the place where so many of my former students have learned the skills they need to succeed in life, the place where they made friends, created memories, and prepared for their passage

In the days after the tornado, someone used duct tape to create an inspirational message on the sign in front of Joplin High School.

into adulthood exists only in memory.

At least 89 people are reported dead and hundreds injured as a result of the first major tornado to hit Joplin in four decades.

Those of us who were fortunate enough not to be in the path of the storm (it hit approximately a quarter of a mile from the apartment complex where I live) waited in the center of a darkened city, praying that loved ones had somehow managed to remain safe in what reporters were describing as a scene from a war zone.

With nearly all power gone in this city of 50,000, the night sky was still illuminated by jagged streaks of lightning in the distance and by the lights from emergency vehicles as they passed every few seconds.

When morning arrived, we were greeted by a sun that seemed almost foreign in light of what had happened.

And now the waiting begins. Every few moments I scan through

Facebook postings, heartened by messages that indicate my students and former students are alive. So far, none have been listed among the casualties through word of mouth, but it may be only a matter of time. Officials have yet to release any of the names of those who were killed.

The Joplin School District has canceled classes for today and they may well be finished for the school year, which had another nine days to go. Three of our school buildings are gone forever and the middle school where I teach no longer has a roof.

Many of my former students received their high school diplomas Sunday afternoon during graduation ceremonies at Missouri Southern State University, commemorating their achievements over the past four years at Joplin High School. Now that ceremony, which should have been a memorable milestone in their young lives, will always be tainted by tragedy.

As I write these words, slightly more than 14 hours have passed since the city of Joplin was changed forever.

The welcoming sunshine of just an hour ago has vanished, replaced by darkening clouds and the steady, insistent rumbling of thunder.

And now we wait.

Nightmare at Freeman

By Kristen Huke

I was at Freeman visiting my sister who had given birth to my newest nephew in the early morning hours of the 22nd. I found myself in the middle of things in the ER late that same day. I've tried talking about it but can't put into words what I saw that night. It's so hard, even this doesn't do what happened justice, but it is a bit of what I saw, and hope none of those people have to suffer through again.

MAY 22, 2011

We had just gotten back to Freeman from a late lunch at Freddy's and a quick trip to Joann's on Range Line. We were sitting in my sister's room, when nurses asked us to go to the birthing center's waiting room because a tornado warning had been issued. My sister, baby and husband were told to get into the bathroom inside their hospital room and wait it out.

From Freeman's first floor waiting room, we could hear rain, thunder, hail, etc. But once we lost TV reception then power... we had no idea what had gone on just a few blocks away.

My mother and father and I emerged from the cafeteria to see if things were ok and slowly ventured up a spiral staircase to see a little debris in the parking lot, but not a lot else. The trees, cars, and doctor's offices to the east looked just fine. Within minutes - it was not.

A frantic nurse came running into the hospital and downstairs almost falling with every step - soaking wet. We soon found out she had gotten caught in the storm, was in a ditch, and a stranger picked her up and brought her to the hospital. She was hysterical. That set the tone for the evening to come.

The first car pulled up and actually parked out in the parking lot. It had 4x4 posts and lumber sticking out its front grill - broken windows - and looked like it had been shot up with a machine gun.

Six people emerged from the car with various injuries and cuts all over. After they were in the hospital, I walked out to the car and couldn't believe they were able to drive it anywhere. Not wanting to be in anyone's way or gawk, I went back into the hospital.

Nurses started coming from departments with extra wheelchairs, beds, and cots, anything they had. But there was a large metal door that separated the ER/tower from the rest of the hospital, and they were unable to get supplies through. The only way was a hallway in the tower, so a bunch of us started hand carrying cots through to the ER.

Out front, things started picking up and soon the front entrance of the hospital was lined with cars in various states of destruction, unloading victims of a terrible storm, some not even knowing who drove them there.

Loads, people piled into vehicles just to get somewhere safe because their homes were gone. Truckloads with people unable to sit up lying on found doors and lumber just to get there.

Several of "us" jumped in to help, not knowing what was to come and how long we would be needed. Three security guards were trying to direct traffic when they saw that they had to just get the people into the hospital. We were told to put on plastic gloves if we were willing to help.

The injured were all in various states of shock, shaking, bleeding, not able to answer simple questions. They would just stare at you, unable to believe what had just happened to them. We were unable to believe what had happened to them because for us to look to the north, Freeman blocked our view of the destruction just beyond our reach. Just on the other side of 32nd Street- we had no idea what they'd been through. Just that they needed help.

A truck with a man and his wife in the back pulled up. He was talking a mile a minute. He did not know the driver; they had been picked up somewhere around the Stained Glass Theater. They were so thankful for the driver; he said they were standing and getting hit by hail when he pulled up to help.

He kept saying, "It's gone... it's all just gone! We'll never have anything there again... It's just GONE!"

He had a large cut in the back of his head and could barely stand, but he was more worried about his wife and refused help. Almost falling, he finally agreed to sit in a wheelchair, and I pushed him into the ER behind his wife as she lay on a gurney.

I kept telling him I would push him as far as I could, but they might try to stop me once we got back to the swinging doors. I'd do whatever it took to make sure they stayed together, but I didn't know if I could keep my promise. Luckily, a nurse ran up to us, and I told her over and over... "You have to keep them together... that's his wife!" I never saw them again.

I saw so many things that will stick in my mind forever. Strangers helping strangers, neighbors helping neighbors. A beautiful elderly lady who was dug out of her house by her neighbors and couldn't move from her La-Z-Boy... so they lifted her, chair and all, into the back of their truck and drove her to the hospital.

Once there, we had no more gurneys, so they once again lifted her and her chair and I made a path for them to get her into the ER waiting room. She sat there for hours.

I brought in another beautiful woman about the same age and sat them by each other. I kept checking on them and getting them water, and as hurt as they both were, they were more worried about others than they were themselves.

Before I left that night, I went back to see how they were, and they had both been taken somewhere... but the old green broken La-Z-Boy remained. I was happy to see it empty, but worried and hoped wherever she was, she was o.k.

Another young man I helped in the door was immediately given a cup of water. He drank it in one gulp and asked for more. I made three trips to the only water fountain I knew of in the tower hallway. Each time I came back with a full cup, he would ask for more. He was so thankful; I was so glad I could help.

Whole families came from blocks away just walking down the streets to the hospital, needing refuge from the storm. Homes and all forms of transportation gone, scared to death, children traumatized, mothers crying, fathers trying to be strong for their families.

An SUV zipped in and everyone getting out looked o.k., but then opened the back of the car to expose a young man who was not. His grandmother was screaming for help. We were doing all we could.

The older woman's daughter and her young daughter were frantically calling for us to help him. Three generations of women begging for help.

While the men were unloading the boy, I looked the young girl square in the eye and as calm as I could told her it would be o.k., that "the nurses were doing all they can, and screaming for help was not going to help her grandmother, it would only make her more upset."

I sincerely thought her grandmother might have a heart attack on the spot. My guess was the little girl was 9 or 10, and I think something clicked with her. Her attention went from complete distress over the hurt young man to soothing her panic-stricken grandmother. That little girl sat with her grandmother the rest of the evening and took care of her. I consider that little girl a hero.

Later, I ran into her mother outside and told her how proud I was of her young daughter. She thanked me and assumed I was a nurse. I apologized to her and told her I was just an artist who decided to do what I could and pitch in. She shook her head and thanked me again.

We quickly ran out of wheelchairs, and instead used conference room rolling chairs to unload victims that were too shaky and hurt to walk. Several of us made trips to the Heart wing of the hospital to rob their linen closets of blankets, sheets, towels... whatever they could spare.

People were pouring in the doors soaking wet with what clothes they had left, no shoes - shredded, torn, covered in glass and dirt. If nothing else, at least we could try to cover them and give them some decency.

A family I sat next to just an hour before the storm was helping find and hand out blankets - they were from Las Vegas here to visit their newest family member - a baby in the NICU, but seeing the need started helping without any hesitation.

On my second trip for blankets - I helped a beautiful young lady and her newborn twins that had been born that morning at St. Johns via c-section. I told them to avoid the ER and head straight to the birthing unit, unfortunately, that was downstairs, and a spiral staircase at that. She said it was no trouble - she had just walked herself down six flights of stairs at St. John's with her husband and twins to get to Freeman... one more set of stairs was not going to stop her. The babies were wrapped in so many blankets they looked like white balls.

When we ran out of gurneys, we resorted to getting people out of the backs of trucks still lying on the door or other debris and sitting them on sawhorses till they could be moved inside.

Doctors and nurses started arriving in shorts and t-shirts, some in scrubs, some pulling suitcases behind them, knowing they would be there for a while. Eyes wide as they approached, they were unable to believe what task was before them. A truck of supplies came from Lamar - and I showed them where to get a large rack to put the supplies on to get them into the building. The rack once held blankets and sheets, but they were all gone.

It was particularly hard to see the patients from Greenbriar Nursing Home. They were so scared. One elderly woman was on a board in the back of a truck waiting her turn to get carried inside.

I stood by the truck and tried to talk to her, not knowing where she had come from. I'm not sure if she couldn't talk back or was so scared and in shock, she was unable. I held her hand until they took her in. She was shaking, wide eyed, cold. Dirt and debris covered her face, ears, hair, and jammed under her fingernails. Someone had written on her forehead "3."

Once in a room just inside the hospital doors, I made sure she was o.k. and replaced her head as it was slightly off the side of a dirty decorative couch pillow. She looked me in the eye and smiled, and in the background another lady in the room was yelling "AMEN," over and over.

Blood on the pillars, walls and floor. I pulled a used towel from a mountain of dirty linens, and with my foot mopped up a line of blood that ran from the scrub store to the waterfall, then there were too many people to maneuver around and I didn't want to trip anyone. I saw a man with a huge blue cart for the linens and told him where the biggest piles were.

The traffic out front started slowing down, but I soon realized that was not a good thing... there was a reason they were not in a hurry. The truck driver was asked to pull around back and if he could possibly leave his truck there for a while until they could get to the DOA in the back. I guess it was another version of a temporary morgue. That was the hardest to see.

Helicopters buzzing overhead, waiting their turn to scoop up a victim from Freeman and transport that person to another hospital. A helicopter with a searchlight scanning over St. John's looking for more wounded. A line of school buses and ambulances to carry people to other hospitals strung out the parking lot to 32nd street.

Packed in the ER waiting room, down the hallway, past the water fountain to the gift shop, people everywhere pacing back and forth. Scared, wondering where their loved ones were. A young man in the foyer was in agony and disbelief. He had just lost his two young children.

And there we were... not nurses or doctors... ordinary people, doing our best. Some of us were meant to be there to run for supplies for the nurses. Some of us were meant to be there to hold a hand. Some of us were meant to be there to carry people who couldn't walk. Some of us were meant to be there to sit with others and pray. Some of us were meant to be there to be strong in the face of devastation where hope could not be seen. All of us were scared to death, but we didn't show it.

I stayed until 2: a.m. Eight hours had gone by, but it felt more like 10 minutes. Mentally and physically exhausted, I got in my car and started to leave the parking lot. I stopped one last time to look back and try to process what had just happened.

All I saw were the lights of Freeman like a beacon in a sea of black nothingness. Blinking strobe lights from school buses and a line of frantic flashes from tops of ambulances.

I drove myself home, probably not the best idea. As I merged onto I-44, I quickly realized I was the only car on the interstate, aside from an occasional ambulance. I almost didn't notice I was at the Range Line exit; it was pitch dark - black.

One police car light was all that lit up Range Line to the north or south. I didn't see the devastation; it was too dark. I think God was protecting me from what I was about to realize when I finally got home to Carthage and turned on a TV.

I simply couldn't believe my eyes. I didn't realize how close we were to being in serious danger. I regret leaving the hospital - I should have stayed.

It has been nine days now, but I constantly relive it like it was yesterday. Seeing the mauled faces of people I may never see again. I'm not scared of it, if anything it has made me stronger, and made me realize life's so precious.

"Don't sweat the small stuff" is an understatement. I have so much to be thankful for. We all do.

I don't write this to say what I did. I just happened to be there. I write this to help people understand what the nurses and doctors at Freeman did, and the challenges they faced in a very dire situation.

I did what I could to help them, so they could help everyone else who was hurt. People flocked to Freeman because they knew there would be help and possibly a bit of hope, refuge from the forces of nature like we've never seen.

Freeman is an amazing facility. But I will never walk through those doors again without thinking and seeing what went on there the evening of May 22, 2011. The day my nephew Gunner was born. The day that changed my life forever.

May your path be blessed with happiness and love,
Kristin Huke - Proud sister of Jennifer Choate, Post-Op Nurse Freeman Hospital & beautiful mother of newborn Gunner Madden Choate

a Lazy Afternoon

By Brennan Stebbins

W e were at the intersection of 26th and Main Street when the first sirens went off. I was with two close friends, Isaac Duncan and Corey Waterman, and we were spending the afternoon driving around in my car and listening to the Kansas City Royals play the St. Louis Cardinals on the radio.

Earlier, knowing severe storms were forecast for the day, I looked up to the sky to the west and saw the clouds steadily building. Now, with the ominous drone of the sirens in the background, I looked back to the west and saw the sky darkening.

It's been said many times by many people in the year since May 22, 2011, but upon hearing the tornado sirens, none of us worried because it's such a common occurrence in the Midwest in May. If anything, it excited us and made the drive more interesting.

We drove east on 26th Street, then turned north on Wisconsin past dozens of old ranch-style homes in the neighborhood near Joplin High School.

Looking out my window to the left, I noticed the red brick home at 2314 Wisconsin, with its large Pin Oak swaying in the breeze. The sky was still growing darker, and the front yard of the house was dark, except for the old gas lamp.

I turned into the parking lot at the high school, and I remember looking up at the tall pine trees at the back of the lot before we pulled out and continued our meandering. A few minutes later, we were driving on Connecticut, and then east on 24th Street into my old neighborhood. We drove past the Rosedale swimming pool, and then past the cream-colored house at 2302 S. Florida where I grew up.

Still listening to the baseball game, we were driving north on Texas when drops of rain began kissing the windshield, and we turned to a local news station to get an update on the weather. There were reports of large hail just west of town. We turned west on 12th Street and then headed north on Florida, crossing 7th Street and then passing behind the Ozark Memorial Park Cemetery.

Coming up on Newman Road, we decided to drive to the Sonic Drive-In near 20th Street to park the car under something sturdy. As we turned onto Newman and drove to Range Line Road, we heard radio reports of people panicking and fleeing the Joplin High School graduation just east of us at Missouri Southern.

The quickest route to Sonic was to turn right on Range Line and drive south for a few miles, and we would surely beat the hail. I felt like making things interesting, though, and we were curious to see what was going on at the college, so we pulled up to the red light at Newman and Range Line and waited to go straight instead of turning right.

It was the longest red light.

Soon we were all talking about how strange it was to be stopped at a red light for so long.

"I should have just turned right, and we'd already be there by now," I said.

Finally, the light changed to green and we continued towards Missouri Southern, where we planned to turn south onto Duquesne Road, drive over to 20th Street and then on to the Sonic and our respite from the weather.

You could feel the tension in the air by now, and we knew the hail was probably just blocks away from us, but it gave us a rush. There was nothing going on at the college; everybody had already left, so we drove on Duquesne to the intersection of 7th Street when we began hearing radio reports of a tornado on the ground at 7th and Schifferdecker, and then reports of a tornado on the ground at 7th and Range Line, just barely west of us.

I looked to my right and thought the radio reports must be wrong, so I turned onto 7th Street and drove west, but didn't get far before my friends urged me to turn the car around.

We turned back onto Duquesne and drove south.

Driving the stretch of road from 7th Street to 20th Street through Duquesne, the radio reports really started to get spooky. We all started to feel for the first time that this was a really serious storm. As we circled the roundabout at 20th and Duquesne, we saw a white Duquesne police car speeding out of the Fastrip parking lot and driving north.

"That guy was sure going somewhere fast," someone said.

Something inside me said this was as far as we were going to go, and I pulled into the lot and parked. We just sat there wondering what to do. Should we go inside the store and wait it out? Should we keep driving? Which direction should we be driving?

We decided to wait in the car and see what happened. The sky to the west was almost black by now, and it was raining heavily. There was another car parked under the roof above the gas pumps, which gave us comfort knowing we weren't the only ones waiting outside.

Within a minute, though, we saw the passengers jump out and sprint to the door of the gas station. Almost simultaneously, the three of us got out of the car and ran to the doors behind them, where Ruben Carter, the Fastrip clerk, let us inside.

I almost slipped and fell when I took a few steps onto the wet tile inside, and there were already about 20 people sitting on the floor in the back of the store, so we joined them.

It was then that Isaac pulled out his cell phone and began recording the video that would go viral within hours, not because of what is seen, but because of what is heard.

***

"Why the fuck did we drive this direction?" Corey asks nobody in particular.

A small child asks her mother if she can go to the bathroom, but the mother says no because the bathroom is at the front of the store.

"Hey, where do you want me to put everybody?" Ruben asks someone on the phone. "At least probably 10 or 12."

A woman counts out loud.

"There's probably 18 or 19," she says.

"Dude, shit is getting real," Isaac says.

Isaac tells a woman about the radio reports of a tornado on the ground at 7th and Range Line. "Yeah, but there's one coming this way on 20th," she says.

"Dude, this is getting real," Isaac says.

Then, more people come to the door, and Ruben walks across the tile to let them in.

It's almost pitch black in the store because the power has already gone out, and I hear a girl crying and her mother trying to soothe her while I look out the window at the roof above the gas pumps looking very weak as it rocks up and down in the wind.

"Is that the tornado, is that what that roar is?" someone asks.

Ruben tells everybody to get down and huddle on the ground.

"Jesus, Jesus, Jesus," a woman says. "Where's it at?"

Now we can all hear debris pelting the back of the building, and any thoughts that this storm might miss us are gone.

"Let's get inside that … what is that room right there?" Corey asks, looking at the walk-in beer cooler.

Another woman asks Ruben if we can get in the beer cooler, but he doesn't have a chance to answer before the windows blow in and everybody knows we're getting in the beer cooler.

The entire group tries to get through the door to the cooler, and it's a mad dash at first before people calm down and wait their turn.

"Jesus, heavenly Father."

"Come on, go. Everybody move inside."

"God? God? GOD?"

"Jesus, heavenly Father."

Kids are crying and people get separated, but everybody makes it inside and I know what Isaac means when he says shit is getting real. There's just a single light bulb hanging from the ceiling and the walls are lined by shelves of cold beer.

Everybody gets on the floor and huddles together.

I can hear that tell-tale sound of a freight train, and it sounds like a dozen of them are running across Range Line. Slowly, they're moving this way.

"We're good, we're good, we're good," Isaac says, trying to comfort everybody. "I think we're going to do it."

With those words, everyone hears the growing roar outside, and we get hit.

"Heavenly Father. Jesus Jesus Jesus. Oh, heavenly Father. Jesus Jesus Jesus."

"I love everyone," Isaac says. "I love everyone, man."

"Yeah, I love all you guys," Corey responds.

I feel my glasses get sucked off my face, and I start feeling around on the floor for them. Eventually I find them, still on my face.

"Jesus Jesus heavenly Father. Thank you, Jesus."

"Are you guys all okay?"

"Yeah, we're alright."

"Stay down. Stay down."

Isaac asks if everyone is okay below him.

"I'm trying not to lay on someone," he says.

"Somebody's on my back."

"Am I hurting anybody?"

Bottles begin breaking. The roof has collapsed and is resting on the shelves of beer, which are holding up the weight but beginning to buckle. Bottles are sliding off and shattering on the floor and people below.

"We need to call somebody," Corey says. "Who should I call?"

"Be careful, there's glass on your back," somebody else says.

The storm passes, and we can see daylight shining through holes in the walls. I'm sitting with my legs under one of the shelving units, which I notice is leaning toward me at nearly a 45-degree angle, and I look between some bottles of beer and see a tree a few feet away. I run my hands down my legs and arms to make sure nothing is missing.

***

The plan is to just stay put and wait for help. Nobody figures the tornado has hit as many areas as it has, and we all assume the fire department will arrive shortly to help us out.

People are calm at first, but it doesn't take long for everyone to get restless. There's no way to stand up and most can't extend their legs. People are getting cramps and sitting on broken glass.

I can see Isaac and we make eye contact briefly, but I can only hear Corey's voice from the back end of the cooler.

People begin wondering out loud whether we should look for a way out. A few people try to crawl to the holes where they see daylight, but they just end up crushing people underneath them.

I sit and look toward the shelves in front of me, wondering what has happened to my car on the other side. There's a strong smell of fuel in the air.

When we start smelling smoke from an electrical fire somewhere in the rubble, people start panicking. Corey, who sits on the west end of the building, is the first person to find a way out, and he relays the good news. It's probably a 10-foot climb up a piece of the metal wall of the cooler, which is at a steep angle, so people stack cases of beer at the bottom as a makeshift ladder.

I was sitting on the east end of the cooler, so I was one of the last people to climb out. I made it to the top of the wall and stood up to jump down to the ground behind the building, and I will never forget looking around and seeing absolute devastation for 360 degrees.

All of us stand there for a few moments, unsure of what to do or where to go. My car is sitting upright in the middle of the store, around where the cash register was just a few minutes earlier. The next day I drove it across the street on flat tires, but a forklift picked it up to move it again and it didn't run after that.

There was gasoline spewing out of the ground, and the strong scent of fuel was now joined by the sickly smells of plowed earth and old, musty lumber. There were no hugs and really no words said at all after everyone was out of the cooler. Gradually people just began walking west on 20th Street, toward a horizon with plumes of black smoke and piles of wet carnage.

I got a call from my father who said my grandpa in Duquesne was fine, but his barn had been destroyed and his house damaged. He hadn't yet reached my grandmother, who lived at 2314 Wisconsin, and I could hear in his voice he was nervous.

So, we began walking west.

the Fire Chief Was a Hero

By John Hacker

He lost his home, and most of his belongings, but once Joplin Fire Chief Mitch Randles knew his family was safe on May 22, he knew what he had to do.

City Manager Mark Rohr said he met Randles on Main Street immediately after the EF5 tornado tore up Joplin.

"I could get as far as J-town then I parked my car and went three blocks and found him at a Mexican restaurant on Main Street," Rohr said days after the tornado.

"As I made my way there, I was shocked at what I saw. There were two deceased individuals right there in a vehicle where I met him. While I was on my way to meet him, he was pulling people out of a basement."

Then the two of them drove to survey the damage when they were flagged down near Joplin High School and helped pull people from a church east of the railroad tracks on 20th Street.

"We went by the high school and across the railroad tracks

Mitch Randles, the Joplin Fire Chief at the time of the tornado, speaks at a news conference in Cunningham Park in the days after the tornado. Photo by John Hacker

near the high school someone flagged us down at a church that had collapsed," Rohr said. "He and I went over and there were deceased individuals in the church. We were working with different people who there, I believe they were church members, lifting debris and moving people out of the way that couldn't benefit from help and pulling people out of the wreckage.

"The fire chief was a hero," Rohr said. "I was very impressed with him and continue to be impressed with him."

In the days immediately after the storm, Randles said he and his family lived at his office at the fire station at 303 E. Third Street while Randles directed the around-the-clock effort to find victims of the tornado.

"My family spent the first three days after the tornado with me in the office," Randles said on May 26. "Two kids, a wife and two wiener dogs, it got kind of crowded, but I've got my family in with my sister now."

Hundreds of volunteer and professional rescuers converged on Joplin from across the country. Randles' job was to coordinate their efforts while trying his best to keep the volunteers and rescuers from being hurt.

He said the help was desperately needed in the days immediately after the tornado.

"We're a department of 80 people. It would be a challenge for us to take care of one block of this," Randles said "We're literally talking about miles of this and there is no way my department could deal with it. We're just not physically capable. It wouldn't be possible for any department, solo, to handle something like this."

Randles said he had to put the thoughts of what to do about his home in the back of his mind while dealing with the rescue effort.

Randles said his wife and children took care of assessing the damage at their home for the first week or so after the tornado while he led his battered fire department in the effort to save lives.

"I haven't seen my home, I don't even know what I'm dealing with," Randles said four days after the tornado hit.

"I've been told, my wife has been out there, my son has been out there, that the home is destroyed. My wife, she's a trooper. She's out doing the things that I need to be doing, but I have a responsibility here."

He said the help of the hundreds of rescuers that poured into Joplin in the immediate aftermath was essential in dealing with the catastrophe.

"We're a department of 80 people, it would be a challenge for us to take care of one block of this," he said. "We're literally talking about miles of this and there is no way my department could deal with it. We're just not physically capable, it wouldn't be possible for any department, solo, to handle something like this."

Death at the Full Gospel Church

By Randy Turner

"It was an awful rumbling, the loudest thing I had ever heard," Latina Puebla said after surviving the tornado that ripped through the Full Gospel Church on South Michigan in Joplin at 5:41 p.m. Sunday, May 22, 2011, just a few moments before evening services were scheduled to begin- the tornado that took the life of her daughter Natalia and sister Sandra Thomas.

Natalia had always been in a hurry during her short life, her mother said. She had mastered the alphabet at 18 months, mastered the piano, and was already sharing her love of music by teaching others to play.

Only 17, she had already completed her first year at Ozark Christian College, where she recorded a 4.0 grade point average.

The brunet, bespectacled Natalia had wisdom far beyond her years and had already created a bucket list. Topping that list was one wish. "I want to be someone that people can look up to," she wrote.

Her mother believes that Natalia could see something awaiting her. Natalia had written a prayer in her journal for Joplin, Latina told

Natalia Puebla

the *Jasper County Citizen*. It read, "God, you said you would spare the city if only 10 righteous men were found. Lord, please spare Joplin!"

The family arrived well before church services were scheduled. About 30 had gathered in the nursery. Children were singing "Praise You in This Storm," when the tornado sirens sounded.

"Get in the middle of the church," someone shouted.

Then the roof collapsed.

"I couldn't breathe," Latina said. At first, she could hear Natalia praying and speaking in tongues. "She was in direct communication with the Lord she was about to see."

Latina could hear her sister screaming because a portion of the roof had fallen on her. The sound grew weaker with the passing of each moment. She no longer heard her daughter's voice.

"I remember thinking that I knew I didn't want to live if she didn't live," Latina said. "I said, 'God, if you've taken my daughter, take me, too, but God had other plans."

Natalia and Sandra and two others, Moises Carmona and his daughter Arriy, died in the church that evening.

Moises Carmona, a native of Mexico, had worked hard to earn American citizenship and to take care of his family. His daughter was only a few feet away from him when their bodies were found.

"The ones who got under the pews didn't have a scratch on them," John Myers, pastor of the church for the past quarter of a century, told the *Tulsa World*, choking up with tears, "but the others... we lost four."

The last Facebook post of Natalia Puebla shows she was ready for whatever happened.

"No guilt in life, no fear of death-this is the power of Christ in me. From life's first cry til final breath, Jesus commands my destiny. No power of hell, no scheme of man, could ever pluck me from His hand. Til He returns or calls me home, here in the power of Christ I live."

I know God Was and is With Me

By Melissa Rainey-Campbell

It all started on Sunday, May 22, the evening that has changed lots of lives forever throughout the city of Joplin, Missouri.

An EF-5 tornado ripped through the central part of my hometown. It destroyed almost everything in its path. Everywhere you turn there is some kind of destruction. So many homes, businesses, churches and schools destroyed. Three-fourths of my family lost their homes that evening.

All I can remember is the terrible noise ripping my house apart as my family and I were huddled together praying in the bathroom, debris flying, glass breaking and scattering, the roof lifting off the back of our home. I prayed for protection for those around me and my family.

After it all settled, the back of my house and roof were gone; our car was heavily damaged. Comforting my children crying and shaking with fear, I began to make my way to find my Dad across the street. The destruction was overwhelming; it was like nothing I'd ever seen in my life.

My husband cautioned carefulness due to debris, downed trees, downed power lines, massive gas leaks, and it was still raining and lightning.

I could finally see my dad making his way out of the debris of my childhood home. My heart felt a small bit of relief. Then I looked up behind where he lived and could see to Range Line Road. There was nothing but rubble. All I could think of was my brother John and his family. There was still that strange kind of quiet shock, I guess.

Our cell phone reception was not working very well. You could not get out, but you could text. Soon we started hearing sirens everywhere trying to get to the injured. We turned to see the high school was on fire. Neighbors were in shock, there was nothing left of our neighborhood to the north of us.

My husband had received word that our employer Mercy/St. John's had been heavily damaged. I then thought of my mom who was there working on the fourth-floor oncology unit. My heart sank because they were saying there were injuries. I began to pray for my mom and my co-workers at St John's, as I was receiving news that my brother and his family were safe, but their home was totally gone.

My husband was called to work and little did I know that I would not see him for the next 24 plus hours. My children and I were taken to the safety of my in-laws' home. My husband kept checking in with me to give status updates of trying to find my mom. My heart was heavy, and I cried and prayed for her safety.

I finally received the long-awaited text that she had been located. She was banged up but had been working to save lives of the patients on her floor. She had to hold on the foot of a patient bed to avoid being sucked out of a window of the hospital. Her hands were bruised from holding on to that bed.

She got her patient to safety and began helping with carrying others to safety down the stairs. The next couple days were a blur going back into town seeing the devastation and going through the rubble of what used to be our home. It was very difficult, but GOD was there with me on my emotional roller coaster!

Seeing people help people, the compassion and generosity has been amazing. Mercy Hospital has been good to us. Brad is working like a crazy man and I am working from our temporary home. My husband's cousin suffered the loss of her daughter on Saturday, June 4, 2011 due to injuries from the tornado. We are continuing to hold her up in prayer during this difficult time.

My grandmother (mom's mother) passed away Saturday evening June 11, 2011. My mom and her siblings really need lots of prayer. I will miss my grandma. Now she is watching over me. She was a very special lady and I loved her so much!

Now my poor baby girl, Abigail, has chicken pox from head to toe. I'm doing all I can to keep her comfortable in this heat. I thank the Lord for my wonderful in-laws who have been here with us every step of the way. Their unconditional love and support have been amazing! I am so blessed to have two such wonderful people in my life.

I know God will not give me more than I can handle. I know he has a plan for Brad and me! I will continue to praise Him in the storm! For those of you who might read this, please keep us in your prayers! We do know God has a plan for us!

Back to the Country for Me

By Gary Harrall

I was watching TV when I heard people yelling outside. I stepped out on the front porch and heard what sounded like a freight train. It was loud and getting louder.

I ran through the house and into the basement. The lights went out and I heard the house collapse behind me in the basement. I saw the door into my basement rip off the hinges like it was nothing.

When I came out of the basement, my first words were, "Oh my God!"

The devastation was amazing. And I am not ashamed to say I sat down on what was left of my foundation and cried.

I walked to my grandma's house over on Indiana Street. I lived at 2315 Kentucky Street.

My place of work, Vitran Express, got destroyed, too. All of our trucks, trailers, freight- destroyed.

I'm moving back to the country where I belong. I can't stand it in town.

Laela's Story

By Kaylea Hutson-Miller

The devastation in Joplin is overwhelming, but the words of local clergy and President Barack Obama left one Joplin High School student with hope that her community will recover.

Laela Zaidi, 15, now a sophomore at the ruined Joplin High School, not only lost her school when the F5 tornado blew through Joplin, but also her home and three homes of family members.

She also knew several students who died as a result of the twister.

Yet, after hearing the President and others speak during Sunday's memorial service, Zaidi is confident Joplin will not only recover, but also be better than ever.

"There was hope in the air," Zaidi said. "We have a very resilient community.

"I left wanting to go hug my world, and help – volunteer doing anything I could for the community."

Having the President speak at the service, she believed, gave community members the push to know that Joplin will survive.

"It was a huge morale booster to have our own President standing there, saying the community will rebuild," Zaidi said. "I believe the healing process has begun.

"Joplin will heal, Joplin will move on."

Zaidi, who is Muslim, said she especially appreciated the words of the Rev. Aaron Brown, of Saint Paul's United Methodist Church, when he said death never wins in the end.

She agreed, adding that one way to honor those who lost their lives in the storm is to celebrate their legacy.

That statement was especially poignant for Zaidi, as she mourns the loss of a high school friend, Will Norton.

"We've all heard his story and are horrified by it, and are all grieving deeply," she said, "but the fact that death doesn't win – I believe there is life after this.

"Will was such a humble guy. We can live, and in doing so, honor him."

Zaidi believes the entire service, whether viewed in person or viewed on TV, touched everyone who experienced it.

"It's sad that it took a tragedy to get him [President Obama] here," Zaidi said. "I feel honored that he was here... He gave us a push. He gave us hope."

LOOKING TOWARD THE FUTURE

When the tornado struck, Zaidi was at a friend's house. Her mother, Vaidi Saba, was at home, taking shelter with several family members, while her father, Dr. Navid Zaidi, was at work at St. John's Regional Medical Center.

Because Zaidi and her extended family lived in the same area of Joplin, she not only lost her home, but also the homes of two aunts and her grandmother.

In all, more than 20 members of her family found themselves directly impacted in one way or another by the tornado.

At one point, many took shelter on the campus of Missouri Southern, in the Leggett & Platt Center.

"I thank God that we are all ok and all alive," Zaidi said. "A

Laela Zaidi

house is a house, you can rebuild it, but you can't rebuild a person.

"My dad said the community will have to start from scratch. [But] I have so much faith, probably even more faith than in my whole life. Things are going to get better."

EVERYDAY HEROES

In his address, President Obama talked about how everyday heroes made a difference in the immediate hours after the tornado struck.

Zaidi agrees.

She is quite proud of how her father, a pulmonary and internal medicine physician with St. John's, has responded during the crisis – providing medical care at medical care at the Missouri Southern shelter even as he found himself finding shelter.

"He truly is a hero," she said, "He doesn't realize the good he's done for the communality."

Not only would Navid Zaidi walk around the shelter, talking to people and caring for them, but she said he made sure they patients knew where he was sleeping, so they could seek him out in the night if something went wrong.

RETURNING TO NORMAL

A week after the storm, as the healing process begins; Zaidi finds herself looking for signs of normality.

"Everyone is appreciating the little things in life at this point," she said. "When the Starbucks re-opened, it was one piece of my life that was back to normal. I could go [there] with my friends."

The other piece of normality may not come, until she is able to see friends on a regular basis.

When that happens, "I'll be the happiest person in the world," she said, adding that she's sure the new high school will be "one of the best schools around" when it is rebuilt.

Kaylea Hutson-Miller is the former editor of the Grove, Oklahoma Sun and is currently speech, drama and debate teacher at Grove High School.

Sarcoxie Soldier Saved Lives at Walmart

By John Hacker

National Guard Specialist Jeffrey Price doesn't consider himself a hero, but his actions on May 22 earned him special recognition on May 26 from Maj. Gen Steve Danner, adjutant general of the Missouri National Guard.

Price, 22, Sarcoxie, a member of the 294 Engineer Co., based in Carthage, worked at the 15th Street Walmart on May 22, when, "it got real noisy from the wind and the rain.

"Then I saw the beams on the roof start pulling off the concrete, so we went to the actual inside because we were in the back," Price said. "We were standing back there where all the associates were, and the beams started moving. Then the panels in the ceiling started moving and then the only way I can describe it is a pop can. It was like a pop can crushing and the next thing I know, I look up and all I can see is sky."

Everyone hit the ground and held on for dear life as the roof was ripped from the store and shelves started crashing down around them.

Jeffrey Price, a Missouri National Guard Specialist, was honored at a ceremony at Missouri Southern State University on May 26 for heroism for his actions as the tornado tore apart the Walmart at 15th Street and Range Line Road where he worked. Photo by John Hacker

Price is a small man and initially his supervisor and another manager jumped on him to protect him.

"He said he thought it was funny because he thought I was a kid, I'm a small guy, so he was trying to protect a kid, so he jumped on me," Price said. "When it got done, me and my supervisor got up, he was the one I was most concerned about because the last time I saw him, he was standing up. That's when I started hearing all the sounds and I kept hollering for him. Finally, I heard his voice and

Jeffrey Price

found out he was okay."

Price said everyone tried to find anything to protect themselves from pelting hail that fell in the minutes immediately after the tornado hit.

Then, Price, his supervisor, who is an ex-Marine, and the others started looking for a way out of the store.

That's when Price's small stature paid dividends.

"The back wall had caved in and it had a gap underneath it and we had tried to see if we could go out that gap, but we decided if we moved anything there it might fall," Price said.

"The inner roof had come down so we decided I was the only one light enough to walk on that roof so it wouldn't hurt anyone, so I climbed up there and helped people up. My supervisor was helping lift them up and I was escorting them across the roof and helping them over."

Price said he considers himself lucky because all he lost in the storm was a motorcycle while others, including his supervisor, lost everything. He doesn't consider himself a hero.

"My boss at work said in his eyes I'm a hero. I don't believe that," Price said.

"I'm not going to tell you I wasn't scared, I was scared to death, but in the same sense, I was seeing people who were just standing there, in shock, and I was trying to get them to get out. I did what I had to do."

a Survivor's Story

By Rhonda Hatfield

As we left a few minutes early from Joel's graduation ceremony at Missouri Southern State University, we hurried to our cars so that we wouldn't get rained on.

Aunt Vicky (Newcomb) rode with Uncle Jackie (Hatfield) and Aunt Vickie (Hatfield) to race back to my house so that she could put the top up on her convertible so it wouldn't get rained in.

I rode with my mom (Diana Painter) and stepdad (Chuck Painter) and Tavis (Beaver) rode with my dad (Harlan Rigsby). As we got home, we noticed that Aunt Vicky's car top was up.

My husband Brent and son Travis (Morris) were out on the patio because Brent was cooking hot dogs and hamburgers. I went into the house and started getting out stuff for the hamburgers.

Aunt Vicky started cutting up tomatoes and onions. I put the grad cap made of sugar paste onto Joel's cake, took a pic and then was off to another errand.

Joel King showed up; Dad and Tavis had already made it back. Joel opened one of his cards and then the sirens blared. We turned to watch the TV and were told that there was a funnel cloud between Joplin and Galena. The gray area took up one-fourth of the screen and once I saw a transformer blow on the screen I said, "that's not a funnel cloud, that's a tornado." With all of us thinking it would do its normal path by going towards Carl Junction we all went back to what we were doing.

A few minutes later the hail came, quarter size and odd looking. Joel, Brent and my dad were all outside and Joel showed us a piece of the hail. The rest of us continued talking and I do remember telling Jack and Vickie that if the tornado came this way it was their fault because it was following them, since they've been hit numerous times. This was jokingly of course.

Then we heard one of the guys come into the house screaming that it was here, and I immediately yelled "My 6 into my bathroom, everyone else into the guest bath," and we ran.

Then I heard it, the large train coming, and I knew we were in trouble. I got a cover and covered Mylee up and stuck her in the bathtub, Tavis was on the left of her in the tub, Travis on the right. I hollered for Joel and I heard him yell that he was getting a mattress. I got on my knees and leaned over the tub watching my children and then it hit. I had no idea where my husband or my oldest child was. I don't remember what it sounded like after that.

Tavis screamed "I love you mommy" and I hollered back "I love you too, Tavis. It's gonna be all right".

I could feel dirt and objects just pounding me. I got hit several times in the back and behind with 2x4s and/or bricks and I knew the next time I got hit that I was gone, and I was at peace with that, but I just didn't want my children hurt.

The wall behind the kids started coming down and I stuck out my arms to it and started screaming, "No."

I was just thinking, "Please God, not my babies," and then silence. It was gone and I leaned up, asked Tavis if was okay, then Travis, pulled the cover off Mylee to check her.

Travis had just gotten hit in the head by a part of the wall. No one noticed any minor injuries on themselves; you couldn't even feel them at this point. All o.k. but I didn't know where Joel was, so I screamed for him. He answered, "Yeah". He had been a couple of feet from me lodged between the toilet and vanity.

Brent had been behind me; he had gotten in the bathroom after the roof had already been ripped off. After I figured out that all my kids and husband were safe we quickly noticed that the rest of our family members were all buried under debris and walls.

We saw an arm of one and that was it. We pulled my Aunt Vicky out first, followed by my mom, Jackie who was in serious pain, then Chuck. Vickie and my dad were buried deep.

While others were trying to get them out, I was trying to find shelter for mom, Mylee, Tavis and Travis to get under to protect them from the rain.

Mom was shaking terribly, and I knew Mylee was cold as well. A minivan had landed just up the street from us and the back had popped open so I put them in there so they could get warmed up. It was so quiet out. You could see siren lights everywhere but so many people were walking around in the streets silently.

I went back to help with my family members. Kevin (Beaver, Tavis's dad) arrived shortly and took Tavis with him so they could go find their other family members. As people passed by, I asked if they could help but any people who were in that area were searching for their own family members and I understood that.

An EMT worker came down through our area. She checked Uncle Jackie out and said it wasn't life threatening, so she continued on. Shawn, Saundra and Walter Emarthla showed up too. Shawn stayed behind and the others went back to Miami. Joel was all over the neighborhood helping, and then he came to me and told me had found our neighbor lady who lived behind us dead in the backyard.

I hollered for dad but heard nothing, but the others were telling me he had been talking. I had thought they were lying to me to keep me from panicking. I walked mom and Mylee up to 24th and Main so they could sit in an ambulance and warm up and then I returned to my home to help find my family members.

My aunt and dad had been pulled out safely, thanks to a construction worker who knew just what pieces of a wall to pull up so that the wreckage wouldn't then collapse again on my dad.

As soon as I arrived back at the house I hollered for my dad and someone told me he was out and o.k. but I didn't believe it until I saw my dad walk around some debris. I just remember hugging my dad and breaking down.

We were all alive.

We searched for something to put Uncle Jackie on because he was in such severe pain. We finally found one of our doors that was very sturdy and got him onto there, then we loaded him in the back of a stranger's pickup, Vickie with him and then off to the hospital they went.

Joel and Brent went to several surrounding houses helping others. Travis's family showed up to check on him, but he had already headed towards their house to check on them. Uncle Tom (Newcomb) showed up. Chuck, me, Vicky and Tom went up to where I left mom and Mylee, but they were no longer there. Somehow I told them, Tom and group, to go on and that I would keep looking.

I went back down by the house looking for anybody that I knew and went back up to Walgreens where I met up with Brent and Shawn. We went to Memorial Hall, then to one of the schools looking for mom and Mylee.

A volunteer drove us all over town helping us to find our family. Finally, I said to take us to my grandma's and there Mylee was, asleep on the couch. That was after 10 p.m. Nearly five hours after the tornado hit. Mom had gone back out with Tom and Vicky. David's (Rigsby, my brother) kids were there as well, David had gone to find dad since he didn't realize he had been pulled out. Rowdy (Cooper, my dad's stepson) had picked Dad up and took him home. Shawn had been picked up and went back to Miami. We finally knew we were all accounted for. Then the search was on to find out where Uncle Jackie was taken and that search ended about 3 a.m. when we found out that he had been taken to Rogers, AR with non-life-threatening injuries.

Aftermath:

Uncle Jackie has several broken and fractured ribs, released from hospital the next day

Aunt Vicky -sprained ankle

Mom -crushed arm

Aunt Vickie -hurt back

Joel -cut head

Tavis -glass in back

Me -sore butt and back, scratched up arm

Dad -fractured rib

Chuck- badly scratched up arms

Travis -sore head

Mylee -one little scratch on her foot

House: Destroyed, 2335 Grand Ave, Joplin, MO

Vehicles: 7 destroyed, 1 found a block away demolished in a neighbor's driveway

Lives: Numerous neighbors dead and we lost one of Joel's best friends, Caley Lantz Hare, 16 years old. He was no doubt the biggest lose we suffered. We can replace everything but him. Lantz was on his way to our house for the birthday/graduation party.

This is dedicated to my heroes H. Joel King who refused to stand by and wait for help to save his family members and surrounding neighbors and Tavis Beaver who was willing to give his young life to protect his little sister and to the one we lost, Lantz Pantz.

McCune-Brooks Deals With Disaster

By John Hacker

When the deadliest tornado to hit the nation in more than 50 years took out half the medical infrastructure in Southwest Missouri, McCune-Brooks Regional Hospital in Carthage suddenly found itself the largest fully operational hospital in the region.

The injuries the doctors, nurses and staff at McCune-Brooks treated in the hours after 5:41 p.m. on May 22 were horrible — and they kept coming — but the staff was up to the task, treating more than 300 injured people in the 24 hours after the tornado.

"After it was all said and done, I was very proud of how this hospital stepped up," said Dr. Robert Arnce, an emergency room doctor who was on duty when the tornado hit Joplin.

"The staff functioned above and beyond their normal capabilities, just rose to the occasion. Their training came to the fore in this disaster."

McCune-Brooks Hospital CEO Robert Copeland speaks at a ceremony welcoming employees of St. John's Regional Medical Center to their new, temporary workplace in Carthage. Photo by John Hacker

A DOCTOR'S PERSPECTIVE

Arnce and the rest of the McCune-Brooks emergency room staff were working their way through a relatively routine spring day that Sunday when the skies turned dark.

Severe thunderstorm and tornado warnings are part of that routine in May in Southwest Missouri and at first this did not seem any different.

"We had heard that there was bad weather coming and of course that's not uncommon," Arnce said in an interview on June 1. "We had heard that there was a tornado cell or supercell approaching Joplin from the west, then we heard it had touched down and it had hit parts of Joplin."

That's when routine went out the window.

"Not too much longer after that, we heard it had hit St. John's," Arnce said. "The EMS community is pretty quick to get everybody

73

up to date and we realized that St. John's was incapacitated, and a lot of the injuries would be coming here so we activated the emergency disaster plan and got tremendous response with that.

"A lot of people had seen it on television about the time the pages went out so nearly 100 percent of our medical staff responded, and we had multiple doctors down here waiting on patients."

Within minutes, the first patients made their way to the McCune-Brooks ER. It was the beginning of a night that would stretch the imagination and present challenges that Arnce had never encountered in his career as an emergency physician.

"The first wave of the injured that came, they kind of had that 100-mile stare that reminded me of what you might see in a documentary on a war," Arnce said. "We had a lot of people who brought their loved ones over here in private vehicles that were without windows, some without doors, just demolished.

"Some even had dead family members in the cars with them. They didn't know what to do with them so they would show up and there might be one in a family with minor injuries, one with major injuries and another family member dead.

"Some people even apologized for bringing their dead family member over here, they just said they didn't know what to do with them. We told them, 'You don't have to apologize; we'll take care of them.' I've never seen anything like it."

The injuries were like what a doctor might see in a combat zone, with sticks, rocks and other debris whipped around so fast it acted like bullets. The injuries were severe and graphic.

"We saw a lot of serious injuries in that first wave, traumatic injuries to the eyes. A lot of people were hit by flying debris and had ruptured globes with objects impaled in their eyes," the doctor said. "They had pieces of limbs cut off, crush injures, open fractures, a lot of lacerations, a lot of bad internal injuries. A lot of the people we've seen have been injured in ways that I've never seen before.

A lot of them had penetrating trauma injuries like you normally think of with people who were shot with a gun."

Arnce said as the night of May 22 and May 23 progressed, he could track the progress of the rescue workers by asking patients where they came from.

"I could tell where the rescuers were because we kept getting people from those areas," he said.

"As they headed down Range Line, we'd get people and we'd ask, where are you from and they'd say I 'm from the AT&T store, I'm from Academy Sports, then I was across the street at Taco Bell. We could track the progress by where the people were coming from as they dug people out."

He said staffers at McCune-Brooks were performing jobs they didn't normally do to help out.

"You had family practice docs, internal medicine docs, OB docs, all down here, out of their element, but pitching in," Arnce said.

Pam Barlet, public relations officer with the hospital, said administrators and front office workers came in and worked to help the medical staff keep treating patients through the night.

"Our patient accounts manager, her staff and volunteers did $600 worth of laundry at Uptown Laundromat because we ran out of linens," Barlet said. "We needed clean blankets, warm blankets, cloths, gowns and other things for all these patients."

Arnce said the top administration was on hand all night and granted emergency privileges to doctors who came from Springfield and Branson to help.

He said those volunteers brought more than just themselves.

"It was interesting, we never ran out of stuff," Arnce said. "We'd get low, literally, we got low on stuff to sew people up with, about that time in would come a group of docs from Skaggs in Branson with two cases of suture material, or in would come four doctors and a bunch of nurses from Cox with material we needed.

"It was amazing. The response was amazing, multiple doctors from multiple disciplines, even multiple cities who came in. The administration was in here and granted them emergency privileges to help and they just dived right in."

A NURSE'S PERSPECTIVE

Linda Carnes, the head emergency room nurse at McCune-Brooks, was not working on May 22. She was attending a birthday party for her grandson at a home east of Carthage when the clouds started moving in.

"We saw the storm coming in and we were looking at it and all of a sudden we saw this debris flying through the air, pieces of plywood and shingles and we were like, where is this coming from?" Carnes said.

"We heard the tornado sirens go off, and then the hail, I mean large hail and in the back of my mind I knew something bad was going on and I knew I probably needed to get to the hospital, but I needed to make sure it was safe for me to travel first."

Carnes ran home, changed into scrubs and arrived at the hospital about 7 p.m. to find that the disaster plan had been implemented and patients had started arriving.

"When I got to work, I was so surprised that, first of all, the entire ER was set up for a disaster, there were hallway beds, there were hallway chairs, clipboards were there, everything was labeled, charts were there," she said. "The staff did a miraculous job of setting the ER up, they did wonderful."

Triage, the prioritizing of patients by the kinds of care they needed, took place at first at the emergency room lobby, but that was quickly overwhelmed, so a second triage center was set up in the main lobby where medical people saw patients who needed treatment, but did not need to stay at the hospital.

Gary Pulsipher, CEO of Mercy St. John's Regional Medical Center, speaks at a press conference at McCune Brooks Regional Hospital in Carthage on July 1, 2011, as McCune-Brooks CEO Bob Copeland, Board members Pat Phelps and Tom Giesert, State Rep. Tom Flanigan and Mayor Mike Harris look on. Photo by John Hacker

Barlet said among the patients that came to McCune-Brooks were 23 pregnant women who came to the hospital for evaluation because they had been scratched and bruised in the tornado and were concerned about their babies.

Carnes said most patients came straight from where they were rescued in Joplin to McCune-Brooks.

"Most of the people I personally took care of knew St. John's was gone, knew Freeman was going to be overwhelmed and so they left their homes, dug themselves out of the rubble of their homes and came straight to McCune-Brooks because they knew they would not get seen over there," Carnes said. "Of course, we welcomed them with open arms and did what we could for them."

Barlet said 22 local doctors responded to the hospital's pages for help.

"We got them here, and then when we opened up the other area, we decided to split the doctors up," Carnes said. "When we did triage, we said they have a laceration that needs to be sutured, we sent them to the outpatient lobby because we had doctors over there who were strictly suturing up wounds and taking care of x-rays.

"We kept the more serious in the ER lobby, the ones we thought might need to go to surgery or had the deeper lacerations that took multiple layers to close or may need to go to surgery to get cleaned out. We had some amputations and some compound fractures, the ones with bones sticking through the skin, that we kept on this side and saw and took care of."

Barlet and Carnes both said the tornado victims were calm and patient as they waited for care.

"My observation of being back here was that the people didn't whimper. They were so accepting of anything that you could give them," Barlet said. "They were waiting in line to be seen and they were so accepting of our situation. I would be running back and forth and there would be one guy in the hallway and he had a blanket on, but he we cold so we switched out the blanker and kept him warm and they were just like, thank you. We'd ask, are you doing alright, as good as they can, and they said yes."

Barlet said McCune-Brooks staffers were starting to wear down, but the patients were still coming in around 2:30 a.m. when unexpected relief arrived.

About 2:30 in the morning, we were exhausted, and this busload of 22 professionals from Cox, who had worked all day at Cox Medical Center in Springfield," Barlet said. "Five of them were doctors and the rest were trauma nurses and techs and they showed up and said what do you want us to do."

"And they brought supplies," added Carnes. "We had run out of laceration kits, they brought laceration kits.

"It was like a godsend. We were overwhelmed, we're just a little hospital, we worked in trauma and lots of blood and crap for hours and then these people showed up, ready, willing and able. It was great because they didn't bypass us and go straight to Joplin. They stopped to see if we needed anything and oh, my god, that was so great."

Barlet said volunteer doctors and nurses came from other places, including Skaggs Memorial Hospital in Branson.

"Then we had another doctor, Stephen Waller, son of David Waller here in town," Barlet said. "He heard about the tornado, got in his car and drove down from Kansas City just walked in and said I'm here. He's an infectious disease doctor in Kansas City.

"Dr. Judy Parton came here and worked in our triage. We had nurses from St. John's who knew they couldn't go to their hospital, so they came here to help, St. John's Springfield, Cox Springfield nursing staffs were here. Those people coming in, they just showed up and we utilized them. They checked in like everyone else and we put them to work."

One problem that concerned McCune-Brooks administrators was that they had no communication with the medical services in Joplin and no way to tell how long the emergency would last or what else McCune-Brooks could be doing to help their cohorts in the heart of the storm.

"We had no communications with Freeman and St John's because the cell phones were down," Carnes said. "Landlines were tied up because of the increased calls. At one point Bob Copeland finally texted Gary Duncan so they could talk and then not long after that, that was probably 2 a.m., finally we got a call from Freeman telling us what they were doing, and we could tell them what we were doing, and we were able to touch base."

Coordination among the hospitals started improving later the morning of May 23 when St. John's set up its temporary hospital at Memorial Hall in Joplin and Dr. Tia Strait, dean of the school of technology at Missouri Southern, set up a temporary hospital at the brand-new health sciences building at the university.

"When St. John's set up at Memorial Hall, we were able to call them and they were able to talk to us about what we could take and what we were treating," Barlet said.

"St. John's called us and said, we have no way to sterilize our equipment, can you sterilize our equipment? So they sent their own tech, and we sterilized all their equipment. Actually, we did it for two or three days, we sterilized all of that.

"Tia Strait was in touch with us from Missouri Southern and they knew what they could send us, what we were able to take care of, and what they needed to send to Springfield. They knew Freeman was pretty well booked so they started sending patients straight to Springfield."

Barlet and Carnes said a big part of the treatment provided at McCune-Brooks was just listening to the patients tell their stories. They said taking the time to listen helped the patients cope with what had happened to them, but it had practical medical applications as well.

"It also helped because you knew the circumstances they were in, so you knew better where to look for injuries," Barlet said. "Even though their legs weren't hurting, a lot of people had injured legs but that's not what they noticed."

"You checked every inch of them," Carnes said. "Their backs had cuts and scrapes, you get them undressed and you look at their backs and stomachs and you look at their legs. You actually touch them all over and ask, does this hurt and ask what hurts.

"We had a little three-month-old baby, I think she was okay, but she had these cuts and scrapes all over here, just like her parents.

McCune-Brooks and Mercy St. John's staff watch as officials announce the new personnel sharing program that will allow more than 100 Mercy St. John's Regional Medical Center employees to work for McCune-Brooks while St. John's is being rebuilt. Photo by John Hacker

They were in a house and had to dig out from all the rubble and we did x-rays and cleaned them all up. We had a team specifically, that was all they did, was clean people up. We took some of the nurse aides and some of the non-clinical people and had them just cleaning wounds."

Arnce, Carnes and Barlet all said the loss of St. John's Regional Medical Center was a blow, professionally and emotionally, to everyone at McCune-Brooks.

"I was kind of teary about it," Arnce said on June 1. "I had worked at St. John's for 13 years and had run the ER before we formed our own company and came over here. I still have a lot of friends over there, a lot of colleagues so my concern was, just like for loved ones, did anybody get hurt or are they alive or not alive.

"First, you locate your family then you start to think about your friends. St. John's holds a kind of special place in my heart and I have yet to go by the building. I don't even know if I want to. I want to remember it the way it was."

Barlet agreed.

"Those are our cohorts, our teammates over there, our coworkers," she said. "We have a lot of PRN people who work over here that work there too. We have a lot of staff that are full time here that are PRN there, per diem workers there. I have family who work there, and I was worried that they were working, and then the patients, it's a tower and they have, like us, lots of windows, and I'm instantly worried about the patients."

Since the tornado, McCune-Brooks has established a talent sharing program where more than 100 St. John's employees, from doctors to cleaning staff, will work at McCune-Brooks for the next two years or so as the Carthage hospital doubles its bed capacity to help fill the gap left by the destruction of the more-than-300-bed St. John's.

Arnce said he finally drove over to Joplin and saw parts of the destroyed area about a week after the tornado.

"The other thing that went through my mind was as bad as it was, and I don't want to minimize how bad this was, it could have been worse," Arnce said.

"If it had gone a third of a mile further south than it was, it would have taken out both of those hospitals. Then what do you do. The other thing I think about is what if it has been during a weekday, all of those kids in school, there would have been people in all of those office buildings west of St. John's that are basically just gone. I don't ever want to minimize how catastrophic it was, but it could have been worse."

Code Black

By Randy Turner

Close to 150 people were in the 15th Street Walmart 5:30 p.m. Sunday, May 22, 2011. On a normal Sunday, you might have expected more, especially when you had hundreds of people who had just left the Joplin High School commencement ceremonies at Missouri Southern State University.

But this was no ordinary Sunday. The tornado sirens had already sounded, but perhaps thinking them something akin to the boy who cried wolf, many Joplin residents were used to ignoring them.

The sirens went off all the time and nothing ever happened.

The last major tornado in the city had been in 1974, 37 years earlier. Thirty-seven years is plenty of time for a city to grow complacent. In that tornado, the fatalities had stayed in single digits, the same as when a 1971 tornado had cut a swath through the city.

So with just 11 minutes to go before the storm hit, for many of the people on Range Line, the hub of Joplin's economy, it was business as usual.

Even as people were still walking the aisles, gathering items, managers at the Walmart store were already preparing for the worst. When they received word that a funnel cloud had touched down in Galena and was heading their way, the store went into Code Black.

Walmart associates began moving customers toward the Site-To-Store area in the back of the building, a procedure they had gone over time and time again during required emergency training.

Just before the storm hit, some people pulled off Range Line, parked their cars in the Walmart lot and raced into the building. One of those people, fresh from buying a riding lawn mower for his dad, was Tommy Carpenter.

"We saw that wall of storm heading at us."

The danger of that wall is that it hid the tornado funnel clouds until it was too late.

As they moved customers back, associates swapped jokes in an effort to keep their spirits and the spirits of their customers up.

Then the lights began flickering. For a moment they went off, and then they came back on again. Finally, it was complete darkness.

Nineteen-year-old Cameron Paul, a Wal-Mart associate, had watched as one woman angrily left the building a few minutes earlier because she was not allowed to buy groceries after the Code Black procedures began.

Paul stood by the front entrance until the winds sucked the doors off the building. He ran to the back of the building, taking any stragglers with him. As he reached the electronics department, the tornado ripped the roof off the building. He watched helplessly as a support beam fell onto a couple and their child only a few feet away from him, killing them instantly.

After that, he kept his head down and waited for the nightmare to end.

"This is where we're all going to die," he thought.

As the tornado hit, another 19-year-old Walmart associate,

Breann Ferguson, shouted, "Get down on the floor," aiming the warning at everyone in sight.

"It sounded like someone was taking a sledgehammer and swinging it around and around and hitting everything in sight," she told a Wall Street Journal reporter.

As she finally hunkered down on the floor, she began praying for what seemed to be an eternity but was actually only a few brief moments.

The Walmart associates tried to keep the customers calm. That is what they have been taught to do, but that was in pretend situations.

This was the real thing.

In the back of the store, customer Debbie Chaligoj's main concern was for her three-month-old grandson Grayson, who was in the store to have his picture taken. It might have been the last picture taken of the toddler had not it been for Tommy Carpenter's decision to ride out the storm at Walmart.

As the storm hit, Carpenter, on his knees, covered Grayson and the car seat in which the child was sitting, keeping him from harm.

From that vantage point, he could hear screams, prayers, and people crying out in agony as they were struck by falling beams or hit by flying debris.

And then as quickly as it began, it was over. As rain poured down with no roof there to stop it, Walmart associates began pulling people out of the debris.

Cameron Paul, whose father was an Army medic, began grabbing first aid supplies that had been blown away from the pharmacy and treated the wounded. At first, some balked at being treated with materials that were partially covered in dirt after the storm, but Paul calmly explained that they would all have to take tetanus shots anyway. That explanation satisfied the doubters.

Debbie Chaligoj was reunited with her grandson. It wasn't until later that she learned the identity of the man who saved the child who came to be known as "the Walmart baby."

As Breann Ferguson passed through the center of the store, she saw a man lying on the floor, lifeless. She said a silent prayer.

The associates began escorting people out of what was left of their workplace. As Cameron Paul guided a child through the store, trying to keep him from seeing the worst, his effort was unsuccessful. The boy said, "There's a dead guy over there."

Cameron did not know how to respond.

It took an hour to get the building evacuated. Tommy Carpenter, the hero who had saved the Walmart baby, found the riding lawn mower he had come to town to get had not survived the storm; it lay crushed beneath his pickup.

That didn't seem to matter much, though, as he looked around and saw mangled cars in every direction, some of them holding the bodies of people who had decided to wait out the storm in the parking lot.

As for the lady who was upset and stormed out of the store because she was not allowed to buy groceries, Cameron Paul hoped she had not become another statistic in the worst tornado to hit the United States in six decades.

People wandered about, since most of them lost their cars to the tornado. Some like South Middle School communication arts teacher Kathy Baker and her three daughters, Breanna, Molly, and Maggie, began the long walk home.

Only an hour earlier, the family watched proudly as Breanna received her high school diploma during ceremonies at the Leggett & Platt Center on the Missouri Southern State College campus.

Three days earlier, Kathy expressed her feelings about her first-born graduating. It seemed like only yesterday that she was taking Breanna to kindergarten for the first time. "I watched her walk in the kindergarten classroom, go to the desk that had her named printed on a strip of paper and begin playing with Play-Doh."

Now that Breanna had crossed the threshold of adulthood, the horror of the last few moments, made Kathy want to hold on to her and her other daughters and never let them go.

But that would have to wait. Their car was gone, and they had a long walk home.

MSSU's New Health Sciences Building Comes in Handy

By John Hacker

In August 2010, Missouri Southern State University started using a facility that had been in the works for more than a decade to build, a state-of-the-art training hospital with 29 hospital beds and robotic patients to allow student nurses to train without fear of hurting a real person.

Dr. Tia Strait, dean of the school of technology at Missouri Southern, knew the potential of the building she now managed, in fact, less than a month earlier, the university and American Red Cross signed a memorandum of understanding to use MSSU facilities in case of a disaster. Turning the Health Sciences Building into a hospital was one of the options.

"We didn't develop it or design it at first to serve as an alternate treatment location, but when several people from the hospitals came through, they said, Tia, you really need to be a part of the Jasper County, Joplin Emergency Health Care Coalition," Strait said in an interview on June 2, 2011, 10 days after the deadly EF5 tornado hit Joplin.

"I started attending those meetings this fall, as well as our safety director here on campus. We signed a contract with the Red Cross to be a sheltering facility three weeks before the tornado," Strait said.

"Really, we were working on this. Last Tuesday (May 24, 2011), McCune-Brooks, Freeman and St. John's representatives were going to meet with me here at the university. We were working on a memorandum of understanding as to how we would all work together in the event of a disaster."

Little did anyone know how soon this capability would be needed.

Strait said she was watching the news from home when a friend told her to check the Weather Channel.

She left her home in Carthage so quickly to go to Missouri Southern to start clearing the Health Sciences building for use as an emergency hospital that she missed a call from someone at Freeman Health Systems asking her to do exactly what she was already doing.

"We pretty much just sprang into action," Strait said. "When I saw St. John's hospital, I told my husband get ready, we've got to go. As we were driving over here, I was trying to reach my department heads, not knowing who had been affected, who hadn't, and those kinds of things, so we could get things going. We started moving simulators and all that kind of stuff out of the hospital beds to prepare for any kind of patients that would come."

Strait said she started with very little, treating people and sewing up wounds with the material and drugs they had in the dental clinic, where the public can come in and have their teeth cleaned by dental students. That quickly changed.

"When we first started treating patients, the only things I had were dental sutures, dental lidocaine and anything that we treated patients within the dental world," Strait said. "But within 24 hours, I bet I had probably close to a million dollars' worth of medical supplies."

"It was a God thing, because God sent me the right people. I was coordinating all of this and trying to get everything put together, but within four hours I had a dispensary. I had Tim Mitchell from

Family Pharmacy in Neosho, bless his heart; he was here within two hours and he pretty much took that and ran with it and I had that pharmacy staffed 24 hours a day with two pharmacist volunteers."

Volunteers started showing up from across the region more quickly than the patients as the community started to adjust to the reality that St. John's, one of Joplin's two major hospitals, was knocked out.

"It took a while because I don't think people really knew we were here," Strait said. "I think Freeman Hospital knew we were here because when I went home Tuesday, I had a call from Freeman.

"They knew that we had that capability and we talked about being a treatment facility in case of disaster, but to begin with here, the halls were full of volunteers. I had to finally move them to one end of the hallway to free up the main entrance where we could intake patients.

"Then I would go to that room where we had all those volunteers and tell them I need you to work here, here and here. Probably the picture that McCune-Brooks saw and Freeman saw was probably a little more traumatic than what we saw.

"Within the first three hours, I bet I had 70 volunteers, doctors, nurses, anesthesiologists, orthopedists, radiology tech, respiratory therapists, paramedics," Strait added. "As the week progressed, I was just utterly amazed at the people that came from all across the country to volunteers. I had a group of physicians from Arkansas, from the medical school in Jonesboro, Ark., they brought up some residents and interns with them that actually stayed with me for three days. They were there 24 hours a day and slept so that, no matter what, I knew I had medical coverage.

"There were other doctors, Girard Medical Center sent over doctors. It just really restores your faith in people, the American spirit and how people really care for one another."

Strait said that for more than a week, a building that was built to teach people how to treat patients, was used to treat the real thing, and take up the slack created by St. John's destruction.

"We have 29 beds, and our simulation center is designed kind of like an ICU, and that's kind of how we used it," Strait said. "Those hospital beds function just like they do in the hospital with oxygen, the medical airs and gasses and suction, so basically we could do basically everything over there except surgery.

"We did not have a surgery center, but in the Justice Center, the Franklin Tech surgical tech program has their tech lab down here and I know that when this started, one of the anesthesiologists and my husband took my keys and got stuff where, if we needed to do surgery, we could have done some minor surgery.

"We just kind of raided their area and I knew they wouldn't care. We have a close working relationship with the Joplin School District."

Strait said while the staffs at Freeman Health Systems, McCune-Brooks Regional Hospital and St. John's Regional Medical Center, after they moved to Joplin's Memorial Hall, saw horrific injuries, the staff at her hospital, saw those with more minor wounds.

"Most of the injuries we saw were broken bones, lacerations, people that had been battered," she said. "We would see people who had a bruise every quarter inch on their body from stuff hitting them. We saw people who really needed to be observed overnight because they had head injuries, those kinds of things.

"Then we tried to find a place for them to go when we released them, other than the shelter. If they were elderly, we tried to find a nursing home. I had one of the individuals who was helping me start calling all the long-term care facilities and assisted living facilities to see, do you have space, can you take somebody. So we tried to find a more stable environment for everyone we saw, or to get them back with family."

Strait said the environment was very orderly and organized.

"It wasn't chaotic at all," she said. "We put the patients in a classroom, we had a couple of classrooms set up where we actually would have a doctor come in and assess the patient and determine whether it was something we could treat right there or if they needed to be kept overnight.

"If we needed to do sutures or set a broken bone, we sent them to the dental clinic because those dental chairs worked for that kind of situation. It was an organized chaos because we didn't know what was coming in, but we had the space to see these individuals and try to keep some semblance of confidentiality and privacy."

Twice in that first week after the tornado, Strait said she and her staff had to move patients from their beds, on the third floor of the building, to the lower floors because of tornado warnings.

Strait said she saw numerous stories and examples of heroism in the 10 days or so the clinic was open, but it was a friend and coworker and his wife who provided one of the most inspiring stories Strait saw.

She said the Dean of the School of Arts and Sciences, Richard Miller, and his wife, Cindy Miller, came to help, but it wasn't until days later she learned they could have been doing something else instead of spending their time at the University.

"Within one hour, this is the resiliency of our people, Dr. Miller and his wife were in the health science building and what they said to me was Tia, we're here to help, put us to work," Strait said.

"His wife is a nurse for St. John's, so I put her to work doing triage. Probably an hour and a half later, someone said, 'Did you know Richard and Cindy lost their house?' I had no idea.

"When I talk to Richard now, and his wife, I asked his wife, 'Why did you come here?' She said I asked Richard, where do we go, and he said we're going to the University because Tia will have her health sciences building up and running."

In the second week after the tornado, St. John's was setting up their hospital in a tent just east of their ruined building and they were still providing care from Memorial Hall. Water had been restored to full capacity at Freeman Health Systems and other hospitals were taking up the slack, so Strait was told she could shut down the clinic at Missouri Southern.

"We were blessed here at Missouri Southern that we weren't harmed by the tornado and we are all just thankful that we can give back and help in any way we can," Strait said. "I think it will make this community closer and even the towns around us, it's going to bring us all closer and I think we all feel we're neighbors and we're taking care of neighbors."

a Graduation Day I Will Never Forget

By Lacy Heiskell

I was outside MSSU after my graduation taking pictures with my family, then it began to sprinkle, and the sirens went off.

Like almost everyone else in Joplin, we didn't think much of it and continued with our picture taking then decided to leave. I was driving my Nissan Sentra and was planning to drop my mother and stepfather off at home then meet up with my boyfriend to go eat.

We were sitting in the traffic of the parking lot when we felt something smash against my car. My mom asked if it was hail and we all replied that we didn't know. It happened again and we knew this time it was hail and still we didn't think much of it.

I started driving and began to turn onto 7th and Range Line when the radio announced that a tornado had touched down there, so I turned my car around and headed down Duquesne. It began raining so hard that I couldn't see anything outside any of my windows and we began to panic.

I pulled over and my stepfather and I traded places. He got in the driver's seat and I went in the backseat He started to drive, making his best attempts to figure out what we should do or where we could go.

Finally, we pulled over, unable to drive anymore due to not being able to see outside the windows. We were on 20th and Duquesne, near the roundabout, and across the street from the gas station Mom tried running out of the car to the building we were next to, but my stepdad quickly grabbed her and pulled her back in.

The next thing we knew, we saw a black wall heading towards us. The driver's side window was the first to blow out and then complete chaos hit. We all ducked down and covered our faces. I remember glass and wood hitting my body and the wind howling. Then my car began to move and I thought "This is it; I'm going to die right now."

I had never been so sure of something in my life and in that moment all I could do was scream, cry, and pray. I started off praying, and then I began begging. I begged God to save my family and me. I later heard that the tornado only lasted about 45 seconds, this stunned me, it felt like hours. Then it was finally over.

My stepdad kept asking if I was ok, but all I could do was cry. I was in such shock and I still am. We didn't know what to do. My roof had caved in except for the last layer of metal. We attempted to drive a little, but all the wheels of my car were popped except one and there was too much debris in the roads to get anywhere anyway.

We finally got out of the car and looked around us, everything was gone, including the building my mom was trying to run into. Cars twice the size of mine where flipped, smashed or wrapped around what was left of buildings.

It looked like someone had taken a bomb and dropped it on that area. Then we began to walk, and the destruction continued. We ran into a woman who was kneeling and crying, her children were in a red truck that was flipped, smashed into the ground, and had another car on top of it.

There were more people walking in the streets, some crying, others not saying a word. We walked for a while and then a family was nice enough to pick us up, complete strangers who were willing to help people in need. All their windows were busted out besides the front windshield.

We drove past Home Depot, gone.

Walmart, gone.

Half of Range Line, gone.

Then a thought occurred to me, is everyone safe? I tried countless times to reach my boyfriend, my family, friends, somebody, anybody, but the phone calls refused to go through. We got almost to my house (I live behind Lowes) and the family couldn't take us any further because of all the trees in our roads so we headed home, unaware of if we had a home to go to or not.

We realized my mother's leg was cut up very bad. A neighbor, who we had never met before that day, offered to help. The man was an ex-EMT and cleaned my mom's wound but told her she would definitely need stitches and should get it checked out before it got infected.

I wore my graduation robe throughout the whole ordeal, and I think that's part of the reason I wasn't injured as bad, just a few minor cuts and bruises. My stepdad walked the rest of the way to our house while we waited for my mom's wound to be cleaned. The man pulled out glass, grass, and insulation out of my mom's leg.

We were very fortunate to be alive and to have a home to go to. My car was destroyed but it kept us alive and you can't put a price tag on life.

I later went back to my car and found 2x4s, glass, insulation, dinner plates, pictures, and blueprints in it. There's not a day that goes by that I don't think about that day. The town I was born and raised in was destroyed in seconds. The school I had attended for the last four years was gone.

You can look at pictures of Joplin but it's nothing like actually seeing it and living through it. The images still make me sick to my stomach though. I have blocked out a lot of images from that day, but I will never forget May 22, 2011. I know God has a plan for me and for Joplin.

In an Instant, Everything Was Gone

By Iris Fountain

Dear Family, Friends, Church Members, Company Employees, and Volunteers,

I want to begin by thanking you all for your outpouring of care and concern, your thoughts, prayers, donations, and phone calls during this very difficult time. As you know on May 22 a devastating tornado ripped through our town. It destroyed our home along with 8,000 other homes and businesses in the Joplin community.

Our lives were going along as usual on that Sunday afternoon. Gene was on the phone with a friend. I was doing the dishes when the tornado sirens sounded. With a quick glance to the sky, we knew something was terribly wrong.

Philip and I took cover in the bathroom and Gene lay on the hallway floor because there was not enough space for the three of us to fit in the small bathroom. We held hands, covered our heads with beanbags, and prayed.

Within a matter of minutes everything we had collected in 36 years of marriage along with our home of 20 years was torn apart. Angie was our stronghold throughout it all. We called her from our cell phone and only had about a minute to tell her that the tornado, that was supposed to be heading towards her house, had hit ours instead. Then due to poor cellular connections the phone went dead after less than a minute.

All she knew is that we were crying and panicking saying that our house was destroyed and was caving in on us.

It took Angie and Robert three long hours to finally reach our house. The traffic was crazy! Everyone was trying to find out about their loved ones. There was debris and power lines all over the roads.

At one point they had to give a group of firemen a ride in the back of their truck with their rescue gear. They were trying to find an 80-year-old lady who was trapped in her house and couldn't get out and was suffering from a puncture wound from the debris.

After helping the firemen get as close as they could to the address, Angie and Robert had to park at a church and walk almost three miles to reach us because there was no possible way to drive into our neighborhood.

As they walked for as far as the eye could see the houses in the neighborhood she grew up in were all but rubble, there was the sound of hissing gas from the gas leaks, and small fires were breaking out everywhere. I can only imagine the horror she and her husband felt not knowing what they were going to find when they finally reach us. After all they only had that one quick panicking, heart stopping, phone call.

Immediately following the tornado, after calling Angie, we looked outside and realized it wasn't only our home, but the entire neighborhood was gone. It was unreal, we were living a nightmare.

We immediately went across the street to find our neighbors climbing safely out of the rubble. Their house was more damaged than ours. They are strong Christian people and other than a small scratch on him they were safe as well. Then together we went and checked for our other neighbors, some of whom we've called neighbors for the last 21 years.

Thankfully, they were all safe. It was a miracle! My neighbor Mary and I stood in the street, in the rain, hugging each other and crying. We kept reassuring each other saying, "These were just material items, we are ok," but tears for our homes were falling down our cheeks along with the rain that was still falling from the dark sky.

By the time the Angie and Robert arrived we had gathered a few necessary things such as medication and a few other things we could find to take with us. It was growing dark very quickly.

Because of the loss of light, we had to leave almost immediately after they got there. I kept trying to save things and had a large pile of items in the front yard that I wanted to take.

Angie told me, "Mom, you can only take what you can carry. That stuff has to stay. We'll come back and get it tomorrow. It's just stuff, you're ok; that is all that matters. We can take care of the stuff tomorrow."

The five of us walked away from our home in the dark with only what we were able to carry in our arms. Robert was holding a leather bag with Philip's kidney pills and a few other small but important items. Gene had our large lab Patty on a leash.

Philip is night blind, so Angie and I took turns holding his arm and guiding him in the dark while trying to juggle our small dog Oscar in his kennel and my purse. That was it.

We were so tired and so much in shock, what a sight we must have been. But it wasn't only us. Everywhere you turned there were people walking their dogs and taking nothing else with them. We were all trying to find a safe way out of the neighborhood. The further we walked the flatter the houses became. There were ambulances and emergency vehicles, parked along the streets. The road was filled with power lines, trees, debris and the ground was a thick layer of mud from all of the rain.

Angie and Robert let us stay at their home that night and for the rest of the week. We had no clothes, so we borrowed their clothes to sleep in. Later it was a small joke about where all of our underwear ended up. We couldn't seem to find it anywhere. Was it in one of the neighbors' trees? It wasn't funny but was a way for us to make light of a horrible situation. We found that if you didn't laugh the only thing left to do was cry. We've done both. We had no idea our life would change forever that day.

After we got home and realized to some extent the amount of damage that had occurred that night, we knew housing would be in short supply and high demand. The next morning Angie woke Gene up at 6 am. Together they sat down with the paper and began making calls.

Many rental houses had already been taken and the list wasn't very long in the first place. The first rental house that we found available we took. We never even looked inside. This was probably one of the smartest things we could have done during this crisis.

Even now almost a month later FEMA trailers are just now arriving in town. They are estimating there may be at least 900 of those. Every hotel room is booked, there are no houses available to rent unless you want to drive an hour to get to work each day. We even have a tent city set up where many now homeless people have been living since Memorial Day.

It was several days before we really knew the extent of the damage. We had no time to watch television or to read the newspapers. We heard whatever they were telling us on the radio as we traveled in the car. That was really it. And that was all that was on the radio for the first two weeks. All music stopped.

The radio became our city's lifeline. With phone lines no longer working and over a thousand people missing in the beginning the radio became a place where people could call in to try to find others.

So while the rest of America knew how bad our tornado had been, it wouldn't be until the next weekend that we would slow down enough to really learn the full extent. We had family and friends who lived far away calling us and telling us all about our hometown. Celebrities from the national news along with the National Guard and even the President were all here. We missed all of it.

As a matter of fact, for a while even the experts didn't know the extent of the damage. At first, they said it was an EF4 with six miles of destruction. But a few weeks later they pronounced it an EF5 with 14 miles of destruction and they announced that 151 lives had been lost. We knew it was bad enough just trying to drive to and from Angie's house.

In the daylight the next day we all drove back to "our home." After living in Joplin for so many years we couldn't even tell where we were at in our own neighborhood. The roundabout and the dead cows in the pasture told us it was time to turn. There were no other street signs or recognizable landmarks left standing. There was just miles and miles of piles of rubbish.

We didn't have the heart or the stomach to watch the news and go see any more of it for ourselves than we had to. Philip told us it was an EF5 as he looked out the window during one of those first car rides.

We didn't need to wait for the experts to tell us that, how could it have been anything less? We already knew that. The pictures and the videos by the way do it no justice. They never do. You would have to see it for yourself to fully comprehend the devastation.

We spent that second day in the pouring rain trying to save as many items as we could. This was a difficult task because our house had no roof. We had to carry whatever we could save out to our shop and try to dry it off with wet towels because everything we had, including the towels, was already wet and covered in sheet rock and insulation.

Through thunder and lightning and in three inches of water on the floor of our home we worked. We worked all day saving as much as we could, and the next, and the next. It rained most of the week. Everything was soaked. All of the wood furniture, our chairs, couches, beds.

We spent three full days at the laundromat trying to wash clothing, curtains, and bedding. Each time the clothes came out we had to wash the washer between the loads because it was full of leaves, sheet rock, and insulation. We managed to save quite a bit.

You realize how quickly that material worth is nothing compared to human life and you had better have your soul right with God. It was almost like the Bible says, "God will come quickly like a thief in the night."

Our bathroom was the only room still intact. Or it was until the house was demolished last week. We walked out of our home unharmed. Not even one scratch. I do believe God had his hands resting on us that night.

I also want to say it was awesome to see how fast everyone came to help on that night and the next day and the weeks to follow. People from all over the country came to help our city, thousands of them.

They drove down the roads offering us gloves, tarps, warm food, watermelon, Gatorade, water bottles, bibles. Complete strangers.

One day a man walked up to Gene and asked, "Do you live here?" Gene answered "yes." This isn't an uncommon question these days. Everyone wants to know if you lived here, if you've filled out these papers, talked to these people, and gone to this place or that. So, boy was he surprised when the man handed him a hundred-dollar bill and walked away.

Some days we would pull up in our driveway to find an army of complete strangers clearing our debris for us. Do you know we'll never be able to thank so many people for all of the kindness they have shown us? How can saying thank you ever be enough especially when you don't even know who all to thank?

If you know my husband Gene, you know he is a man full of pride. He is not one to take handouts from anyone. But just this one time we were able to convince him that he couldn't do this all by himself. That even with Angie and Robert helping there was no way we could do all of this by ourselves. We had no choice but to accept and embrace the help.

When you go through a crisis like our family has with our community you realize so many people really do care. Thank you does not seem like much for all you have done for our family during our time of need.

We don't know what will happen tomorrow. We are taking it one day at a time. We are mentally and physically exhausted. But your support and acts of kindness have given us the strength to go on and to start over again.

Thank you from the bottom of our hearts. Each and every one of you has helped to make our situation a little more comforting and bearable knowing that you have offered so many gifts and prayers. Your generosity is amazing. God bless you all!

an Incredible Ride

By John, the Maintenance Guy

Note: The following was written by John, who described himself as "a maintenance guy from Freeman Hospital."

OK everybody. Here we go. What a ride it has been. I just woke up from crashing finally. I was at work at Freeman Hospital when the tornado hit. I was the only maintenance man on the evening shift. The alert sounded, said it was a warning for Carl Junction, which is 10 miles north of where we were. I started all the generators, 10 of them, just in case.

When the storm hit, we did not realize what had happened only ¼ mile north of us at St John's, not until the caravans of people started coming in. St John's took a direct hit, blew out all the windows, then had a gas leak and an explosion. The tornado was about eight blocks wide and went through Joplin west to east. It never left the ground.

We had people coming in pickups with wounded, cars with all the windows blown out, people on boards, doors, tables. We emptied four conference rooms of the rolling chairs... about 100... to use as wheelchairs.

We had four triage areas going full blast, one at each entrance. People were lined up for 10 blocks or more just to get to our driveways.

We had just gone through an earthquake drill last week, so everyone knew where their supplies were. It was calm chaos. Hundreds of wounded, covered in blankets, sitting in chairs, lying on the floor in rows, blood everywhere.

The nurses and doctors were great. Our phones were out instantly. The cell towers were inundated, couldn't get out. We couldn't call for reinforcements. They just started showing up from everywhere. EMTs, nurses, doctors, local and even from out of town.

The few in the kitchen started making sandwiches. We brought out all the blankets we had, brought up rolling supply carts of bandages, cases of bottled water. We formed small groups of volunteers to manage traffic so the ambulances could get in and out. School buses of injured started coming in. Truckers were bringing in semi loads of injured. There were no lights in Joplin. We have a six-story tower and all you could see were blue and red lights everywhere. I personally took the first six bodies and started a temporary morgue.

The stories people were telling were beyond belief. We had probably 10 or 12 dogs that people had brought in with them running somewhat loose in the hospital. There was smoking in the hospital on a no smoking campus. There were cries of pain, sorrow and yes, even joy, when people would find loved ones.

The situation in town is way worse than you see on TV. I came home in the dark and did not know where I was because of the destruction, until I came to a roundabout in the road and realized I had gone a mile too far. I couldn't get through to Sandy on the phones and people started coming in from the area I lived in with horror stories of total destruction. The Home Depot you see on TV is just blocks from us.

Finally, another employee came in and said his mom was ok and she just lives two blocks from us. The tornado just missed my son by two blocks as well. My daughter-in-law is a therapist and has no office building to go to anymore. Her father is a dentist who also has not office left.

Joplin will take years to rebuild. It is kind of like the Twin Towers. You can actually see all the way through town, end to end.

The high school is gone. A major business street, going east and west on the east of town is flat on both sides of the street for two miles, with nothing left standing. Thousands of people have lost their homes, and their possessions, and their income because their places of employment have vanished off the map.

On the other hand, Thank the Lord, I have my home, my possessions and my job. I never had to serve in combat, but surely this has to be somewhat similar in relation of chaos. I kind of know what the Japanese must feel like after the tsunami now.

Yes, I know some of the dead in Joplin personally. Freeman Hospital still looks kind of like it did that night. We still have stuff everywhere. The floor is still dirty because Joplin has virtually no water pressure. We barely have enough water to run our sterilizers for instruments. Only two bathrooms work in the hospital. I don't know why they do.

The water company has so many broken pipes in houses that are gone, that it can't get the pressure to come up. A large area of the roof blew off and the rain collected and ran down in between the layers of roofing and into the areas full of pipes and wires and is still dripping and of course, the rain won't stop so we can fix the roof.

We have buckets all over the halls and even have a couple of areas of rooms we can't even use because the water keeps coming out of the ceiling area. We have removed hundreds of ceiling tiles that have gotten wet and were coming down anyway.

The fire alarms keep going off all the time because the wiring system is getting wetter and wetter with all the leaks. We have to check each alarm to make sure there is no fire and then silence it. Please pray for us. A lot of people's lives are changed forever. Mine is. And I am all right. Thanks for all of the calls. Sorry the phones still don't work very well. We are on a curfew with National Guard at hundreds of intersections. A 15-minute drive to home took me an hour. Only my Freeman badge let me through. Maybe I will write more later. Now I'm going back to sleep.

the Day That Changed Everything

By Shaney Delzell

It started off as a normal Sunday. I was hanging out with my family and my best friend Maddie. We knew a storm was coming in, but we didn't know how bad it was going to be.

When the sirens went off the first time, we all loaded up in the car to leave the house because we lived in a trailer. We decided to go to the Fifteenth Street Walmart. When we got there, a police officer told us to go to the back of the store, where everyone else was.

My mom, Maddie and I had met my mom's best friend's daughter, Cheyanna, at Walmart. She had just gotten off work. Maddie and I had to go to the bathroom. When we got out, the police officer wouldn't let us leave that area because it was the Walmart "safe spot," and they had just spotted the funnel cloud. I called my mom and had her and Cheyanna come back to me and Maddie.

About the time they got back there, my boyfriend, Kyle, had texted me and told me there was a tornado down on Seventh and Range Line. His dad is the battalion fire chief so he would know more than anyone at Walmart. When Kyle called me, the tornado was closer to Fifteenth Street. I was on the phone with him when it hit and the last thing I said to him was "I'm getting hit! I'm getting hit!"

About that time, the police officer was telling everyone to get down and cover their heads. My group was pushed into the men's bathroom. We took shelter under the urinal. Cheyanna and I under one, Maddie and my mom under the other.

I made myself as small as I could get to fit underneath the urinal. The next thing I knew we were all praying, and then the urinal busted, and the roof and walls caved in. I would probably be dead if I had not been under the urinal, because where I would have been was where everything fell. I wasn't even paying attention to the sound that the tornado was making. I was focusing on keeping myself calm.

When the tornado had passed, the first thing my mom did was scream my name because no one could see me. Then this very generous man pulled Maddie out and dug me out of the rubble and pulled me on top of the roof to get out.

The first thing I saw was St. John's Hospital and that it was destroyed. And the first thing that popped in my head was my dad, is my dad okay?? He stays in the house. When everyone that was with me was pulled out, Cheyanna was handed babies! When that family had got out, we took off walking to what used to be the front of the store, to try to find a way out. We were being told to pick up whatever we could find to cover our heads from the hail.

When we got halfway through, I saw my dad, and I started crying tears of joy because he was still alive. He had skirted the tornado, and was dodging trees, houses, and a whole bunch of debris, to get to us at Walmart! He thought he was going to die. My mom's car was nowhere to be found. We saw Cheyanna's and it was able to be driven. It won't even start now. We got to Elaina's and her family was so nice to us. They got us dry clothes and blankets.

We were sitting there listening to the radio about all the destruction. We sent my dad right down the road to where our house should have been. He came back to get me and my mom after Maddie was with her parents who live right next to Elaina. My dad told us our house was gone and took us home to get what we could.

And still to this day June 26th, 2011, we have no home.

the Voice of Joplin

By Randy Turner

The story of the Joplin Tornado may have received more attention than any event in southwest Missouri history.

Unwillingly, our city found itself featured on page one of major newspapers in the United States and throughout the world. We watched as Diane Sawyer of ABC, Anderson Cooper of CNN, and reporters from every major network and regional television station found their way to a city that few of them had ever seen before it was touched by tragedy.

One of the "bigfoot' reporters had a familiarity with Joplin- Brian Williams, NBC Nightly News anchor started his career at KOAM and lived in the area that was wiped off the map by the tornado.

During much of the time that the networks and the reporters from Kansas City, St. Louis, Tulsa, and Springfield television stations were here, we were not seeing any of their reporting.

The storm knocked television and cable service off the air in Joplin. Some of what was being done could be viewed via the internet, but not in those hours just after the tornado. In a time when any tidbit of news was vital as Joplin residents tried to find out what was going on around them, there was no way they could wait until the next day to have the Joplin Globe put events into context.

The need was immediate; the need was now.

And that need was met by radio, more specifically, News Radio KZRG and the Zimmer Radio Group.

Relying on Zimmer stations during weather emergencies is nothing new for those of us in the Joplin area.

During a recent ice storm, when electricity was out, it was Zimmer that put all of its stations into public information mode. The same thing occurred each time the area was threatened by severe thunderstorms or was put under a tornado watch. It was that reliability that enabled Joplin residents to know where to turn when skies darkened, and the winds began to pick up.

Seeing that it could be one of those days when the weather would be a major concern, KZRG News Director Josh Marsh reported to work Sunday afternoon and broadcast the first tornado warnings, for southeast Kansas, at about 4 p.m.

"That's what we usually do," Marsh said in an interview with Ignite TV. It was obvious, he added, that what was coming could be far worse than just threatening weather.

"This was one of those days when you are really concerned because of just how hot and humid it was and a cold front was just passing through." The big concern, he said, is that it was going to be "a nasty situation."

And then it happened.

"I don't think anyone was prepared for what was going to happen," Marsh said. Marsh was talking with the city of Joplin's emergency director Kent Stammer "when he said there was a tornado on the ground."

"Your mind doesn't jump to an EF-5 and you don't think it's going to go through the middle of Joplin," Marsh said in the Ignite Church interview. Soon KZRG, just like most of Joplin, was bathed in darkness. "Our generators kicked in and we kept broadcasting. We had no radar, just a microphone and a few lights on our mixing board.

"It was unreal."

As the heart of Joplin was laid bare by destruction, Marsh felt the same fate was going to befall his workplace. "We were watching huge stuff flying past the window. We thought the studio was going to be hit."

At home listening to him, it was amazing just how calm Marsh remained. I knew something had terrible had happened to my city, but just how bad it was became clear when I heard the live broadcasting of a KZRG reporter who was driving through the streets after the tornado.

"It's horrible; it's horrible," he said. "The high school is gone."

I thought it was exaggeration. I prayed it was exaggeration, but as he kept providing information on apartment housing that been blown away, on people roaming the streets after their homes had been destroyed, it became obvious that he was providing an accurate description of the horror that Joplin had become.

As Marsh sat in the nearly pitch-black studio, he worried about his wife and whether she had survived the storm. "I kept trying to help people," he said. "It was scary. I didn't know if my wife was safe. There was no way to get a message to her."

Thankfully, she was uninjured.

From the first moment the tornado struck, and for the next few weeks, KZRG and the Zimmer stations became the center of our community. It wasn't just Marsh; it was every on-air personality from each of Zimmer's seven Joplin stations, including seven who lost their homes. People who normally listened to rock or country or syndicated talk shows tuned in hour after hour as up-to-date information was provided.

At times, what we heard was heartbreaking. Such was the case when a man named Frank Reynolds called to tell listeners about the search for his 16-month-old great-nephew Skyular Logsdon, a fighter who had survived a premature birth. Reynolds left a number for anyone with information to call him.

The child's body was later discovered.

But there were also tales of triumph mixed in with the sadness. KIX 102.5 Program Director Rob Meyer, another Zimmer employee who kept broadcasting after losing his home. "It really doesn't feel like work when you feel like you're doing some good."

And there were times when the radio station was able to relay good news to its listeners. When they were able to reunite family members, "the feeling was great," Meyer told KY3 in Springfield. "It was incredible."

And through it all, the Zimmer stations were wall-to-wall local coverage, 24 hours a day.

"We kept on broadcasting," Marsh said. "We knew that's what we were supposed to do."

If Joplin city or school officials held a press conference, it was live on the Zimmer stations. Whenever there was an update on the number of dead or what needed to be done with debris, it was covered live.

It was not the official moments that made the coverage so riveting and made it a lifeline to Joplin residents for days after the tornado, but the conversations between on-air personalities and those same residents.

They passed on information as people tried to find out where their loved ones were. They listened to survival stories, they took the questions provided to them by listeners and posed them to official sources. And more than anything, they provided a consistent message of hope and optimism even during the darkest hours.

"It was incredible to see the hope that was springing out of the darkest places," Marsh said. "That was the one thing that kept us going, the hope."

Some of that hope was provided by Marsh, whose skill with words is not limited to speaking. He wrote his feelings about the tornado, sharing them both on his blog and on air.

The post, simple titled "Hope," concludes in this fashion:

We will still have our sorrow and grief to share. But eventually that bright summer will come when we can shed it. Until then we will wear it together and share our tears and our stories. Emotion will pour out and we'll let it come, til it comes no more.

Hope is alive and well. It remains in the hands and hearts of our neighbors. It is a belief in each other. It is the trust we place in our neighbors. It is the expectation that we will heal.

Note: The Zimmer Group provided wall-to-wall storm team coverage for nine days on all six of its stations.

On-air staff involved were Josh Marsh, Chad Elliott, Rob Meyer, Steve Kraus, Randy Brooks, Hank Rotten, Jr., Joe Lancello, Chris Hayes, Darrin Wright, Kyle Thomas, Sam McDonald, Ryan Keith, Jennifer Wilson, Brett James, Michael Johnson, Daron Harris, and Audie Renee. Support staff included Christie Ogle, Kris Bullard, Mel Williams, Pat Whatley, Lauri Lance, Kathy Stockdale, Sherry Cable, Larry Boyd, and Tina Robertson.)

Lucky to Have a Home

By Denton Williams

Just after tidying up our house and finishing some chores, I had sat down to look over my communication arts papers, along with my Missouri Driver's Guide PowerPoint for my reading teacher.

I sat myself down onto the couch, when I heard this loud noise. It was strange... but oddly familiar. It was the first of the two tornado sirens. Not being in any hurry, because the sirens have sounded and nothing happens time and time again, I walked toward the back door, where my parents are sitting outside, enjoying the weather, oddly enough, under the circumstances. But I was seeking reassurance, and instructions.

"Relax," my mother replied to me, "It's all towards the west of us."

I tend to be very cautious anyway, so I put on my tennis shoes, and grabbed my phone, and other small things that I may need if we take cover. I sat them all in a pile, and once I did, the sirens turned off. My friend, Rylee Hartwell, was shopping at Walmart with his mom, and he called my cell phone once the employees began to escort the shoppers into the back of the store. He wanted me to check the weather.

I turned on the speakerphone, and I played the Severe Weather Alert, "Foxcast", and his last response over the phone, other than goodbye, was: "Well, the way it sounds, it sounds like it is moving away from us" Which it was, until the massive tornado changed its direction of destruction.

I returned outside to talk with my parents, when my dad was standing up, and announced that he was going inside to check on the weather. I looked at the sky, and I saw these really dark clouds, almost black. My dad glanced at it and told my mom, "Watch that cloud, that looks kind of funny," he told her,

"I remember just standing there, kind of mesmerized, the cloud was sort of spinning, but I thought, that is too big to be a funnel cloud, and just after that, I heard a train. Not in the distance, but as if it was rolling up our street."

As soon as she said that my dad told us to get into the closet, my mom first, then myself, and my dad didn't get in. We were by the window, watching the storm, saying things like: There goes the light pole, and a huge limb just blew down from our tree to the other side of the road!

I sat there praying the only two prayers that I could get out through the fear: "Protect me, O Lord, now and at the hour of our death," and the Lord's Prayer. After about five minutes, which seemed like 45 minutes, the storm ever so slightly calmed down, and so we got up, and went to look through the windows at our backyard, and front yard.

Once most of the heavy wind was gone, and heavy rain remained, we went outside. One light pole was blown over, had knocked down our fence, and was laying on our pool side. the light pole attached to it, on the other side of my house, was blown toward my house, the cord was the only thing keeping it from blowing into our house. Our patio furniture was blown over upside down and every which way and our table was in two pieces and on different sides of the yard.

I remember thinking: Thank you, O powerful God. You have proved that you are a very merciful God.

I walked down my street and the most damage that I could see was one house that lost all of their shingles, (the only one on our street), and one house had a tree fall, and a branch damaged the roof.

But a few days later, I was going for a walk to look around, and I realized: One block away, they had fairly bad roof damage. Two blocks away, people had to replace their roofs and windows. And from there, on for one more block, each house you walk by, gets a bit worse and worse, until the end of the block, where people have nothing. Three blocks from total destruction.

I am lucky to be alive, with a home.

the Story That Affected Me for Life

By Shanti Navarre

O f all the stories that have broken my heart and made me cry, this one has torn me up in a way I can't even explain. I volunteered Tuesday night and I was assigned to missing persons. I knew I couldn't handle the phones, so I volunteered for data entry, inputting the information on the missing folks.

Will Norton's name was on the list multiple times. I'm sure many of you are familiar with Will, as he was one of the horror stories that made national news.

Will was literally torn from his father's arms and sucked out of the sunroof of his Hummer. He was reported missing by numerous people.

When I was working, he was coded as "found" but apparently had gone missing a second time because, as we were down to one hospital, injured folks were being farmed out to hospitals far and wide, and often the loved ones were unaware where their people were.

The entire town... hell, the nation... believed that Will was one of those. So he was on our missing persons list as "found" and became somewhat of a beacon of hope and light for our ravaged town.

Will Norton had survived.

A couple days ago, in our constant quest to find ways across town to the storage units and not be in the way of the thousands of emergency responders and cleanup volunteers, and with streets being open one minute and closed the next, and in our ignorance early on as to the complete extent of the damage (remember, we had no internet or cable - all of our news was via texts and calls from people, like Cheyla , my daughter who was in Tennessee, or my friend Carol in Arkansas who kept us posted on the second storm that came through and sent us scurrying to our basement. We thought we could come across the west end of town on Schifferdecker. At that point, we were unaware of the damage to that area, much as we were unaware for days of the destruction on Main. We thought the worst of it was the length of 20th Street.

As we traveled north on Schifferdecker the destruction became more and more obvious. There were police directing traffic, which was backed up, but we were able to get through. As I pointed out the duck ponds to my brother, Dad and I were mourning the loss of the "duck crossing" sign and sad for the "displaced ducks." The wreckage was not as severe as further east but still phenomenal and very, very moving.

Here comes the part that I will have trouble with for years to come. Last night I saw the news report that Will Norton had been found. He had never been transported to a hospital. He had never been "found" in the first place. It was all misunderstanding and/or miscommunication.

One of our bright lights in this horrific tragedy is extinguished.

His body was in the duck pond literally as I was pointing the pond out to my brother. I feel somehow personally responsible, like I should have somehow intuitively known that he was there. He was there and I was there and if I'd known he was there he would still be alive. I know that's ludicrous but there it is.

Cheyla called me at midnight in tears, accused me of being wrong. "You said he'd been found." And so I had. We cried together, but she was more than upset.

"You didn't know him, Mom. You didn't sit with him in classes." Cheyla told me that Will was "really smart," and funny, and talented, and friendly with everyone, and that he was going somewhere with his life.

Cheyla will have to grieve Will in her own way. I can't help her. They weren't close friends, but she knew him and liked him. I will grieve in my own way, and I never even met him.

Will Norton's story is only one of thousands, but for reasons unknown to me, his has affected me for life.

How Will Norton Led Me to Joplin

By Rose Fogarty

It was May 25 and I had finally collapsed in bed from yet another fast paced, stress filled day at work. I had heard about the tornado in Joplin, Missouri, which happened three days before, but because of my schedule I had not been able to sit down and read or listen to one news story. Until that night.

As I do most nights, I pulled out my iPhone as I lay in bed and started to catch up on the news. I started reading about Joplin and began to pay attention. Then, I read about Will Norton and became overwhelmed with sadness.

Will Norton, an 18-year-old with a promising future in film production ahead of him, died tragically on his way home from his high school graduation. I can now expand on the initial story I read because I had the fortunate pleasure of meeting Will's Aunt Tracey, which I will go into later.

It was Sunday afternoon and Will had just walked across the stage to receive his diploma from Joplin High School. He wanted to stay back with his father Mark to take pictures with his friends, which tragically would be his last photos.

His mother and sister Sara headed home in the car before them to get ready for guests who were arriving for his graduation party. As Will was rushing home with his father Mark, they were frantically trying to avoid the storm and ended up driving right into it.

Being the exceptional human being he was, Will, even though terrified, started quoting scripture to his father to calm him, who was also terrified and in the passenger seat of his Hummer SUV. They were a Christian family who read the Bible, yet Will's father had never heard Will recite those exact scriptures before. The family feels that it was God speaking through Will during his final moments on this earth.

As the tornado grew fiercer there was no way around it, Will turned to his father and said, "I'm scared", and then he was gone. The tornado sucked out the sunroof and pulled Will out with it.

His father's arm was severely injured trying to hold onto him. The SUV still had Mark in it and was being flipped around like a toy car. Mark had to be cut out and rushed to the hospital with severe injuries. Will was missing.

To think of this happening to my own son, who is 11 years old, I found myself overcome with emotion.

As I read article after article about Will being a YouTube star and went to his site, www.youtube.com/user/willdabeast88883333. I discovered here, hundreds of videos that Will had made over the years which led him to want to pursue a film career.

He was on the way to this dream by getting accepted to Chapman University in Southern California.

As I watched video after video, I found a beautiful, energetic, funny, charismatic, talented and handsome young man who brought life to any situation. Will lived life to his fullest and shared his spirit with everyone he touched.

After watching for about 20 minutes, I found myself sitting up in my bed bawling like a baby. I knew I had to do something to help these poor people, whose town had been completely obliterated. I felt connected to Will now, as so many people all over the world felt after watching his videos.

If there were one purpose to Will creating those videos, it was to bring Joplin to the world's stage. He certainly got my attention and made it personal for me. I was completely devastated for this boy who did not deserve to lose his life.

I started watching on CNN and paying close attention to the destruction, to the people looking for loved ones. I saw Will's Aunt, Tracey (Norton) Prossler on CNN with Anderson Cooper. She was pleading for people to look and find Will, she just knew he was still alive. I had reached out to Tracey on the "Help Find Will Norton" Facebook page. I felt I needed to connect with her personally, but I still didn't know why.

By now, there were 50,000 people on this page, so I was not getting through all the comments, I didn't even know if she saw or read all of my posts on the threads of hundreds.

Within a week, Will's body was found in a pond near the accident site, which was less than ¾ miles away from his home. It was about this time that I received an email from a friend of mine, who started brainstorming about a mission trip to Joplin.

I immediately joined and told myself whatever I was going to do was going to be in honor of Will Norton. There were other victims of course, but Will's story haunted me. Within a span of about 5 days the St. Lou Crew for Joplin (https://www.facebook.com/pages/St-Lou-Crew-For-Joplin/176174329106856) was formed, united and ready to drive to Joplin with two 53-foot 18-wheelers full of donations, a 24-foot trailer and about 10 cars filled with approximately 30 people. We had gotten radio and TV coverage, and the people of St. Louis really came together to drop off much needed items for the people of Joplin.

Not only did they drop off items, but some also got out of their cars and stayed to help load for hours upon hours. It was incredible to watch the city come together.

We were told by many not to go down, stay out of the way, they don't need help… but we went anyway. We were on a mission and nothing was going to stop us from stepping up and helping those people.

As I left my house in the early morning of June 3, I had Will on my mind. I was leaving my kids for the weekend, missing their school picnic, but I knew there was someone else's child who needed my help more.

I went to Will's Facebook page and snapped a picture for my iPhone screensaver. I wanted to look at Will's smiling face all weekend as I worked. I knew my phone would be connected to my hip, because I had made several contacts in Joplin and they were all stored in my phone.

In those contacts were the members of Baby Skyular's family, who we were able to fill two garages full of goods which we pulled from the collections on our trucks.

As the caravan started to pull away out of Dierberg's parking lot, I was rushing around still hanging signs on people's cars. Everyone was yelling, "let's go, let's go," so I jumped in my friend's RV and off we went.

We got onto the main road and I went to grab my phone to start working and making calls. It was not there. I panicked. This was BAD. I was in charge of the delivery to Skyular's family, and their phone numbers were all stored in there. I needed contact with my children, and I had a following on Facebook that were waiting for pictures and posts, and it was so important to share our experience.

The people who were traveling with me started making calls to other members in the caravan. Someone in a car even drove back for me and checked the parking lot and store. We kept calling it and could not hear the ring, so we knew it was gone.

I was completely devastated and inconsolable. Of all days to lose my phone, God decided to pick this one? I was so upset, I was crying all the way to Rolla, Missouri, which was a 100-mile, hour and a half leg of the trip.

I felt sorry for the people who were riding with me, because believe me; it was a spectacle in that RV. I felt like I failed Will and Skyular and we had not even arrived in Joplin.

We stopped in Rolla to get gas and I jumped out of the car. By that time, I had prayed about it and decided I needed to let it go or my trip would be ruined. I figured I would be able to track down Skyular's family through Facebook on someone else's iPhone, so I was comfortable with my backup plan, yet still distraught. Then a miracle happened.

As I got out of the RV my friend's little girl came up to me and said, "Rose is this your phone?"

Time froze for a second as I was trying to make sense of it all. How in the world was she holding my phone and where was it this entire time? As I grabbed it with elation, Will's picture immediately showed up as my screensaver I had placed that morning.

The voices were in a fog as I was trying to process, and I could not believe what I was hearing. My phone was on the outside of the car, on the step, for 100 miles on a very windy and bumpy highway, all the way from St. Louis to Rolla, with Will Norton's picture as my screensaver. Will Norton protected my phone all the way there, no doubt in my mind.

There were hugs and laughter and disbelief. What a miracle it was and what a wonderful way to start off our trip. Will was definitely with us and guiding us safely to Joplin.

As we headed back on the highway, I knew I had to make contact with Tracey, Will's aunt. She had since accepted me on her personal

Facebook page, and knew the St. Lou Crew was heading to Joplin, but we had yet to speak.

Although I was worried to infringe on her privacy, I took the liberty to call her personal cell phone, because I absolutely had to tell her this miraculous story. She answered, in her sweet angelic voice (yes, she really is that sweet) and I started sobbing telling her the story.

She immediately said, "Rose, please contact me when you get here, and I want to come meet you in person." This was the beginning of the engine running full speed ahead for the St. Lou Crew for Joplin.

There were many other miracles that happened once we were down there, which I personally felt was my guardian angel in Will. Like when the St. Lou Crew for Joplin were walking into Ground Zero, with everything bombed out for miles, no plant or animal life around us. Suddenly, a Cardinal bird flew right across our front row. That was Will Norton.

Like when I was searching through rubble with tears in my eyes. I knew we were short on tools and something told me to search in this particular spot. I uncovered the one and only tool I found the entire weekend; a saw, which was needed at that very moment, by a man who was trying to get to some personal items buried in the rubble. As I passed it to him and watched him cutting through a tree to get to these items, I thought in my mind "That was Will Norton."

Like the poor girl who just wanted to help our mission, who got six barbeque pits donated from Anheuser-Busch. She was so worried because one of the lids flew off on Highway 44 on the way to Joplin. We found the lid, on the side of the highway, unscathed on the way home two days later. That was Will Norton.

Like the man who drove our injured crew members to get a tetanus shot. He said, "I will take anyone who needs to go, I work for the Lord". That was Will Norton.

Tracey, her husband Jeff and sons Matthew and Dillon came to our barbecue Saturday night, directly across from St. John's Hospital. As soon as she walked up to me, we hugged and cried.

What was supposed to be a few minute meeting turned into a several hour visit, from someone who has become a sister to me in one short week. We have great plans going forward and the St. Lou Crew is headed back for a second mission the weekend of July 22.

Will Norton will always be in my heart. I feel that Will made me so upset and connected to him because he was guiding me to Joplin. If I had not lost my phone, I don't know that I would have ever met Tracey in person and we would not be able to collaborate on the amazing things we hope to accomplish going forward, united in Will's memory and honor.

God must have needed a special one, as Will Norton is clearly as special in heaven as he was on this earth.

Tornado Ends School Year for Most Inspirational Teacher

By Randy Turner

"**S**he's racist."

I blinked twice and reread the beginning paragraph of a two-page paper one of my eighth-grade students had written about the teacher across the hall from me. That word did not describe the Andrea Thomas I know, my colleague and friend for the past four years.

Eighth grade reading teachers have a short shelf life at the school where I teach. The first one I taught beside, eight years ago, a tiny young woman with the look and voice of a teenager, became the first teacher at the school to have the embarrassment of having students throw furniture out her second story window.

I didn't expect anything different when Andrea took the job. She, too, looked like she would have fit in easily with a high school class. That was where the resemblance ended.

Of all of the young teachers I have worked with over the past dozen years, I have never met one who was so prepared to be in a classroom. She knew what she wanted to accomplish and constructed a plan that would enable her to achieve that goal. I was designated her mentor for that first year, but it would be no understatement to say that I learned far more from her than she did from me.

Over the course of the next four years, I had the privilege of watching her thrive as one of those teachers who goes the extra step for her students, no matter what their race or social status.

This was a woman who put her stock in her God, her family, and her students. By no stretch of the word could she be labeled a racist. So, I kept reading.

It did not take long for the student, an African American girl, to get to the point." She initially considered Andrea to be racist, but it wasn't the teacher who was the problem.

"I was the one who needed to grow up."

The student changed her attitude and work habits and reading became her favorite class. "Mrs. Thomas wanted to make sure I didn't fail," the girl wrote. "That is why Mrs. Thomas should be named the Most Inspirational Teacher at East Middle School."

Each year, my eighth graders write a paper declaring their choice for Most Inspirational Teacher. The students vote on the winning paper, not their favorite teacher, but for the essay, the one that does the best job of extolling the virtues of a teacher who has made a difference.

And for this young woman, that teacher was Andrea Thomas. That award would have been presented a week from this Friday, June 3, on our last day of school. Mrs. Thomas would have received a certificate and a copy of the winning essay.

The auditorium in which that ceremony was to take place is no longer standing. The winning essay, which was on the desk in my classroom, may no longer exist and if it does, it is highly unlikely it is in a presentable condition.

From what I have been told, my room and Mrs. Thomas' room were hit the hardest by the tornado that caused extensive damage to the building, which had only been standing for two years.

In the grand scheme of things, an essay and a certificate do not mean much, especially compared to the horrible devastation that Joplin has suffered from the tornado that tore the heart out of the city and has cost at least 116 people their lives and countless others their homes and property. But it would have been nice for Andrea Thomas to have been named the Most Inspirational Teacher...on her last day at East Middle School.

It would have marked the perfect ending for a frustrating year for Andrea, who reluctantly came to her decision to resign after she realized her long, exhausting hours of work before and after school were taking away from her time for family and church.

Andrea has bigger problems to worry about.

She and her husband lost their home to the deadly tornado, but even that never caused her to waver in her faith. After the tornado hit Sunday night, she did not ask her Facebook friends to pray for her,

"Please continue to pray for our city," she wrote.

As for the problems faced by Andrea and her husband, Joe, she brushed off their new homeless state. They can stay with family. "Our needs are being met."

With so many suffering, I can't help but think I am being selfish, but it would have been great to have taught alongside Andrea Thomas for nine more days and for her students to have another two weeks with this young teacher with the tough exterior and the marshmallow heart.

It would have been nice to have had a chance to say goodbye.

Originally published in the May 23, 2011 Turner Report

Calm in the Storm

By Andrea Thomas

O n Sunday evening, when Joe and I had planned to be with some of the youth from our church celebrating the approaching arrival of summer, we sat huddled in our bathtub as a tornado demolished the world around us.

At about five thirty, we learned that a storm was approaching and let another youth leader know we were going to wait out the storm at home.

Moments later, the sirens sounded. We remained on the couch watching the TV. The anchors were saying that a funnel may have been spotted, but they could not confirm that a tornado was headed our way. Then, what I would guess was five minutes later, the woman said, "I think those in the Joplin area should probably take cover."

At this point, we went to a bathroom, which was a central room in our home. Joe joked about toilet water flying on us, and we both left the bathroom again to watch the TV. I sat in the hall for a few minutes, and then, we both returned to the bathroom.

The world was silent, but the power went out. I knew, then, that something was very wrong. I lit candles, but the candles made Joe nervous. He blew them out. We sat. Joe said, "My ears are popping."

I said, "We are in a tornado." And then, we heard it.

The storm was loud; the cracking and popping of our house was louder. I remembered hearing the story of a woman flying in a bathtub with her children and surviving. I thought the roof was going to be ripped from above us, and we would fly, too.

I prayed aloud, "God, command your angels concerning us. God, now. God, you are our refuge. You are our stronghold. You are our protector."

Then I listened. Joe and I both laid lower in the tub. The house shifted. Glass was breaking. I wondered, "How much longer?" Then it ended.

I wanted to get out then. Joe was concerned. I finally convinced him that the worst must have been over. He said he felt cold air and dirt. I felt cold water. He began to open the door. I asked him to let me light a candle; I thought we would open the door to the bathroom and see the backyard. I couldn't have imagined outer walls would still be standing, but they were. I didn't see the debris and glass at first, but Joe did. He reached for my shoes, which were near. We found him some shoes in our room, which appeared to be undamaged. Then we went to our living room and kitchen.

Glass was everywhere, water was pouring in, metal pipes and pieces--not from our home--laid scattered around our home. We opened the front door.

The frame of the glass door was present, but the glass and metal handle from the door were no longer there. Across the street, our neighbors' homes had two walls standing and no roofs.

We went out into the pouring rain, turned right, and ran up the street to check on other neighbors. Everyone appeared to be okay. We ran back, jumping over downed power lines, which were everywhere. We went back into our home. We changed clothes because we were completely soaked, and we didn't know what to do. We grabbed coats and went back out.

Joe went across the street because we could not see our elderly neighbor. I called to other neighbors, asking them to seek shelter under what remained of our roof. Some came but others walked around dazed. Then others appeared. Joe returned.

The neighbor was not found--we learned later she hadn't been home. Joe started grabbing for coats and blankets. Then I did the same. We had something to give to people that had nothing.

A couple took shelter in our garage. I asked Joe to find something for them to sit on. We tried to help them by calling their family, but the phones weren't working. We tried and tried. Our next-door neighbors wanted to flee.

We helped move massive trees from their driveway. We never went past their home. If we had, we would have known a damage much more severe. Literally, three houses down, there is nothing.

Nothing.

We smelled gas and decided we needed to find family. We gave a neighbor the keys to what remained of our home and the keys to my car. We didn't know if we'd ever see my car or some of our more expensive items again, but it didn't matter. We had something to give.

Somewhere in the midst of it all, I realized that I had taken off my wedding ring to fold laundry. I had set the ring on a table that had set under one of the shattered windows. The only thing I wanted from my home was my ring. At first, I thought it wasn't even worth looking for, though. I went to help others. I thought of the ring again and went back inside. Then, I prayed, "God, please help me."

Within minutes, I had the ring in my hand. In the midst of the darkness and shattered glass, I recovered my ring.

We grabbed a few clothing items, still in laundry baskets, and we headed out the door. My grandparents pulled in the driveway then. They had come to find us. They couldn't reach us; no one could. We told them we were leaving. They got back in their car and headed to find other family members, which proved to be difficult.

Joe and I made it to my aunt's home. We couldn't connect with the rest of my family. They knew I was "okay" but at that time didn't know that we had experienced the tornado.

I thought my brothers were okay, but then, learned that no one could connect with them. Joe's family didn't really know how we were; we headed to their house. I tried to stay in contact with my parents as they tried to reach my brothers and tried to get to me.

Soon, I learned that my oldest brother was okay. Three hours after the tornado, I learned my youngest brother was fine. Four hours later, my parents made it to me. It was a joyful reunion.

We took my parents back to my home; it was, then, I learned the devastation was beyond what I had known. We left and headed to my parents' house. I couldn't sleep that night. Every time, I closed my eyes, I heard the walls crack around us. I prayed and gave thanks for what I saw as God's provisions.

***

I really didn't sleep much the first night, Sunday night. When the sun rose, I did too, ready to go to my home. My parents and Joe made a plan. Joe, my mom, and I headed for the house. My dad headed to Carthage to get supplies. We went through Duquesne, around the roundabout, and took 20th Street.

I couldn't believe what I saw.

I drove 20th in the direction of my school every day; nothing looked the same. Buildings were gone; cars were overturned, mangled, stacked. Trees had disappeared. We made it to our neighborhood. One man stood across the street at what had been his mother's home--our elderly neighbor, who Joe could not find the day before. He told us he had spent the night on her driveway. He had stayed to defend our neighborhood. We were overwhelmed with what we saw, but we began to salvage our belongings. Soon other neighbors arrived. I learned, then, that we had lost a little boy from our street.

About an hour after we arrived, the skies grew dark again. I wanted to seek shelter. My mom drove me to her parents while Joe and my brothers, who had come to help, tried to cover the massive holes in our roof.

Time moved so slow; my grandfather--Hal, "Pawdad"--made me some breakfast, which was fruit because they had no power. Then he found a radio and batteries for me. Finally, Joe and my dad arrived. Then one of my aunts and her girls came. Soon, we all had a plan and places to go. We were off again.

Joe and I went to his parents. They had power, TV for news updates, and running, clean water; their home was like returning to a normal world for us. No one was home when we arrived, but we fed ourselves, showered, and tried to talk, for really the first time, about all that had taken place.

When we had rested enough, we returned to our home. I found a few more items and left in my car, which had been spared, to go to my parents. Joe continued working. Time continued to move slowly.

Finally, Joe arrived at my parents, and we decided to spend the night at his parents. We returned to their home, and they shared their dinner with us. They also watched TV with us. Lisa, Joe's sister, who had come from Texas to help prepare and attend for a wedding--for Becca, Joe's youngest sister--gave up her bed for us. I finally felt I could try to sleep.

Before I fell asleep, I found a Bible, and I read. I needed to hear from my Savior. He had wrapped us up and protected us from the storm, from downed power lines, from images far worse than collapsed homes, but other lives had ended. I wanted to be reminded that He understood. We had so much to be grateful for, but we also had so much to mourn.

***

On Tuesday, we woke with the sun again and returned to our home. Soon, friends and family arrived to help.

Within three hours, everything we could take was loaded and on its way to one of a few family members' homes. I don't really know how it all worked out. It seemed overwhelming to me, but people came and worked until there was no more work to do.

Teri Byrd--one of my mom's friends--and her grown kids, Jennifer and Taylor, helped a ton and even took our dirty, wet laundry, which had been scattered to their home to wash it and pack it for us.

Jennifer made decisions about what could be saved and what couldn't. She thought to save things that hadn't crossed my mind, like a doormat; I'm sure others made decisions too as they packed.

Joe's parents, Tonna and Tom, and his sister, Lisa arrived and packed. My friend Kristen, and her friend along with her friend's cousin arrived, and packed. I know they did a ton of work; they never complained.

I remember at one point, Kristen handing me water. She didn't ask me; it was like she just knew it was time someone told me to drink something. A teacher-friend, Will, showed up and helped move heavy items.

Other teachers tried to make it to me but couldn't reach me. They helped others, even at some point, calling students in hopes to confirm that all our students are okay. My uncle, Lindy, and cousin, Kellen, came. My brothers came and brought a friend. My brothers covered more windows and other massive holes in the roof. They helped pack and move what could be saved.

When we heard that another storm was on its way, I wanted

to remain in shelter for the rest of the day. Joe and I headed to his parents; on the way, though, we stopped at a McDonald's. Comfort food for Joe.

When we arrived, I was able to shower and feel some comfort again. We spent the afternoon discussing various topics--we told our story, we listened to others, we discussed the upcoming wedding. Some much to look forward to even in midst of certainty.

I fell asleep early hoping to sleep through the night but not expecting to; at nine-thirty, Lisa and Tonna woke Joe and I to tell us the sirens were sounding. I jumped over Joe, who was slightly dazed, and grabbed the blanket off of him as I headed to a safer place. I sat praying in the central room in their home. Tom and Lisa listened to the news in the living room and explained to me that any tornado was headed North. I prayed for the people living in that area. Soon, I also entered the living room. Tom retired as Tonna had already done. Joe soon followed, but Lisa stayed awake with me and watched the news. When I was convinced that I could sleep in peace again, I went to bed.

***

I'd call Wednesday my favorite day since the tornado hit. Joe and I had a ton of work to do to set up our living arrangements, but we decided those arrangements could wait. We went to our church, where my aunt was helping to direct the organization and storage of much-needed supplies arriving via truck and semi from around the country.

I need to interject and tell you that for a year my aunt has been working with an organization in Arlington, Texas, called Mission Arlington.

Mission Arlington was founded to meet the needs--physical and spiritual--of the community of the area. They do a terrific job of bringing food, furniture, and other supplies in from businesses and individuals and sending those supplies out to those in need.

My aunt was impressed with the organization and has returned to Texas almost monthly since first working with the organization last summer. She kept thinking something like it needed to be started in Joplin.

We joined my aunt and other volunteers on Wednesday morning and helped organize. I had the privilege--literally, it was a privilege--of helping a woman and her daughter load their car with supplies for three families they were sheltering. The woman and I embraced, before she left. I'm not a big hugger, but I have loved hugging every person including perfect strangers since the tornado hit. I helped another family find tubs. And I tried to help another man by trying to figure out where he could shower.

Some of the other church members asked about my story; I told a little. It is still hard. I understand that we lost two neighbors, and there are people around us without family support, who need support. I am so thankful for a church who loves. I am so thankful they gave me a way to love too.

We left the church to go to my grandmother's--Gram's-- and used a real computer for the first time. We also had dinner with my parents and slept at our new temporary home for the first time; we are staying at my parents.

Joplin Forever Changed Our Hearts

By Tanya Sneddon

T here was no question in my heart whether or not there was going to be a mission to Joplin. The question was what could we really do once we were there.

However, my husband and a neighboring couple decided to pull what resources we could together. We staged a plan of action to buy as much breakfast and lunch/dinner items as we could, thinking we might be able to help at least a handful of people, once we arrived in Joplin.

I had not been there in so long; things had changed over the many years. Yet I couldn't even begin to orientate us. So we slowly pulled into town not sure what direction things got bad at or even just where to go. We found ourselves silently pulling down the road in complete disbelief of what we were seeing.

Curfew had just lifted at 6 am. It seemed as if it was going be hard to find somewhere to put the tents and start feeding. We had found our way upon the only green grass in sight that had not been littered with debris.

A security officer stood there looking at the job at hand. We asked are you hungry?

He responded with a laugh. "Of course." He had mentioned they were eating MRE's the past week. So we knew there was a service that could be done here. We then explained what we had planned.

He was extremely excited to have just started his shift next to a pancake and sausage breakfast, along with a cookout for lunch and dinner. There was a huge need for some kind of food service or something on the hospital campus. We just had no idea they did not have enough time to get outside of the destruction, eat and return on time.

We found everyone from doctors, surgeons, nurses, MASH unit coordinators, national security, construction workers, you name it. They were in our line multiple times a day sharing their brave stories with us. Each one amazed us with their strength, courage and care for others.

At that point, it sank in, a lot of them had lost family, friends, and things, yet still day after day they returned to their jobs, doing whatever it was they could do. We had served close to a couple hundred.

That is when the donations started to roll in. Along with two very cute kids who came from over a hill with arms full of food with their family. It was great; we were able to get lots of food through money and food donations.

With the local family's help, we were able to get the word out on what a great thing had developed. So we were able to run the tent for the next three days.

At that point, we had to return home. We left everything from the grill Sutherlands donated to food with the family to carry on for another two weeks.

From the point we left there had been many foods brought prepared and served. There came a point where the women left in charge had no idea what she might be feeding the crews that day. It warmed my heart to see the residents of Joplin getting up, standing strong, and rebuilding their great city.

Joplin, you have forever changed our hearts.

Joplin's Apocalypse Now

By Randy Turner

In a few hours, it will be exactly two weeks since a tornado ripped through my city and changed it forever.

I was one of the lucky ones. The tornado missed the apartment complex where I live by about six blocks. When I look outside the window, everything appears the same. It is an area that is seemingly untouched by the disaster.

Appearances can be deceiving, and in this case, are very much so.

When I listened to the radio coverage during the 10 or 15 minutes before the tornado hit, I thought it was coming my way, and there was not much I could do since I live on the second floor. I covered myself with an old blanket and a pillow and waited for fate to deal its hand.

The radio announcer continued to follow the path of the tornado as it moved away from where I lived and tore its way through the central part of Joplin. Since that time, I have blogged almost nonstop, a coping mechanism. A reporter covering the tragedy described it as survivor's guilt. That would probably be an accurate description.

For the first 36 hours after the tornado, I did nothing but offer my own thoughts, link to the best articles and videos and try to offer a service to those who were seeking information, any information, about the disaster.

Midway through the second day, I wandered into what once had been the heart of Joplin. In the school district where I teach, there are three middle schools. The one where I teach lost its gymnasium, auditorium, band room, and commons area, while classrooms suffered damage and much of the roof was blown away.

That damage was nothing compared to what I encountered when I went to the apartment complex behind the 15th Street Walmart, one of the dozens of business structures that were destroyed.

I was serving as a guide for someone else who needed information about the tornado as part of her job, but I felt more like Martin Sheen's Benjamin Willard in Apocalypse Now as he continued a search that grew more nightmarish with every step.

For as far as the eye could see, structures that had once stood proudly over Joplin's landscape had been shredded. Every once in a while, I saw a sight that reminded me that this area had once served as home to hundreds of people, a matching pair of red flowers hundreds of feet from each other, a child's doll somehow intact in contrast to its surroundings.

My apartment was fine, and I was grateful for that, but this was the area of town where my students lived- I correct myself, the area of town where my students once lived. The existence we all had taken for granted was no more, my students were uprooted now and maybe forever.

Through Facebook conversations with my students, I had learned that one of them, a tall redheaded eighth grader who was unfailingly polite in non-classroom settings, but occasionally a bit overzealous in class, had not been accounted for since the tornado. His apartment was one of those that would never again serve as a home.

I asked a few people about him and, as you might expect, in a large apartment complex with hundreds and hundreds of tenants, the people I talked to did not know the eighth grader.

Finally, I came across a man and his daughter quietly removing belongings from the remnants of an apartment. It was an apartment that was clearly damaged, but it appeared to be in a bit better condition that some of those surrounding it.

I asked about my eighth grader. "I don't know him," the man said, as he loaded a box into the back of his car. I thought it was another dead end, but he kept talking. "The apartment manager said everyone was accounted for and nobody was killed."

As hard as that was to believe as I looked at the kind of scene I had only seen before in post-nuclear holocaust films, I felt much better. My student was undeniably suffering from the loss of a home, but he was safe.

The man continued to talk, volunteering information I had not asked for, but information that he clearly wanted to tell.

"My son was killed," he said, leaving the four words hanging in the air.

I said nothing, but the exhilaration I felt seconds earlier had vanished.

"He was the manager at Pizza Hut," the man said, stopping once again. I had heard the story. Chris Lucas, 27, a veteran, had sacrificed his life, saving customers and workers at the restaurant as he guided them into a cooler.

"He has two little girls," Terry Lucas said, adding that another child was on the way.

He talked for a while longer, about everything from his son's acts of heroism to the young man's love of fishing.

It reminded me of the time 17 years earlier as a newspaper

reporter when I had interviewed the mother of a murdered eight-year-old boy. For the most part, you don't talk, you just listen. They have a story, and they want to tell it. They need to tell it.

When I returned home, it was back to blogging; it wasn't much, but it gave me the feeling I was contributing something, adding a touch of understanding to something that clearly is not understandable.

That night, I received a phone call from one of my eighth-grade students, a tiny brown-haired girl who always seemed on top of the world. It was clear a few moments into the conversation that, despite her bravado, she had been deeply affected by the events of two days earlier.

While her home was untouched by the tornado, it was evident she did not fall into that category. She had been in the middle of the city when the tornado hit. She talked of having to walk by people who had been killed.

"It didn't bother me," she said. "I'm going to be an EMT. I will have to get used to it."

For the next 30 minutes or so, she told me how much it did not upset her.

Clearly, it did.

What upset her the most became clear. Many of her friends had lived in the apartments where I had been only a few hours earlier. Those friends were alive, but they had moved in with relatives or friends, away from Joplin, some even out-of-state. She was hurting because she might not see her friends again. The people she had counted on for support through hundreds of problems that now paled in comparison were scattered, likely never to be together again.

I was grateful she had someone to talk to about it, and even more grateful that I was that someone. Again, it gave me a feeling that I could be of some use.

In the two weeks since the tornado hit, I have blogged one obituary after another, more than 100 of them. I have linked to stories of courage and bravery, links to sad stories of those who did not survive, inspirational stories of the way a city, a state, even a nation, came together to support Joplin.

Though I was sitting in my living room blogging my way through it, I felt hope when I heard the words offered by Rev. Aaron Brown, Gov. Jay Nixon, and President Obama at the memorial service one week after the tornado.

After a time, I continued to blog about the tornado, but I no longer felt guilt about having the St. Louis Cardinals game in the background.

The blogging will continue for the time being, lasting well past the time, I am sure, that the nation's eyes are focused on my city.

It's what I do.

Originally published June 5, 2011 on Daily Kos.

the Volunteer Spirit of Samaritan's Purse

By John Hacker

During the time she coordinated volunteer efforts for Samaritan's Purse, there was a certain kind of volunteer that stood out.

She recorded the names and directed the efforts of hundreds of volunteers, some from the Joplin area, some from other states.

The ones she will remember most are those who were already suffering from the wrath of the May 22 tornado.

"I had people who came in to volunteer and I asked them, 'Were you in the tornado?' and they would say, 'My home was completely destroyed, so I thought I would come in and help someone else.'

"I cried every time.'

Manning the gates for the Joplin effort of Franklin Graham's international relief organization, Samaritan's Purse, brought a lot of tears for Della Bergen, but also much laughter and satisfaction.

The one thing she did not see during her time volunteering in the tornado-ravaged community was selfishness.

Even among the children, people were putting others first, she said. "We had a toy giveaway at Forest Park early on. Kids came in. There were toys all over. You would think the kids would be grabbing five or six toys, but they were reluctant to take one.

Volunteers with the national group Samaritan's Purse help remove debris from a home in Joplin in the days after the Joplin tornado. Photo by John Hacker

It is so hard to imagine the spirit of these kids."

One child, she said, was not concerned about toys, but about the Bible he had lost. Mrs. Bergen was able to locate a Bible for the boy and when he left, his mother was holding a toy, while he was clutching his Bible.

"That made me cry."

The Bergens' tornado story started with their volunteer help, but it could have easily been different. On Sunday, May 22, they were having a special dinner at their Carthage home to celebrate their future daughter-in-law Kelsi Loyd's

graduation from Missouri Southern State University. Both Kelsey and the Bergens' son, Micah, were planning to head back to their Joplin homes after the dinner, but Mrs. Bergen, seeing the beginning of the storm, convinced them they should stay in Carthage.

The Bergens knew that everyone was safe, but with

communications spotty in Joplin after the tornado, Kelsi's mother was frantic about her daughter's whereabouts until she located them at the Bergens.

The volunteer work began from Stephen and Della Bergen the next day after getting the call from Samaritan's Purse. And with that work came the stories, one after another.

"Speaking with the survivors and listening to them tell their stories and telling how God protected them.

"Two days after the tornado, a man showed up. His daughter was pregnant with twin boys." She and her mother had hidden in a closet when the tornado hit, saving their lives, but everything else was lost, including all the gifts from the baby shower and the nursery they had worked on as a labor of love was no more.

Mrs. Bergen and Lindsay Blue took this case on as a personal mission, collecting car seats, cribs, and anything else they could get for the young family.

After the babies were delivered by C section, Mrs. Bergen and Ms. Blue took the materials to the family, which got everything it needed.

Stephen Bergen has also collected stories, working out in the field, coordinating volunteer efforts.

"We had an elderly gentleman who wanted something in his basement. His son said not to go because the basement was filled with sewage."

The intensity with which the man wanted what was in the basement piqued Bergen's curiosity. "When they were gone, I put plastic bags on, went down there, and found a trunk floating."

In that trunk, Bergen said, were dozens of letters. "They were love letters written from his dad to his mom in World War I.

It wasn't just the elderly who had belongings that held special meaning to them. One of Bergen's favorite stories concerns a 15-year-old boy named Chase who had one item he had lost that he

Thousands of volunteers, including those from the national organization Samaritan's Purse, came to Joplin in the weeks after the tornado to help Joplin residents rebuild their lives. Photo by John Hacker

dearly wanted to recover- his wrestling medal.

Chase's searches had been unsuccessful, but when a number of Samaritan's Purse volunteers joined the hunt, the medal was located 15 minutes later in a tree.

Another favorite story concerned an old family Bible lost in a swamp-like area but found totally intact under a piece of furniture- the only place in which it could have remained undamaged.

Though the work has been hard, and it has nearly completely eliminated their personal lives, the Bergens would not trade a minute of their volunteer efforts.

"Every day is a challenge. It has been incredible to see all of the people who have come from all over the U. S. to help out." Mrs. Bergen said.

"Every day has been a blessing."

a Return to East Middle School

By Randy Turner

As I circled around East Middle School, where I was teaching eighth grade communication arts (English) until our school year ended nine days early due to the horrific tornado that ripped through Joplin Sunday evening, I dreaded each step, knowing I would see something that would increase the pain I was feeling.

I had walked with *Daily Beast/Newsweek* reporter Terri Greene Sterling from where we had parked in a driveway close to 13th and Duquesne to the roundabout. The sound of sirens that had punctuated the night air Sunday had been replaced by a chain saw symphony as homeowners and those who rushed to the area to do whatever they could do to help, began the slow, painstaking process of clearing a landscape that would have seemed unthinkable...still seems unthinkable...just two days earlier.

As we turned onto 20th, heading east toward my school, we came across a couple celebrating one of the small victories that have served as a counterpoint to the death and destruction, a beloved pet

Photo by Randy Turner

cat had been found alive and uninjured, hiding in a small crawlspace beneath the rubble of what once had been a home.

It wasn't all good news for the couple, which had slipped into the bathroom for protection when the tornado hit. They were okay, the kids were okay, the cat was okay...but the family has two cats.

The second was still among the missing.

As we talked to them, they unearthed a precious family picture, unharmed by the forces of nature. Earlier, they had been able to salvage irreplaceable photos of the wife's sister, who died a few years ago.

The scene was the same as far as the eye could see, on both sides of the street. Homes were leveled; debris was scattered. What appeared to be some kind of costume was hanging precariously at the top of what was left of an oak tree.

We gingerly stepped around any wires that were strewn across the street, though they were not likely to still pose any kind of danger. Finally, after stopping to talk to a few more survivors and workers, we turned into the driveway at East Middle School.

My room, at the end of the eighth-grade hallway, is at the first corner of the building we reached. I could tell nothing about its condition; boards were covering where windows had once been. I had been told Monday that my room and the room of eighth grade reading teacher Andrea Thomas at the end of the hall had suffered the most damage, primarily from the sprinklers, which had been activated. It seemed silly in the midst of such devastation and destruction, at a time when at least 122 people had lost their lives, but I confessed to Terri Greene Sterling that the only things I worried about as far as my classroom was concerned, were the papers on the Writers' Wall of Fame, where the best work of my students is displayed each year, the older papers from my top writers of the past, which I display at the beginning of each year to give my new students examples of excellent writing, and my collection of books on the American civil rights movement, which students use each year when we do our third quarter research project.

None of those things really mattered, but I could not help thinking of them.

There was nothing to see from our vantage point outside of the building, so we walked to where our gymnasium once stood. The floor was still there, as was a fierce Joplin Eagle standing guard on the back wall, but the other walls had vanished. I did not even want to think about the auditorium, which has been the pride and joy of East Middle School. How was I going to be able to gaze at the debris of a place where so many memorable moments had been packed into two short years?

It was the place where Lara Stamper and her drama students had staged the school's first ever musical, *Disney's The Aristocats*, just a few weeks earlier, the place where concerts were performed in the last two weeks by Kylee Tripoli's orchestra, Nick Moore's band, and on the last performance ever given in the auditorium, just five days ago, Julie Yonkers' choir and the Joplin East Middle School Show Choir.

I thought about the two benefit shows we had staged to raise money for the school the past two Novembers, with performances from history teacher Rocky Biggers' group, the Victorymen, Stone's Throw Theatre's Godspell cast, Hannah and Tammy Cady, my band, the ironically named Natural Disaster, and scores of middle school and high school students.

It was apparent when I turned the corner- the auditorium was in ruins. And then I saw the American flag, a source of pride in good and bad times, and an incredible thing of beauty when it stands proud in the center of such desolation.

I remembered how the flag stood proudly in the auditorium during our Veterans Day Assembly and our observance of 9-11. It is remarkable how much meaning such symbols have in times of despair. There is nothing like the majesty of the American flag.

God willing, there will be a new East Middle School standing someday soon and the creation of new memories will begin. The EMS I had grown to love in its two short years of existence was no more, but the memories remain forever.

Originally published in the May 25, 2011 Turner Report

Finding "Hi" In My Joplin Classroom

By Randy Turner

It was one of those days all teachers have. It started with a few admonitions for students to stop talking. Once one student stopped, the next would start, and soon there were outbreaks all over the classroom…and this was my fourth hour class, the class that came through for me on those days when all of my other classes were afflicted with that contagious wildness that comes from changes of weather, cycles of the moon, or vast right-wing conspiracies depending on which veteran teacher is doing the talking.

It was almost impossible to get anything going for more than a few minutes, and in the middle of this tsunami of adolescent conversation, the right hand of the one girl who had not been talking, the one girl who almost never talked, thrust forward with the urgency of someone who had a vital message to deliver.

"Sabrina," I said, looking in her direction.

She smiled and said, "Hi."

The rest of the class looked at me. If anything was going to cause this cranky old-timer to snap it would be that one-word rebellious

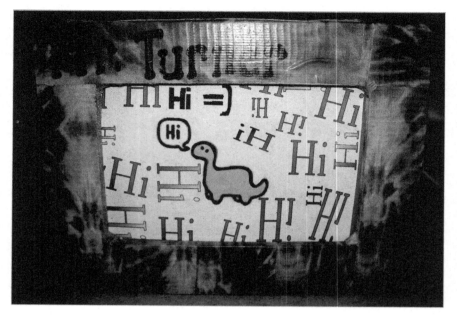

Photo by Randy Turner

statement. And looking back on that day, nearly two years in the past, I recall that my first instinct was to chastise Sabrina for wasting my time.

But the face that was looking at me was not one of someone who was trying to irritate me or to provoke me in any fashion. It was the face of a thoughtful, considerate eighth grader who knew just when her teacher needed someone to offer a friendly "Hi."

My growing anger dissolved in a blink and somehow I was able to steer my class back to learning how to develop their writing skills so they could succeed in high school and later in life.

That simple word would have remained a "hi" point of the 2009-2010 school year for me, but it became a scenario that repeated itself often throughout the year.

On a few occasions, Sabrina's "Hi" came when the class was slightly unruly. Most of the time, it was just an acknowledgment that everything was okay. The one thing I never considered it to be was an interruption of class.

The 2009-2010 school year, the first in our new East Middle School building, ended much too soon, and on that last day, Sabrina didn't disappoint me. The right hand darted out, I called her, and she smiled and said, "Hi."

I was going to miss that word of encouragement. Sabrina realized that, too. After class, she presented me with one of the most cherished mementoes I have from my dozen years in the classroom- a multi-colored wooden frame with "Mr. Turner" written in black letters on the top and a cute blue creature saying "Hi," surrounded by 20 "Hi's."

A big smile covered Sabrina's face. "Now I'll be able to say 'Hi' to you every day," she said.

I am sure the damp spots on my face at that moment were due to the humidity.

Every day during the 2010-2011 school year, I glanced at that gift that kept on giving. On the normal days when the stream of education was flowing in the proper direction, it brought a smile to my face. On days when the storm clouds were brewing over my corner classroom, it made me realize that this, too, shall pass.

When I received word after the May 22 tornado that decimated the city of Joplin that East Middle School had been severely damaged, I imagined the worst and my first visit to what was left of the campus did nothing to dispel my fears.

The auditorium, the gymnasium, the band room, the commons area, all were gone, leveled by nature's fierce fury. I was unable to get into my classroom that day, but I heard that it was one of those that received the most damage.

Last week, the East Middle School faculty was called in to remove personal belongings. I did not recognize the room I had called home for two years.

My Writers' Wall of Fame, posted papers of my students' best work, had somehow survived, except for a few that had slipped off the wall and fallen into the small lake that had been created when the sprinkler system was activated.

My collection of books that I used each year during the third quarter for our research project on the American Civil Rights Movement had not been damaged at all. Other items were unsalvageable. The first I noticed, which had somehow broken away from the others in a cosmic act of irony was a copy of the school's tornado procedures. I walked over to my desk, skimmed through the books and papers that had been strewn about. The one thing I did not see was Sabrina's gift.

I looked at the floor. If it were there, it would be damaged beyond repair. There was no sign of it.

Again, I looked at my desk and on the front right-hand corner; I saw a portion of the frame, buried under papers and a couple of textbooks. I lifted those items and, there it was, face-down on the desk. I turned it over and there, slightly dirty, but still intact, was one of the best gifts any teacher ever received.

Despite the destruction that surrounded me, that collection of "Hi's" was enough to put the smile back on my face.

When East Middle School reopens in August, and the construction process has already begun, I will be surrounded by an entirely new room, a new teacher's desk, new furnishings, all interchangeable with all of the other classrooms in my building.

The one thing that I will have that my fellow faculty members will not is that gift that will hold the same position of importance in my new classroom as it did in my old one, the gift that even a tornado could not destroy.

I will still have my daily reminder that it is a good thing for a teacher to get "Hi" in the classroom.

Originally published June 5, 2011 on Huffington Post

Daddy, I'm Home

By Mitch Randles

On May 22, 2011 at 5:41 p.m., the City of Joplin and its residents underwent a life changing event. A tornado of such fury and destruction laid a path of devastation through our city leaving it scarred and unrecognizable.

As I first surveyed the damage from the storm, I was fearful that our city would never recover and be the hometown that we had all grown comfortable with and accustomed to.

Emergency responders and volunteers descended upon Joplin to aid in search and rescue, the removal of debris, demolition and reconstruction of homes. They were like angels from heaven.

Without all of the assistance that was received I have no doubt that we would not be as far along in our recovery efforts as we are today. I believe that everyone from Joplin, the four-state area, and possibly the entire country felt the effects of the tornado, not just those in the tornado's path.

I don't think there is a single resident of the Four States that didn't know someone who had lost a loved one, their home or their place of employment. It affected each and every one of us in some way.

As we continue with recovery and rebuilding efforts there have been several times when people have asked about a single individual who has made a significant difference either in the rescue or the recovery efforts, and I cannot come up with a single name or even a group.

There was no one person or group which stood out. We all stood out; we were a community of people who were placed in an extraordinary situation and each one of us stepped forward. This was a group effort from the moment the storm struck the city. No one put themselves first- we all looked to help others no matter how bad the individual circumstances were.

We all believed that our friends and neighbors needed assistance first. I have never in my life been prouder of our city, our citizens, our friends and our neighbors. We were united in a cause as never before, and I believe that Mayor Mike Woolston summed it up perfectly when he said" We aren't going to let some F5 tornado kick our a**".

With the one-year anniversary of the storm quickly approaching, I find the city still working feverishly on the recovery and rebuilding efforts, working on getting back to normal.

But I believe that the normal we knew on May 21, 2011 was forever taken from us on May 22. I once thought that things would go back to being the same, but shortly after moving into our new home, my wife and kids were talking about having the family out to our new home for the annual holiday celebrations. That is when my daughter Sabrina looked at me and said, "This is our house- it isn't our home. That was taken away from us."

Reality really came crashing back to me. I thought about how many other residents must feel the same. I think that Sabrina got it right. We will never go back to the normal we knew before. We are currently creating the "new" normal with each piece of debris that is removed and every building and home that is rebuilt.

Looking forward I know that the buildings and homes will be

replaced and that our city will recover. Our community is too strong not to have that happen. But I pray that each and every one of us affected and touched by this tragic event are able to find closure and have the "new normal" which I long for.

For each of us that will come in our own time as the emotional scars heal. For me, I wait for the day when Sabrina looks at me and says," Daddy, I'm home."

This article was originally published as the foreword to the book Spirit of Hope: The Year after the Joplin Tornado by Randy Turner and John Hacker

One Year, One Community, One Direction

By John Hacker

L ike the tornado, it started small on one end of town with a few hundred people gathering at the roundabout at 20th Street and Duquesne Road and moving west.

Like the tornado, it grew quickly into a powerful wave with thousands of people joining them at 17th Street and Range Line Road.

Like the tornado, thousands of people formed an unstoppable force sweeping across Joplin.

Unlike the tornado, this force came not for destruction but for construction, not for death but for life, not for an end but for a beginning — a new beginning for two cities ripped asunder exactly one year before.

The Unity Walk on May 22, 2012, marked exactly one year after the Joplin tornado with a march in the opposite direction that the tornado traveled.

"It was symbolic," said Joplin City Manager Mark Rohr as he prepared to lead the crowd west from 17th and Range Line. "We're walking against the wind toward Cunningham Park and we're doing

Thousands of Joplin residents, volunteers who had come to help, and others, returned to Joplin on May 22, 2012, one year after the tornado and walked the damage path from 20th and Duquesne Road west to Cunningham Park to remember those who were lost and reunite with new friends and old friends. . Photo by John Hacker

it as a group. The purpose of the Unity Walk and the Day of Unity is to stay together.

"That's what's been the secret to our success so far and led us to the point where we're at and that's what's going to take us home in terms of completing the rebuilding process. We thought it was important to highlight that, to remind people of that and to urge them to continue to work together until we reach the point where we're rebuilding the city."

EARLY WALKERS

Duquesne Mayor Denny White estimated that between 300 and 350 people gathered at the Duquesne Road roundabout for his city's portion of the walk.

Duquesne is a much smaller city than Joplin, but proportionately, it might have suffered even more than its larger neighbor.

The tornado destroyed more than 40 percent of the structures in Duquesne, between 300 and 400 homes damaged beyond repair.

One of them belonged to Cindy Sundy.

"This walk is, it's hard to put it into words, but this walk is victory," Sundy said as she walked west on 20th Street toward Range Line Road.

"It means that we've come through on the other side of what should have been the worst day of my life, but I actually realize it was the best day of my life because my son, my husband and I were trapped in my house, the walls exploded around us. Any one of us, or all of us could have lost our lives and we didn't.

"So it really puts it into perspective what's important. The stuff, everyone says it was stuff. It was important stuff. There's stuff I miss, but not near as bad as I would have missed my husband or my son or my best friend who lived across the street, or my dog, who wouldn't come in the bathroom with us, but still managed to survive. So it's victory."

Sundy said she heard that the weather was going to be bad, so she took a shower because "I don't like to shower in a thunderstorm."

"I flipped the TVs over to local channels when I saw the sky to the west get dark," Sundy said. "They were showing their weather cam, you could see transformers blowing and they said there was a tornado on the ground, but it was rain-wrapped, it didn't look like a funnel cloud, but it was a tornado, and we should take cover.

"At this point it was on the west side of town. It was west of the TV stations, so I went and got my husband and told him, they say there's a tornado on the ground. He being a man wanted to go see, so we went and stood on the driveway and we talked about where we wanted to go, do we want to go in the tub in the bathroom, or do we want to go under the house. Well, there are spiders under the house; I'm not going there. So we chose to go to the tub."

As the winds tore at her house, she, her son and husband huddled in their bathroom. The tornado hit and tore into the home.

"It sounded like there was a 747 parked in our driveway with all of its engines on at once," Cindy Sundy said. "And then we were in the eye of it. At first, I thought it was over, we had made it, and then when the other wall hit, I remember then praying with everything I had because I didn't think there was enough house left to protect us.

"When the roof went, my husband immediately laid on top of my son and me, we had both felt the suction and if he hadn't done that, there's no telling what could have happened. A bathroom wall fell on us and that's what kept us in.

"My husband crawled out and the dog was waiting for him. She was fine, covered with leaves, covered with debris, but she was fine. Our house and neighborhood were completely gone. It was surreal, but like I said, I've come to realize that was the best day of my life."

Sundy was joined by people who didn't live in the tornado's path, but who were affected, nonetheless.

"We're here because some parts of me feel guilty because we didn't lose our home and I just want to be with those that did and let them know that we're behind them," said Joyce Wall, who walked the Duquesne walk with her niece, Adison Wright, and Adison's mother Amy Wright.

"We were lucky enough that our home wasn't hit, but we had a graduation party going on in our house for Amy's daughter and Adison's sister," Wall said.

"If they hadn't been in our house at that time having a graduation dinner, there might have been some injuries or deaths. We had about 22 people in the house; some that lived up by the hospital and some that lived down in Duquesne."

"I'm basically here just to show the strength and power behind our community," Adison Wright added. "And to show that, yeah, our entire town got wiped out but still, after all of this and after all the volunteers leave, our community is still going to be here to rise up and walk to show that we're still strong and we're still going to be here even if it happens again. We're still here and we're going to have that strength."

Duquesne Mayor Denny White said the one-year anniversary was an important milestone for residents of the entire area.

"It's been a very tough year," White said. "There's been a lot going on, but we've worked hard to rebuild and we're happy to be here today and have this moment. In the beginning, Joplin had more of the limelight than we did, but as time went on, we got our fair share and we're not unhappy about anything. We're just happy to be here."

Joplin City Council Member Mike Woolston, who was mayor of Joplin at the time of the tornado, walked with the Duquesne crowd as it moved to meet the Joplin contingent of the walk.

Woolston said Joplin and Duquesne are partners in the reconstruction and must work together to reach out to all who have helped and all who need help.

"That's why I'm here with Denny, I called him to ask him a couple of days ago if he'd mind if I started the walk with them," Woolston said. "Because it is a partnership and I think the community needs to see that and I hope they buy into it because our futures are more or less intertwined in terms of going forward.

"As a percentage, Duquesne probably took greater loss than Joplin did in terms of houses and those kinds of things, and many people don't recognize that.

"It's a long walk and it'll be difficult for some people, but I think it's symbolic of the difficulty that we've encountered in the past year since the tornado, but just as we have overcome in that area, we'll overcome today. The walk is symbolic to a lot of people in terms of how we conquered the tornado. We'll conquer this walk today as a symbol of our resiliency and the spirit of today."

Thousands of people walk west on 20th Street on their way from Duquesne to Cunningham Park on May 22, 2012, the first anniversary of the deadly tornado. Photo by John Hacker

SECOND BEGINNING

The beginning of the walk for a majority of participants was almost three-quarters of a mile into it for those who started at the Duquesne Roundabout.

Thousands of people gathered at the 17th Street entrance to the Walmart parking lot as police prepared to clear the path for the Unity Walk.

For Jody Kirk, Joplin, the walk was a deeply personal event. She walked the distance carrying a sign honoring her father, Stan Kirk, who died in the 15th Street Walmart when it was hit.

"It's very much a part of my healing process," Jody Kirk said. "Seeing all these people out here today is so comforting and therapeutic for, I don't think just me personally, but as a community.

"We've all lost something whether it's a relative or a house; we've all lost a part of our community, so I think it helps with the healing process for everyone. This is a beginning, even from May 23, in Joplin we showed what coming together as a community was like and we are, as a community, so strong and we'll continue to be strong and this is the beginning of a new future. Thank you so much for everyone coming out."

Myra Pickering, Duquesne, remembers the path the Unity Path would take and what it looked like a year earlier.

"A year ago today, it was a path of total destruction," she said. "Today it's a path of everyone being together, working hard, showing the partners that we made that you can't keep us down. I'm here just to show that we can overcome anything if we work together. I think it's a good idea, this walk."

Laura Pyle, Carthage, had relatives who lived on the path she and her family planned to walk on May 22, 2012.

"We have a lot of friends and family that are in Joplin," Pyle said. "Joplin is part of where we grew up, so we've just come out and helped a lot throughout the year so we're here to support and keep going.

"The walk is a good way to bring everyone back together and just have that day to all get together and walk through everything, see what's changed, see what's come back, what's new, what's different and get the perspective a year later on how much it's grown back and become once again."

Ann Ingram, Carthage, said she may not live in Joplin, but everyone in the area was affected by what happened on May 22, 2011. That's why she decided to participate in the walk.

"I was in Joplin with my family in Academy less than an hour before the tornado," Ingram said. "So it's one of those things where there's not a whole lot in Carthage to do on a Sunday, it's a gorgeous weekend, you want to get out and do something and you're probably going to get out and go to Joplin. This is a chance for us to show our support for them. If anything ever happened in Carthage, I know it would be the same way, Joplin would come out and show their support for us."

Joplin City Manager Mark Rohr walked with residents from Walmart to Cunningham Park. Rohr said the anniversary brought out many different emotions in him and everyone participating in the event.

"It's a day to walk together, it's a day to be unified," Rohr said. "We'll see what comes after this, but today we're all coming together and we're all sharing some experiences together. The emotions have to do with the attitude with which we've approached our recovery process.

"Undoubtedly it was a horrible thing, and a lot of things were lost, a lot of lives were lost and there's two ways to approach it, to sit and worry about what happened to you or to work on improving things and that's what we chose to do."

STEEPLE RISING AND GROUNDBREAKING

A little more than 2.5 miles into the walk, residents paused to mark two major reconstruction efforts that reached milestones on the first anniversary of the tornado.

The Joplin School District marked the day with groundbreakings at several schools, including Joplin High School during the Unity Walk.

Across Indiana Avenue from the old Joplin High School site, the Church of Jesus Christ of Latter-Day Saints raised a big white steeple on its Joplin Stake office, which replaces the one destroyed in the tornado.

The steeple-raising ceremony at the LDS Church featured a talk by Lee Allphin, one of nine people who were in the church and rode out its destruction in a women's bathroom.

Next to him stood Ruby McBryde, who was 8 at the time and the youngest person in the building at the time of the storm.

"Ruby is a very special young lady," Allphin said. "A lot of our children in our area suffered this tragedy, but as the savior said, suffer the little children that they should come unto me, forbid them not for such is the Kingdom of Heaven.

"I believe we can learn a lot from the youth and the young people who have suffered and had experiences here. But this is not a time of sorrow but a time of rejoicing and rebuilding.

"There were eight of us who crowded into a small women's restroom here in the former building. The building went down around us. Debris was flying everywhere. Smells and sounds, many of you experienced that the same as we did. There were hundreds of stories just like ours, but we felt protecting hands guarding us and protecting us."

LDS Stake President Creed Jones, who lost his home in the tornado, also spoke at the steeple raising. He said he hoped the reconstruction of the LDS church would serve as beacon to other churches struggling to rebuild.

"We recognize that there were 27 or 28 churches that were

Joplin Mayor Melodee Colbert-Kean leads the crowd down 20th Street between Range Line Road and Connecticutt Avenue on the May 22, 2012 Unity Walk marking the one-year anniversary of the tornado that killed 161 people. Photo by John Hacker

destroyed," Jones said. "I'm told that there were about 48 places of worship that were affected one way or another through the tornado, so this is just symbolic of one for many here."

Rick Nugent, another who survived the tornado and attended the steeple raising one-year later, said the event was "certainly bringing back memories that have been there all along."

"It's a great moment to think that I can be here with my friends and I'm still here, alive and we were spared that night," Nugent said.

"It's pretty awesome to have all these people here. It's great to feel all that support. It's been inspiring to see how people have stepped up and all the volunteers that came in and everybody helped each other. It's very inspiring."

WALK ENDS AT A PARK AND A SYMBOL

The massive river of people left the high school grounds and headed west on 24th Street and across Main Street to the grounds of the old Irving Elementary School.

There, organizers set up a fair of sorts, with food and games for the kids. All along the route, bottled water was available for free and handed out by volunteers.

The walk then moved south to 26th Street and approached its end at two symbols of the tornado — the ruined St. John's Regional Medical Center building and Cunningham Park.

Crews have been tearing down the nine-story St. John's building since January, a long and painstaking process made necessary because of the mineshafts that lace the ground under this part of Joplin.

The shell is still recognizable and was used as a background by media and residents for photos and video on May 22, 2012, just as it was in the days after May 22, 2011.

Joplin's oldest park, Cunningham Park was also destroyed in the tornado. The iconic bandstand in the middle of the park was erased, the pool destroyed and hundreds of old trees, some dating back to 1898 when it was known as Cunningham's Grove, were blown down.

Thomas W. Cunningham, Joplin's mayor in 1897, gave the grove to the city to be used as a park. Since the tornado, it has become a gathering place for events such as the 10th anniversary of the 9/11 attacks on America and the six-month anniversary of the tornado on Nov. 22, 2011.

It would serve that role again on May 22, 2012, as thousands gathered in lawn chairs and on the grass for the unveiling of a brass monument to the 161 people who died in the tornado.

Duquesne Mayor Denny White was at Cunningham Park to greet the throng that had grown from that modest gathering a few hours before four and a half miles away at the Duquesne roundabout.

"It couldn't be any better than this," White said. "If you expect better than this, your expectations are too high. Just look out ahead of you, there's still a sea of people approaching and there's been a sea going the other way already. It's been well worth it to be part of this, it really has. I haven't seen a sad face out here today, and that's a testimony to the people of this area. These people are tough; they've gotten right back in and gotten back with their lives. We couldn't ask for more than what we had today."

Jeff Piotrowski is a storm chaser from Oklahoma who followed the storm into Joplin with video camera in hand. He has returned to Joplin many times since the storm and has produced a video of his experience.

He stood on 26th Street watching the crowd file by and remembered.

"Twelve months later and you think of the biggest tornado in U.S. history that took a heavy toll in Joplin," Piotrowski said. "Now we're here 12 months later and you think about all the rebuilding.

"Here's a whole community, 6,000-plus buildings, and all the people that live here, people from around the country are here in Joplin just as I am and it's a celebration of moving forward. Twelve months of unbelievable things these people have been faced with.

"Here today we had the two school dedications, the high school dedication, we had the church steeple raising, and we had businesses opening up and just look at Cunningham Park. Look at the people. We see 8,000 or 9,000 people here it's unbelievable. It's just a great moment in history that I don't think we'll ever repeat itself, ever."

PEOPLE GATHER

Thousands of people gathered on the lawn at Cunningham Park at around 5:15 p.m. for the final ceremony of the anniversary day.

The program included speeches, people placing items in a time capsule and the unveiling of the brass plaque featuring the names of

Mark Norton, father of Will Norton, the 2011 Joplin High School Graduate that died in the tornado minutes after graduating, carries an item relating to Will Norton to the time capsule set up in the monument in Cunningham Park that features the names of the 161 people who died in the tornado. Photo by John Hacker the 161 people who died.

Mark Norton, father of Will Norton, the student who graduated from Joplin High School on May 22, 2011, then was killed minutes later while on his way home with his father, placed one container of items into the time capsule, set in the base under the plaque honoring the tornado victims.

Mark Norton suffered serious injuries when the vehicle he and his son were riding in was caught up in the tornado on Schifferdecker Road and destroyed.

"Physically, I'm pretty much healed up," Mark Norton said. "I was much luckier than so many people that got hurt and I didn't have internal injuries like so many people did. Mine was all structural, but it's nothing compared to the emotional things people suffered. I'm doing fine."

Mark Norton said he was deeply moved by the care shown by the community to him and his family after the storm and by the turnout for the anniversary ceremony.

"I think it's an accomplishment to get through this first year," Mark Norton said. "Now we can see so many good things that have happened and in the midst of the tragedy. It's a really warm feeling to see all these people here with all the love and kindness and support shown by the volunteers. It's touching to us to see what's happened to this community."

Norton said faith was helping his family cope with their tragic loss as he healed physically from the terrible wounds he suffered.

"They say you take one day at a time, but sometimes I think you take one hour at a time or one minute at a time," he said. "You have difficult days, but you just get through.

"We know we'll see our son again someday and so now you just go through life and look to that time. We have strong faith, and we know he's in a better place and we still have a son, he's just not here with us today, physically."

Brian Mora also survived the Joplin tornado and attended the May 22, 2012 service.

"I was downstairs in my office and I started hearing the sirens going off," Mora said. "I started hearing the winds getting louder and louder. My mother got into the downstairs laundry room and I got into the downstairs hot water closet. After the horror was done, I went outside, my mother and I went outside and we saw the devastation all over the place, houses all over the place, windows broken out, some houses were completely leveled, there were cars flipped like pancakes."

Mora and his mother lost their home and both their cars, but they came out of it with an introspective outlook on life.

"We have to rebuild in order to really move on with our lives," Mora said. "We really do need, at some point, to start rebuilding ourselves and renewing ourselves and making efforts to think about what we've done in our lives. If there are things we haven't done or we would like to do, it's a good idea to get out and do them.

"There are a lot of wonderful things and we have to learn to get out and appreciate life. I've spoken with a cowboy church pastor in Texas about some of the problems affecting us and there are a lot of things you need to get out and do."

As he did one week after the tornado and six months after the tornado, City Manager Mark Rohr spoke about the people who died in the tornado and how they will be remembered in Cunningham Park.

"We lost 162 fellow citizens as a result of the devastating storm that struck Joplin Missouri at 5:41 p.m. on May 22, 2011," Rohr said. "Although no longer here in body, they surround us and envelop us in spirit. Their names will be forever commemorated on the plaque that we dedicate here today. Their earthly presence will be reflected in the 161 trees planted in Cunningham Park and their spirits infuse and permeate our daily lives and our efforts to rebuild our city."

Rohr spoke again about the "Miracle of the Human Spirit," a term he coined to describe what was happening in Joplin in the wake of the tornado.

"We gather amongst the 130,000 registered volunteers that have helped us clear away the debris from the storm and have helped us in the process of rebuilding our community," Rohr said.

"Mere thanks are not enough but please know you are part of the miracle of the human spirit and a very special movement that has occurred here now, and you will forever be an important part of the city of Joplin."

The keynote speaker at the anniversary event was Hal Donaldson, co-founder and president of the Springfield-based Convoy of Hope, a group that has played a big role in helping victims since the day after the storm.

Convoy of Hope has committed to building a number of homes and, in fact, dedicated the first of these completed homes on May 22, 2012.

"Twelve months ago, we began a journey from uncertainty to hope," Donaldson told the crowd. "But as you know we have not traveled this road alone. People from across the country have joined with us by giving of their time and their resources and offering their prayers. I know tonight on this one-year anniversary, I speak for thousands and thousands of Americans when I say, tonight we stand together with you as one, proud to call this our adopted home."

He talked about how Joplin and Duquesne had shown the nation three principles for overcoming disaster and paving the way for healing and restoration:

• Finding solutions is more important than fixing blame.

• Focusing attention on a common vision works better than "being enslaved by division."

• You can find the courage to persevere or wallow in pity.

"The future of Joplin, Missouri will be built upon your brave shoulders and rest assured the same faith and character and values that have carried you through this crisis will be there to help you navigate the challenges of tomorrow," Donaldson said.

"I'll close with this. There's no denying this has been a long and arduous journey, but my friends, through it all, we are stronger, we are united, and we are determined that this city will soon be better than ever. God Bless You."

God Was With Me

By Randy Turner

The smile never vanished from Sarah Kessler's face as she listened to the names of one student after another being called onstage to receive their diplomas.

It takes a while to go through 431 names. Fortunately for Sarah, her last name was closer to the beginning of the alphabet so she would have to stand in line for much less time than some of her classmates.

It had been an exciting evening for the tall, slender ("I'm a beanpole," she says) senior. About an hour and a half earlier she had been in a room with the President of the United States. It was not her voice that said, "Oh, my God, the leader of the free world,"-that was a classmate- but she could understand the awe.

The Joplin High School Class of 2012 listened to seemingly endless speeches- from High School Principal Kerry Sachetta, Superintendent C. J. Huff, Gov. Jay Nixon, and yes, from President Barack Obama "the leader of the free world," in a ceremony that started a few minutes late.

All of the speakers praised Sarah and her classmates. "You are an inspiration," the president had said, but somehow Sarah did not feel like an inspiration. As she waited, she thought back over the past

Joplin High School graduate Sarah Kessler greets Missouri Gov. Jay Nixon and Joplin Superintendent C.J. Huff at the May 21, 2012, graduation ceremony. Photo by Mike Gullett

year, the path that led her from the most horrifying moments of her life, some spent in this same building, the Leggett & Platt Center on the Missouri Southern State University campus, to where she was today, a few moments from receiving her diploma- her ticket into adulthood.

It still brought a shudder to her every time she thought about the events of May 22, 2011.

That weekend had been a big one for the Kessler family. A day earlier, the wedding of Sarah's older sister, Kate, had taken place. Sarah and her brother, Will, provided music for the occasion- Sarah on her beloved violin, Will on guitar.

"My entire family was in town," Sarah recalled. The family stayed for another big event the next day, Will Kessler's graduation with the Joplin High School Class of 2011.

The family watched with pride as Will received his diploma, had pictures taken afterward, and then Will left. "He had a party he was going to, so he left before the rest of us," Sarah said. It was shortly after Will left that the tornado siren sounded.

As the rest of the Kessler family was about to leave, a security guard stopped them. "He told us we had to go to the basement. We didn't have a choice. We were all wanting to leave."

The guard escorted the family to the locker room area with five or six other families to wait out the storm. "We were down there for a quite a while," Sarah said. It was there that they received word that Home Depot had been hit. "That's when we started to get nervous about my brother because we live a block from the high school. One of the easiest ways to get from the college to my house was down 20th."

Scaring the Kesslers even more was their inability to contact Will. There was no phone coverage in the locker room. "That was the scariest 30 minutes in my life, not knowing where my brother was, or even if he was still alive."

Finally, they were able to contact Will. He had been driving through the heart of the storm. "He said he prayed the whole time he was in the car. He just got a new car, and he is a good driver. Thank God for both of those things. He said he was dodging flying cars, flying trees," Sarah lowered her voice, "flying people."

Will Kessler ended up at a church at 26th and Connecticut.

Now that they knew Will was all right, the family piled into two cars to head toward their home, which they now knew had been in the path of the tornado.

"We went down Range Line, but that wasn't going to happen. It was mass chaos everywhere, so we drove down side streets. It was terrifying; the closer we got to home, the worse the destruction. We wondered if home was going to be there."

As what would normally be a 15-minute trip had already taken more than a half hour, Sarah's dad received a call from Will.

"Where are you?" her father asked.

"Home."

"Do we have a home left?"

"Sort of."

Still seven blocks from home, Sarah's dad stopped the car, jumped out and began walking. Sarah's cousin took the wheel. After what seemed an eternity, Sarah was close enough to see her house.

"I will never be able to forget that. We were on Indiana and I can remember driving up to 20th Street. I could see clear to the hospital. There was nothing there. I saw the school, then I looked slightly to the left. Our house was built a little better than the ones around us. It was the least damaged. The lower level was still standing. You could see a part of the upper story where my brother's room was."

The first words she said when she saw what was left of her home will be forever burned into her memory. "I remember looking at it, crying, and saying to my cousin, 'That's my house. That's my house.' All I could think was it was gone."

At that point, Sarah got out of the car, stepping over downed power lines, walking between cars. "I walked the path between the school and my house, the same as I had done every day since my freshman year."

She spotted Will and ran to him, hugging him. The two stood crying. They checked on neighbors to make sure they were all right and then went into their house to see what had survived.

Much of the family's irreplaceable sentimental items, including photo albums and papers, were unharmed since they were under their parents' bed in the lower level. "We were able to salvage quite a bit," Sarah said. "We were fortunate."

And the one possession that Sarah cherished above all others- her violin- was also undamaged, as was her brother's guitar. "We had played my sister down the aisle at the wedding and when we got home, we left the instruments downstairs in the hallway." Had they taken the instruments upstairs where they were normally kept, they would have been swept away.

"That was about the only happy thing that happened that night. I love playing the violin. It has always been special to me."

For the next few weeks after the tornado, Sarah and her family stayed with Matt Proctor, president of Ozark Christian College, his wife, Katie, and their six children. Some of the time Sarah stayed with Rebecca McMillin, her best friend since kindergarten.

The Kessler family lost some of its animals, but "we found two of our rabbits and two of our cats." The family also had two dogs, Hank, a yellow lab, and Rusty, a golden retriever.

After a few days, Rebecca McMillin talked Sarah into going to the Humane Society to see if her dogs were there. "I didn't want to go. I was afraid I wouldn't find them." When they walked into the building with the dogs, "I saw Rusty right off the bat. I went up to the cage and he started barking." When he was released, he ran to Sarah. "Basically, he almost knocked me over. It was so good to see him."

Sarah was never able to find Hank.

A new home had to be found for Rusty after the Kesslers moved into an apartment, where they would have to stay for quite a while before their house could be rebuilt.

In the days following the tornado, many friends helped the Kessler family through its ordeal, including some they had never met before. "The people from our church (Central City Christian Church) were there for us. They helped us with our house and helped us move into our apartment."

The summer was a blur for Sarah. After a couple of weeks dealing with the aftermath of the worst night of her life, Sarah had an opportunity to get away from it all for a short time, as she traveled with Ozark Christian College's Highest Praise Choir, playing her violin. "It was nice to get away," she said. "It was such an encouraging environment."

When she returned, it was not to the home she had known for her whole life, but to a place she had never seen before. "I didn't quite have a room. My room was full of boxes, so I stayed on the couch in the living room for a while, but that was okay. It took us quite a while to get everything put in its place. It was mass chaos."

It was also not the home she knew. "We had just remodeled our house, spent the last two or three months before the tornado just totally redoing it. We had a beautiful new deck. I told everyone that next year, we would have to have all of our study parties at my house.

"Obviously, that didn't happen."

Sarah threw herself into volunteer work, helping Forest Park Baptist Church's Mission Joplin. Sarah's plans to spend her summer looking for colleges were tossed aside. That would have to wait.

Before she knew it, it was time for her senior year of high school to begin, not at the historic building she could walk to every morning, but in a box store at Northpark Mall. "I thought it would be poorly put together. When school actually started, it was so much better than I could have possibly imagined. It's not the best, obviously, because it is not a permanent facility, but it worked."

Sarah will never forget the first day of school at Northpark Mall. "It was all hugs and laughter and smiles. Even with people you barely knew, it was like, 'Oh, my goodness. I know you. You're alive.' "

That spirit continued throughout the school year. "The student body seemed to be closer. There is something that links us all together."

As the school year passed, there were many positive moments such as using another tornado survivor, her violin, to earn a I rating at state and being a part of the Prom Court. "That was something totally unexpected." Her fourth year as a member of Key Club, a service organization, was also a highlight. Sarah was lieutenant governor on the Missouri/Arkansas Board.

And while she didn't have a deck for study parties, she had something even better. "We have a roof at our apartment," she said. "The other night my dad and I had a candlelight dinner of beans and weenies on our roof."

Even though the Kessler family will soon move back into a house, Sarah confided, "I kind of like our little apartment. We all secretly kind of like it."

The experience of living through the tornado has helped strengthen Sarah Kessler's faith. "I'm a Christian. I'm very proud of that. One of the biggest lessons I have learned is to trust in Him no matter what. No matter what the situation is, He will take care of you."

God helped provide for her family, Sarah said, with everything from saving her brother Will the day of the tornado to helping them to cope with the aftermath of the storm.

"I went through, maybe not quite depression, but I wasn't my normal, bouncy self for a while," Sarah said. "When that happened, I needed to reconnect with Him. I learned that the more I make an effort in my relationship with God, the more joyful and hopeful I was, the more content I was."

By this time, Sarah had moved to near the front of the line. In a few moments, her name would be called, and she would leave Joplin High School forever. The next stop for Sarah will be Missouri State University in Springfield where she will study music education.

"I've always wanted to be a teacher since I was little. I like helping other people learn and I have a lot of patience. Teaching comes naturally to me."

"Sarah Kessler."

A smile spread across her face and there was a spring in her walk as she stepped forward to receive her diploma. She turned to her family in the audience and smiled, then she took a brief moment to give thanks.

The path to graduation had not been an easy one for Sarah Kessler, but the moment had arrived, and she knew this was never something she could have done alone.

"One big lesson I have learned this year is that even when you can't feel God's presence, that doesn't mean He's not there. God has promised us he will never leave us."

This time, Sarah felt His presence.

a Tale of Survival

By Andrea Queen

On May 22 of this year, our morning started out like any other. We woke up and went to church at Forest Park Baptist Church, with Pastor John Swadley. His message that morning was over Romans 5:6-8 and his message was "It's Not Fair" in reference to what happens in our lives may be unfair, but the mere fact that God had to send His own Son to Earth to die for our sins was unfair.

We went on about our day as usual and had settled in to watch the St. Louis Cardinals play the Kansas City Royals. In the bottom of the eighth inning, we began to hear rumblings about how bad the weather was supposed to get, so we grabbed a couple of backpacks and got prepared to stand outside and watch the weather coming in.

About that time, my grandmother came by the house to bring me a beautiful red rose to plant. We stood outside talking about the clouds and how the weather was supposed to be getting more severe. I finally convinced her to go home, but she told me that she needed to run by Wal-Mart first and then she was going straight home. I wish she had just gone home instead.

At about 5:30, the Cards and the Royals had just entered the 10th inning, tied at 7 all. Then about 10 minutes later - the game

Photo by Andrea Queen

ended with the Cards on top 8-7. Five minutes after that, we got the call that we needed to take shelter; there was a possible tornado on the ground. I contacted both of my parents and begged them to take cover just in case.

Five minutes after that, we got confirmation that a tornado was on the ground at St. John's and that we needed to take cover. The boys and I grabbed our backpacks that we had ready and we snatched up four blankets to lay down underneath us under the house in the crawlspace.

Then, as we had just gotten under the house, my husband and I looked at each other and we both knew what was coming. The four of us held hands and said a prayer of protection and faith. Something told me in the pit of my stomach that this was it – it was really happening, and we were right in the path of the monster.

Within two minutes, the wind ceased to blow, the air became

green and we heard something that can only be described as evil come in our direction. After a couple of minutes, I saw the hatch get thrown off of the crawlspace entry and the wind whip something that resembled a tree limb across the opening.

That was the last thing I saw before I climbed on top of our youngest son Jackson, who is six. My husband, Franklin II, crawled on top of our oldest son Franklin III, who is 12, and held on to him for dear life.

As the tornado got closer, the noise was deafening. All four of us were being pelted by dirt, debris, and driving rains that were thrown under the house where we were taking shelter. The pressure forced our ears to pop repeatedly and all I could do was pray.

When it hit, there was no screaming, like you would imagine. We were all calm, silent and determined to survive.

Our youngest son Jackson, hollered at me, "Mommy, you're squishing me!" I replied, "I know baby, I know…."

To that he, hollered louder, "No, Mommy! Squish me harder!" What else could I do but oblige him and do my best to hold him to the ground and pray that it would be enough to keep him safe.

When the tornado hit, I could hear the shattering of glass, the sound of screeching metal and the sound of sheer destruction. In what seemed like an eternity later, but was maybe only two to three minutes, the storm finally passed.

Then I smelled the natural gas.

The gas meter was located about five feet from the entrance to the crawlspace and had literally been ripped apart. We had to get out from underneath that house quickly. We knew that we had a lot of damage but weren't quite prepared for what we all saw when we crawled out.

A huge tree that was maybe seven feet around, that had sat about 15 feet from the house was on its side and maybe two feet away from the edge of the foundation where we had to crawl out.

There was siding, a bedroom door, and other debris crowding our escape hatch, other than just the tree. Franklin was able to finally maneuver things around and get out first and lifted Jackson out and off to his right and Baby Franklin crawled out right behind his Daddy.

I was on my way to crawl out and my husband began screaming to get back under the house quickly. The wind picked up again, almost to an intensity that we had just experienced, golf ball sized hail began raining down and Jackson's feet left the ground. He threw Jackson back down under the house to me and we scooted back just in time for Franklin III and his Dad to get under before we got hit by either a downdraft of sorts or another small spin-off tornado.

The natural gas was now completely overwhelming. We decided that we just had to get out before we couldn't breathe due to the fumes, so we crawled out and were still getting pelted by hail, driving rain and strong winds.

We climbed up and stumbled over what used to be our master bedroom and jumped off the foundation and began to look around. All we could see was devastation.

Our entire house had been completely swept off the foundation leaving nothing but the subflooring we had hidden under.

All we could do was stand in the street with the boys surveying the damage around us. Not thinking that the entire neighborhood was struck, we decided to walk west to get out of the destruction. As we walked and walked, we realized that there was virtually nothing standing. We crawled over downed power lines, felled trees, our neighbors' belongings, pieces of siding and roofing and breathed in the streaming natural gas.

Then the ammonia odor hit.

The General Mills factory about a mile away lost an ammonia tank and we were directly in the direction of the wind. My husband and I both remained completely calm as we led our children out of the destruction left behind.

We walked for about a mile and a half until we found refuge in a house that still had a garage standing. After about 20 minutes, we decided to travel north on Duquesne Road toward my mother's house. We walked another mile and a half to my mother's house to come in out of the rain. In all, we walked about 3 1/4 miles to get out of the path of the tornado.

Then it occurred to me that my 78-year-old grandmother had been in Wal-Mart when the tornado struck. She left my house about 30 minutes before the tornado hit Joplin. We didn't hear word from her or anything about her until around 2:30 in the morning.

A nurse from St. John's Mercy in Springfield contacted me to let me know she was in terrible shape, but still breathing. She had been carried out of Wal-Mart on a door and transported to Memorial Hall in the back of someone's pickup truck.

She had been sitting behind a cinder block wall, which used to comprise one of the bathroom walls of the store. When the tornado hit Wal-Mart, the cinder block wall came tumbling down on top of her.

My grandmother, Delores Rowan, stopped counting the blocks that hit her head after the sixth one fell. She suffered numerous contusions, lacerations, bruises, and a concussion, which included a serious brain bleed.

When she tried to cover her head with her hands, a block ripped her hand from the impact, causing her hand to tear from in between her middle and ring fingers to the middle of her hand.

Miraculously, she stayed in the hospital only five days and came home to us. She is still recovering, but lives for her great-grandbabies, (her words, not mine).

The next morning, on May 23, 2011, we left my mother's house at six in the morning and went back to our "pile."

When we reached our house, it became apparent that we received a direct hit and our car and truck had been thrown through the house at a direction to which, had we been hiding in the bathroom, we would not have survived. All that was still standing of our house was a section of siding about two feet long by 10 inches high.

Also, upon closer inspection of the foundation we were hiding under, we found that the subflooring had started to rip up from the foundation. We figure that had the F5 lasted for another 20-30 seconds, we would have lost our cover and been completely exposed.

While we were looking around at the "pile" it also became apparent that we were missing several appliances, such as a refrigerator, that should have been easily recognizable. However, even though we couldn't find one of the computers, we did find a thumb drive, which was plugged into it. Nothing around us made any sense. There was no rhyme nor reason as to what we could and could not find from our house. It is still hard to comprehend so many weeks later.

It was so disheartening to look at all the destruction around us. And I felt guilty for being alive at that moment, because I knew that several of my neighbors had perished. Many of our other neighbors had been seriously injured. I shielded the boys from one of the scenes of some person's ultimate demise on our way out of the rubble.

It occurred to me that our story was referenced the day before, by our pastor. It was unfair. There was nothing fair about anything that happened between 5:41 and 6:00 pm on May 22, 2011.

Only by the grace of God did we escape the grasp of the tornado that evening with only minor bumps, scratches, and bruises. Only by the grace of God, did we survive to tell our tale of survival. And, only by the grace of God, did so many come to our rescue in the coming days, weeks and months.

Ground Zero

By Jeff Wells

Hot and humid. I couldn't relax. I may have slept four hours. I felt uneasiness in the Joplin air late on Saturday, May 21, 2011.

When the morning came, I asked my wife what she would think if we headed back to our home near Dallas a day early. She said that sounded like a good idea and we made plans to leave midday on Sunday, May 22. I never thought that restless night would be the last I would spend in the house where I grew up.

My parents purchased 2201 S. Illinois Ave. in June 1981. They bought it from the original owners — the Coffey family. The full-brick home was one of the oldest in the neighborhood. It was built in the early 1960s by Walt Ruestman (who built all the homes on that block of Illinois). The house's exterior bricks were old nineteenth-century bricks that were salvaged from the infamous House of Lords saloon and brothel that stood on Main Street during Joplin' rowdy mining days.

My mother is someone who has spent almost all of her life caring for other people before herself. My father, aunt, and grandfather all suffered long-term health problems and are all deceased. My mother helped care for them in addition to being a single parent

Barbara Wells' home at 2201 Illinois Ave. Barbara and her mother, Syble David, who lived nearby, survived the tornado. John Hacker. Photo by John Hacker

and a working mom.

In fact, my mother never stopped working after she graduated from Carl Junction High School. She even worked full time as she pursued her degrees from Joplin Junior College and Missouri Southern. She retired in 2010 after more than twenty-five years working at the corporate office of TAMKO Building Products.

True to her character, my mother spent the first year of her retirement working rather than enjoying the fruits of her labor. She improved her home on Illinois, helped my 87-year-old grandmother maintain her independence, and volunteered at the Spiva Art Center.

She didn't go on any trips or indulge in retirement. She saved for a year and was planning to install central air conditioning during the summer — the old house never had it. Of course, if the house had cool air then we might have not considered leaving Joplin a day earlier than we intended.

My wife and I left Joplin about 1 p.m. The skies were a gorgeous blue as we drove through Oklahoma. About an hour before the storm struck Joplin, John Hacker called to warn us of the approaching storm (not knowing we'd already left). I called my mother and she said she wasn't concerned. She said she had clothes on the line. I suggested she might want to bring them inside.

As my wife drove through southern Oklahoma, I pulled up the local Joplin police scanner traffic on my telephone. I heard a chilling call from a storm spotter that a dangerous tornado was on the ground near 20th and Central City Road.

I called my mom, told her to call my grandma and tell her to get in the bathtub and for her to then do the same.

"Jeffrey, the storm sirens aren't even going," she protested. Just as soon as she said the words, I could hear the siren next to her house activate. "I've got to go," she said. "Bye."

It was 5:37 p.m.

My mother called my grandmother with the warning. She then locked the doors to her house and put on her shoes — her normal routine during storms. She heard the tornado as she walked down the hallway and realized she didn't have time to retrieve her purse. She closed the bathroom door as the lights went out and the windows exploded. My mother and grandmother usually just sat in their bathrooms during storms.

Getting in their bathtubs probably saved their lives. My mother laid down in her bathtub, as if soaking in a bath, and clutched two bed pillows. She heard the front wall of the house collapse then a tile wall fell on her. The wall stayed intact — mostly — and covered two-thirds of the tub like a lid. My mother was trapped in this sarcophagus, but it protected her on almost every side from the flying glass and debris that injured and killed so many people.

A friend told me that the security cameras at Joplin High School show the storm was over my mother's neighborhood for six minutes.

The National Weather Service estimated the winds there reached 210 miles per hour.

My mother's home, her prized possession, crumbled around her.

She says she heard the bricks grinding together and clanging against the side of the bathtub that protected her. She said she felt two distinct waves of the storm. She experienced the eye phenomenon.

After surveying the debris, we're confident the storm's first round of fury destroyed the house. A telephone pole across the street snapped and acted as a wrecking ball crashing into the front of the house. The bathtub protecting her was dangerously exposed as the second wave crumbled what was left of the house at the top of the hill. My mother, understandably, suffered a heart attack.

After the storm passed, my mother decided to stay there in the tub until she heard someone near. She didn't have a clue how widespread the devastation. Then she smelled gas. She knew she had to find a way out. She didn't have the strength to lift the wall above her. She twisted and contorted her body until her head was at the foot of the bathtub. There was a small hole and a shaft through the debris. She could see the blue sky above.

She removed one of the yellow pillowcases and waved it as high as she could. Neighbor Pete Box heard her cries for help and pulled her up and out of the rubble.

I can't imagine what she thought when she stood there atop of the ruins of her house. I climbed up there days later and it was a sickening vantage point. I could see everything from St. John's to Range Line — the neighborhoods gone, the churches gone, the high school gone, my mother's home — all gone.

Standing there, her chest pounding with pain, she had to have been one of the first to realize the extent of the devastation. She said she worried about her mother who lived alone exactly one mile almost due east. She felt helpless because she knew there was no way she could help her.

My mother knew she needed help. Mr. Box helped Joanne Schenk from her house and my mother and Ms. Schenk left to find help. A minister from Neosho, Barrett Anderson, drove past them at 22nd and Indiana. He was trying to get to a friend's house. He knew that it would be impossible to reach his destination and decided to help the two women. It took more than an hour, but he finally got them to Freeman Hospital.

I continued to listen to the police scanner and KZRG on my phone as we crossed into Texas. I was already getting panicked calls from friends and family. I, too, felt helpless. My mother was finally able to reach me on Mr. Anderson's phone. She managed to say, "Jeffrey, I have chest pains and I'm going to the hospital. The house is gone," before the call dropped. I wouldn't hear from her for another six hours.

I went to a Walmart in Sherman, Texas, and started buying everything I thought people would possibly need. My wife and I gathered cartloads of food, water, and supplies. My in-laws, who live in Fort Worth, saw Mike Bettes report on the horrible scene near Cunningham Park on the Weather Channel, jumped in their car, and headed in our direction. They met us in Sherman and we loaded their vehicle. I knew my mom was hurt and headed to the hospital. I assumed, given everything that I was hearing about her neighborhood, that my grandma was dead.

Evan Young, a friend of mine from Webb City, and his family fought their way to my grandma's house. Her neighbors told them that they had dug in the remains of her house and didn't hear or see anything. They assumed she wasn't home.

They almost abandoned the search when Doug Adams, her neighbor's son, heard her weak cry for help. They pulled her from her bathtub, and in another miracle, she had only a small scratch. Another good Samaritan took her to the hospital.

My friend called me with the good news just before we left the

Walmart to begin our trip back to Joplin. My mom was able to get through to us as we passed though Muskogee just after midnight. She was at Freeman and grandma was with her.

My mother had sat for hours in the crowded lobby of Freeman Hospital waiting for a chest X-ray and wondered if her mother was alive or dead. Did the storm somehow spare her house? Was my grandmother sitting there physically safe, but worried about my mom. Was she trapped?

There were thousands of people crowded into that building. My mom heard a woman cough. She told Ms. Schenk, "That sounds like my mother's cough." Unable to stand, my mother looked around and didn't see her. The woman coughed again. Ms. Schenk stood and said, "Barbara, it's your mother." She was sitting several rows away.

The reunion of my mother and grandmother was brief. My grandma was taken downstairs and examined. They put my mother in the emergency room with the more serious cases. We arrived at the hospital at 2 a.m. but weren't able to see them or even get confirmation that they were still there. Freeman was out of power and overwhelmed.

We heard that the hospital staff and volunteers performed admirably in the hours immediately after the disaster, but by the time we arrived everyone was starting to wear down. Two hours passed and we had no information.

A woman slept under a pile of blankets across the room. When she woke up and sat up, I saw it was Ms. Schenk. Her wounds were minor, so the hospital didn't treat her. I was glad that I was able to use one of the first aid kits I bought to help my mother's neighbor of 30 years and one of her closest friends.

Two hours later, someone wheeled my grandma into the lobby. "Is the family of Syble David here? Will someone claim her?" The man was going to place her on the bus to the shelter at MSSU. "I'll claim her," I cried. That was one of the happiest moments of my life.

The hospital staff finally confirmed that my mother was in the ER but wouldn't let me go back there. I heard horror stories from families that discovered their loved ones had been evacuated to Tulsa, Springfield, or further away hours earlier and that they weren't notified until hours later. I couldn't sit and wait any longer. I went outside and started looking inside every window and down every corridor. I peered inside every ambulance. I saw people in the worst condition. It was like a war or horror movie.

Men and women lie covered in blood with severed limbs, head wounds, and broken bones. Some people looked like they'd been in a blender filled with glass — they had been. I cringed about what my mother would look like when I found her.

Finally, after hours of persistence, the staff allowed me into the ER to see my mother. Just in time. They were preparing to load her on an ambulance. She was ashen but looked physically OK. She was clearly in a lot of pain. I went back to the lobby and asked my wife and father-in-law to take care of my grandmother.

The crew allowed me to ride in the front of the ambulance as they transported my mom to Mercy Hospital in Rogers, Arkansas. I knew my mother would be fine when I heard her joke with the emergency medical technician that she was going down to Arkansas "to call those Hogs." My parents used to attend Razorbacks' games years ago.

My mother was hospitalized until the Wednesday following the storm. My grandmother stayed at my cousin's house while my wife and father-in-law tried to salvage what they could of my mother's possessions. They had a lot of help.

A group of U.S. Marine Corps recruiters were among the first volunteers to assist — a thrill for my father-in-law who is a retired Marine officer. Then, in my father-in-law's words, "the cavalry arrived."

TAMKO provided crews and trucks to help employees, retirees, and their families. The TAMKO team labored for days at my mother and grandmother's houses. Unfortunately, there wasn't much worth salvaging, but they sure tried.

My wife secured my mother and grandmother a room at the Days Inn. Because my mother was in the hospital for the first few days after the storm, we weren't in a position to find her and grandma an apartment, a rental house, or another temporary place to live until later that week.

By the time we started looking, all of the rental units in Joplin were gone and the real estate market was becoming a feeding frenzy.

On Wednesday, the doctors told my mother to go home — where exactly was that she asked — and rest, but my mother, almost immediately upon returning to Joplin from the hospital, said she was going to rebuild on Illinois.

She asked me to call Mike Landis, a homebuilder and friend, to schedule a meeting and get started. As we continued to try to salvage family photos and heirlooms, my mother and grandmother filed insurance paperwork and, following the advice of city officials, registered with FEMA.

Things seemed to be going as well as possible. We felt extremely blessed. The death toll continued to climb, and it seemed an even bigger miracle that my mother, grandmother, and uncle, who lived down the street from my mother, all survived. Then the second disaster struck.

My grandmother was unable to get her blood pressure medicine for several days following the storm. About a week after the tornado, we had just concluded a meeting with an insurance adjuster when my grandma slumped over in the hotel room.

My grandfather had suffered two strokes, so we knew the signs. An ambulance arrived quickly, and she was to the hospital in less than 15 minutes after the onset of symptoms.

My grandmother's condition forced my mother to temporarily postpone her plans for rebuilding on Illinois. She knew she had to find a place before my grandmother was discharged.

We couldn't find an apartment and the housing market was crazy. My mother wanted to find a house near the hospital with no steps and suitable for someone in a wheelchair. She made a bid on one house but was outbid by someone who paid significantly more than the asking price.

My grandmother was hospitalized for almost three weeks. In that time, Jennifer Reaves from Keller Williams worked miracles for us.

In the midst of the craziest real estate market Joplin has ever seen, she helped us find them a house, make an offer, get an inspection, and close in less than a week. Amazing.

My mother closed on her new home 30 years to the day after she and my father bought 2201 S. Illinois Ave. She told us at closing that when she retired that she never imagined she would ever buy another home.

Back on Illinois Avenue, Samaritan's Purse helped remove the debris from my mother's property. After the debris was removed, friends and a group from the First Presbyterian Church of Colorado Springs, Colorado, toiled with me in the sun for hours cleaning and sorting bricks.

We salvaged approximately 2,000 of the House of Lords bricks. A contractor told me that should be enough to build at least a partial façade across part of a new house. My mother hired a crew to demolish the foundation. More volunteers came and raked and bagged loose debris. Unfortunately, several times over the next several months, contractors hired by the city and utility crews would drive across the lot leaving ruts and trash or dig trenches and leave rocks and piles of dirt.

The intersection of 22nd and Illinois is no longer my mother's address. It's ground zero.

It still amazes me that my mother and her immediate neighbors survived considering the intensity of the storm at that point and because many people died within a few hundred yards of her house. A photo of the neighborhood immediately after the storm is featured on the cover of the book 5:41 Stories from the Joplin Tornado, co-written by my friend John Hacker.

That intersection witnessed the worst of the storm's fury and, fittingly, provides an excellent view of Joplin's recovery. New churches, homes, and the new Joplin High School are being built nearby. I hope my mother is able to rebuild there soon.

Will There Be a Christmas Tree?

By Marty Oetting

Debris and rubble tell stories. They give clues to what used to be and reasons to ponder what might again be in the future.

I had occasion to think long and hard about these things over the Thanksgiving holiday weekend when I made my first trip back to the Joplin area following the May 22 tornado.

I may live four hours away in Columbia, but a big part of my soul was deeply disturbed by the disaster and I felt the pain and struggle from afar. I have been in Joplin, in spirit. I sensed the pain, even if I didn't feel it physically like so many who were there.

I lived in Joplin in the 1980s, graduating from Parkwood High School in 1982 and worked at Red Baron Pizza on 20th Street. (It was only there a couple of years.) I also was familiar with St. James United Methodist Church on 20th Street as my father was a district superintendent for the Methodist churches in southwest Missouri. We lived on the corner of 28th and Illinois.

More importantly, I drove up and down 20th Street every day for many years. It is an important part of my memories of growing up. Shopping at Dillon's. Watching trains at the 20th street crossing of the KCS. Watching little league games. Filling up at the Sinclair at 20th and Range Line. And just driving up and down that road every day.

I have always had a fascination with tornadoes and severe weather. When skies would threaten, my friends and I would hop in the car and chase severe storms, hoping to get a glimpse of a funnel cloud.

While a student at Missouri Southern, we even did a special series on the anniversary of the tornado that hit Joplin in the early 1970s for the Chart newspaper. We never saw a tornado while I lived in Joplin.

But that was not the case on May 22, 2011. I had been visiting my parents in nearby Carthage that very weekend and brought them back to Columbia to celebrate my son's high school graduation. But this isn't about my story of the storm and how I survived it. I was two hours away when it hit, and believe me, many of your stories in Joplin are so compelling that I feel my heart race and my hair stand on end when I read your accounts of survival.

And so it is – Thanksgiving weekend 2011 I find myself in the parking lot of what was left of the shopping center on 20th and Rhode Island that used to house Red Baron Pizza. It was leveled by the center of the tornado, most of the debris hauled away long ago.

I walked around and looked at the foundation and rubble. Soon I realized it told a story. I began to see things begging for further inspection. I found a large piece of the instrument panel from a car. I found a CD billfold that held several home-made compact discs. I found a windshield wiper. I found a woman's shoe. And not too far away, another woman's shoe.

But then I saw two things that really hit me. The first was a child's knitted glove. It was just lying on the pavement near the foundation. I wondered where the other glove was, and more importantly, where is the little girl who wore those gloves? I wanted to believe she was celebrating Thanksgiving with her family in a new location. But I also knew there was the possibility she and her family are not all still here.

The second thing I saw was a string of Christmas tree lights. They were knotted up in a tight, tangled wad. I wasn't sure if they were left that way from the last holiday celebration, or if they were tangled in the winds of the tornado. But I knew this – they would not be decorating a Christmas tree this year. Where did they come from? How far did they fly in the wind? Would that family have a Christmas tree this year?

I will always remember the Joplin tornado, and how it destroyed the physical location of so much of my childhood. There was Cunningham Park, where I went swimming and played tennis. And Main Street, where I visited different restaurants while riding around with friends on Friday nights.

I think of my high school, which was so sad to see in a pile of rubble and twisted beams. My old house survived but looked forlorn, stripped of all trees and in need of roof repair. And then there was that old pizza restaurant with the salad bar that looked like a biplane cowling, now nothing but a flat foundation.

So I decided I wanted to keep some things found in the rubble, to remind me and others of the awesome power of Mother Nature and the struggle to overcome the disaster. I found an old brick in the rubble from Red Baron Pizza. I found a small shard of split wood framing. I found a shredded and twisted piece of siding. And I found a piece of metal flashing that was twisted in an odd shape from the wind.

They all went in the back of my car and came to Columbia with me. I will arrange them in a display that will serve as a tribute to memories of the Joplin I once knew and the resilience of a community after tragedy.

And each Christmas, when I am getting out the lights to decorate, I will always think about my chance discovery of a string of lights in Joplin after the 2011 tornado. And I will wonder, will they have a Christmas tree?

This Town is My Home

By Laela Zaidi

In the hours before the May 22 tornado, I remember the afternoon being filled with laughter. The beautiful day was a reminder to my friends and I that summer was around the corner, just two weeks away. I anticipated it not only because of the freedom, but it was the summer after my first year in high school. My plans were to spend it with old friends and new and to play tennis for my upcoming fall season. It seemed as if nothing could bring me down; I was content with life.

Of course, nothing could prepare me for what would happen hours later. The beautiful afternoon turned ugly as a massive EF-5 tornado tore the town apart and destroyed countless homes and businesses- including my home, three of my family's homes, my dad's office and the hospital where worked.

My high school, which I also lived across the street from, was torn to pieces.

A few days after the tornado, I climbed to the top of what was left of my home. Standing on a grey slab (what used to be my room) I looked over the damage. There was nothing in sight except endless debris, chewed up homes, and, in the distance, the shell of St. Johns. A realization came upon me; the unchanged life I had known for 15 years in this town would never be the same.

With nowhere left to go, 20 members of my family to look after, and the possibility of more tornados, my parents decided to move everyone to the MSSU Red Cross Shelter for a week.

My sister, who lives in Chicago, came down and stayed with me at a friend's. However, this situation couldn't last forever. A quick decision was made that we would move to Monett, Missouri. This small town, just under an hour outside of Joplin, is where my mom commutes to work three times a week.

With my dad out of work in town, it seemed like the only choice. My aunt and her three kids followed us there.

Despite what had happened in Joplin on May 22, it never crossed my mind to actually leave. My house may have been gone, but this town has been my home for 15 years.

Once moving what little we had to Monett, this dawned on my parents as well. My dad signed up with Mercy St. John's and we found a new house in Joplin. By August, we moved back in town. Nothing felt better than being reunited with my friends, seeing familiar faces, and being home.

Of course, our new house still didn't feel right, but at least I was back in a familiar place. The uncertainty of living in Monett made me feel homeless, lonely, and depressed.

Despite the genuine sympathy from those I met there, nobody could relate or understand the emotional rollercoaster of losing your home, high school, and neighborhood in a natural disaster.

After a summer spent in misery, I felt so much joy to be back where I should be. The support of friends, family, and familiarity of the town helped in getting back to some sense of normalcy, and it has been encouraging to watch businesses and homes spring from the rubble.

One aspect of life forever changed, one both individually affecting citizens of Joplin and collectively, is school.

For 2,000 students, the loss of our only public high school has changed the way most of us think of school spirit forever. The first home football game clearly proved this.

Luckily, our off-campus football stadium was spared from the tornado's path. The filled stands were vibrant in our school colors and nothing could bring the energy of the crowds down.

Because of the loss of our building, the high school was split into two campuses. One for 9/10th graders, at a building recently used as a middle school, and a modern, newly built campus in our mall for 11/12th graders.

While both are "Joplin High School," everyone can agree the high school experience in Joplin is definitely far from normal.

In order to make up for the hundreds of textbooks lost, JHS has adopted "21st-Century Learning." Every student has his or her own Macbook laptop, and most work is done electronically. Classroom projects are done through video editing, presentations, and various other technology outlets.

To most people, this seems like a unique way to learn. In reality, the ability to focus on work and be productive has become near impossible. The quality of education hasn't increased, and there is nothing healthy about spending seven hours a day on a computer screen. Being a lover of books, paper, and pens may leave me biased, but many students feel just as frustrated at times as I do.

Like any change, especially dramatic ones such as this year has seen, time and patience are needed for them to be broken in. The new learning strategy Joplin Schools has adopted has much room for improvement, and without older kids to look up to in the hallways (in a place where many of them recently went to middle school) the chance for freshmen to grow up and mature proves much more difficult. Despite all this, the chance to continue our education, on time, has been the greatest blessing. High school life is far from normal, but knowing our teachers and administrators are doing everything they can to make it the best it can be is the greatest comfort.

Throughout the year, the skeleton of JHS stood as a reminder of comforting memories; My history teacher's closet where his students hung out and did homework, the classrooms, the teachers I said hello to everyday (some whom I don't see anymore) are all things I still miss.

Often, I revisit those places in my mind. One last time I walk the hallways, sit in the classrooms, and say my goodbyes. I venture across the street and lay in the backyard of my beautiful three-story home.

Sometimes I even drive past those places and envision those buildings still standing as they once did. Years from now, the old Joplin High School and the red brick, green mansard roof home of mine will be forgotten. But hopefully, there will be something bigger and better in their place.

The land where my house once was will be a part of something that provides young adults an education and opportunities for generations to come. While these places leave me finding myself heartbroken today, one day I hope to look at them with pride in what my community has rebuilt in their place.

Until then, the story of what took place on May 22nd will be told as one of resilience, human spirit, and what it truly means to not have a house, but rather a home shared with an entire community.

Pushed to the Breaking Point

By John Hacker

"I t is my opinion that weaknesses are generally just strengths that are pushed too hard."

In Joplin, on May 22, 2011, many, many strengths were pushed to the breaking point. One of the people pushing those strengths as hard as possible was Keith Stammer, Joplin's emergency management director.

Stammer talked about that day with people who know and feel his struggle, emergency managers and meteorologists at the National Weather Service's Severe Weather Workshop on March 2, 2012 in Norman, Okla.

An interesting thing about Stammer's presentation is he spoke for more than an hour to a crowd of more than 100 that hung on his every word, but he used no notes, only a slideshow.

Each image evoked memories of a specific place, or event, or casualty, or triumph on May 22 and the days that followed.

Each memory burned into his brain by an event that emergency management directors try to prepare for, but hope they never have to work — a major catastrophe in their town.

And how do you prepare for something like what happened to Joplin on May 22, 2011? It is hard to practice for something that seems impossible to imagine.

"If I had walked into that exercise design committee meeting with this scenario in my back pocket, I would have been laughed out of the room. They would have said let's do something we know," Stammer said. "Well, not now."

PRELUDE TO DISASTER

Stammer gave the crowd a mental picture of Joplin before the storm.

"We sleep 50,000 more or less. On a given workday, population swells by 5 with almost 250,000 people.

"You can watch the headlights come into town in the morning. You can watch the taillights go out of town at night. The thing that makes that significant as far as May 22 was May 22 was a Sunday evening; it was not a Monday evening. So Sunday evening at 5:41 was a lot different than a Monday evening at 5:41 and for that, we are most grateful, it made a big difference in terms of the number of people in town.

"Joplin does not own its own utilities, gas water, electric owned by for-profit companies which makes it a very interesting situation when you are running an emergency operations center and trying to coordinate all of the utility activities that happen."

He also talked about what he was doing on May 22 prior to 5:41 p.m.

"We were under tornado watch as of about noon that day. I was sitting at home watching the Cardinals play, had my iPad on watching the radar and also, I was on NWS chat with the Springfield office talking about what was going on.

"At about 4:30 p.m. we, being Kathy and I, decided it was time to go down to the EOC. She goes with me; she brings her knitting and sits in the EOC and we visit.

"Things started getting crazy, turned on sirens at approximately 11 minutes after (5:11 p.m.), then decided to turn them on again about 20 minutes after that (5:31 p.m.)."

THE STORM

At 5:41 p.m. something happened that shocked meteorologists.

Steve Runnels, warning coordination meteorologist, attended the conference in Norman and described for his peers how this storm was different from any other he had seen.

"An EF 5 tornado, capable of producing 200-mile-per-hour-plus winds, only occurs one out of a thousand tornados. Even at that, the type of storm that produces such a tornado, called a supercell, is a relatively rare event. We get maybe 10 days or two weeks out of the year when we see supercells and maybe three or four of those produce tornados.

Was Joplin rare in terms of intensity? Yes.

"But even on top of that, supercells like to form in an environment where they are the only storm in the region. They require a strong inflow into a rotating updraft to survive. What was really strange about the Joplin event is that we had supercells that were forming and then merging within other cells. It was an event that normally the environment does not produce the types of storms that we saw that day.

"The other thing that perhaps was a little bit strange from a supercell's perspective was that the tornado itself was masked in rain. So you had three-quarters to one-mile-wide tornado with lots of debris, but on top of that you had rain further blocking visibility.

"These factors together really went into the fact of making this an odd event. Like the Picher Tornado that occurred back on Mother's

Day, 2008, this event does show that there are times when the National Weather Service can forecast tornado outbreaks a week in advance. AKA the storm system that came through in 2003, but there will be other times where the day before or even the morning of the tornado, our forecasts are being further refined."

THE STORM HITS

Joplin's Emergency Operations Center, or EOC, is located at the Donald E. Clark Safety and Justice Center at 303 E. Third St. about 20 blocks north of what was to become the path of the most destructive storm in recent memory.

It's where Keith Stammer goes to coordinate services when disaster strikes. Stammer had set off the sirens twice on the evening of May 22, once for a tornado warning sounded in the north end of Joplin and a second time for a warning the Weather Service issued further south shortly after 5:30 p.m.

Stammer was talking to one of the local radio stations when the tornado struck.

"KZRG was talking to me on the cell phone and they said why are the sirens going off and I was explaining why the sirens were going off, we had a report of a touchdown and they said thank you very . . . I looked at my cell phone and said why did you hang up on me? Then I realized the cell phones were down and I looked, over and our phones were down, and the cable was out, and the Internet was down. We had backups for all of that, but the tornado just ripped all of that out of there, so we did not have access to all of our phone lines."

Stammer said he had some communication and reports of damage were starting to trickle in.

"We did have cell text messaging. It was kind of spotty, but we used that quite a bit. We do have a robust radio system on 800 megahertz; we have towers on the north and south sides of Joplin. None of that was affected.

"A big thing for us as opposed to Tuscaloosa, Alabama, was that they lost their police station; they lost their EOC all through the path of that tornado, none of that was true with us. It went through a residential area. We lost two fire stations. 95 percent of primary and secondary streets were impassible. We lost the street signs, streetlights, traffic signals. . ."

EVACUATING A HOSPITAL

Stammer talked about the incredible events transpiring at Joplin's largest hospital. St. John's Regional Medical Center, located at 26th Street and McClelland Boulevard, took a direct hit from a tornado that had rapidly spun up to incredible strength.

Security camera video, shot on May 22 and not released until May 2012, show winds sweeping through the hospital's emergency room waiting area, rendering it to shambles in seconds.

"Five years ago, I attended evacuation exercise at St. John's, where we practiced taking people from upper floors to lower floors, practiced surging from the building to the parking lot. That was in all of our plans, if the hospitals needed to surge, they needed to expand someplace, they would just go to the parking lot because all their equipment is there, doctors are there why go to a different location. We evacuated something like 50 pretend patients in something in the neighborhood of two to three hours and were quite pleased with ourselves.

"St. John's had 180 patients that night plus the doctors and staff that were there. That entire building was evacuated in 90 minutes flat. They did an outstanding job, it's amazing what you can do when you have to."

Stammer talked about the damage the nine-story, 40-year-old hospital sustained.

"The hospital itself, you may have heard various stories about it being moved off its foundation. What actually happened was the top three floors of the hospital twisted about four inches. Those of you who know the engineering understand concrete and steel do fine job up and down. Left and right, not so much, so when that happened, the building was done.

"They are in the process this year of starting to take it down by jackhammer and by backhoe and balls. We wanted them to blow it up, I thought that might be kind of fun, but the problem with Joplin is that it is totally undermined with old lead and zinc mines and the engineers said we really don't want to lower streets for a mile around. (Laughter) You think that's funny, but I can tell you that two years ago, St. John's, on one side, had a three-story parking garage and that parking garage sank three inches, so they had to take it down. So that's a very real concern in that area.

"It's coming down, St. John's Hospital is rebuilding, they have a temporary building, they've put up semi-permanent buildings, they are going to be in the process of putting up a permanent building on I-44. Sisters of Mercy and St. John's, which is now called Mercy, are not going to spend $1 billion in erecting a new medical facility. It's going to be very nice; it's going to be state of the art, and they did a fine job."

TEMPORARY MEDICAL FACILITIES

Stammer talked about the temporary medical facilities, set up to support Freeman West Hospital, which had suddenly become Joplin's only operating hospital and emergency room at exactly the time when the city needed all the medical help it could get.

"The state of Missouri has what is known as a medical mobile unit, I know Dottie Brinkle, she's the director of nursing for St. John's Hospital. Our elder daughter used to babysit her daughters.

"She called me up and said Keith I want the MMU and hung up. I said yes ma'am. I called the state and they brought in the whole unit, it's a MASH-type hospital that will handle 60 beds and the National

Guard set that up, they're known locally as the MONG, the Missouri National Guard, they helped set that up.

"Memorial Hall, owned by Joplin. In 2007 we had an ice storm come through. Lost power for a week, and we set up a shelter there in Memorial Hall. We had a nursing home or two and several residents who had no power, and we ran a shelter there for an entire seven days.

"We said well, that worked out very well. What we're going to do is incorporate that into our Local Emergency Operations Plan, part of our after-action review, so the next time we have a disaster, we know we go to that shelter.

Apparently, the medical review committee was also in on that because as soon as this happened, the doctors at St. John's marched themselves down the street to Memorial Hall, walked in the door and said we're here to take over, this is now our building.

"In a matter of an hour or two, they were doing surgery on the basketball court. Most impressive. We ran there for quite a while until they could get quarters set up in other places. Doctors set up offices there for practice. That's not how we exactly envisioned it, but you do what you have to based on your past experience and the situation you find yourself in at the moment. Again, our hats off to our medical community and the work that they did."

INFRASTRUCTURE

Stammer described the massive damage to the utility infrastructure of the city. He also showed pictures of the damage to the Empire District Electric Company substation on 26th Street and Wall Avenue.

"We had widespread electrical outages, damaged or missing distribution points, you can see the top right hand, that is an Empire District Electric Company substation that was totally gone just from the wind, fires around the area and that didn't do us a whole lot of good because there was no water for a three-mile area.

"When the houses were destroyed, we refer to that as smoothing, when the houses were smoothed all the utilities were still there, but it broke off all the access. So it broke off the gas, broke off the water, broke off the meters. They had to go around and turn off every individual water line to every house in that entire area, the same thing for all the gas lines. It took about three days to get the water pressure back up."

He also described the response from 110 outside municipal public works departments that sent people and equipment to help.

"Within 36 hours after the storm, 100 percent of the primary and 70 percent of the secondary streets were cleared. I remember Sunday night, the city manager, Mark Rohr, came into the EOC, all the department heads had come in and, in one conversation, I remember he turned to the director of public works and said job one is to clear the streets. Why are you still standing here? Go clear the streets. So that's what we did all Sunday night. SEMA, the State Emergency Management Agency, was there on Sunday night, FEMA came in on Monday morning, actually they started coming in the middle of the night and as soon as dawn broke they were out. They said they really could not believe that you could get to the locations. We needed that done."

"HUNDREDS DEAD"

Stammer talked about the shock in the reports from his first responders as they fanned out in Joplin that first night.

"Honestly, folks, our first responders said, when they went out in the field, we have hundreds dead. Just looking at everything out there. The police department and ambulance people, they were discussing how to set up a triage. We practiced triage before; we had gone through that kind of thing, but always on a smaller scale. They figured out all you had to do was pull an ambulance into a residential area that had been hit and turn on their lights. When you turned on your lights, they literally came out of the woodwork."

He said the residents of Joplin themselves became first responders that day.

"A man and his two dogs came in and bought the house in my neighborhood after the storm, I think the dogs were cosigners. He said they rode out the storm in an interior room, multiple walls and between him and the exterior in a closet holding on to the door of the closet to keep the wind from pulling it open.

"When it was done, he kicked the closet door open; all that was left was a closet. He looked over to one side and he sees some debris move, so he went over and helped his neighbor dig out. The two of them looked over on the other side and saw a hand waving from the debris so they went over and dug a woman out and that's kind of how they survived. As far as triage was concerned, people were trying to help each other all the way around.

"We had 5,000 emergency personnel from 435 agencies come to Joplin. Our city manager was extremely straightforward about this, he said we will not stop looking until there is no one to look for, so that's what we did.

We started search and rescue that night, we brought in dog teams, we brought in search and rescue teams. Urban Search and Rescue teams out of Arkansas, Oklahoma, Kansas, Kansas City, St. Louis, Mo. These are teams that have all the equipment, the hard hats the ropes, they know how to do all this stuff. And they can just go through a big box store in literally 45 minutes; it was quite amazing.

"We had a lot of dogs, some 80 different search and rescue dog teams, we made six passes across the city from east to west and from west to east going back and forth. We found our last live person on Tuesday afternoon. Physicians were telling on Wednesday, people had a 50 percent chance survival if they were trapped, Friday it's like about 10 percent. Wanted to make sure we hadn't missed anyone.

"Another thing was from the air. People brought in helicopters and we flew every treetop, every building, every roof that we could. They brought in search and rescue teams as far as CERT, Community

Emergency Response Teams, put them on the ground in the path going down to Newton County. Dive teams, we dove every pond, every swimming pool, every golf course hazard from one end to the other just to make sure we didn't miss anything."

FEEDING VOLUNTEERS AND VICTIMS

One big problem was feeding the victims that were coming out of the rubble and the massive army of volunteers that was going in to search and clean up.

"Feeding stations were set up everywhere. Tyson Chicken came in and set up right outside the EOC and it was really nice, chicken for breakfast, chicken for lunch, chicken for dinner and sometimes they put eggs with it. (Laughter) I went to see them and said I only have one requirement; you don't turn anybody away. The first several days, anyone that wanted to eat could come up and do that.

"The health department was pulling their hair out. They're used to doing inspections of food services and talking about cleanliness. Yeah, 40 feeding stations opened up simultaneously, that doesn't count everyone who owned a grill.

"Because the volunteers came in and people just took their grills out of the garage and started cooking hamburgers and hot dogs and handing out cokes. The health department went by and said I'm going to pretend this didn't happen and went down the street to something else."

FAITH-BASED RESPONSE

Stammer talked about the role of churches in Joplin's response to the disaster.

"I'm going to tell you right now, those, from an emergency management standpoint, this job cannot be done without the faith-based organizations. Every major denomination of which I am aware of in the United States has a division for emergency response; they all know each other. They all work together on these and they specialize in different things, not the least of which is, God bless 'em, those Southern Baptist women who know how to cook. They came in one time with a trailer and said we're here for two weeks. I said okay, great, they said we need a location; we have our own people, all of our own food. I asked how many can you do, she said we can do 1,200 meals a day. That's what they do.

"The Latter-Day Saints called and said we can put 600 boots on the ground over the weekend, where do you need them. The Presbyterian Church specializes in the housing of volunteers later on, the Mennonites, they have people who pull off their jobs, they give up their vacations and they come in and work with people who have no money, but they get their roof put back on, their carports repaired that type of things. They work with their own NGOS, non-governmental organizations. They work without NGO liaison out of the EOC.

"Here's the key in all of this operation, how things went. For seven years I've been there, and we've done this before, we do exercises, we do drills, we do after-action reviews and for me the one key thing was this, there was not one major player who walked into the EOC that I did not already know.

Any faith-based, any governmental organization, any business that came in to talk, we'd all seen each other. The statement is the disaster scene is not the place to exchange business cards. We want to know who you are, that's how things worked, and it worked very well when we did it."

VOLUNTEERS COME IN

Stammer praised the response of Americorps, the federal office coordinating volunteers that come into the city to help.

"Anyone familiar with Americorps?" he said. "They're good kids aren't they. They march to a little different drummer. In the EOC on Sunday night, one of my people could not remember the name but they remembered them from 2007, they said where are the hippies?

"Oh, you mean Americorps, Bruce is already coming, they are authorized to respond, they were in St. Louis, he called and said we're en route, we'll be there at about 3 o'clock in the morning. They helped out a lot; we had to divide out the debris into five different piles, white goods over here, metals over here, vegetation debris that's hauled off separately.

"The other thing they did is ran our volunteer registration area, which was a godsend because it helped us get people's names and addresses and who are you and when you come in and when you leave. That gives us volunteer hours.

"Another rule worth of repeating: all disasters are local, they start locally, they end locally. They may rise to national prominence as ours did somewhere in between, but at some point, with all due respect to all of you who have come, all you foreigners are going to go away at some point, and we are going to be left here to handle it ourselves so we're not giving up local control.

"The volunteers did a wonderful job. Missouri Southern State University, they're a nice college, a drive-in sort of place; only 950 dorm rooms. There is no alcohol, no smoking, it's kind of like come in, get your education, leave, thank you very much. It's a great college.

"They had just signed a memorandum of understanding with the American Red Cross two weeks before to act as a shelter. When this happened, they stepped up. We filled up their dorm rooms, we filled up their gymnasium, FEMA came in a few days after the tornado and said how many people, how many structures, we didn't know, we were guessing. They said how many shelters; we said one. They said one? I said it holds 1,000 people. If it fills up, we'll go get another one. The most we ever had were 650.

It's kind of interesting; people take care of themselves around here. That was our first question, where did everybody go? They went with family and friends, the churches were grabbing people off the street, calling parishioners and asking can you take three, yes, here's six thank you very much. It was amazing and it worked real well for the first three weeks."

"THE FISH"

One of the most important contributions from the federal government, in the early days of the disaster, was helping to map out the tornado's path.

"If you don't get anything else out of this evening, please get this. This is our map of the destruction of the tornado running from west to east through Joplin.

"Basically, it fired up on the west side, it gained its strength, you can see that outlined against the white, that's the damage path itself, then it went over to the east side of Joplin, approximately six miles, began to spool down a little bit, made a right-hand turn and went on down into Newton County down toward Diamond, Mo. approximately 13.8 miles in all.

"Our first responders refer to this particular map as the fish, because of its shape, so they came into the EOC and said do you have any more maps of the fish? Initially, our fire chief got into a helicopter and sketched out the damage area. This particular map was brought to us by benefit of FEMA and the U.S. Geological Survey and their satellites. This has been of multiple uses for us.

"One thing that has been rather nice is that we've had multiple communities ask us for copies of this as an overlay and they then took that overlay to their communities and said this is what happened to Joplin, coming through a residential area, what would happen to us if the same thing happened?"

"Let me just say right up front, I'm going to sound like a PSA for FEMA and that's fine. We saw the stories of Katrina; the FEMA of today is not the FEMA of back then. They are very collaborative, they were very cooperative, they helped us in any way, shape or form that they could, not the least of which is they brought in this satellite data map and so we could do some grid work on this for search and rescue and for rebuild.

"They zoomed in from a satellite to each individual property and identified it as destroyed, majorly destroyed, partially destroyed, lightly destroyed, by looking at them.

"For many of you in the industry, you know this is true, for the rest of you who are not in the industry, those stories about the government being able to look down from the sky and read your license plate — they are true. And I know that's true because I asked for an electronic copy of this, they say no. Why not, because you can zoom in on these places as well. They gave us printouts all we wanted, but we never did get an electronic copy of it.

"We used this in our discussions we've had on after-action reviews since then. That map pretty much is the story, you can see where it started out small and got wider and then went across the city from west to east."

STATE AND FEDERAL RESPONSE

Stammer said the state and federal agencies that responded were generally very helpful and respectful of the local control he and the city sought to maintain.

"The state emergency response and the federal emergency response to us was outstanding. Again, we have worked with the Missouri Emergency Response agencies for years, they know us by name, they've been to our EOC, I have most of those people on my speed dial on my phone, I have 420 names on my phone, which is just a work phone, so if you called me and your name did not show up, you went to voice mail.

"FEMA came in and did some rather innovative things for us. Number one, I told you about the map. Another thing that was interesting that they did was they provided us with a full-time administrative assistant. She knew everybody and their emails and their super-secret phone numbers, so when the city manager came by and said I need to talk to that one gal who came by and handed out the stuff that had to do with the housing, she said oh yeah, that's so and so, I'll get her for you. She was wonderful.

"The weather service brought in an embedded meteorologist, Kevin Hoover, we love Kevin, he got along with everyone real well, he has that southern drawl that just kind of makes everyone melt. He likes to eat; we had lots of chicken. (Laughter)"

Stammer talked about coordinating all the different agencies in town at the height of the response.

"We would do a briefing at 7 a.m. and 7 p.m. every day. We had what was called an incident action plan. It was a bible for us. It listed what our objectives were for that day, who was in charge of the objectives, when we wanted those done, what equipment and supplies were required.

"Everyone that was out in the field their position, their cell phone numbers, the day's weather report, any other materials that we needed, hazardous materials reports, anything like that was all part and parcel of that IAP, and very quickly word spread amongst all of the other organizations that we need one of those IAPs, we said fine, there's a price, you have to come to our 7 a.m. meeting and Kelly would give us the weather report at 7 a and 7 p, every day.

"Probably one of those lessons learned, one of the things we didn't do well there, we should, instead of printing 50 copies of the IAP for department heads, we should have printed like 300 and handed them out to every cop, every firefighter, everybody in the health department so they would know exactly what our plans were for that particular day."

THE EOC

The nerve center of Joplin's response to the catastrophe was the Emergency Operations Center, a Cold-War-era bunker in the basement of the Donald E. Clark Safety and Justice Center in the north part of town.

It is a very nice place," Stammer said. "It has full power, electricity, in a basement. My standing joke is when we have storms, I can stand there; watch the radar, drink a latté and a tornado goes over the top and we say what was that? I have no idea; we are under two feet of stressed-reinforced concrete. We had quite a few crews set up there."

The help from the state came in the form of more than rescue crews in the debris area. The state sent teams to help with the reams of reports and paperwork that comes with keeping track of the living and dead, those evacuated and those searching for survivors. He said as trivial as it might seem to worry about paperwork, those reports and documents were important to keeping track of the search, keeping people safe and wasting as little time as possible.

"Incident Support Teams, they were a godsend to us. An incident support team, if you've been through the National Incident Management System, I'm trying hard not to say NIMS and ICS and all that, if you've been through the Incident Command training through the National Incident Management System, you'll know you have a standardized method of arranging yourself. You have an incident commander, you have a public information officer, a safety officer, a liaison officer, then you have four department heads for operations, planning, logistics and finance and admin.

"We had all those people. Some of them weren't in town; some of them were victims. My police department PIO, it took him 30 minutes to get out of his basement. He radioed in and said, 'I'm out of service.' A week later we saw him. One of my primary backups as incident commander, the same story on him. We have in the state of Missouri Incident Support Teams that are trained to come into a city or a town, an area, to help support in this particular situation.

"I called Ryan Nichols, emergency management director in

Springfield, about 7 p.m. that night, I'd been calling him all night because I needed this and that. I finally called him and said I need an IST; they were there in two hours."

Stammer said the terrorist attacks on Sept. 11, 2001 changed everything when it came to emergency management in America.

He said it freed up money for preparing for disasters as well as terrorist attacks.

"Now thanks to the funding that was available after 9-11, when you call for a fire department you get a truck, maybe two, they have radios that can be tuned to different frequencies, they will bring a mass casualty trailer, they will bring a hazmat trailer, and often times they will bring a communications trailer.

"The incident support team out of Springfield brought all their own stuff in terms of forms and everything they needed to run an office and they brought their own communications trailer, which was a microwave relay truck. We didn't have phones, so they just set it up, pointed it back toward Springfield and for the next 11 days we ran off of Springfield's phone system."

Mercy Joplin Opens Component Hospital

By John Hacker

An unknown Mercy employee said it best as she was walking into the ribbon cutting for the new Mercy Joplin Hospital on April 11; "It's the most permanent-looking temporary building I've ever seen."

The startling thing in first seeing the new Mercy Hospital Joplin – the factory built, trucked-in replacement for the building destroyed by last May's tornado – is how attractive and permanent it looks.

Joplin has a new hospital as of mid-April, and this one isn't tents or trailers.

"This facility is a concrete and steel structure that will serve as our last temporary home until the opening of the new Mercy Joplin in 2015." Said John Farnen, executive director for planning, design and construction for Mercy Health System.

"With additional services and conveniences for our patients and guests, the facility will have Labor and Delivery, a Pediatric Unit, an expanded Emergency and ICU department and up to

This aerial photo taken in February 2012 shows two of the temporary locations Mercy Joplin Hospital occupied between the destruction of St. John's Regional Medical Center on May 22, 2011 and the completion of the new hospital at I-44 and Hearnes Boulevard in March 2015. The tent hospital is above and the component hospital is under construction below. Photo by John Hacker

120 beds. Mercy is proud to be able to bring back these important services to Joplin."

The new facility will offer patients all the comforts and most services they would expect from a Mercy hospital. With steel construction that is sturdier than the old St. John's Regional Medical Center, the new Mercy building is a testament to modern technology and overtime workers coming together to build a complete hospital in eight months.

The new facility includes a full-scale emergency department. Surgeons can again conduct complex, open-heart procedures. Mercy doctors can deliver babies again. Patients can rest in rooms with monitoring features and communication capabilities.

From the beginning of the day on May 22, 2011, to April 15,

2012, this will be the fourth new facility opened and operated by Mercy doctors, nurses and staff. That includes the old St. John's Regional Medical Center that was destroyed in the tornado, the temporary hospital that was opened at Joplin's Memorial Hall for a few weeks immediately after the storm, the tents installed to the east of the old St. John's that served for the past seven months, and this 110-bed component hospital, assembled in a record eight months.

Farnen said the company took lessons learned from May 22 and incorporated them into this building.

There will be flashlights, new communication systems, new battery lights not just emergency power," Farnen said. "It includes a protected emergency supply area, additional safe areas and training for future events and safer egress paths.

"The new design will incorporate a harden structure for the utilities. The generators and all power switches will be housed in a reinforced concrete and brick structure. All utility lines will be buried in a tunnel from the plant to the Hospital. Fuel tanks will also be underground. The old hospital had outside above ground fuel tanks and generators exposed to the elements. This reinforced plant will also have storage area for emergency supplies that can be accessed through the tunnel to the hospital or a loading dock for off-site facilities. We will also have a covered dock area for storing emergency trailer to protect it from weather."

Mike McCurry, Chief Operating Officer for Mercy Health System, paid tribute to the staff and coworkers that have had to adapt to these new facilities every few months since their original beloved building was destroyed.

"Imagine that your entire work environment and the tools that you use and the process that you follow, the building that you are in, the people that you are around, it all just up and changes every few months," McCurry said. "All of it, every bit of it, so nothing is the same, the building is not the same, the tools are not the same, the beds are not the same, the docs are not the same. It's everything imaginable that we're asking them to adopt to and change and the magnitude of change is immense."

McCurry said the change has been unprecedented, and that same staff will go through an even larger change in 2015 when the massive new Mercy Joplin campus, under construction on 50th Street, opens.

But Mercy had a choice.

"The choice was to just simply be out of business for three years," McCurry said. "We were so concerned that if we let that happen, valuable talents would atrophy or leave the community. We knew we could get the hospital opened back up, but if there's nobody there with the talent and the know-how and frankly the compassion of the community to run it, then it's little good."

The modular hospital is stronger even than the old St. John's building, with glass windows and walls built to withstand 200 mile-per-hour winds.

And the speed in which this building was assembled and erected is also unprecedented.

McCurry said no one has ever built a hospital of this size in eight months.

an End and a Beginning

By John Hacker

Crystal Harvey spent 16 years working at the St. John's Regional Medical Center building at 26th and McClelland Boulevard, but that building was so much more than just a place to work.

"My grandma passed away there, I've had two uncles pass away there," Harvey said on Jan. 29. "I met my husband there and he was born there."

Even though the May 22 tornado made that building unusable, it was still hard for people like Harvey to watch as a wrecking ball took the first of the thousands of swings that it will eventually take to bring down the massive building.

Fortunately for Harvey and her co-workers, January 29 was not only the beginning of the end for their old workplace, but it was also the beginning of the beginning for their new workplace as Mercy and its employees and city leaders turned the dirt at a groundbreaking at the future home of Mercy Joplin on 50th Street.

Screenshot from Mercy Hospital YouTube Page

"It was very tough to see that wrecking ball hit the building," Harvey said. "It is closure to the end of one era and we came directly here to the beginning of a new era. And it's good to close it and begin it all in the same day."

Harvey was one of hundreds who attended the dual ceremonies on Jan. 29.

Under a tent in the parking lot on the east side of the tornado ravaged former hospital, co-workers and Mercy leaders joined Joplin leaders to watch the beginning of the process of tearing down the building.

In the ceremony, co-workers described the history of St. John's through the eyes of the founders, Sister Mary Francis Sullivan, who led the effort to build the first St. John's hospital in the late 1800s, and Sister Mary Austin O'Donahue, who led the hospital as it moved to the 26th and McClelland area in the 1960s.

They also heard from Bishop James Van Johnston, leader of the

Springfield-Cape Girardeau Diocese, Sister Mary Roch Rocklage of the Sisters of Mercy, Mercy CEO Lynn Britton and Mercy Joplin CEO Gary Pulsipher, among others.

After watching the wrecking ball take the first whacks at the side of the building, the crowd drove to the new site on the old Messenger College property east of Hearnes

Boulevard on 50th Street, led by a wooden cross that once hung in the old St. John's and will spend the rest of its days in the Mercy McCune-Brooks Hospital in Carthage.

Here they heard from the same leaders about the new, $950 million hospital that will be built there before grabbing shovels of their own and joining hospital officials and dignitaries in breaking the ground for the hospital.

"It was nice to have closure for the old building," said Justin Gilstrap, who works in radiology for Mercy Joplin. "My wife was born there, both my sons were born there, my grandmother passed away there, my mother had bypass surgery almost 21 years ago there and she's still alive. This was also important to acknowledge that something new was coming. We've been looking forward to that."

We Will Have School

By Randy Turner

"Which one is the superintendent?" a photographer for one of the cable networks asked the middle-aged woman standing a few feet from him.

She pointed at the man standing a few feet away from the makeshift podium that had been set up in front of the shattered remnants of what only two weeks before had been Joplin High School.

At first, the photographer did not believe her. School superintendents were older, distinguished gentlemen, wearing suits and fighting the effects that too many chicken dinners at too many educational seminars can create for the waistline.

These, however, were not ordinary times in Joplin, Missouri, and C. J. Huff was not an ordinary superintendent. Maybe he had been a couple of weeks before, in those blissful days before an E5 tornado destroyed one-third of the city and damaged or destroyed 10 of his schools, including the one a few feet behind him. Normalcy was a thing of the past for Huff and it would be a long time before it would ever return.

A brisk wind whipped through the gathering crowd as they waited for the superintendent to speak. This was the first meeting

Joplin Superintendent C.J. Huff speaks to the media with other school superintendents and members of the Joplin Board of Education behind him on May 23, 2011 at North Middle School. Two days later, Huff would tell the world that Joplin schools would be open for business on time for the 2012-2013 school year. Photo by John Hacker

of school district personnel since the tornado- a family reunion of sorts, and the audience was filled with the same dreadful fears that had taken hold of their lives since 5:41 p.m. on May 22.

Had their colleagues survived? Were the students who had sat in the classrooms a few days before ever going to have a chance to move on to the next grade, or to grow to adulthood?

They also had to worry about their jobs. It was almost a certainty that there would be fewer students whenever school started again. Would there be the need for as many teachers, as many secretarial staff, as many custodians? Was there a possibility that this gathering might be the last time they would ever see each other as co-workers and colleagues?

As the photographer took a closer look at C. J. Huff, his earlier doubts had been erased. Though he had cast aside the suit and tie in favor of a maroon baseball cap with a proud "J" for Joplin and looked more like a Sunday golfer than a community leader, it was clear that this was the man in charge.

The face was boyish, but a closer examination showed the stress of having to deal with a crisis few school administrators had ever faced, the slight redness in eyes that had not been closed many times since the tornado.

Huff and his staff had been at the biggest event of the 2010-2011 school year, the culmination of 13 years of schooling, the high school graduation, held at Missouri Southern State University, when the tornado sirens sounded.

It seemed like an eternity had passed. In the days since, school officials and teachers had mounted an unceasing effort to locate every employee and every student in the school district.

It was no easy task. Phone service was down in many areas. Those whose homes had been hit by the tornado were staying in hotels or with relatives, some out of state.

It was a task made easier due to the advent of social networking. Many students were located by teachers through Facebook.

And there were other concerns. The administrative office building had been hit by the tornado. The team had to spread to different buildings and somehow manage to coordinate their duties. After some trial and error, they had established a working rhythm.

Their ability to do was aided by the members of the Board of Education. In a meeting, two days after the tornado, Huff told them, "We are going to start school on time."

Their reaction to that seemingly impossible goal did not surprise the superintendent. "They didn't question the decision. They got out in front and took care of business.

"These folks on a normal day work long, hard hours at the job and deal with patron calls about everything from overcooked chicken nuggets to angry cheerleader moms."

The board also included a board member who had lost her home. "They were all affected by the tornado."

Despite all of this, the board never hesitated to do what needed to be done. "They knew getting our kids back to school and out of the rubble was the best thing we could do for our community."

The first order of business was to give Huff and his staff the ability to do what needed to be done without having to call a school board meeting for approval every day. They approved a Missouri School Boards Association policy granting authority to Huff to make emergency purchasing decisions without board approval.

At the same time as the hunt for staff and students continued, Huff and his team were making arrangements for temporary buildings that could house the students when the 2011-2012 school year began, a task made all that much more daunting by the fact that school was scheduled to start just 87 days after the tornado.

And now on Memorial Day, May 30, 2011, just eight days after the tornado, Huff prepared to address the "family gathering."

The crowd quieted as a man stepped to the microphone and said, "How about a great hand for our superintendent of schools, C. J. Huff?"

Huff adjusted the microphone and wiped sweat from his forehead.

"First of all, it's good to see the family here. I miss you guys. I want to thank you for making the time to join your Joplin Schools family today as we celebrate life in the midst of destruction."

"Memorial Day is set aside to honor those who have given their lives to defend those principles we hold most dear. I was thinking about this last night and the parallels to our situation are striking. Our soldiers don't choose the battles they fight. They suit up, show up, and do their jobs. We didn't sign up for this war either. But true to form, in the past week you have pulled together as a family, supporting one another through prayer, words of encouragement, volunteerism, and action. No task was more daunting than our primary mission following the tornado last Sunday evening- the mission- locate and account for all of our family members."

At that point, Huff's voice began to falter, and tears streaked down his face. He took a few seconds to collect himself as he prepared to deliver the most difficult portion of the most difficult speech of his life.

"At 3:16 last Friday, I received a text message- "he stopped again and took a deep breath.

'Are you all right?" someone asked, the question picked up by the microphone.

Huff nodded and continued his sentence, "that indicated that mission was complete. As a result of your diligence and unwavering fortitude in the face of insurmountable challenges, 100 percent of our family are accounted for."

The hoops, hollers, and applause began, but the news was not as positive as Huff's words indicated. All of the family members had been accounted for, but not all of them had survived the tornado.

"I personally believe that all things happen for a reason," Huff continued. "I believe in God and I believe 3:16 last Friday had significance for all of us. It was a great moment of relief for our family, but more significantly, I believe there were biblical implications, as well.

"John 3:16 says this- For God so loved the world that He gave his only begotten son that whosoever believe him shall not perish but shall have eternal life."

Huff paused, took a deep breath and collected himself once more. Many in the crowd, understanding the words that would come next, were also fighting tears, some unsuccessfully.

"Today, we grieve the loss of eight members of our family. We lost seven children and one educator. Today, we celebrate that we are all together again in body and in eternal spirit. Please join me in a moment of silence to honor the family members who are no longer with us."

After the moment of silence, Huff began what he knew would be the most important part of his speech. With all of the death and destruction that had hit Joplin eight days earlier, with all of the school buildings that were damaged and destroyed, Huff had to point his family toward the goal that would pull them all together- the goal that became a rallying cry for the community that sounded across the nation.

It would have been easy to use the tornado as an excuse for canceling summer school and delaying the beginning of the 2011-2012 school year. Not one person would have questioned that decision had it been made.

Huff, his team, and the Joplin Board of Education never considered any option other than full speed ahead.

Will Norton is With Us In Spirit

By Randy Turner

Will Norton was light years ahead of his classmates (and most other people) when it came to effective use of social media.

The Joplin High School senior built a nationwide YouTube following and was also a master at Facebook, Twitter, and Tumblr.

His mastery of 21st century communication made it that much more ironic when for days on end, the most important message Will was waiting to receive was coming his way in an old-fashioned envelope courtesy of the U. S. Postal Service.

The message Will wanted to receive more than anything was an acceptance letter to Chapman University.

"He loved the campus, the town of Orange, and the excitement," his father, Mark Norton, said. "He just felt so comfortable there and he had heard so many good things about the university and the friendliness of students and faculty."

After his visit, Will waited for word. "The day he received the

Will Norton at graduation on May 22, 2011. Photo from 'Help Find Will Norton'

acceptance letter, his mom and I were watching him reach into the mailbox. He had this huge smile, and he hadn't even opened the packet. I asked him why he was smiling."

"Of course, I was accepted, Dad," Will replied. "They don't have to send you an entire packet to turn you down, just a letter."

"He was so excited to be accepted," Mark Norton said.

Will was so enthused that he joined the Chapman Class of 2015 Facebook site and immediately began making friends with his future classmates.

On Friday, May 21, Linda Zhou, a Chapman freshman from Anaheim Hills, noticed "someone had reblogged one of my blog posts of a picture of Chapman University on Tumblr.com. I recognized his username, willnorton, from the Chapman 2015 page. I looked him up on Facebook and requested him as a friend so I could share my excitement for finding a fellow soon-to-be Chapman freshman on Tumblr as well as Facebook.'

Their friendship started the next day. "We talked via Facebook messages and discussed our majors, our excitement, and he shared his YouTube account with me. That day was my prom day, so I did not get a chance to have a thorough, continuous conversation with him and I didn't get to check out his YouTube videos until the next day.

"I sent him a message on Sunday about how I enjoyed watching his videos and how honored I was to be talking to such a star. He never got a chance to see that message."

Sunday, May 22, was the day Will Norton graduated from Joplin High School- and it was also the day he died.

The day was scheduled to be a complete celebration of Will's passage into adulthood, with his graduation to be followed by a party at his home.

With bad weather approaching, the methodical droning roll call of seniors' names was quickened as the ceremony continued. When the final name was called, Will's friend and classmate Becky Cooper said, "We turned our tassels together, then we threw our hats in the air, and it was all over."

The students had to go into another room to pick up their diplomas. "I went and took pictures with my family and people were filing out. I remember my aunt saying, 'Becky, there's sirens going off,' but I told her to ignore it. The sirens go off all the time."

With rain approaching and the winds picking up, Mark Norton told his wife Trish, daughter Sara and niece Whitney to go on. He told them he would wait for Will and ride home with him.

Shortly after they left, Will emerged from the building. "I hugged him and congratulated him." As they walked to Will's Hummer, the tornado siren sounded.

"We got nervous, but they stopped." As Will drove home, his father received a call from daughter Sara. "She said they were home, but the power was out, and the storm was bad."

As Mark Norton talked to his daughter, something hit the hood and the window on Will's side blew out.

"Will asked me what to do and I told him to turn into Summit Ridge Subdivision. He began reciting Bible verses and praying."

The tornado, which had winds in excess of 200 miles per hour, picked up the Hummer and flipped it over. "All of the windows blew out. I put my left hand on Will and held on, but somehow, he must have flown out of the sunroof.

"Once the H3 stopped flipping, I looked over and Will was gone."

Mark Norton shouted for his son, but there was no answer. When rescue workers arrived, he told them to look for Will.

"They couldn't find him."

For the next few days, the smiling face of Will Norton became the face of the Joplin tornado, thanks to the Help Find Will Norton Facebook page started by his family.

The search for Will Norton went national, as the media told the story of a young man who had built a sizable following on his Willdabeest YouTube videos, which showed his potential as a comic filmmaker, a talent he planned to hone at Chapman University.

One of those who followed the coverage was Chapman President James L. Doti, who began researching Will Norton as the search continued.

"I have to tell you, this young man in every way, shape, and form, was a superstar," Doti said. In addition to his filmmaking prowess, Will Norton has a nearly perfect GPA and "some of the highest ACT scores I have ever seen."

For the next few days, the hunt continued, and one of those following with interest was incoming Chapman freshman Linda Zhou. "I couldn't believe- I didn't want to believe- that he had gone missing."

It was the same emotion that another Chapman freshman, Allie Reidy of Palos Verde, had. "It was a strange thing for me. Even though I had only spoken to him once, it completely turned my world around. I was so devastated, and I never thought I would cry for someone that I barely knew, but he had shown me so much kindness. And by reading what everyone else was saying about him, I knew he had affected many other people's lives.

"I followed all of the updates in their search for him and I prayed every day that God kept a firm hand on him, and I guess he did, just in an unexpected way."

Five days after the tornado, Will's body was discovered.

***

Two weeks after the last time she saw Will Norton's luminous smile, his classmate Becky Cooper saw it once again, only in a way she had never expected.

When she entered Christ's Church of Oronogo, Missouri, for what was termed "a celebration of Will Norton's life," the first thing Becky saw, on a large screen television, was that smile, over and over, in a loop as Will's life was replayed for the hundreds who gathered to pay tribute.

Some of the photos were taken from the good times with his family, some with his friends at school, and others from his celebrated YouTube videos.

"Will loved watching YouTube videos and made his first video about his pet sugar gliders (an Australian flying squirrel)," his father recalled. "It was such a hit; he was instantly hooked. His views skyrocketed (some of his videos have been viewed more than 50,000 times) and he was encouraged to keep filming. Eventually, YouTube asked him to be part of their partner program so he could share advertising revenue. He loved that because it let him purchase better filming equipment. He just loved creating videos that people got joy from watching."

The eulogy for Will was presented by Rev. Aaron Brown, whose church was also a victim of the tornado that had taken Will's life. Just a week earlier, Rev. Brown had spoken before a nationwide audience at the Joplin Tornado Memorial Service at Missouri Southern State University.

When it comes to Will Norton, Rev. Brown said, "Death doesn't get the last word."

And for those who came to mourn for the teenager, the tears were mixed with smiles and often with heartfelt laughter.

The highlights of the celebration were provided by Will himself, in one of his Willdabeest YouTube videos.

Stories were told about a young man who had celebrated life every day, through videos, through social networking, through flying (he already had a pilot's license) and through building a large network of friends.

"Will was an All-American kid," his classmate Savanah Sweeton recalled. "I had two classes with Will this year, one of which I sat quite close to him, so close I could reach out and touch him. Small things like reaching out and touching someone seem miniscule living an everyday life until that person is no longer a part of this life."

As the celebration of Will's life continued, Becky Cooper found herself laughing several times, sometimes at Will's videos, and often as others told stories about her friend. "I laughed because someone mentioned how his dad always made lunch for him every day. Well, I used to eat part of that lunch every day.

"Will always put others first and he always took the time to ask me how I was doing and what my plans for the fall were."

"I'm going to miss him."

One of the speakers at the service, Joplin High School Principal Kerry Sachetta, spoke about the graduation, something that had only taken place two weeks before, but now seemed an eternity. "I was able to shake Will's hand for the last time." The principal presented Mark and Trish Norton with a replacement diploma for their son.

Rev. Brown concluded the ceremony by saying, "Will would not want to be remembered as a young man killed in the Joplin tornado. He would want to be remembered for how he lived.

"Will knew how to enjoy life, didn't he?"

***

Though Will Norton never attended a class at Chapman University, officials say his presence will be felt.

Part of that, advertising/marketing Professor Cory O'Connor says is due to Will's innovative use of social networking.

"Will was a very talented young man. He brought people together through his community, through his Twitter and YouTube videos, you get a sense of who he was, and how excited he was about coming to Chapman.

"I am convinced that Will's life was meant to teach us all something. He left for us a biography of who he was through his two Twitter feeds and his YouTube videos."

Chapman University will also pay tribute to Will Norton when freshmen arrive in August, according to Nancy Brink, director of church relations. "Our tradition has been to honor students who have died, and we are going to do that for Will."

Will's name will be added to the Memorial Wall in the Fish Interfaith Center, Ms. Brink said.

It will be the first time that such an honor has been given to someone who had yet to attend a class at Chapman, she added.

"We were looking forward to Will being a part of our freshman class," Dean of Students Jerry Price said. "Will wanted a career in

TV and film. It was his desire to come out here to pursue this passion that really resonated with us."

Before Will was found, Price said, "We talked with his family and found out how much Chapman meant to him."

That included a bedroom full of Chapman posters, University President James Doti said.

Doti hopes that Will Norton's short life will serve as an inspiration for Chapman students. "He lived a whole life. It is a tragedy to lose such an incredible young man.

"When I tell students about Will Norton, hopefully, they will be inspired by his life and take these years at Chapman with more seriousness and dedication.

This was a great tragedy. We are always going to consider Will to be a member of Chapman's family.

"He is with us in spirit."

This article was originally published in the Fall 2011 Chapman University magazine.

a Day of Miracles – Joplin Schools Start On Time

By Randy Turner

It was the first day of school and a sixth grader did not know where the office was in our new East Middle School building.

He asked eighth grade science teacher Mike Wallace for directions. Wallace, glancing down at the end of the hall, told the youngster, "Go down the hall and turn right at the governor."

Whether the child knew who Missouri Gov. Jay Nixon was, I have no idea, but the presence of the governor in our hallways and the national media at every new or refurbished building in the Joplin School District made our first day of school Wednesday a memorable one.

Normally, so much media might be considered intrusive, but not on this day, just three months after an EF-5 tornado destroyed or heavily damaged 10 of our 19 schools.

On this day, the national and world media were welcome because it was so important to thank the world making it possible.

In the days after the May 22 tornado, the idea that school would start on time seemed an impossibility. Joplin High School, a center of the community, had been blown apart by nature's fierce fury,

Irving Elementary Principal Debbie Fort greets a student on the first day of school. State of Missouri Photo

leaving the words "Op High School" for all to see.

That did not last long. Within a couple of days, someone had added two letters to that sign, an H and an E, turning it into Hope High School, and setting the stage for the complete resurrection of the Joplin School District.

The effort began with school administrators and board members who had to create solutions because there was no blueprint for how to deal with this kind of devastation.

Teachers and staff were brought into the equation and the Joplin community, parents, students, business owners, and people who had no connection to elementary and secondary education except for paying the taxes that support it. The restoration of Joplin schools and the idea that they could open on time, only 87 days after the tornado, became the goal of an entire community.

And that community extended far beyond the city limits of Joplin. There was much need in this community and in this school system and people from across Missouri, the nation, and the world, stepped in to take care of that need.

Millions in donations came, brought about in part by the national media that brought attention to the difficulties we were facing.

The United Arab Emirates chipped in with a half-million dollars and the promise of another half-million in matching funds to provide laptops for every Joplin High School student as a part of the school district's One-to-One initiative.

Most of the effort was steered successfully through the district's Bright Futures program, an initiative started two years ago to help provide equipment for schools and to cover the needs of the poorest children in our community.

So when we saw reporters with their cameras and notebooks approaching us and our students Wednesday morning, we met them with deep gratitude.

They were the ones who allowed us to express our thank you to a

Gov. Jay Nixon provides a backpack to Quinton Anderson and all other students on the first day at Joplin High School. Anderson's parents were killed in the tornado. State of Missouri Photo

world that adopted the Joplin community and made it its own.

A simple thank you can never repay the many acts of generosity that made opening day in the Joplin schools a success, so we are going to try to show our appreciation in the best way we can, by giving 100 percent of our effort to make the best use of the schools that the world made possible.

Six-Month Anniversary

By John Hacker

Six months after the tornado tore its deadly path through Joplin, hundreds of people gathered at a park that has come to symbolize Joplin's recovery to remember, mourn and try to move forward.

On November 22, 2011, city, state and federal officials gathered with residents in Cunningham Park to mark six months since 161 Joplin residents and others were killed in the May 22 storm.

Chris Piquard, who lost his mother, Marie Piquard, in the storm, attended with his father, Lloyd Piquard, to remember and move on. The two saw the name of their mother and wife on a temporary version of a bronze plaque that will soon grace Cunningham Park as part of a series of memorials around the park at 26th Street and McClelland Boulevard.

"The milestone is hard," said Lloyd Piquard. "It makes it hard on me, but I know where my wife is, she's in heaven with Jesus."

Chris Piquard said it was important on the six-month anniversary

Maria Kumbier and her children, Asa Kumbier, 9, and Coe Munch, 12, stand together with their lights held high during the ceremony held Tuesday, Nov. 22, at Cunningham Park marking the six-month anniversary of the EF5 tornado that devastated Joplin. Photo by John Hacker

to remember those who died.

"I think it's something that memorializes not just the fact that Joplin, most of it was destroyed, but the fact that we did lose those loved ones and they will be remembered," Chris Piquard said.

"Closure is something that we're never going to get as far as we're never going to forget who was lost or what has happened, but it is a milestone that we came to and it is a part of the recovery that Joplin needs to go through."

City officials joined Missouri Gov. Jay Nixon, U.S. Rep. Billy Long and local clergy to lead the ceremony that saw hundreds bring lawn chairs to brave chilly temperatures and remember.

Joplin Parks Director Chris Cotten spoke about the trees that were uprooted in the park.

"On the morning of May 22, 2011, 61 oak trees stood tall and proud in Cunningham Park," Cotten said. "More than likely, some of them had stood prior to Cunningham Park's establishment in 1890. They had witnessed countless family events, observed babies napping under their branches, watched young children grow old and shared lovely spring days and crisp fall evenings with our seniors as they entered the twilight of their lives. By 6 p.m. that evening, like the city of Joplin, they stood broken and shattered.

"The largest of those oak trees had a width of 43 feet, stood 50 feet tall and had a canopy of 60 feet. If it was not the oldest tree in the park, it was certainly one of the oldest. Like the mighty oak tree, strength and courage among Joplin residents were not lacking immediately following the tornado's aftermath."

Cotten said the city plans to plant 161 trees in a rebuilt Cunningham Park, one for each of the people killed in the storm.

He talked about a bronze plaque, containing the names of all 161 victims, which will be placed in the park.

He described a new fountain that has been set up in the park.

"In November of 1908, the work of installing a fountain,

Matilyn Perry, Webb City, takes a picture of her mom's name on the plaque in Cunningham Park listing the 161 victims of the May 22 Joplin tornado during the Nov. 22 six-month anniversary ceremony where the plaque was dedicated. Sharyl Nelson was one of those killed in the EF5 tornado that tore through Joplin. Photo by John Hacker

purchased by the Women's Park Association for Cunningham Park, began," Cotten said "That fountain was nine feet in diameter and the water was to fall from three levels. In May of 1909, that fountain came to life in Cunningham and was described as located at the foot of a slope in the southeast corner of the park. For reasons lost to us through time, that fountain was removed in the 1920s, but the base was left behind. For years and years, it was used as a planter and its history as a fountain was forgotten.

"After the storm, its true history was again discovered, and today, some 80 years after its predecessor was shut down, water will again flow in this fountain basin."

Now a new fountain has been installed with three levels, the top level with five streams of water, the middle level with 22 streams and the bottom with 11, to mark the date 5-22-11.

Governor Jay Nixon compared Joplin to the "the house of the wise man described in the gospel of Matthew."

"The rain descended, and the winds blew and beat upon that house and it fell not for it was founded upon a rock," Nixon told the crowd. "The storm shook Joplin to the core, but its rock, its foundation of faith could not be moved. In six short months, the tornado's wounds, some still visible, some hidden deep within us are healing. Brick by brick and board by board, Joplin is rising from its granite foundation of faith. And everywhere we look, we see change.

"Cunningham Park has been transformed into a vibrant oasis of beauty and peace, a living memorial to those who lost their lives and the tens of thousands of volunteers who opened their hearts in Joplin's hour of need."

Nixon spoke of his admiration of the "unwavering courage, compassion and true grit," shown by Joplin residents.

"Your fight and your faith have proved to the people of our state, our nation and the world that the spirit of Joplin is unbreakable," Nixon said.

"From day one, help was here when and where it was needed most. In all, more than 400 first responders and law enforcement agencies from every corner of our state and many other states dropped everything they were doing to help Joplin. We owe these brave men and women an enormous debt of gratitude.

"The success of our partnership is a shining example of what we can accomplish when people of good faith rally around a common goal. I know that Joplin's journey has really barely begun, and I'm here to tell you that we'll be here with you until that job is done."

Joplin Mayor Mark Woolston talked about the strength he had seen in Joplin's residents in the reconstruction work that happened in the summer and fall of 2011.

"In the immediate aftermath of the tornado, city staff, school district personnel and the Chamber of Commerce set the tone that this is not the type of community that is going to let a little F5 tornado kick our . . .," Woolston said, pausing instead of using the word he used on CNN immediately following the storm. "We're not going to let this storm defeat us. That is just as true today as it was the first day following the storm.

"The sense of community that has been realized here is, to my knowledge, unmatched anywhere in the country, and that sense of community is what brings us here tonight. Not only have we lost 161 members of our community, we've lost a part of ourselves. That loss is something from which we are not ever likely to recover.

Though we may never recover from the loss of 161 lives, we will, slowly, but surely, move forward. As we move forward to Thanksgiving, let us be thankful for the lives that were spared. For those that avoided destruction, for those that volunteered to help us and for those who continue to help us recover. In this community, we care for one another."

Remembering the forgotten School

By Randy Turner

During a recent teacher in-service day, staff members from Joplin East Middle School where I teach, left the warehouse where we are conducting classes for the 2011-2012 school year (and probably the next year or two) and returned to the building that we called our own for the last two years for a farewell ceremony. I stayed at the warehouse.

It was not that I was making light of the planned ceremony. I am sure it helped some to find closure after the May 22 tornado that destroyed that building; I just did not have a strong connection. It was a brand-new building, less than two years old, and while I had some wonderful memories in those two school years, I did not feel a need to say goodbye.

The building where I taught before those two years was an entirely different matter.

Before moving into East Middle School, I taught at South Middle School for six years. It was an old building, one of those made in the 1920s that did not have a smooth transition into the computer era. South did not have a gymnasium; it had an auditorium with an extended stage that was used for physical education classes. The computer lab was a converted boys' bathroom.

The classrooms, at approximately 500 square feet, were smaller than the ones in the warehouse and desks were jammed into every corner with a cruel efficiency. An entire area of the basement was shut off due to asbestos. We had no playground area, just a fenced-in gravel lot with basketball goals and picnic tables that had been donated to us by our hard-working parent-teacher organization.

By all definition, South Middle School was a dump compared to the spacious, modern school building we left it for prior to the 2009-2010 school year.

Yet I loved that broken-down building like no place I have worked in the past three and a half decades.

It was difficult during the following year when North Middle School students moved into that old buildings while renovations were taking place on their campus.

During that first year at the new East, I had to go to South during the school day on one occasion and it was not the same. The halls seemed darker, the laughter nearly non-existent. This was not my South. I made the mistake of stopping by Room 210, which had been home to me for six years. There were no traces of that home. It was just another classroom.

After serving as a temporary building for North that year, the old South building was vacant last year for the first time in more than 80 years. I did not even think about it until May 22.

The same tornado that destroyed our state-of-the-art East Middle School, also ripped through the stately building with the grim, institutional look on 22nd Street. I checked out East two days after the tornado. It took me more than five months to visit South.

After I read that our board of education had awarded a contract to demolish South, I had to make one more pilgrimage to the place that had been such an important part of my life. It was broad daylight on a Sunday when I parked my car in the gravel lot in the same parking place I used every morning at 6:45 a.m. during the school year.

As far as I could tell, I was the only person in a two-block area. The houses in this older part of town, the ones that survived the tornado, are mostly boarded up with prominent no-trespassing signs. As 40-mile per hour winds whipped through my old school, despite the daylight, there was a sense that I was walking in another world.

Most of South's windows are gone, but the wind whipped through the blinds, all of which were intact, slamming them against the wall in a macabre symphony. Creaking metal sounds could be heard every 10 seconds or so. Sections of the building were gone and the front door, the one I had walked through thousands of times during those six years was covered by a sign warning of asbestos contamination.

I looked up at the second floor to the window of my Room 210 and the ghosts of thousands of wonderful memories came back to me. There was Jessica in her front row seat, working diligently on her Elks Lodge essay, filling in even the margins on her paper and then turning in 750 words for an essay that did not allow more than 250. After that, Jessica did a masterful editing job, eliminating 501 words and winning the contest.

There was Andrew causing people to roll in the aisles with inappropriate laughter with his interpretation of a character during our reading of the play, "The Diary of Anne Frank."

I could see Fox's always empty seat, and then when I looked down at the floor, I saw her scribbling away in her notebook.

After thinking about those days for several, long minutes, I walked back to my car and left South Middle School for the final time. I appreciate the public ceremony for East. I am sure it helped my fellow staff members deal with the loss of their workplace. But to me, South Middle School was home, and a quiet, private goodbye was just what I needed.

Originally published in the March, 23, 2012 Turner Report

I felt His Hand

W hen people speak of the sounds they hear when they are in a tornado, many say it sounds like a train.

That was the sound Jordan Aubey, senior reporter for KOAM-TV, heard, but it was unlike any train Aubey had ever heard.

"We live by the train tracks, so it's not unusual for us to hear trains," Aubey said. This sound, which he heard late afternoon on May 22, 2011, was different. "You didn't hear the wheels. It was just a straight freight train sound."

Aubey went out the front door of his second story apartment and stepped straight into a nightmare. "All I could see in front of me was a whirlwind. It was scary." He returned to his apartment, debris swirling around him.

"I thought of Mom and Dad, specifically that Mom has always cared for me. She'd give her life for me. I knew that. I pictured her face learning I didn't make it. I pictured Mom crying and holding her hand up to her face. I pictured Dad the same way.

"I said to myself, 'That's not going to happen.' "

Aubey climbed into the bathtub just as the roof was torn off the apartment. "I heard windows crashing. My ears were popping. When your ears pop, the tornado is right there.

The bathtub came loose. "That was when the real fight began."

Aubey found himself being torn away from the bathtub and spinning in the tornado.

"I don't remember landing," he said, but he found himself on the asphalt street with the remnants of a wall atop his right leg.

"I prayed. I had an intimate talk with God."

After several minutes of exertion, he managed to pull himself from under the wall and asked for help. Two people carried Aubey into what was left of the apartment building.

An off-duty nurse took him to Freeman Hospital, where he remained on a stretcher on the floor for an hour and a half. Aubey suffered a broken hip and had to have a rod installed.

The veteran newsman, who has never been comfortable when he becomes a part of the story, knew that despite the pain, he was a fortunate man.

"It was proof positive to me that there is a God.

"I felt His hand."

Jordan Aubey is the anchorman on KOAM's News at 9 on Fox 14 and continues to thrive as a senior reporter for the station. This story is taken from an interview with Tim Hetzner of Lutheran Church Charities. The interview can be found at https://www.youtube.com/watch?v=eu5tyEhiZTs. More information about Lutheran Church Charities can be found at www.lutheranchurchcharities.org.

Restoring My faith In Humanity

By Emily Evans

May 21, 2011 was forecasted by Christian radio host Harold Camping to be the date of "the rapture," and adolescents everywhere were having a field day mocking it on social media.

My three roommates took great joy in arranging an entire outfit right down to shoes on a chair out on our front porch. They snapped a picture as if the occupant of the clothes had been suddenly swept away and posted it to Facebook.

I tried to act disdainful toward their giggles and semi-adolescent prank, but I actually did think it was pretty funny. The picture is still online, but now it's more sobering than humorous.

I don't think any of us would have been laughing if we had known that at the same time the very next day we would be walking out of a basement to meet a sight which was in fact very much apocalyptic.

May 22 was my day off from work, and I was happy to have a day to spend with my roommate and girlfriend at the time, Aileen.

Photo by Emily Evans

We spent most of the day relaxing, and I'm sure nothing of note happened, because I don't remember anything aside from the very moment our other two roommates Ericka and Emily T. came home.

They had been out running errands and were delayed because I asked Ericka to pick up my medication from Walmart, so they doubled back to 15th Street before coming home. I only remember this detail because since then, Ericka has marked it as being the first in a chain of events that somehow resulted in the perfect timing that saved our lives.

Somewhere between 5:20 and 5:41 Ericka and Emily nearly busted down the door. Ericka quickly uttered something to the effect of "the guy on the radio said that there is a confirmed tornado in Carl Junction and we're going to Stone's Corner to see it. Do you guys want to come with us?"

After a hurried conversation in which we stated that we wouldn't actually be chasing the tornado but would rather park nearby and try to see the funnel cloud, I went against my better judgment and agreed to go.

Ericka had always wanted to see a funnel cloud and I had always advised against it, but I thought that maybe I could keep them from doing something more reckless if I went along. The car ride that followed changed our lives forever.

After grabbing our things, we ran out to the Blazer then we drove, and listened to talk radio about the storm. We only made it a short distance from our home before we were pulled over by a police officer.

This visit ended quickly as he received a message of some sort on his radio and let us go, urging us to go back home out of the storm. We were reckless young adults and most of us really wanted to see that tornado, so we kept driving.

Moments later, the man on the radio announced that a tornado was seen in Joplin, going down 32nd Street by Freeman Hospital. Ericka asked us whether she should turn right or left, trying to decide which report to believe. My friends sometimes looked to me in these types of situations so when I found everyone looking at me, I told her to go to 32nd Street. This was a moment of well-meaning deception. I thought that the first report was probably more accurate. I was wrong.

We drove to and parked at Schlotzsky's on the corner of 32nd and Main Street, because we were all starting to get a little spooked. We only wanted to see a funnel cloud – not get close to it. But as soon as Ericka put the car into park, the sky went dark and it started to hail like I had never seen before in my life.

I got a very bad feeling and locked eyes with Emily T., who looked the same. She spoke up and we got the hell out of there, but we turned the wrong way. We were literally driving into the storm.

Then Aileen saw a transformer blow blocks ahead of us, and I noticed how strange the dark sky looked against the leaves that were just too green. We were in danger and we knew it, I sent a text to my parents and my younger brother that simply read "I love you," on the off chance that it was the last chance I would get to tell them.

Just then Emily T. remembered that the Sadler family lived just a block away and they had a basement. We turned down their street and by the grace of God their van was parked out front. We sat there for a split second.

Ericka turned around and asked if we should stay or try and make it home, but before anyone could answer the tornado sirens went off. We all ran from the car and halfway to their door the sirens stopped. We didn't know at the time, but it was only blocks away from us and had been sucked into the tornado.

All four of us were beating down the door of a family we hadn't seen in over a year, hoping and praying that they were upstairs to let us in. Ericka yelled that it was she and her roommates, that there was a tornado coming and to please let us in.

Quickly, Mrs. Sadler answered the door, completely unaware of what was going on outside. She was on the phone laughing at the idea of a tornado hitting Joplin, which was the attitude most of us took at first.

The kids were playing without a care in the world and the Weather Channel was on the television.

We begged them to listen to us and get in the basement, but no one was taking us seriously until one of the young boys yelled "Yay, our first tornado!" opened the door before we could stop him, and almost got sucked out the door.

At the sight of this, we all hurried to the basement, and shut the door. Mere seconds passed before we heard what sounded like a tree falling on the house – but it was the tornado taking the roof.

We huddled in a circle together in the nearly empty basement for what felt like hours, but only lasted minutes. First, one of the windows broke out and we moved. Then some papers and small toys left on the floor lifted off of the ground and levitated in circles.

The other window broke too so we moved to the middle, with our arms interlocked around the children. I still couldn't describe the feeling, or the sound. They say that tornados sound like trains, and I guess that's true, but this was the loudest, most powerful, most evil "train" I had ever heard in my life.

We didn't just hear it either. The most terrible part of this memory is the feeling. The feeling of indescribable power and destruction, the instant realization of our frailty, the vulnerability, the panic. Everyone was panicking.

Ericka pushed her nerves aside to calm the rest of us and everyone protected each other: Ericka protecting Emily, Aileen protecting me, Mrs. Sadler and Abby Sadler protecting the children.

Suddenly, parts of the floor above us started falling on our heads and I was certain we were about to die. In what I thought might be my last act I yelled for everyone to pray – and they did. It didn't last much longer after that.

As the storm moved on, we broke the huddle. I remember feeling so strange when I realized that we were o.k. We were covered in rainwater, though I don't remember being rained on, and the Sadler boys were screaming for someone to call 911 while reciting their address over and over.

In retrospect this seems silly. Half of the town was gone and 911 wasn't going to do us any good, but most of us were on autopilot. We tried making the call several times before realizing we would never get through.

The baby was shivering, and Ericka gave him one of her shirts, because she was wearing two. To calm my nerves, I almost lit a cigarette, but someone (probably Aileen) stopped me because the gas line was obviously busted.

We stayed in that basement for quite some time before any

of us realized it was safe to go out. But when we did emerge, the most devastating sight my eyes have ever seen was there to meet us. Everything for as far as I could see was gone – the houses, St. John's Hospital, everything.

For a while we took shelter in the senior center across the street. It only had half a roof left but it had clean water and places to sit.

While there, we each were able to get at least one phone call through to a loved one, and every single one of us gave our contacts a wrong location. My call was to my brother, Carl. I told him we were at 32nd and Jackson, but we were really at 27th and Jackson.

The rest of the night consisted of a five-hour walk through all the places we mistakenly told our loved ones to find us, with long waits at each stop just in case they did.

From 27th and Jackson to 32nd and Jackson – from there back to Schlotsky's – from there down Main Street and left down 20th Street toward our home.

Walking down 32nd Street we passed a church sign that said "Don't worry! He's got the whole world in his hands!" and I stopped to take a picture.

I still love the perfect timing of whoever it was who decided what message the sign should read that day.

We stopped at Schlotsky's to wait for Ericka's mom, because that is where Ericka said we were. Aileen and I were talking to a man in the parking lot and I looked up just in time to see my dad's van drive past – but they didn't see me. My heart sank, but we had to stay there a while longer.

Ericka and Emily T. had separated from us to go see if Emily's dad was o.k. because we were told the high school was completely destroyed and he lived just blocks from there.

After night fell, we had to start walking again; neither of us was sure if we had a home to go to, but that's where we were headed.

During this time, we met a Pizza Hut employee on Main Street who had stayed to hand out drinks and let people use the restroom. I will forever be thankful to that young man. It was hours after everything had happened and there he was helping people after everyone else had gone.

We stopped at 20th and Main to check our friend Tosha's house and see if she was ok. The house was in bad shape, but her car wasn't there. We were almost home so we kept walking down 20th and just then a guy ran past us.

I shouldn't have thought much about it, everywhere you looked people were frantically trying to find their loved ones – but there was something about the way that kid was running. It was my brother Carl.

I called his name, and I could swear he stopped and turned in midair, and we ran and hugged. I don't think I've ever been happier to see him. When my dad and stepmom had to stop looking for me and put our baby brother to bed, Carl got out on foot and kept looking.

That night was hard, I couldn't sleep, couldn't stop thinking about what had happened and what could have happened. I thought about all of the people who had lost their lives and couldn't understand why I hadn't.

We all slept on the floor at my dad's house because he was lucky enough to still have power. But I was up all night, with pieces of someone's floor in my hair and my scalp, wet, and dirty, and confused. I tried to call in to work around 3 am…but the Webb City Waffle House where I worked was one of the only places still open and there were only two waitresses on shift. I showed up at 6 a.m. for my shift, too dumbfounded, guilty, and obligated to even tell my boss that I had been in the tornado. He did eventually find out, but he didn't send me home.

We had to feed the town.

We called in our best workers, but we were stepping all over each other in that tiny store and I was practically a zombie, nothing felt real. I worked over 40 hours in the three days following the tornado, I served so many people…people who had been through it, too, but were less fortunate than me. Why?

I couldn't stand the fact that I had been spared, I didn't lose anything – anyone. It broke my heart every time I saw another broken soul walk through that door. I felt guilty for feeling broken – guilty for being alive.

The truth is, if I hadn't gone along; if we hadn't been pulled over; if Ericka had never doubled back to Walmart for my medicine; if we had gone the other way; or done anything differently I might not be here writing this story – the Sadler family might have still been in their living room when the tornado hit – anything could have happened to any of us. But it didn't. We were less than a minute away from death, and for some reason we were spared.

May 22 is a day that will make me wince for the rest of my life, but it will also remind me of a strength I didn't know I had; of a town that stood up and fought when it could have laid down to rest; of a nation of kind hearts and pure souls who came to us in our time of need.

May 22, 2011 changed the course of my life, and who I am as a person. It brought destruction and mayhem, but it also taught me the value of life, of friendship, of love, and perfect timing – but most importantly, it restored my faith in humanity.

Courthouse Janitor Killed In Tornado

By John Hacker

C o-workers remembered him as quirky, yet a hard worker and a man who will be missed after almost 18 years working in the historic Jasper County Courthouse in Carthage.

Officially, Randy Mell, 49, Webb City, was listed as missing as of Saturday, but his co-workers know he won't be returning to work.

Jason Shryer, supervisor of maintenance at the courthouse, and Lucy Pendergraft, Mell's co-worker at the courthouse, said they got the word at 10 a.m. Thursday that Mell had been killed when the storm destroyed the Stained Glass Theatre, 1318 W. 26th Street, Joplin, next door to the demolished St. John's Regional Medical Center.

"He would look through the paper through the list of activities, events going on, if they were going to have a charter bus taking people to some concert somewhere, if it was a good concert, he'd buy himself a ticket," Shryer said.

"Whatever was big that weekend, you would get an update

A memorial table was set up in the Jasper County Courthouse in Carthage to honor Randy Mell, a long-time custodian at the Courthouse. Mell was killed when the Stained Glass Theatre, which was located near St. John's Regional Medical Center on 26th Street in Joplin, was destroyed right after the conclusion of a production. Photo by John Hacker

on how it went that next Monday. It didn't matter, if there was an activity somewhere, he would go. That may have been why he was at Stained Glass Theatre."

Shryer said Mell had worked as a janitor at the courthouse since 1993 and was a fixture in the halls and offices of the historic building.

"A very polite guy, he was a hard worker, too," Shryer said. "Always tried to keep himself busy. It might be the wrong thing, but he always tried to keep himself busy with some kind of work around here.

"Lucy and I would be off painting something, we'd ask what's Randy doing. You would go out there and find him buffing the floor. I'd say, Randy, the floor could wait this week, let's go paint. Okay, he'd say."

Lucy Pendergraft said being in the courthouse by herself made her nervous, but Mell was always there early in the morning to look out for her.

"For the last 14 years of working together, every morning, if I was not here yet, he always watched for me," Pendergraft said. "He would watch for me from a window and see if I was o.k. I would wave to him and he would go on. Now I'm going to be missing that face in the window. Every morning, 5:30 in the morning he was here."

Shryer said Mell was a regular at sporting events in Webb City and Carthage, as well as plays at the Stone's Throw Theatre and other events.

He said courthouse workers have heard that Mell may have died a hero, helping to usher people into the basement of the Stained Glass Theatre as the tornado approached.

He said witnesses at the theatre told another courthouse co-worker that Mell matched the description of a man who held the door to the theater's basement open for people attending a play, but he was killed when the theatre disintegrated before he could get in that door himself.

"It's unverifiable, but we're sticking with it," Shryer said. "I'm sticking with it in my heart because that is Randy. I told him a few times, one you're older than I am and two, I'm not a woman so quit holding the damn door for me. He'd say okay, okay, but he'd still hold the door. He'd be two steps behind me, and he'd take a double step just to get in front of you to get the door."

Lucy said Mell touched her life in so many ways and she thought he might still be touching it even after his death.

"As soon as I got the news, I said we're going to do something for Randy, I want to lower the flag," Pendergraft said on Friday.

"We probably got the news at 10 a.m. Wednesday and I said

we're going to lower the flags for Randy. The wind was blowing so hard and I didn't look at the clock, but I was lowering the American flag and I was facing the courthouse and I look at the top in the tower. I looked again, I said Jason, do you see what I'm seeing? Now Randy is a guy of routine; he's got to follow his routine. Jason looked at the clock and said oh my, it's Randy's lunch hour. It was 11 o'clock right on the dot. I screamed 'Randy, go to lunch.' I was getting goose bumps, but he's telling us 'I'm okay, I'm going to my lunch hour now.'"

God Kept Us Safe

By Angie Williams

On Sunday May 22, 2011, my family and I got up to get ready for church. I took a few moments to check Facebook. God laid it on my heart to post as my status: Joshua 24:15 "...But as for me and my household, we will serve the LORD."

If you don't have a personal relationship with Christ, I pray you will find him today.

Little did I know the horrific event that would take place later that day.

After we got home from church and had eaten lunch, the girls and I took an afternoon nap while daddy had to go to work. After we woke up, I started to do dishes and was going to get dinner ready. Adley was watching a movie so we didn't have the local news station playing, completely unaware of the weather.

Treay called, which is unusual, to tell us to watch the weather. I turned the TV on to the news station and he and I decided together we were safe that the storm was heading north of us, so we hung up and I started back to what I was doing. Then my mom called and said, "Do you know you are under a tornado warning?" I said "Really?" and then the sirens started going off. I hung up and took the girls to the bathtub and sat down. The sirens quit so we got out of the bathroom and started to resume our evening.

I put Averie in a stand-up bouncer seat in the living room and Adley was sitting on the couch. My mom called again to check on us. While on the phone, I continued to look through the windows keeping an eye on the extremely dark sky.

When looking out my front window the sky to the left was a pretty light blue while the sky to the right was black. I kept hearing the weatherman saying the storm is "over the heart of Joplin."

I thought, "Is that me?" Then I noticed hail sporadically falling out the front window. I told my mom who was still on the phone that it was hailing. She said, "Get in the hallway this is not a good sign."

So I told Adley to get in the hallway and I picked Averie up still in the bouncer seat and placed her in the hallway. I went to Adley's room and grabbed her bed pillows and her special puppy dog and blankies then shut her bedroom door. I went to my bedroom and grabbed just a few more bed pillows and shut our bedroom door along with Averie's bedroom door and the hall bathroom door. These things I don't always do...

Then something told me to remove Averie from the bouncer seat and hold her in my lap, so I took her out and put the seat back in the living room. I realized the TV was too loud and it wasn't telling me anything worth hearing. It was playing Seinfeld, so I got up to turn it down so I could hear more of what might be happening outside.

Seconds after I sat in the hallway, the hail and extreme winds began banging on the front of the house. Still on the phone with my mom, I was giving her a play by play of what was happening. I said, "It's hitting the front of the house and it's really strong," then the power flickered, and I let out a shriek then it flickered back on then off.

I heard the sound of a train.

I told my mom and she said, "That's it. Cover your heads and get as low as you can! Get low!"

The force pushing on the house got stronger until it ripped through the house taking everything in its path. The noise was unbelievable; it was so loud! The wind was strong, and the skies were dark.

All I could do was cover my babies and yell "God PLEASE keep us safe! PLEASE put your Angels all around us!" I begged and pleaded God to keep us safe.

The tornado seemed to go on and on, the thought of what it would be like to wake up in Heaven passed through my mind. The pillow that was on my head flew immediately off and I thought man it's me against the tornado now, so I got lower down on my girls. I begged God to "PLEASE let it end! PLEASE let it end!"

When it finally came to an end and I sat there checking on the girls and I hear a voice that I know very well yelling "Ang? Ang? Ang?" It was my mom! She had been on the phone the entire time the tornado ripped through my house! I couldn't believe it.

I had to search a little through debris and I finally found my phone. First words out of my mouth were "Everything's gone!"

It was so surreal. I covered the girls with their daddy's coat that landed nearby us. It had started to rain huge raindrops. I sat there thinking, "What do I do?" "Where do I go?" "Should I stay here or go for help?" I decided I needed to get the girls to safety. The lightning was striking extremely close and the rain was really coming down.

So I had Adley stand up and then I stood up with Averie (we did not have to crawl or dig out, just stood up from where we were sitting, everything was gone around us, not a single wall was standing) then picked Adley up and carried both girls in my arms along with Adley's favorite blanket and stuffed puppy dog and carried them barefoot to a nearby church. I can't believe I carried them that far not to mention barefoot. I didn't look around much, I was too afraid of what I would see.

The girls and I just held each other close and walked to where we knew we would be seen. I walked to 20th and Wisconsin. I heard screams and cries. It broke my heart knowing there were injured or even trapped people, but I had to keep walking to keep my girls safe. My mom still on the phone tried to figure out a place for me to go, but communication was hit and miss.

Once I reached the church, we were all cold and tired and scared. We sat down on the church parking lot. Everywhere we looked had been destroyed.

A nice Christian couple drove by and saw the girls and me sitting all alone in the middle of a deserted parking lot and told us to get in their truck. I am so blessed by this family. They gave us towels and blankets to warm up. They drove to the grandparents' house and got the girls new t-shirts to wear; Averie was beginning to turn blue because she was so cold.

Both girls were so brave and barely cried. Adley was worried about daddy and so was I, but we couldn't reach him by phone. I knew in my heart he was o.k. Adley and I said a prayer for daddy trusting that God had took care of him, too.

The sweet family took us to the home depot parking lot where I saw a highway patrolman. My mom had told me that a trooper would be looking for me, so I knew I had to talk to them. I finally got to talk to a trooper, and he helped get word to my dad where I was. This nice trooper drove my girls and I down 20th Street to my mother-in-law's house, which thankfully was not hurt by the tornado.

Not much long after I arrived a familiar vehicle sped into the driveway and it was my mom and dad! I have never been so relieved to see them in my life! I gave my mommy a huge hug and started to cry.

a Tiny Survivor

By John Hacker

If only the little white dog at the Carthage Humane Society on Tuesday could talk, what a tale it could tell, to paraphrase the Hoyt Axton song originally about a cat.

Glenda Erwin, director of the Carthage Humane Society, said she believes the dog, found Saturday in a field near Diamond may have survived almost three weeks buried under wreckage dumped there by the tornado that hit Joplin on May 22.

How the dog, a shih tzu named Bentley by one of the shelter workers, got to that field is a complete mystery, but Erwin said the dog is recovering well from a number of minor injuries.

The dog has a wound in the middle of its face where something apparently hit it and had grass and wood splinters embedded in its skin under hair that appeared to have been matted by storm winds and debris.

"It's an incredible story," Erwin said. "I don't believe that dog could have crawled into that debris from what the person who brought him in said."

Erwin said a woman was in tears when she brought the dog in with a number of children.

Erwin said the woman dropped the dog, which was wrapped in

Glenda Erwin, director of the Carthage Humane Society, hold the tiny dog tnamed Bentley by the shelter staff, that was found on Saturday, June 11, 2011, about three weeks after the Joplin tornado, in a pile of tornado debris in a field near Diamond. Photo by John Hacker

a towel, off at the shelter and left before workers could get her name. Erwin said workers took the dog to Central Pet Care in Carthage, where veterinarians and workers shaved the matted fur off the dog and treated its injuries.

"It was 2:30 p.m. and everything worked just right," Erwin said. "If Central Pet Care hadn't been open, we would have had to keep the dog as it was until Monday, but they were open and they were able to clean it up and treat it right away."

Justina Sampson, a veterinary technician at the shelter, said the owner told them she had heard the dog crying around a pile of debris in the field about a week ago, but they had not been able to find the dog and had to leave.

On Saturday, they returned and heard the crying again, this time louder and more desperate. The woman was able to locate the source and pulled the dog from out from under the debris.

Sampson said the dog's eyes had ulcers like they had been hit by dust and debris and the fur was matted in a way that was different from animals that have been neglected.

She said pieces of particleboard and fibers that appeared to come from a carpet were embedded in the fur and pieces of grass had actually embedded themselves in the dog's skin.

The dog appears to be deaf and may be blind as well, although it's not clear if those conditions are a result of injuries from the tornado or were previously existing conditions.

Erwin said she was going to Joplin on Tuesday to look at pictures of missing pets to see if a dog matching Bentley's description had been reported.

"We want to see if the owner is still out there," Erwin said. "If we don't find the owner in a week or so, we will put him up for adoption."

I Am Proud to Call Joplin My Home

By Taylor Robinson

Who would have thought such a tragedy could happen to Joplin?

Trust me, that is not what was on my mind when I was at Grand Lake in Grove, Oklahoma. The weather was so nice. Beams of sunlight peeked through the clouds and the water felt good on my skin.

After a while, it started to get cloudy, so we headed toward the docks. The wind blew through my hair as we rode to the campground. We hooked the boats up to our trucks. It was around 4:30 p.m. Our parents started talking, so my friend, Kayden, and I went inside her camper and got some snacks.

Kayden's parents were in the middle of building a camp, so they were carrying logs to the side of the shelter. My parents and their friends stayed to help, and all of the six kids let out a small cheer. We got to hang out longer!

We went inside Kayden's camper and started to play Monopoly.

After about an hour, we got bored. All of the kids came outside with Kayden and me. The time was now a little after 5:40 p.m. We wanted to listen to music on Kissin' 92.5. We were ready to sing and dance, but that excitement quickly disappeared.

My parents' friend turned on the radio in her Jeep and what we heard was definitely not music. A guy was talking loud and fast in a panicky voice. I heard him say something about a tornado in Joplin and I was a bit confused. I mean, nothing ever hits Joplin, so I figured it was a minor tornado that blew about five shingles off a couple of roofs.

I was wrong.

We listened a bit longer and the reports of damage kept getting worse. My mother logged onto Facebook and the news feed was overflowing with comments about this tornado. My mom came across one that said 18th Street was gone.

That was my street!

I choked back tears and tried to stay strong so I wouldn't worry the younger kids who were with me. I was scared because I did not know what Joplin was like or if it was as bad as everyone said it was. I longed to know if Joplin was o.k., if my friends, family, and neighbors were still alive and if my house was affected.

The little kids didn't know what was happening, and for a moment, neither did I. Kayden already had tears streaming down her face. All of the four families rushed to their cars. We were soon on the road heading for Joplin.

So many questions were running through my mind and I had a lot of mixed emotions. My uncle sent a picture of the front of my house. It did not look horrible. After a few seconds, though, I noticed that only our garage was standing, and it was barely up. I let out a small whimper, which suddenly turned to tears. I remembered that my dog was at home in the house when the tornado hit.

We texted my uncle to ask and he said there was no sign of

Buddy. I tried to stay strong for my sister, but it kept getting harder and harder to choke back my tears. I started to see the destruction as we drove down I-44. These houses did not look too bad, but we drove further, and the damage was much worse.

I saw people in hospital gowns being aided and guided down the street. We checked on my grandma and her house was fine, but she wasn't there. We got back in our car and tried to find our way to our house.

The police made us park our car on 24th and Connecticut. We had to walk the rest of the way. I had never seen so much damage in my life. Wires, trees, cars, and many other things were mangled and all over the ground. I saw people walking the streets with leaves and debris in their hair and on their bodies.

When we reached my street, I ran down the road, hopping over wires and tree limbs. I looked at what was once my home. My family and I walked up our driveway and our relatives and neighbors surrounded us and gave us hugs. I kept trying to see the house, but they thought it would be too overwhelming. I requested to see my room.

I stopped breathing. I started choking, trying not to cry, but I couldn't hold it in any longer. I fell to the ground bawling. My aunt took me in her arms and held me there until I calmed down.

My room was completely gone; I had nothing left. Broken pieces of my belongings were scattered across the floor and the lawn. My sister's room was crushed. Pile after pile of debris, some walls, and bedroom furniture. The kitchen, living room, bathrooms, my parents' room, and the other rooms in the house had all of the contents scattered and destroyed.

It was hard to take in reality and understand what was happening, and the next several months after this disaster felt like a dream, but Joplin is coming back stronger and better than ever and I am proud of the hard-working citizens, but most importantly, I am proud to call Joplin my home.

Taylor Robinson was a seventh grader during the 2011-2012 school year.

Duquesne: the Stepchild of the Tornado

By Cindy Sundy

We live in Duquesne (or as I refer to it, the "stepchild" of the tornado) and there was little left of our entire neighborhood. My husband, son, and I were huddled in the bathtub which was the only wall left standing.

Our location was in the eye of the storm so when it appeared that the winds were dying down, we hoped that it was over but then the other side hit. I'm pretty sure that I was alternating between prayer and profanity at that time because I knew there wasn't enough left of the house to keep us alive much longer but somehow we made it.

Our dog wouldn't come into the bathroom with us and I couldn't find our cat before we had to hunker down with just our hands covering our heads. Gypsy, the dog was OK but plastered with mud and leaves and insulation, so we know she was exposed but we don't know where she rode it out. We never found a hair of the cat.

I will never forget that when the roof blew off and we were being slammed with hail, rain, and debris, my husband, Gary, immediately laid across my son and me to hold us down and all I could think about was what he was exposing his back to. He got some bumps

Photo by Cindy Sundy

and bruises, as we all did, but it could have been so much worse.

Oddly enough, on the one-year anniversary of the storm, when I woke up and realized what day it was, the first thing that I thought of was that had been the best day of my life.

It should have been the worst day - it could have been the last day - of my life but thankfully we all came through it. We rebuilt in the same location and we have a storm shelter. I have a lot of problems with storms now, but having this shelter gives me some sense of security.

This is part of our story and it's sometimes hard to believe that it we went through it. Our story has a much happier ending than a lot of others and I will always thank God for that.

Avenue of Hope

By John Hacker

Peace Lutheran Church, located at 20th and Wisconsin Avenue was one of dozens of churches destroyed in the Joplin tornado of May 22, 2011.

Their church home was destroyed and members have been meeting in the Bethany Presbyterian Church at 20th Street and Main since then.

Twice, however, since the storm, they've held special services on the parking lot of their church. The first was on May 29, 2011, a service to affirm that they were still a church family one week after that family was made homeless.

The second was one year after the storm, on May 20, 2012, when they held a service they dubbed Praise on the Parking Lot in a tent near the concrete slab where their church home once stood.

TWO PASTORS

Two pastors have played a big role in this church's existence since the tornado.

Pastor Kathy Redpath was appointed to take the leadership post three weeks after the tornado. She replaced interim Pastor Bill Pape, who served for several months before the tornado and a little more than a month afterward as the church searched for a permanent leader.

Redpath, who had been serving as pastor of a church in Mankato, Kansas, described how she found out she was coming to Joplin and how a simple piece of art, dubbed the "Joplin Cross" played a role in her finding out.

"I first saw that cross in the Synod Assembly in Kansas City, I was still serving in Mankato," Redpath said. "I had heard the news from Joplin but had no connection to it whatsoever. They explained it the first day of the assembly. The Synod Assembly is all the churches in Missouri and Kansas, Lutheran Churches, we gather once a year.

"I marveled at it and heard the story about it, and it was later that day that Pastor Janice Kibler talked to me. She knew I was looking for a new call and she said I have a seed to plant with you. We were in a crowded, noisy hallway and I'm trying to hear what she's trying to say and she's talking about the Joplin tornado, and I thought I know about that, get to what you want to say. Then all of a sudden, I realized what she was saying. So I said, you want me to go to Joplin, is that it?"

What Pastor Kibler, who represents the Synod and has been in Joplin many times, including the May 29, 2011, and May 20, 2012, services in the parking lot, didn't know, is she chose a pastor for Joplin who had experienced the power of a tornado before.

"I said, are you aware that I lost my first home in Ohio in a tornado years ago and she did not know that piece," Redpath said. "While (the people of Joplin) will always identify with the 22nd of May, I will always think of the 10th of May because that was the date of ours. It was 1973 and we were living in a trailer. There was a tornado warning and we got out of the trailer, we got into a cement block building that had been put up there as a utility building. There were a dozen people in there and when we came

The Cross at the destroyed remains of St. Mary's Catholic Church stands among an ocean of debris around the area of 25th Street and Moffett Avenue on May 24, 2011. The church built a new location on Central City Road west of Joplin, but the cross at the former location has been preserved. Photo by John Hacker

out again, I fully expected to wash my dinner dishes. I never found my dinner dishes.

"We knew the man who had built it and what it turned out, he for no reason other than he wanted to do it, he put extra reinforcement in that building. There were at least a dozen people in there and we would have had nowhere to go if it weren't for that building. It wasn't an EF5, I don't know what it was, but it was not as devastating as Joplin, but in that trailer park, there had been 34 trailers and 31 of them were totally destroyed. The other three hung on by a thread, but they were gone and a couple of deaths there.

"That's the story I come out of, so I can identify with their stories and they can understand that at least I have some connection, even if it's not the same connection. I remember what its like to walk out there in the dirt and say, that's my grandmother's china in pieces. I still get choked up about it and that's why I say, the stories will always be there. Whether we want them to be or not, they are there."

Redpath said taking over the church in the wake of such devastation has been tough, but she has had help.

"My question to them, because my first meeting with them was when we were deciding whether this was going to work out or not, there were about a dozen people gathered, part of what was supposed to be the core committee, the council, whatever they could gather that day, and I said to them, "How does it feel to be a church without a building?' " she said. "And we reminded each other that church exists whether or not there's a building there."

Redpath said she has had to minister to people who have suffered extraordinary loss, but some of the ministry had already started before she got to Joplin.

"By the time I came and moved in in August, those people were on their way to dealing with it the best they could," she said. She said churches and groups from across the country have reached out to the Joplin community and to their church specifically.

"The list that the secretary has of all the individuals, congregations, Boy Scout troops, Girl Scout troops, just all kinds of groups that have sent things, financial gifts, blankets, we've had blankets galore, is amazing," she said. "We've had some unusual things, the one that sticks out in my mind is one church, I think it was in Pennsylvania, wanted to give us a Christmas Tree. So they ordered from Home Depot or somewhere, and had it delivered, but then separately, they sent us a box of handmade ornaments. Nobody duplicated that one."

At the May 20, 2012, service, Nan Borg, a former member

Peace Lutheran Church Pastor Katharine Redpath talked about the ornate cross that hangs behind the pulpit in the group's new sanctuary at their new church on St. Louis Avenue on May 19, 2013. The cross was made of broken glass collected from the original church in the days after the May 22, 2011 tornado by young people from Sedalia who helped clean up after the tornado. The volunteers took the glass to an art teacher who helped them create the cross. Photo by John Hacker

Peace Lutheran Church member who moved to Good Shepherd Lutheran Church closer to her home in Carthage, presented her former church with a banner made by her present church members.

Redpath said that gift was emblematic of many of the gifts they've received.

"That was huge," Redpath said.

FORMER PASTOR RETURNS

On May 22, 2011, Peace Lutheran Church was a church in transition. The pastor at the time, Bill Pape, was an interim pastor driving more than 120 miles each week from Kansas City to take care of church business and conduct services.

Pape was in Joplin when the tornado struck and, had he not made a fateful decision, would have been in the church at the time the tornado struck.

"I was in the building after the worship service," Pape said. "I was doing some writing and stuff, but it was such a pretty day that I decided to go for a walk. I was going to go for a walk and come back, but I got in the car and thought I can come back tomorrow. So I drove off or I would have been here when the tornado hit and wouldn't be here talking to you."

Pape conducted the first service for the battered congregation in the parking lot. The lot had to be cleared of debris before the service could be held on what turned out t0 be a cool day on Memorial Day weekend.

Most members attended that service.

Pape, who was replaced a few weeks later, returned to Kansas City, but he was back on May 20, for the service.

"I came back to see all the people and to see the liveliness of the people," Pape said. "It was good to see how close they are to each other and how close they are to the God they worship.

"It was a congregation that I knew would come back."

Pape said the loss of the building was a huge blow to the congregation and could have been a death blow, but it has not destroyed this family.

"It was a very big loss for the people," Pape said. It was something you were familiar with and liked. They are remembering baptisms, weddings, funerals, that were held there and now all of a sudden it's gone.

"All you see is a cement platform slab. I don't know if they will rebuild here or somewhere else. Once they get to the new building, eventually it will become who they are."

A MEMBER SURVIVES

Kathrin Elmborg lived across the street from Peace Lutheran Church, on Montana Place. She was a member of Peace Lutheran and that church played a huge role in her life.

Elmborg, who walks with a walker, moved to Joplin 10 year ago from Kansas City and grew up on a farm in Central Kansas. She had just moved into her home at 102 Montana Place two months ago and was starting to feel at home.

"I had moved there to live next door to my granddaughter and her family," Elmborg said. "I was happy as a clam in my little house that I had fixed up. I lived right across the street from the church, then the tornado came and blew it all away.

"I was sitting, watching TV and my granddaughter called and wanted me to go to her in-laws to the basement and I said ah, no, it's just another storm, I'll stay home. All at once, the lights went out, my back door in my kitchen blew open so I thought I'd better shut my door or it will rain in. So I went to the back door and I tried to force it shut. Then the walls were tumbling down and the roof was gone and everything was falling down, and I was trying to close back door.

Elmborg believes God's hand was involved in her survival. She said she fell to the floor and the refrigerator and some cabinets fell and formed a tent over her that protected her.

"That's what kept me safe," she said. "I stayed there trying to close that door and when the tornado went over, I swirled around and sat down on the floor and then the refrigerator leaned a little bit and my cupboards leaned a little bit and there I sat, safe as if I had good sense. If I'd gone to the hall or bathroom I probably would have been killed."

Elmborg said members of her church family came and pulled her from the rubble of her home.

"I have no idea how long I was in there," she said. "I know it rained because by that time I was getting cold and wet and it was raining on me. I sat there for a while and pretty soon I heard our secretary's husband calling for me. They had come over here to see if the church was okay and they thought I was in my house so they called my name, and I answered him and he said he was so relieved to hear me answer him. So he and two other young men moved one of my walls and they pulled me straight up out of the rubble and rescued me.

"There was a couple here from church who put me in their car and they took me to another church member's home and she checked me out. I had a few cuts and abrasions, glass cuts and things like that. Then they took me to their home and one thing I remember as we went north on Main to 171, all the emergency vehicles coming in already. It wasn't dark yet and there was all the emergency vehicles coming in. It was a steady stream.

"I had what I had on my back, and that wasn't much, so I had to borrow clothes and that was uncomfortable. I knew the church was destroyed, we came out and could see that everything was destroyed. My granddaughter's home was completely demolished. It looked like a war zone and you can talk all you want, but until you see it, you can't understand it. My nephew from California came home maybe a month later to Kansas City to his mother's and they came down and he said I've seen the pictures and everything, but he said until you look at it, you don't understand the enormity of it."

Elmborg returned to her old neighborhood a few times during the week to try to salvage what she could from her home. She said the experience was a surreal mixture of terrible times and great fun.

"This was a couple of days after the tornado when we were sorting through junk," Elmborg said. "People would stop and work for a couple of hours, people we didn't know. We'd joke and laugh and I said, if this wasn't so horrible, it would be a lot of fun. That's the way it was, it was a wonderful experience but it was the most horrible thing you could ever go through. If you can figure that out, I don't know.

"Young people would stop and ask, can we help you for an hour or two? As I said, we joked and had fun and it was horrible, but we were having a good time, which doesn't make sense."

Elmborg became even closer to her church family. In some ways, she symbolized the church's efforts to rebuild and stay positive in the wake of such horror.

Elmborg said coming back to the church after the tornado to worship in the parking lot was important.

"It just meant our family was still intact and we would survive," she said. "That service after the tornado meant a lot, it meant we're still here. Today's service, I thought was excellent, it was very upbeat and it meant we're here.

"The church is probably three-fourths of my life. We're like a family. I've been associated with lots of churches, but this little Lutheran Church is different. I've been a Lutheran all my life, but this is like family, everyone cares for everyone else."

THE JOPLIN CROSS

During the May 20, 2012, service, Peace Lutheran members were reunited with pieces of their old church that had traveled the country since the tornado.

A cross, made of curved wood and standing on a thick wooden base covered with fragments of stained glass stood on the altar in front of them in that billowing white tent where they held that Praise in the Parking Lot service.

On May 29, 2011, James Williams accompanied his wife, the Rev. Janice Kibler, to the service in the Peace Lutheran Church parking lot.

Williams, who works with wood, had an idea and a purpose for his visit. He wanted to make something to symbolize what had happened in Joplin.

He had no idea that some pieces of debris and 45 minutes would take on the life that they have taken in the year since the tornado.

"I just went through the rubble and I was trying to find something we could make a little cross out of," Williams said. "We were thinking about something smaller but I was digging through the rubble and I found that piece. It was a piece of laminated interior beam and it had just been completely ripped apart because those beams were probably six or eight inches thick. This was just a piece of it that had ripped and it had the curve of the beam. It was about 10 feet long and I said that's it. Then I saw the end of the pew lying in the rubble and the cross was made then. It took 45 minutes for me to cut it up and screw it together.

"The stained glass was just pieces I picked up in the rubble and the brick isn't even attached, it has just traveled with it. It was one of the bricks in the building and it has stayed with the cross for a year. It's been to Orlando, it's been to Chicago for a Bishop's conference. It's going to two churches next week and the Sunday after, and then back to the synod assembly and then I know it has one more church and then I think it will come back to Joplin."

The cross almost did not get made because Williams said he forgot the pieces in his haste to get out of the neighborhood before it was shut down to allow President Barack Obama to tour the devastation.

"I had this stuff laid off to the side until the truck was empty, then the truck was empty and we took off," Williams said. "We got all the way to the highway and we were in a hurry to get out of town because Obama was coming. We went all the way out there and I realized, I forgot the wood. We turned around and came back and it took us two hours to get out of here.

"We were tempted to say, you know, maybe we don't need to make a cross, but we did. I'm glad we did too. I had no idea it would take on this life. With everybody wanting to see it, it has just gone all over."

Pastor Kathy Redpath said she first saw the Joplin Cross, as it was quickly dubbed, at the Synod Assembly in Kansas City, where it was displayed.

Kibler told the congregation about the cross at the May 20, 2012, service, where it was displayed in Joplin for the first time.

"This cross has been on a road trip," she said during the service. "We took it last year so we could have it at our Synod assembly just two weeks after the tornado. From there, people at the assembly started asking, can we take it home to our congregation so we can talk about hope and resurrection and life. So it has been on quite a road trip through Kansas and Missouri. It even went to Orlando for the church-wide assembly. The presiding bishop, Mark Hanson, caught wind of this cross and said we want that at Orlando as well. So I brought it back for you today, but I'm going to take it again because the road trip isn't finished. You will get it back shortly. There's a notebook here, as it has gone to different congregations people have put in pictures and notes for you, notes of encouragement. So again, thank you for your witness. You are living through something that a lot of us are watching, observing and giving thanks to God for you."

Murlin Hintz, a member of the Peace Lutheran Church, gets emotional when talking about the group's destroyed building, but he was engrossed in the notebook that accompanied the cross.

He recognized the curve in the wood that made up the cross.

"What a surprise for us today that it was picked up by the pastor's husband and brought back after being in so many places throughout the country," Hintz said. "This beam right here was actually one of the beams that was in the sanctuary and this is part of a pew and the stained glass and brick and it was just so cool to see this that I had to look through this book. Also, in this book there are former members that were members of Peace Lutheran that have now moved someplace else and they wrote notes and things and wished us the best.

"It's just awesome. I just looked at it a little more thoroughly so I wouldn't miss anything and it's just neat to see all these names."

GOD'S LIGHT

Also at the May 20, 2012, service, Nan Borg, Carthage, a member of the Good Shepherd Lutheran Church in Carthage, returned to a church she called home for 17 years.

She brought with her a banner, created by members of the Good Shepherd Lutheran Church as a gift to Peace Lutheran and its members.

"It displays the love of Jesus through the sun and through the cross on which he gave his life so we could live," Borg said. "Karen Moll is the head of the banner group at Good Shepherd and I didn't realize they were even making it, then at Bible study just this past Thursday, three days ago, they said we have a gift for you to take to Peace Lutheran, because I am a former member at Peace Lutheran. So I was just thrilled and it worked out beautifully that it could be presented at this particular service on this particular day. And even though it will be a shile before it can hang, it certainly is a gift from one Lutheran Church to another."

Borg recalled her time at Peace Lutheran and the tornado that destroyed a church that held many fond memories for her.

"I was a member up until about two and a half years ago," Borg said. "It's so hard to think about May 22. We had a wedding that weekend and I came over and I couldn't find the church. The roads were so clogged and I was crying so hard, so I had to come back another day and pull up and be able to spend some time. I was a member here for about 17 years, taught adult Sunday school for the same amount of time and was very involved and this church is an extremely community oriented church. I've always been very touched at how they reach out. Even when they're hurting, they reach out. In fact I think it was like a month after the tornado, they were having a bake sale so they could give to the literacy council. They are a precious group of people.

"It was very touching to be here today. And because I know these people and I've known them for so many years, they are very welcoming. So I was very glad to be able to present the banner."

Cliff Eighmy, a member of Peace Lutheran and a friend of Borg's from when she was a member, was moved by the gift from the Carthage church.

"It just makes you want to cry in happiness because people out there are thinking about us and they care," he said. "That's something that should be said, there's been so much support from people outside this community, donations and help from literally thousands of people, have come to this town and to our congregation to help."

Murlin Hintz was also moved by the gift.

"It means so much and there's been so much of that from all over the country that have poured in here, not just into Peace Lutheran but all of Joplin really," he said. "That is a very, very special thing for a church to do. The lady that presented it to us, she used to be a member of this church so it was quite a surprise to her that they gave it to her to forward on to us.

"It's something that this church will always have after these decisions are made where to build, what to build, what kind of a building that kind of thing. Then there was another cross that was given to us from a church in Sedalia, Mo. There was a group in here that helped with the cleanup and they picked up a lot of the stained glass that was in the windows and they made this cross using the stained glass and it's all lit up. It is just awesome so that will be something that we'll always have in our new church as well."

A PROMISE TO REBUILD

The Peace Lutheran family continues to meet faithfully every week at Bethel Presbyterian Church. Their former lot stands bare and cleaned of debris.

Members have formed a committee to decide whether they want to rebuild on the lot they own at 20th and Wisconsin or move to another location.

Hintz, who serves on that building committee, said the congregation is anxious, but it wants to make the right decision for its future.

"Some of us are getting kind of impatient," Hintz said. "It's been a year now and we don't have any building plans on their way yet and there are other churches that have been rebuilt. One of them had their first service Easter Sunday and they were located just over on the other side of the railroad tracks. But we aren't rushing into anything.

"We need to look way ahead and this is where we're at with

decisions now. Past memories are great, we never forget those but we need to look on ahead as to where is the best place for us to be for the future of Peace Lutheran Church here in Joplin and so these are the things we're dealing with now. Where can we best serve our mission to the community. This is what we're struggling with."

Redpath said the congregation is being deliberate in its decision because it is so important. She said the decision whether or not to build on their old location is a big hurdle.

"It's not ruled out, but it's also not decided," Redpath said. "I would like to think — in fact, I know — that we will be back. God will see to that.

Tornado Teaches the True Meaning of School

By Randy Turner

President Barack Obama will speak at the Joplin High School Graduation Monday night.

On Tuesday, the one-year anniversary of the tornado that destroyed one-third of this community and killed 161 will be observed with a unity walk that will cover the path of the tornado and end at Cunningham Park with a moment of silence at 5:41 p.m., the exact moment the tornado occurred.

Joplin will be the center of attention Monday, but on Friday, May 18, just three days before Air Force One arrives, the most important moment for 160 eighth graders at East Middle School where I teach had nothing to do with the anniversary or the president.

It was their last day of middle school and they were spending it in a converted warehouse, directly across from a dog food factory that continually offered an aromatic gift to the surrounding atmosphere.

The East Middle School building the children had attended for two years, what had been a brand-new building, was just a memory. The auditorium, the gymnasium, and commons area were destroyed by the EF-5 tornado; the rest of it was razed recently.

During the 2011-2012 school year, East students took physical education classes in a modular building and performed drama and musical productions in the auditoriums of the district's other middle schools, miles away.

Instead of the state-of-the-art auditorium that had been the pride and joy of the old East, students sat on the floor during assemblies and most of our last half day was dedicated to an East tradition- the annual talent show and awards assembly.

My Journalism Club students were set up at a table in the back of the cafeteria about 20 minutes before the program began. In front of them was an array of laptops that they would use to live blog the show, something we had never done before.

Darin was set up with the camcorder, while Jennifer, one of our two editors, Karly, Megan and Austen were on our blog website doing previews. Amy, the other co-editor, was on our Facebook page providing anyone who might have been online an opportunity to know what was going on this final day of the school year. Two sixth graders, Emma and Katy, were ready to take pictures.

At 9:30 a.m. the students began moving into the commons area, taking their seats on the floor.

For two and a half hours, I watched in awe as my students worked continually on a last day when their friends were relaxing. All of them had to leave their posts several times, either to accept awards for their academic accomplishments, or to perform.

It was a program filled with young girls singing Taylor Swift songs, or at least I think they were Taylor Swift songs, and students receiving awards for making the honor roll every quarter or for having perfect attendance.

The end of the program brought the teacher dance with faculty members showing their willingness to make fools of themselves (though a few of them are excellent dancers).

Jennifer Nguyen, left, and Alyssa Wescoat console Megan Hickey immediately after the conclusion of the talent show/awards assembly. Photo by Randy Turner

The final act was the concert choir's rendition of one of those goodbye songs that make the rounds this time of the year.

As I watched my journalism students, I saw the tears flowing. They knew this was their last day of middle school, but the song brought the point home.

And just like the high school graduation that will come Monday, the room was filled with young people who are ending one stage of their lives and preparing for the next.

A speculator on hug futures would have made a killing. I watched as three of my students shared a group hug, with Jennifer and Alyssa consoling Megan.

Hours after the final day of the 2011-2012 school year drew to a close, I received an e-mail message from Jennifer telling me she had posted a final story on our website. Since Jennifer is one of the best writers I have ever had the privilege of teaching, I quickly called up *East Middle School Roundabout* and read her story. It included the following passage:

I remember thinking for countless hours how I couldn't wait for summer. I couldn't wait to be out of school, to just be lazy! Many eighth graders were especially looking forward to the joys of high school! The time for relaxation and vacation was definitely anticipated...and soon enough, the time came.

This school year went by like a breeze, and before we knew it, the end of school was soon approaching. This meant the end of middle school for the eighth graders, and the beginning of high school as freshmen. You would think we would be happy for summer, for a break.

Yes, we were happy, but we were also sad. The school year just went by too fast!

Too fast? We were in a warehouse, feeling forgotten in the nether regions of the school district. When the dignitaries came, they went to the mall high school, not to see this group of students who had been just as misplaced, just as much lost in the wake of the most horrifying incident of their young lives.

Too fast? Jennifer was right. The end of our educational adventure had come much too quickly.

Jennifer touched another emotional chord with her final words:

Tears spring to my eyes as I close with my final bid of farewell to East. Through all the good times and the bad, we have overcome and made this school truly unforgettable. This is why I will always remember you.

Goodbye East. I love you.

In her words, Jennifer hit on the reason why the Joplin Tornado could never bring East Middle School down. It was just a building that was destroyed, one that had packed many memories into its two years, but just a building.

Those unforgettable kids, the Jennifers, the Amys, the Megans, the Austens, the Darins, and all of the rest of them, the ones who sat in our makeshift classrooms and walked our warehouse halls this year and those who will be there next year as we wait for our new building to be built- they're the ones who make the school.

The circumstances that brought us together in this industrial park we call home were horrific, but what a wonderful school year.

the Photos

Randy Turner | John Hacker

Photo by Bob Webster, Creative Commons

Creative Commons

Joplin East Middle School. Photo by Randy Turner

Joplin East Middle School. Photo by Randy Turner

Photo by Elissa Jun, FEMA

Photo by Elissa Jun, FEMA

Photo by Steve Zumwalt, FEMA

Photo by Jace Anderson, FEMA

Home Depot on Range Line was completely destroyed. Photo by FEMA

A 26th Street resident helps with debris cleanup. Photo by Rossyveth Rey-Berrios, FEMA

Photo by Steve Zumwalt, FEMA

Forest Park Baptist Church volunteers assist with debris cleanup. Photo by Rossyveth Rey-Berrios ,FEMA

Photo by Jace Anderson, FEMA

Irving Elementary. Photo by Jace Anderson, FEMA

Photo by John Hacker

Photo by Steve Zumwalt, FEMA

Photo by Suzanne Everson, FEMA

Photo by Stephanie Gregory

Principal Debbie Fort examines damage at Irving Elementary School.
Photo by Steve Zumwalt, FEMA

Jodie Neal looks at what is left of his home in Duquesne. Photo by Randy Turner

Joplin High School. Photo by John Hacker

Photo by Stephanie Gregory

Photo by Stephanie Gregory

After the 15th Street Walmart was decimated in the tornado, Walmart officials began the rebuilding process almost immediately. Joplin residents crowded into the new store when it opened in November. Photo by Steve Zumwalt, FEMA

Dillon's was destroyed during the tornado and never reopened. Photo by Ashlyn Griffberg

Photo by Trisha Raney

Photo by Trisha Raney

Photo by Ashlyn Griffberg

Photo by Ashlyn Griffberg

The destroyed St. John's Regional Medical Center and the two temporary locations that replaced it on the right in this Feb. 19, 2012 aerial photo. The tent hospital is above and the component hospital, under construction, is below. Photo by John Hacker

The damage path of the May 22, 2011 photo as it crossed Main Street around 26th Street. Downtown Joplin, which was unharmed, is top center and Main Street runs down and to the bottom left corner of this picture which looks from the south to the north. Photo by John Hacker

Connecticut Avenue from 32nd street at the bottom across the tornado damage path around 20th Street to Campbell Parkway near the top. Photo by John Hacker

East Middle School occupied a building in the Crossroads Industrial Park for the 2011-12 and 2012-13 school year. Photo by John Hacker

A shattered Joplin High School in this February 2012 aerial photo. Photo by John Hacker

The tornado damage path along 20th Street looking east from Joplin High School in this Aug. 6, 2011 aerial photo. Photo by John Hacker

The parking lots around the destroyed Joplin High School became staging areas for relief supplies and volunteers in the weeks after the May 22, 2011 tornado. Tents can be seen in the parking lots and the flattened Franklin Technical Center is on the left side of the picture. Photo by John Hacker

St. John's Regional Medical Center and the medical building south of the hospital were both damaged beyond repair in the tornado. Photo by John Hacker

The aerial view from the south looking over Freeman West Hospital and the destroyed St. John's Regional Medical Center, as seen on Aug. 6, 2011. Photo by John Hacker

The tornado damage path as seen from the east over Duquesne to the west. The damaged East Middle School is in the lower center of this picture, taken on Aug. 6, 2011. Photo by John Hacker

A tent hospital was set up immediately after the tornado just east of the destroyed St. John's Regional Medical Center to give St. John's employees a place to work and help Joplin recover from the tornado. Photo by John Hacker

Randy Turner | John Hacker

the Messages

Death Does Not Get the Last Word

The following transcript is from the Joplin Ministerial Alliance's portion of the Joplin Tornado Memorial Service held Sunday, May 29, 2011 at Missouri Southern State University.

FATHER JUSTIN MONAGHAN, ST. MARY'S CATHOLIC CHURCH: Heavenly Father, we take time to pause, reflect, and pray. Amidst the pain and heart of this devastation we have no doubt about your presence among us.

You are infusing in each of us from near and afar a strength and resilience that is a special gift. You are calling our already close-knit community to new heights and determination and purpose. We hear the mission you have entrusted to us, and with your help we will put our hands to the plow.

We are grateful for the support you are sending us and for the backing of our governor and state and for the enormous support from our president and our country at this time of renewal and restoration. Father, we open to your will. Amen. Please be seated.

REV. RANDY GARRIS, COLLEGE HEIGHTS CHRISTIAN

President Barack Obama hugs a woman who lost a loved one, during the memorial service for victims of the tornado in Joplin, Missouri, May 29, 2011. Official White House Photo by Pete Souza

CHURCH: Welcome and thank you for coming to today's memorial service. Customarily, a greeting would include such words as "ladies and gentlemen" and "honored guests."

But when there has been deep shared pain, when a community has suffered greatly and cried much together, and when the compassion and the kindness extended to one another has gone far beyond the scope of words, a more tender language than "honored guests" or "ladies and gentlemen" is heard.

Words like "friends" and "neighbors" and "family" and "brothers and sisters." Words like "us." That's who gathers here today with us. Thank you for your coming. Thank you for your role in each other's lives. Thank you for what you mean to one another.

A prayer which was led by Father Justin Monaghan who by the grace of God in a stout bathtub survived the destruction of the church of St. Mary's, a congregation of the Lord, on 26th Street. And physically and metaphorically the cross still stands. (APPLAUSE)

GARRIS: There's a three-fold purpose to this gathering. The first is to grieve. The loss of even one human life is a tragedy. And we have lost scores. We also gather to pray God's blessings as we rebuild our lives, asking God to lead us as we rebuild around the things that matter most.

And we gather to celebrate the kindness that people have and are giving to one another. Our foundation has not moved. It's still in the same place. We still have a solid place to stand.

In Romans, the eighth chapter, Apostle Paul wrote these -- these words, "What, then, shall we say to these things? If God is for us, who can be against us? He who did not spare his own son, but gave him up for us all -- how will he not also, with him, graciously give us all things? Who shall separate us from the love of Christ? Shall tribulation or distress or persecution or famine or nakedness or danger or sword? No, no.

In all these things, we are more than conquerors through him who loved us. For I am confident that neither death nor life, nor angels nor rulers, nor anything present nor anything to come, nor powers, nor height or depth or anything else in all of creation will ever be able to separate us from the love of God in Christ Jesus, our Lord."

And now with the hymn of promise, the chancellor choir of the First United Methodist Church under the direction of Larry Sandburg (CHOIR SINGING) (APPLAUSE)

GARRIS: Pastor Aaron Brown has been a good friend of the four-state area, a faithful partner in the gospel, and a shepherd of St. Paul's United Methodist Church. It, too, is a congregation that has lost much, including its worship center. He'll have our message this afternoon.

REV. AARON BROWN, ST. PAUL'S UNITED METHODIST

CHURCH: We're all trying to -- trying to process our stories and understand them in the context of what's happened, and I thought I'd take the liberty of telling you about mine about Sunday.

Our family lives south of the city of Joplin. And after the tornado, I drove as far as I could into town and ran to the home of one of my closest friends. His house was gone, but he and his family were safe.

From there, I was able to run to our church on 26th and Monroe and found that about a third of it was gone, and I just had to know if everybody inside was safe. And there was one person in the church at the time the tornado hit, and she was safe. She hid under a dishwasher in our kitchen.

I went out to the street and what I saw was that people were just running. I didn't know what else to do, so I just ran alongside people and I said, "Can I help you find somebody?" And I dug through houses. And I prayed with a young couple whose friends didn't make it out of their house.

And across the street from there, there were two elderly people that had died in their own backyard. I don't know their names. But there was just a lot of running and digging and hoping and praying. That's what I remember.

I got called back to the church and the kids' wing of our church miraculously was still standing and it became a triage center. It's ironic, the classrooms that the children had played that morning, laughed around and learned about Jesus around, they became the place where wounds were being treated, and broken bones were being set, and emergency surgeries were being performed.

Tables where kids had been making crafts a few hours earlier became beds of comfort and rest for the wounded. We have all spent the last seven days looking for family and friends. We've all had moments of unbelievable relief at hearing somebody's voice, and we've all had those moments of heart-sickening pain and hearing that somebody that we know didn't make it.

Late Friday night, I deliver the news to Mark and Trisha Norton that their son Will, his body had been identified. Eighteen years old, absolutely overflowing with life and faith. He had just graduated from high school hours before he was killed. Will is one of -- from what I've heard recently -- one of 142.

What is the word of comfort for us today? The word of comfort today for Will's family and all of those grieving comes from the God of the universe, the God who took human form and walked among us. He suffered. He knows what it's like for us when we suffer.

And Jesus said this. He said, "Do not let your hearts be troubled. Trust in God. Trust also in me." He said, "In my father's house, there are many rooms. If it were not so, I would have told you." He said, "I'm going to prepare a place for you. And if I go and prepare a place for you, I will come back and take you to be with me, so that you also can be where I am." He said, "Before long, the world will not see me anymore, but you will see me. And because I live you also will live."

And then he also says, there a few verses later, he says, "Peace I leave with you, my peace I give to you. I do not give as the world gives, so do not let your hearts be troubled and do not be afraid."

To these families who died, I think God is saying right now is death does not get the last word. I think God is saying to those families right now, this is what I wanted you to see in the resurrection of Jesus, that death doesn't win ever. Even when you think it does -- (APPLAUSE)

BROWN: God is saying to you families who lost someone, even if it looks like death wins, it doesn't get the last word. Life wins. Life wins. (APPLAUSE)

BROWN: And I'll be honest. I don't know the faith stories of all those that have died. I don't know their faith stories.

But I know this -- that God's grace is wider than we can ever imagine, that heaven is real, and that this life is not the only life that we see. I need to be honest and confess, some of us are asking, why? Why did God do this? Why did God allow this, so much death so, much destruction?

But listen -- Jesus never promised to protect us from the storms of life. He never promised that life would be easy or convenient if we chose to follow him.

In fact, almost all of his disciples, they were tortured to death. What he did promise was very simple and powerful: to be with us. To be with us through the storm, to be with us as we grieve, to be with us as we stand at the gravesite of our loved ones, to be with us and listen to us and guide us. And our challenge is: will we let him?

As hard as it may be, pray, as hard as it may be, talk to God. As hard as it may be, listen to his words. Let him love you. Let him love you. Listen, God didn't do this to Joplin to punish us. Read the book. Jesus took our punishment for us. Read the book. (APPLAUSE)

BROWN: This happened -- this happened because life on this side of eternity is unpredictable. It's chaotic and it's broken. God says this, "For God so loved the world he gave his one and only son and he hasn't stopped loving the world."

You may wonder at times, but the fact is that God loves you and God loves Joplin and God is walking through this tragedy today and he will make a way where it seems like there is no way.

You know, when Jesus was crucified, everybody -- I mean, everybody, they thought it was the end. The disciples had forgotten everything that he told them, that their world had come crashing down around them. There was this eerie darkness that covered the land.

And for parts of three days, there was no hope. But then, but then -- then Easter. Death is swallowed up in victory. Light crushes the darkness. Life wins. Life won then. And life wins now.

And now, what do we do? We get busy. Jesus didn't come back from the grave just to point us to heaven. He came back from the grave to give us a mission that those who call on his name would be the light of the world.

His mission is for us to get busy, get busy serving, get busy rebuilding our city which I love. And by the way, I think it is the center of the universe right here in Joplin, Missouri. (APPLAUSE)

BROWN: Let's get busy. Let's get busy loving more deeply than we ever have loved. Let's get busy taking care -- you get busy taking care of your soul. Get busy connecting to God, the God who knows you by name and loves you more than you could ever imagine or believe.

And for those of you who have lost loved ones, get busy living out their legacy. They may have lost their lives, but none of them would want you to stop living yours. Get busy living.

We are not a people without hope. We are people from whom hope and light and life shines to the ends of the earth because God is good all the time. And all the time, God is good. (APPLAUSE)

BROWN: In the name of Jesus, the Lord of life, and the Lord of light, and the Lord of hope, and the Lord of new beginnings, that is the good news, amen.

the Long Journey

Gov. Jay Nixon delivered the following message at the Joplin Memorial Tornado Service Sunday, May 29, 2011 at Missouri Southern State University.

Thank you, Pastor Gariss. To the families of those who were killed and injured; to the families of those who are still unaccounted for; to the people of Joplin who have endured this terrible tragedy; to the thousands of Missourians and citizens across the nation who have opened their hearts to help us heal; to the hundreds of firefighters and emergency responders who came without hesitation to climb over piles of rubble in search of survivors; to Pastor Garris, Pastor Brown, Father Monaghan, Lieutenant Colonel Kilmer, and the wonderful choir from First United Methodist Church of Joplin; and to President Obama who is with us today – thank you all for coming.

It is an honor to be here, joining the thousands of Missourians observing this special Day of Prayer. We stand on hallowed ground, to bear witness to the destructive power of Nature and the invincible power of faith.

We have come to mourn what the storm has taken from us, to seek comfort in community, and to draw strength from God to build anew. It seems inconceivable that just one week ago, the people of

Joplin were going about their daily lives, doing the ordinary things people do on a Sunday evening: Cooking supper. Watching TV. Walking the dog. Attending their sons' and daughters' graduation.

And then came the whirlwind. Nearly a mile wide and six miles long, with 200-mile-an-hour winds – churning and roaring, tossing cars and toppling trees, pounding homes, businesses, schools and churches to rubble.

But that storm, the likes of which we have never seen, has brought forward a spirit of resilience –the likes of which we've also never seen.

What our nation has witnessed this week is the spirit of Joplin, Missouri. And we are humbled and awed by it. You have given "Love thy neighbor" new meaning. The parable of the Good Samaritan in Luke, Chapter 10: verses 25 to 37, begins with a conversation between Jesus and a student of religious law. It starts with a legal question and ends with a moral imperative.

The student asks Jesus, "What shall I do to inherit eternal life?" And Jesus turns the question around and asks: "What is written in the law?" And the student, who is well-versed in the Talmud and the Torah, replies: "Thou shalt love the Lord thy God with all thy heart, with all thy soul, with all thy strength and with all thy mind. "And thou shalt love thy neighbor as thyself."

And Jesus replies: "Thou hast answered right. This do, and thou shalt live." But then the student, wanting greater clarity than the law provided, asks Jesus, "And who is my neighbor?" And Jesus tells him the story of the Good Samaritan.

From that parable, our charge is crystal clear. Good Samaritans do not pass by those who are suffering and in need. They show their compassion with action.

In Joplin, you see Good Samaritans everywhere you turn. You see them over in the gym at this university, where hundreds of volunteers make sandwiches every day. You seem them passing

Gov. Jay Nixon delivers remarks at the Joplin Tornado Memorial Service.
Photo by State of Missouri

out blankets and pillows, sunscreen and flashlights to our neighbors made homeless by the whirlwind.

You need a flashlight. Because it gets pretty dark here at night – especially when you're standing in the street, staring at the lonely pile of matchsticks that was once your home.

If you had been in the ER at St. John's Mercy Medical Center last Sunday evening, mere moments after the tornado struck, you would have seen Good Samaritans rushing frantically to reach the wounded and the dying.

Shattered glass and bleeding patients everywhere, water and gas spewing from burst pipes, one doctor stumbled through the darkness with a flashlight in his teeth, following the wail of a wounded child.

You see Good Samaritans at every checkpoint in the destruction zone, where police officers and citizen soldiers of the Missouri National Guard keep watch over wet socks, teddy bears, cherished wedding photos and crumpled wheelchairs – all that is left of our neighbors' worldly goods.

You see them in the churchyard, men sleeping on cots under the stars, after driving all night to get here from Tuscaloosa. These men were so touched, so moved by the kindness of strangers in their hour of need, that they just had to come to Joplin.

Good Samaritans – on a mission from God. God has chosen us for a mission, too: to grieve together, to comfort one another, to be patient with one another, to strengthen one another – and to build Joplin anew.

Not just to build it back the way it was, but to make it an even better place. We know that all those who perished here are already in an even better place. But for us, the living, there is work to do. God says: "Show me." Show me.

The people of Missouri were born for this mission. We are famously stubborn and self-reliant. Practical. Impatient. But whatever may divide us, we always come together in crisis. And once our resolve is set, no storm, no fire or flood can turn us from our task.

In the pale hushed stillness before dawn, when the chainsaws have fallen silent, if you listen very closely – you can hear the sound of that resolve, like a tiny silver hammer tapping, tapping, tapping inside our heads.

In the days to come, the satellite trucks will pack up, leave town and move on. Joplin's story will disappear from the front pages. But the tragedy will not disappear from our lives. We will still be here in Joplin – together – preparing for the long journey out of darkness into light. And we will need more hands, more tools, more Good Samaritans at every step.

This tragedy has changed us forever. This community will never be the same. We will never be the same. The grief we share at this moment is overwhelming. That sorrow will always be part of us, a stone upon our hearts.

But those we love — those we lost — are safe with God, and safe in our hearts. And in our hearts, the joy they gave us lives on and on. Nothing can take that from us. We can, and we will, heal. We've already begun.

Together, we can, and we will, rebuild — upon a granite foundation of faith. What we build on this hallowed ground will be a living monument to those we lost: mothers, fathers, our precious children.

It will be a monument to the will and determination of the hundreds of men, women and yes, even children, who helped their neighbors dig out of the ruins — a monument to the search and rescue crews who came swiftly to aid the quick, and the dead.

By God's grace, we will restore this community. And by God's grace, we will renew our souls.

One year from today, Joplin will look different. And more different still in two years, and in three years, and in five. But as the years pass, the moral of our story will be the same: love thy neighbor. May God bless.

Joplin Taught the World

President Barack Obama delivered the following message at the Joplin Tornado Memorial Service May 29, 2011 at Missouri Southern State University. The official transcript is from the White House.

THE PRESIDENT: Thank you. Thank you so much. Please, please be seated.

AUDIENCE MEMBER: I love you, Obama!

THE PRESIDENT: I love Joplin! (Applause.) I love Joplin.

AUDIENCE MEMBER: We love Joplin!

THE PRESIDENT: We love Joplin. (Applause.)

Thank you, Governor, for that powerful message, but more importantly, for being here with and for your people every step of the way. We are grateful to you, to Reverend Gariss, Father Monaghan. I'm so glad you got in that tub. (Laughter and applause.)

To Reverend Brown for that incredibly powerful message. (Applause.) To Senator Claire McCaskill, who's been here, and Congressman Billy Long; Mayor Woolston. To Craig Fugate. It doesn't get a lot of attention, but he heads up FEMA, our emergency

President Barack Obama speaks at the Joplin Tornado Memorial Service.
Official White House photo by Pete Souza

response at the federal level. He's been going from Tuscaloosa to Joplin and everywhere in between tirelessly doing outstanding work. We're grateful for him.

Gail McGovern, the President of the National Red Cross, which has contributed mightily to the rebuilding efforts here. Most of all, to the family and friends of all those who've been lost and all those who've been affected.

Today we gather to celebrate the lives of those we've lost to the storms here in Joplin and across the Midwest, to keep in our prayers those still missing, to mourn with their families, to stand together during this time of pain and trial.

And as Reverend Brown alluded to, the question that weighs on us at a time like this is: Why? Why our town? Why our home? Why my son, or husband, or wife, or sister, or friend? Why?

We do not have the capacity to answer. We can't know when a terrible storm will strike, or where, or the severity of the devastation that it may cause. We can't know why we're tested with the loss of a loved one, or the loss of a home where we've lived a lifetime. These things are beyond our power to control. But that does not mean we are powerless in the face of adversity.

How we respond when the storm strikes is up to us. How we live in the aftermath of tragedy and heartache, that's within our control.

And it's in these moments, through our actions, that we often see the glimpse of what makes life worth living in the first place.

In the last week, that's what Joplin has not just taught Missouri, not just taught America, but has taught the world. I was overseas in the aftermath of the storm, and had world leaders coming up to me saying, let the people of Joplin know we are with them; we're thinking about them; we love them. (Applause.)

Because the world saw how Joplin responded. A university turned itself into a makeshift hospital. (Applause.)

Some of you used your pickup trucks as ambulances, carrying

the injured -- (applause) -- on doors that served as stretchers. Your restaurants have rushed food to people in need. Businesses have filled trucks with donations. You've waited in line for hours to donate blood to people you know, but also to people you've never met.

And in all this, you have lived the words of Scripture: We are troubled on every side, yet not distressed; we are perplexed, but not in despair; Persecuted, but not forsaken; cast down, but not destroyed.

As the governor said, you have shown the world what it means to love thy neighbor. You've banded together. You've come to each other's aid. You've demonstrated a simple truth: that amid heartbreak and tragedy, no one is a stranger. Everybody is a brother. Everybody is a sister. (Applause.) We can all love one another.

As you move forward in the days ahead, I know that rebuilding what you've lost won't be easy. I just walked through some of the neighborhoods that have been affected, and you look out at the landscape, and there have to be moments where you just say, where to begin? How to start?

There are going to be moments where after the shock has worn off, you feel alone. But there's no doubt in my mind what the people of this community can do. There's no doubt in my mind that Joplin will rebuild. And as President, I can promise you your country will be there with you every single step of the way. (Applause.) We will be with you every step of the way. We're not going anywhere. (Applause.)

The cameras may leave. The spotlight may shift. But we will be with you every step of the way until Joplin is restored and this community is back on its feet. We're not going anywhere. (Applause.)

That is not just my promise; that's America's promise. It's a promise I make here in Joplin; it's a promise I made down in Tuscaloosa, or in any of the communities that have been hit by these devastating storms over the last few weeks.

Now, there have been countless acts of kindness and selflessness in recent days. We've already heard the record of some of that. But perhaps none are as inspiring as what took place when the storm was bearing down on Joplin, threatening an entire community with utter destruction. And in the face of winds that showed no mercy, no regard for human life, that did not discriminate by race or faith or background, it was ordinary people, swiftly tested, who said, "I'm willing to die right now so that someone else might live."

It was the husband who threw himself over his wife as their house came apart around them. It was the mother who shielded her young son.

It was Dean Wells, a husband and father who loved to sing and whistle in his church choir. Dean was working a shift at the Home Depot, managing the electrical department, when the siren rang out.

He sprang into action, moving people to safety. Over and over again, he went back for others, until a wall came down on top of him. In the end, most of the building was destroyed, but not where Dean had directed his coworkers and his customers.

There was a young man named Christopher Lucas who was 26 years old. Father of two daughters; third daughter on the way. Just like any other night, Christopher was doing his job as manager on duty at Pizza Hut. And then he heard the storm coming.

It was then when this former sailor quickly ushered everybody into the walk-in freezer. The only problem was the freezer door wouldn't stay closed from the inside.

So as the tornado bore down on this small storefront on Range Line Road, Christopher left the freezer to find a rope or a cord or anything to hold the door shut. He made it back just in time, tying a piece of bungee cord to the handle outside, wrapping the other end around his arm, holding the door closed with all his might.

And Christopher held it as long as he could, until he was pulled away by the incredible force of the storm. He died saving more than a dozen people in that freezer. (Applause.)

You see, there are heroes all around us, all the time. They walk by us on the sidewalk, and they sit next to us in class. They pass us in the aisle wearing an orange apron. They come to our table at a restaurant and ask us what we'd like to order. Just as we can't know why tragedy strikes in the first place, we may never fully understand where these men and women find the courage and strength to do what they did. What we do know is that in a split-second moment where there's

little time for internal reflection or debate, the actions of these individuals were driven by love -- love for a family member, love for a friend, or just love for a fellow human being. That's good to know.

In a world that can be cruel and selfish, it's this knowledge -- the knowledge that we are inclined to love one another, that we're inclined to do good, to be good -- that causes us to take heart.

We see with fresh eyes what's precious and so fragile and so important to us. We put aside our petty grievances and our minor disagreements. We see ourselves in the hopes and hardships of others. And in the stories of people like Dean and people like Christopher, we remember that each of us contains reserves of resolve and compassion.

There are heroes all around us, all the time.

And so, in the wake of this tragedy, let us live up to their example -- to make each day count -- (applause) -- to live with the sense of mutual regard -- to live with that same compassion that they demonstrated in their final hours. We are called by them to do everything we can to be worthy of the chance that we've been given to carry on.

I understand that at a memorial yesterday for Dean, his wife decided to play a recording of Dean whistling a song he loved -- Amazing Grace. The lyrics are a fitting tribute to what Joplin has been through.

Through many dangers, toils and snares I have already come;

'Tis Grace that brought me safe thus far and Grace will lead me home… Yea, when this flesh and heart shall fail, and mortal life shall cease, I shall possess within the veil, A life of joy and peace. May those we've lost know peace, and may Grace guide the people of Joplin home. God bless you, and God bless the United States of America. Thank you.

Miracle of the Human Spirit

Joplin City Manager Mark Rohr delivered the following remarks Sunday, May 29, 2011 during a ceremony at Landreth Park.

Being the Joplin city manager, typically, if you've been watching during the week, I prepare statements to read to the press. Beneath the monotone, there's a turbulent sea and that is my way in terms of planning and dealing with things to try and be as structured as possible.

Today I speak from the heart. I do have some notes, I do have an outline to help me if I lose my way, but the message comes from the heart.

If I have trouble getting through this, I apologize to the citizens in advance.

Approximately a week ago, the city of Joplin suffered an unspeakable tragedy. We lost family members, loved ones, friends, neighbors and fellow citizens. We suffered inestimable losses in terms of property within the city of Joplin. But I have always been of the opinion that out of something bad, something good can happen if you have the right perspective.

And what I've witnessed here in the last week is the miracle of the human spirit. It has reaffirmed my belief in mankind.

The people behind me, my department heads, have worked in excess of 100 hours this week to recover from this tragedy. We have had innumerable volunteers come into Joplin from literally all over the country. We have had help from other government agencies throughout the region, state and nation come to Joplin to help our citizens.

We have received countless emails and messages from throughout the world extending their condolences to the city of Joplin and pledging their help to enable us to recover. We have had excellent assistance from our state and federal government and if you heard the messages today, they pledge to stay with us throughout.

In my past experiences in life, when someone close to me has passed away or some other tragedy has occurred, I always talk to other people and say, man that really slows you down, that really requires you to sit and put things into perspective and try to determine what is important and what isn't important. But like most people, that wears off in a few days and you get caught up in the pace of your everyday life and, in the circumstance that surrounds you, slowing down and gathering perspective wanes.

I tried to think of a way to commemorate those people who lost their lives in this unspeakable tragedy and what I came up with is a request that I am making of you here today; that we capture and invoke the miracle of the human spirit that we have seen here in Joplin and we utilize it, and we channel it.

And if I forget, you remind me, and if you forget, I'm going to remind you. We direct that spirit toward rebuilding Joplin better than it was before the storm and we return our lives to a state of peace, love and prosperity as soon as possible.

Joplin, This is Not Just Your Tragedy

Before they delivered remarks at the Joplin Tornado Memorial Service Sunday, May 29, 2011, President Barack Obama and Gov. Jay Nixon toured the area damaged by the tornado and spoke the local and national media.

PRESIDENT OBAMA- Obviously, the scene speaks for itself. When we were in Tuscaloosa a few weeks ago, I talked about how I had not seen devastation like that in my lifetime. You come here to Joplin and it is just as heartbreaking and in some ways even more devastating.

I want to thank the outstanding work that Governor Nixon, the Mayor, all the congressional delegation, as well as the First Lady have done -- and the Red Cross -- in helping people to respond. But obviously it is going to take years to build back. And we mourn the loss of life.

We're going to be going to a memorial service and try to help comfort the families and let them know that we're praying for them and thinking about them. We had a chance to meet some of the folks who lived in this community, and just harrowing stories but also miraculous stories.

I met an 85-year-old gentleman who has a -- still has a lawn service. He explained how he had just gotten his chicken pot pie out and the storm started coming and he went into the closet and came out without a scratch.

And so, there are good stories to tell and happy stories to tell here, but obviously there's been a lot of hardship as well.

The main thing I just want to communicate to the people of Joplin is this is just not your tragedy. This is a national tragedy and that means there will be a national response.

Craig Fugate, who has probably been the busiest man in the federal government over this last bit of months, has been on the ground since just the day after this happened, and he's helping to coordinate with an outstanding team of state and local officials.

We're going to do everything we can to continue whatever search and rescue remains. We are doing everything we can to make sure that folks get the shelter that they need, the support that they need.

We're working with the Governor to make sure that we cut through any red tape that's necessary with respect to rebuilding here. And then we're just going to have a tough, long slog.

But what I've been telling every family that I've met here is we're going to be here long after the cameras leave. We are not going to stop until Joplin is fully back on its feet.

So to all the volunteers who are helping out -- one of the things that's been incredible is to see how many people from out of state have driven from as far away as Texas, nearby Illinois, people just coming here to volunteer -- firefighters, ordinary citizens.

It's an example of what the American spirit is all about. And that gives us a lot of encouragement at a time when obviously people are going through a lot of hardship. So, thank you again, Governor.

GOVERNOR NIXON: Thank you, Mr. President.

THE PRESIDENT: Would you like to say a few words?

President Barack Obama greets Hugh Hills, 85, in front of his home. Hills told the President he hid in a closet during the tornado, which destroyed the second floor and half the first floor of his house. Official White House Photo by Pete Souza

GOVERNOR NIXON: Just that we've been out -- I've been here every day, trying to work early to late, trying to back up the local officials, what they needed, trying to coordinate the federal response, trying to make sure we green-light the necessity to move forward.

Today is a day of remembrance, as we move here to the memorial service. The loss not only of life, not only of injuries and property is significant. It's going to take a higher power to keep the strength of this community resolved to get this done. And we're confident that it will happen.

We're especially appreciative, Mr. President, you focusing your attention right here, the entire world's attention right here, to help us in ways that will make a lasting difference to this community. God bless you, my friend.

THE PRESIDENT: Thank you. And one last point I want to

President Barack Obama makes a statement to the press during his tour of neighborhoods devastated by last week's tornado in Joplin, Missouri, May 29, 2011. Official White House Photo by Samantha Appleton

make, obviously in the rebuilding process there are a lot of families who are thankful that they're okay. But they've been displaced.

It's not just their homes; many of them lost their means of transportation. The school has been destroyed. And so, for all Americans, to take a little bit of time out and make a contribution to the American Red Cross or other charitable organizations that are active here in Joplin, that can make an enormous difference.

Even if it's just $5, $10, whatever you've got to spare -- because one of the things that's striking about this -- and I felt the same way when I was down in Alabama -- this can happen to anybody.

The difference between you being in the path of this twister and a few blocks away, you being okay, is a very slim, slim margin. And so, we've all got to put together because here but for the grace of God go I. Thank you very much, everybody.

Billions In Iraq, Afghanistan, Nothing for Joplin

The following was presented as a portion of a speech to the Faith and Freedom Coalition by businessman Donald Trump June 3, 2011. Trump refers to comments made by Senate Minority Whip Eric Cantor, R-VA, that financial aid for Joplin's recovery should only come if accompanied by corresponding cuts to other budget items.

So we go into Iraq and we spend $1.5, think of this, $1.5 trillion dollars and then a certain Republican representative two nights ago, Rep. Cantor, who I like, said we don't want to give money to the tornado victims and yet in Afghanistan, we're spending $10 billion a month, but we don't want to help the people who get devastated by tornadoes, killed, maimed, injured.

We don't have money for this, but we're spending $10 billion a month in Afghanistan, we're spending billions of dollars in Iraq, where they have the second largest oil fields in the world.

"We're spending billions and billions of dollars, but we can't help people who get hit horribly by the tornadoes and then what's going to happen? We're going to leave Iraq and as sure as you're sitting there, and by the way, this is not 95 percent, this is not 99 percent, this is 100 percent. It's already being planned. Iran will take over Iraq- maybe without firing a shot because we've decapitated their army.

Randy Turner | John Hacker

God Remains With Us In Joplin

The following remembrance by Bill Pape, pastor of Peace Lutheran Church, was written just after church members held their May 29, 2011, services in the parking lot of their building, which had been destroyed in the tornado.

I have told the story many times since Sunday, a little over a week now, about Peace Lutheran Church, a congregation of the Evangelical Lutheran Church in America (ELCA) in Joplin, Mo. The church building was completely leveled by a tornado there May 22.

I have been told by a therapist-pastor that sharing that story is a way of living with guilt over what happened in Joplin and to me. As the interim pastor of Peace Lutheran, I stay in Joplin only three days a week, commuting from my home in Kansas City, Missouri.

I rode out the tornado in the motel basement. The motel was south of the storm's path. But my therapist-pastor friend was right. I was experiencing what I had only often heard about and always thought I would never do: feel guilty about being alive. I kept wondering, "Why did I decide not to go back to the church building?"

After seeing the destruction of the church, I am absolutely positive that I would not be writing this reflection today if I had gone back. I'm dealing with this guilt. But as the days continue, I find that there are many things that just need to be done. The Monday morning after the storm, as a number of us were walking through the rubble of the church building, we wondered: "Where are we going to hold worship on Sunday (May 29)?" We decided to meet in the parking lot to let the world know what the people of Joplin know: we are still a congregation.

God is and will always be with us. The service was chaotic, and it was spiritual. A number of newspapers, magazines, radio and television stations -- local and national -- came. I was wired up to six different stations. I don't even know who they all were, although I knew ABC, NBC and CNN were now part of my body. The rains had finally left, so the weather was beautiful except for the 35-mile-an-hour winds.

But most importantly, God was there. You could just feel it among the 100 people who attended worship that Sunday morning. The service itself, along with music (we had a keyboard loaned to us, hooked up to a battery, and a flutist), the prayers, the sermon and Holy Communion gave people a chance to celebrate and weep over lost homes, lost jobs, lost friends and families. God was there. Where does Peace Lutheran Church go from here?

At this moment, we still don't have a place to worship for Sunday, June 5. We know the parking lot is not going to work Sunday after Sunday. We have had two congregations offer to let us worship with them. But we have not yet had the time to sit down and decide where or how we might accept one of these generous offers. We are meeting tonight to begin the process.

We have no hymnals but have been offered some. No musical instruments, although we have been offered an organ. We have no risographs, copy machines, etc. We have lost all the past bulletins that

Pastor Bill Pape returned to Joplin on May 20, 2012 for the church's Praise in the Parking Lot service on May 20, 2012 marking the one year anniversary of the storm. Pape was interim pastor of the Peace Lutheran Church at 20th Street and Wisconsin Avenue on May 22, 2011 when the tornado destroyed the building. Heled the church in a worship service in their parking lot one week after the tornado, then was replaced by Pastor Kathy Redpath in the summer of 2011. Photo by John Hacker

would help us remember how we did certain worship services. We have lost many other things that we just took for granted would be there every Sunday morning for us.

What we do have are committed and dedicated members who are ready to do whatever is necessary for us to move forward. What we do have is the ELCA Central States Synod in Kansas City, Mo., and ELCA members and congregations from all over the United States who have pledged to help us recover. And what we do have is the power and love of our God, Jesus Christ, and the Holy Spirit. How can you not make it all happen when you have that kind of back-up team? To God be the glory! Amen.

I Will Keep the Spotlight On Joplin, Missouri

Nationally syndicated radio talk show host Rush Limbaugh made the decision to come to Joplin July 4, 2011 while conducting a contest on his program that allowed people to compete to have him bring a truckload of the brand of tea he was promoting to their communities.

While many of the people who entered the contest voted for their own communities, when Limbaugh announced Joplin as the winner, he noted that a great number of those who voted for Joplin were not from the city. He delivered the following remarks at Landreth Park.

Thank you all very much. Thank you so much. But I can't hear you. I am a little bit hard of hearing. I have got to tell you, folks, thank you so much for allowing me to be a part of this tonight.

It's a thrill and it's an honor for me to be here among all of you. It's the 4th of July. Do you know what we are celebrating today? We are celebrating a revolution. We are celebrating the most unique revolution in the history of humanity. Most revolutions install dictatorships. No, I am not going there tonight, folks. Um. Our revolution.

Rush Limbaugh

Have you ever thought. I ask myself frequently as I have gotten older. The country I have gotten more and more in awe of. I have asked myself. We are 235 years old today. There are countries, civilizations, thousands of years older than we are. In 235 years, we have become the most powerful, the most benevolent, the most productive, the richest society in the history of the world. How did this happen? And realize that even to this day, the United States today produces 25 percent of all of the world's economic output.

Twenty-fiver percent. How did it happen? My friends seriously, we are no different DNA-wise than any other human being anywhere in the planet. There is nothing special about us genetically. So what is it about us as Americans that is special?

(Crowd shouts "Freedom.")

I heard a key word from the crowd.

(Crowd shouts "freedom" again.)

The word is freedom. But I want you to stop and to think about something very seriously. This country has produced opportunity and prosperity unlike the world has ever seen before. The first reason is that our founders. This country is a miracle. Our founders believed in the power of the freedom of the individual.

Not the power of a government to dictate for people. The individual.

They knew that people using their God given gifts, their own ambitions and desires could exceed their own expectations. Could-could-could realize their dreams and in so doing could create the best and most prosperous country in the history of civilization. But there is one other element to American exceptionalism.

This is a term that when people bandied about, we say "We are better than everyone else. We are exceptional."

That is not what it means. The history of the world is oppression, tyranny, and dungeons. Not here. We are an exception to the way human beings have always lived on this planet. This is a nation blessed by God.

It is our exceptionalism. This is not a country chosen by God. We are blessed by God because of our founders. It is all in our declaration, folks. We are all endowed by our creator. There it is. With certain inalienable rights. Among them, life, liberty, and pursuit of happiness. That's all up to us. This country turns Americans loose. It turns individuals loose. And look what has happened in 235 years. Even to this day.

We run the world, but we do it benevolently. We liberate people from tyranny when there is a disaster anywhere in this world. We are the first to arrive.

Now you, those of you here from Joplin, MO, you may not know it yet, but you are the essence of what the founding fathers had in mind. You are the epitome. You are the people who make this country work. What happened here is something that you are not going to erase. You will never forget it from your memories. You are going to build back. This is going to get fixed. It is going to be rebuilt. It is going to be better than it ever was. You are going to show the rest of the country how it is done because you represent the best of what this country has to offer.

You understand the principle of hard work and self-reliance. You understand the difference between self-interest and selfishness. You are not selfish. You are all going to be working your own self-interest to you rebuild your lives.

And in the process, everybody else's lives will be rebuilt right along with yours.

American exceptionalism is simply the result of our founding father's understanding that our government is not to determine the equality of outcomes of life because we are not all the same.

Our country was determined to permit equality of opportunity and what you do with it is your business.

We are 235 years old. We are here on Independence Day. We are celebrating the greatest miracle in the history of human civilization. And as I grow older, I just turned 60. I know don't look it.

I just turned 60. I become more in awe. More appreciation for this country each and every day. I am from Missouri. I am from Southeast Missouri. I am from Cape Girardeau.

I know that people have asked me "Do you think you would have succeeded as you have." And who can deny my success?

"Do you think you would have succeeded if you were born in the northeast?"

Yeah, but not the way I have. I don't think there is any doubt the fact that I am from the heartland of this country. It allows me to be able to understand and relate to and be one of you. I have never changed.

We are all part. We are all part of a great part of this country that understands the concepts of hard work and self-reliance, respect for our neighbors, love, doing the best we can, playing by the rules, understanding none of us are perfect. We are there for each other when time requires it.

Joplin, Missouri you are defining that. You are showing the world how it is done. I am honored. I am really honored to be here. We have this new little company that we have started. We wanted to bring a truckload in. We made sure. We didn't want to intrude. We wanted to add to. We wanted to be a part of your event tonight. Show a little gratitude. Come and keep the spotlight on your city. The one thing that needs to happen. We must not forget what happened here. I know you are trying to tonight.

I understand that.

People say, "What are you going to do?"

What I am going to do is keep the spotlight on Joplin, Missouri. And what you are doing. And how you are overcoming something that was just thrown your way.

So, thank you all very much, I know you have a lot to do. You have a great band coming up. You have fireworks coming up tonight. You have a great future! You are Americans. We are all Americans. We are celebrating our 235th birthday.

And remember, there is no stopping you whatever you want to be. You define it! You can do it! The best you can! Go for it! And I'll see you later. Thank you all very much! Have a great Fourth of July!

the Schools Are the Heart and Soul of Joplin

The following remarks were presented by Gov. Jay Nixon to administrators, teachers and staff at Joplin R-8 School District opening day ceremonies August 13, 2011.

Good morning! It's great to be here for the start of a new school year in Joplin, Missouri - the toughest town on God's green earth.

Less than three months ago, I stood on this very same stage, in this very same spot, for a memorial service. That was one week after the tornado had struck. What you have accomplished in the 85 days since then, is astonishing - far beyond what anyone would have thought possible.

Except maybe one person.

When C.J. Huff told me back in May that you were going to start school on time, I sincerely wanted to believe him. Well, he's a man on a mission, and a man of his word. He says you're expecting 92 percent of the students to return this year. That's a great number -for any school district in America.

And we all know that this wouldn't have been possible without each and every one of you here this morning. Whether you are a principal or a parent, a secretary or a science teacher, a coach or a civic leader, a cheerleader or a trumpet player - your determination, sweat and optimism were crucial to this mission.

It's a testament to Joplin's commitment to its schools and its children. It reflects the strength of our partnership, which has brought every possible resource to bear to help Joplin recover and rebuild. And we're not done yet.

You are helping the healing process for this community, because going back to school means getting back to normal. So today is a milestone, and a cause for celebration.

We're celebrating the fact that life in Joplin is not a tornado emergency anymore. We're celebrating the mountains Joplin has moved - literally - in just 85 days. Mountains of what Joplin used-to-be have been moved to make way for the Joplin, soon-to-be.

It's exciting to see the "Now Hiring" signs popping up along Range Line Road. And it's great seeing all the cleared lots, just waiting for new houses and families to come back and rebuild their neighborhoods. A lot of progress has been made, and we're not stopping now. Not 'til every ounce of rubble is out of here.

This hasn't been an easy time. Some of you lost your homes and possessions. Some of you lost friends and family members. Getting ready for school has meant putting your needs and emotions second, and the needs of your students first. Because you have to be strong for them. They'll be looking to you every day - for reassurance, for guidance and for discipline.

Some days they'll need a shoulder to cry on; other days, they'll need a firm hand to keep them on track. And as we all know, students rise to meet our expectations.

Today is also a celebration of the mountains you will move in the next month, and the next year, and the next decade. Because much remains to be done in our schools. We want Joplin schools to be the pacesetter, to lead the statewide push to move all Missouri public schools into the nation's Top Ten by 2020. We need to educate our children for the challenges of global citizenship in the 21st Century; to rebuild a strong and competitive economy; and to reclaim America's place as one of the most innovative, well-educated and prosperous nations on earth.

Our goal is nothing short of excellence - and together, we will make it happen in Missouri, starting right here in Joplin.

Right now, you are the glue holding things together in the wake of so much loss. In about 19 minutes, 14,000 people were made homeless. Thousands lost their jobs; hundreds lost businesses. A hundred and sixty people lost their lives. But Joplin didn't lose its faith, or its heart, or its soul.

The schools are the heart and soul of Joplin.

In a very real way, you are the key to the future of this community: to its stability, its growth, its prosperity. When the schools come back, stronger and better than ever, more families will want to stay and raise their kids here.

Families like Leanne and Randy Ford and their two sons: Duncan, who's 15, and Grayson, who's 17. The tornado destroyed their home, all their belongings, and Randy's dental office.

In those first chaotic weeks, they did some soul-searching. They thought about moving to Carthage, or Webb City, or even to the West Coast.

In the end, they knew there's no place like home, no place like Joplin.

When families like the Fords stay and rebuild, businesses stay and rebuild. Family-owned businesses like Jim Bob's Steak and Ribs have already started. I visited the Gambles at the end of June, to let them know the state stood ready to help local business owners rebuild, so they can start rehiring folks so eager to get back to work. And while we were standing there, looking at the spot where the restaurant once stood, the mailman walked up. He handed them their mail. And then he asked them if they knew where his bass was.

The mailman had caught a big old bass and had it mounted. His wife didn't consider it home decor, so he hung it on the trophy wall at Jim Bob's. The Gambles actually found that bass in the rubble and promised it would have a place of honor as soon as they reopen.

I tell that story because it says so much about the kind of friendly, close-knit community Joplin is. The eyes of the world are on Joplin once again this week, and there's a lot of wonderful things for folks to see.

They'll see the transformation of a big, empty box into a sleek, high-tech high school. Thanks to the generosity of people all over the world, Joplin will be getting twenty-two hundred new laptops - one for every high school student.

They'll see hundreds of little kids marching down the halls at Cecil Floyd, Duquesne and Emerson Elementary, with brand new backpacks stuffed with donated school supplies.

They'll also see the best of the human spirit in action.

They'll see what people with common sense can accomplish when they put the common good before self-interest. And they'll see the unstoppable forces of tenacity and teamwork. And what an outstanding team we've got here in the Joplin schools.

Educating our children is a high calling, and those who answer the call are heroes in my book. Public schools have always been, and will always be, a beacon of hope and opportunity for all. No one is turned away.

Some children come to school hungry or homeless. Some bear the burdens of poverty and neglect. But when a child of want, and a child of wealth, walk through Joplin's schoolhouse doors, they enter as equals - both precious in the sight of their Creator.

We must work together to help each child fulfill the promise God has placed in them, and to carry out the sacred trust He has placed in us. Here in Joplin, we are a team.

The team includes everyone in this auditorium, and thousands more. It includes the legions of carpenters and masons, electricians and plumbers who worked around-the-clock to get the walls up, the lights on, and the water running in every school. It includes scores of businesses that dug deep for cash, football gear, books - whatever it took to get Joplin schools open for business, even if their own businesses were still struggling to get back on their feet.

The team includes the doctors and nurses, technicians and cooks who have pledged to stay and care for this community until a new hospital is built.

The team includes every family and every student, whether they're living in a FEMA trailer or a house upon a hill. And it includes the hundreds of churches and thousands of pilgrims still making their way to Joplin.

More than a thousand Boy Scouts from across the Midwest put in 10,000 hours in Joplin's schools a couple weeks ago: painting playground equipment, spreading mulch and picking up debris. The temperature hit one hundred and six that day.

A fifth-grade teacher drove down from Central Michigan - 850 miles each way - to help unpack and assemble furniture at the new high school, before her own school was back in session. There are hundreds more stories like these.

Disasters happen every day around the globe. So what is it about Joplin that draws people so powerfully? I'll tell you what it is.

The people of Joplin never acted like victims. Not one; not ever.

Yes, a terrible tragedy occurred, and the losses were staggering. And you stepped up with courage, determination and true grit. You started looking for opportunities to make Joplin even better.

As great as the needs were - and will be - you never took it for granted that the world owed you something. You know that the only way to get anything in life is to work hard for it. And you worked hard for it. You put your shoulders to the wheel and haven't stopped. If you did, you might collapse. So don't. School starts the day after tomorrow!

When the world sees so many positive, tangible signs of what your hard work has accomplished, it inspires confidence.

Folks can see that an hour spent in Joplin makes a difference in Joplin; that a dollar planted in Joplin, blooms in Joplin. That makes them want to be part of Joplin's comeback story. And finally, I think what draws folks to Joplin is that you have made it so easy to help you. You're organized. You're energized. And you never forget to count your blessings.

This is how all good parents raise their children and all good shepherds raise their flocks. I know you want the lessons the children learn in class this year to stay in their heads as long as possible. You want your students to use their Joplin education as a springboard to their dreams - whether they want to be doctors or dancers, engineers or entrepreneurs.

This year, you are teaching them life lessons, by the example you have set. You are showing them that from great adversity, great blessings flow. You're showing them that when you get knocked down, you pick yourself up, dust yourself off, and keep on going. You're showing them that hard work really can turn dreams into reality. And I guarantee you: those lessons will stay with them for the rest of their lives.

Not in their heads, in their hearts.

There's a lot of uncertainty in this life. We can't control the weather. We don't know when the first kid will be able to dive into the swimming pool at Cunningham Park, or when the first new house will be finished. We don't even know how many children will show up at the right schools - or the wrong schools - on Wednesday. We can't see the future, but one thing is clear.

Brick-by-brick and board-by-board, Joplin is rising: -one life, one house, one business and one school at a time.

The spirit of Joplin, Missouri can move mountains. Just watch us.

Thank you.

Moving Forward Together

The following remarks were presented by Joplin R-8 Superintendent C. J. Huff to administrators, teachers and staff during opening day ceremonies August 13, 2011.

So to explain my thoughts to you, I am going to have to go back to the Joplin High School Auditorium in August of 2008 at the same event. That was the day I had my first opportunity to meet all of you. Those of you who were there that day will remember it was more of a roast of a new guy in town as opposed to a kickoff event.

I remember a now a skit where one of our young students was asked to play yours truly dressed up in a makeshift diaper. And whoever wrote the script—Cosetta (Cox)—thought that it might be cute to make fun of the unfounding rumors that I might be slightly directionally challenged. It was all in good fun.

When it was my turn to speak to you--1,100 of you. My message was a simple one. I wanted to define our current reality. I shared what I had already learned about you and our district by talking to our patrons, our parents, and our students of the Joplin Schools. Then I left you with my one wish it went like this:

"But if I could have one wish to today to make our district even stronger for our kids it would be this: I would wish that everyone left this auditorium today feeling as though they were on the same team. Not NEA, MSTA, Independent, Republican, Democrat, classified, certified. Not elementary, not secondary, not Royal Heights, not McKinley, not North, South, or Memorial. Not teacher, not administrator, not workman.

If I could have one wish come true it would be that we could all leave here together working as one unit- one cohesive team working together toward a common goal.

Each of you is a part of the whole. I want to make this point very clear. You are all educators in Joplin School District because we all come to school every day to do good things for kids. This is my one wish in 2008.

In the early morning hours on May 24th, I lied awake on a nurse's cot in the middle school counselor's office doing what I am sure many of you were doing at that hour. Wanting to be with my family, worrying about the thousands of members of our schools that had yet to be accounted for.

(paused to collect himself as tears began to form)

Just trying to make sense of it all. Trying to figure out the answer to the question of what do we do now? What do we do? So I did what any good superintendent who believes of the possibilities of 21st Century teaching learning tools would do. I got up from my cot and walked over to the computer and goggled "disaster response for dummies."

<Applause>

No luck. So I had to go to Plan B.

I took a look at my team--all 1,106 of you. You may be surprised to learn that I have been paying attention these last three years.

What I came to realize at 2 a.m. on May 24th is that we have a phenomenally, talented team. I have watched departments work together to overcome other natural disasters: blizzards, ice, and freak windstorms.

We have even moved a few buildings: North to old South, old South to new East, Memorial to New South, old South to new North, Washington to Memorial just to name a few. It was good practice. We worked together, side by side. And accomplished those moves ahead of schedule and injury free.

I have seen teachers, grade levels, departments, and buildings pull together to accomplish amazing things around assessments, PBIS, RTI, graduation rate, PLC, ALL training, and Bright Futures.

Great things were happening to Joplin Schools right up to the afternoon of May 22nd, 2011. Which culminated in the graduation of the second largest class in last fifteen years over 450 students who had received in excess of $3.2 million in scholarships.

All of that changed at 5:41 that day. But by early in the morning of May 23rd, following the aftermath of that storm, our good works continued.

The transportation department went to work. Our bus drivers came in and turned our buses into ambulances and rescue vehicles. They saved lives.

The technology, maintenance, and payroll departments did the unthinkable. With hard hats and flashlights, they waded through water, and sifted through debris in the basement of the administration building to restore power, bring our servers online. And they made payroll on time.

So at 2 a.m. on May 24th, as I reflected on our school family and our achievements, it became clear that my one wish had been granted. We had become one cohesive team-- one cohesive team working together towards a common goal. For in the Joplin Schools, we do the work that needs to be done. When it needs to be done—for every child--every day--no matter what. Nothing stops us. (Applause)

Because of who we are, we have made people from all around the world believers. Together we have made possible what so many people believed was impossible.

Our children are coming back to us in one day, 22 hours, 35 minutes, and eight seconds. (Applause) August 17 is going to happen. I now am looking past that day and I challenge each of you to look past August 17 as well.

On this day as we begin looking forward, if I could ask one thing, one wish, I would wish for you to have faith; faith in your abilities to make a difference in the life of every child. Everyday no matter what. Faith in your colleagues, faith in your community and faith in my leadership and the leadership of your board of education to guide us towards that collective vision for the future of the power of the kids.

To illustrate this idea of faith, I would like to read to you what I shared with the class of 2011 on their graduation day:

"When you walk to the edge of all the light you have and take that first step into the darkness of the unknown. You must believe one of two things will happen. There will something solid for you to stand upon or you will be taught how to fly."

If there is one thing you have learned about me these past three years, I hope it is this:

I will never ask anyone in this room to do anything that I wouldn't do myself. Today I ask you to ask that you take that step with me into the darkness of the unknown. I ask that you grant me one more wish. I ask that you have faith in the school family that we have become.

August 17 marks not only the start of what promises to be an outstanding school year, but also an opportunity to move forward; fearlessly; courageously; boldly; and, intensely focused-- together.

I thank you in advance for the good things you are going to do for every child everyday--no matter what. Now let's get to work. God Bless.

the Tornado Can't Strip Away Our Hopes and Values

The following remarks were delivered by City Manager Mark Rohr November 22, 2011 during the six-month anniversary observance at Cunningham Park.

I don't know if everyone remembers where that term came from, the miracle of the human spirit, was the one-week moment of silence we held right over there.

At that point of time, before we observed the moment of silence, I had the opportunity to say a few words and I tried to describe what I had seen in that week since the tornado.

It was the outpouring of love and support that I had seen, and it occurred to me that the perfect term for that outpouring of support and what we had seen was the miracle of the human spirit, and it's grown exponentially since then.

We saw a lot of support that first week and it's grown over and over since that point in time. We're thankful to the guys for putting that song together, it's a wonderful song.

I want to personally thank everyone here for coming out today to be participants in this very important moment in the city's history. We gather here today to pay tribute to those that we have lost as a result of the May 22nd tornado.

We gather here today to thank the many that have come to Joplin to help our town and we gather here today to look towards Joplin's future. I asked you on May 29, right over there, to honor those that we've lost by channeling our efforts and feelings and emotions for the departed into our overall recovery efforts. You, the citizens of Joplin, have done so in ways and to extremes that I never dreamed of at that moment of silence observation held that day.

Joplin stands as a shining example to our state, our country and to the world of what the time-honored American virtues of compassion, hard work and dogged determination can accomplish.

Today we dedicate the first of 161 trees in Cunningham Park that will serve as the living embodiment of the spirits of those that we have lost. These trees will be nurtured by our tender hands, and those of our children, and our children's children, in this hallowed ground that we now sit on.

They will transcend the temporal limitations of those of us in attendance here today as a living reminder of those no longer with us. I dare say that these trees will be among the most well-kept in the state of Missouri, Mr. Governor. (long pause)

To the 113,000 registered volunteers that have come to Joplin's aid, mere words and actions expressing thanks are inadequate in acknowledging your efforts. You have reaffirmed my faith in mankind, but more importantly, you have demonstrated to the world what can be accomplished by setting aside egos, agendas and the demands of your own lives to help your fellow man. It is a lesson in life that we all need to remember, and we all need to live long after the fog and the emergency and its aftermath have lifted. You, the volunteers, are the living embodiment of the miracle of the human spirit.

In a humble attempt to express our gratitude, we have created a memorial to our northeast that reflects, in concentric circles, the four stages of our disaster recovery, along with a metal band representing the miracle of the human spirit.

At the center of the memorial, we would like to have a bronze sculpture with figures representing the volunteers and actual debris from the storm cast in bronze. This debris will serve as a touchstone for you and succeeding generations to come to return to Joplin and commemorate your experience in this very special human movement.

In the same manner that you helped Joplin, your offspring can demonstrate their participation in this unique effort by simulating their assistance in lifting the debris in the sculpture.

We are also blessed here today to dedicate two distinct water features in Cunningham Park. The use of water is intended to demonstrate the growth and regenerative properties of that element. What really do we all have but this moment in time amongst our friends and relatives, and our hopes for a bright and verdant tomorrow?

The tornado can take away that which we own, but it cannot strip away our values, beliefs and our hopes for a better future.

On that fateful day in May, nature let loose a powerful force that cleaved our city in two and rendered unspeakable damage. But in doing so, it unleashed an even-more powerful force, much stronger than the winds that day. It is a force that has drawn this town together and has united us in a common effort that will make Joplin better than it was before.

We are forever linked by our common experiences on that very uncommon day. We are brothers and sisters of the storm, we are survivors that will not be defined by the tornado, but rather the manner in which we responded to our circumstances that were thrust upon us and in that spirit.

I say to those Joplinites that have sought refuge elsewhere, you may have been welcome in your new circumstances, but those who surround you can never fully identify with what happened to you like all of us here today can. And I bid to you today, come home to Joplin, come home to Joplin, come home to Joplin.

Thank you.

In This Community, We Care for One Another

Joplin Mayor Mike Woolston delivered the following remarks November 22, 2011 at the six-month anniversary observance in Cunningham Park.

In a little less than two days, we'll gather with our loved ones to celebrate Thanksgiving. And this year, in spite of what we've been through, we have so much for which to be especially thankful for. But this evening we gather to acknowledge and memorialize the loss of 161 members of our community.

Those with whom I'm acquainted know that I'm not very good at expressing my feelings. I've always found it difficult to convey to people how I felt about them.

I think this event tonight offers that opportunity. Not only for me, but for all of us to talk about the pain we feel, to acknowledge the loss we've suffered and to continue the healing process.

Make no mistake, the tornado of May 22 affected all of us, some lost their jobs, some lost their homes, some lost their loved ones, but none of us lost hope.

Since the storm there have been many anecdotes being told about family helping family, which you might expect; friends helping friends, which is a pleasant surprise; and of some people helping complete strangers, something which, for many of us, was completely unexpected.

In the immediate aftermath of the tornado, city staff, school district personnel and the Chamber of Commerce set the tone that this is not the type of community that is going to let a little F5 tornado kick our ---. We're not going to let this storm defeat us.

And that is just as true today as it was on the first day following the storm.

The sense of community that has been realized here is, to my knowledge, unmatched anywhere in the country, and that sense of community is what brings us here tonight. Not only have we lost 161 members of our community, we've lost a part of ourselves. That loss is something from which we are not ever likely to recover.

And though we may never recover from the loss of 161 lives, we will, slowly but surely, move forward.

As we move forward to Thanksgiving, let us be thankful for the lives that were spared, for those that avoided destruction and those that volunteered to help us, and those that continue to help us recover. In this community, we care for one another.

Rebuilding Joplin Honors the Memory of Those We Lost

The following remarks were delivered by Gov. Jay Nixon November 22, 2011 at the six-month observance in Cunningham Park.

We gather together to mark a milestone in Joplin's journey of recovery and rebirth, six months to the day.

We gather to remember those who the storm has taken from us and reflect on the kindness of our fellow man and to rekindle the spirit that has carried us so far so fast. There's no doubt that the last six months have been some of the most difficult and most rewarding of our lives.

Joplin's a bit like the house of the wise man described in the gospel of Saint Matthew. The rain descended and the winds blew and beat upon that house and it fell not for it was founded upon a rock. The storm shook Joplin to the core, but its rock, its foundation of faith could not be moved.

In six short months, the tornado's wounds, some still visible, some hidden deep within us, are healing. Brick by brick and board by board, Joplin is rising from its granite foundation of faith. And everywhere we look, we see change.

Cunningham Park has been transformed into a vibrant oasis of beauty and peace, a living memorial to those who lost their lives and the tens of thousands of volunteers who opened their hearts in Joplin's hour of need.

Businesses from Range Line to Main Street have opened their doors and are hiring again. The new high school is bustling with activity. Families are starting to move out of the FEMA mobile homes and back into the community. More new houses are springing up each and every day.

In Joplin, the sun rises every day on a different place and sets every night on a better place. So much change, so much progress, none of it has happened by accident.

From those first terrible moments in the storm's wake, the rescue, recovery and rebuilding of Joplin have been a team effort. Some things are just too big to tackle alone. And the simple truth is that we are stronger together than apart. Teams who work together, win.

The astonishing progress we see all around us is a testament to the resilience and resourcefulness of this community. I've said it before and I'll say it again, Joplin is the toughest town on God's green Earth.

From day one, you have shown unwavering courage, compassion and true grit. Your fight and your faith have proved to the people of our state, our nation and the world that the spirit of Joplin is unbreakable.

From day one, help was here when and where it was needed most. In all, more than 400 first responders and law enforcement agencies from every corner of our state and many other states, dropped everything they were doing to help Joplin. We owe these brave men and women an enormous debt of gratitude.

The success of our partnership is a shining example of what we can accomplish when people of good faith rally around a common goal. I know that Joplin's journey has really barely begun, and I'm here to tell you that we'll be here with you until that job is done.

Everything has progressed faster in Joplin thanks to the tremendous outpouring of volunteers.

The numbers are staggering. At last count, 113,167 volunteers have logged 688,774 hours of service. They came from all faiths and all walks of life, from Alaska to Florida, from Sweden to Japan, each one so moved by Joplin's story that they wanted to be part of it in whatever way they could. Cajun chefs drove up from Louisiana to make gumbo for hungry volunteers. It was good, too.

Missouri cattlemen grilled steaks for firefighters and police. Church groups and chainsaw crews came from Iowa, Nebraska, Colorado and Tennessee, heavy equipment operators brought backhoes and forklifts, buckets and cranes. Crew members of the USS Missouri took a week of shore leave to help haul debris. A thousand Boy Scouts painted playground equipment in sweltering, 106-degree heat. Inner-city teens came from Philly to help sort clothing.

Americorps volunteers sifted through the rubble and found two Purple Hearts and reunited them with the heroes that had earned them. A little girl in Indiana emptied her piggy bank and sent her life savings to a church in Joplin, $52 in nickels and dimes.

Joplin is living proof that the Lord helps those who help themselves. Just moments after the storm had passed, the people of this community mobilized to help one another. And when volunteers began to arrive, you made them feel welcome; you never took their generosity for granted. And because of that, donations and volunteers are still pouring in.

Ask any one of them and they'll tell you the same thing. They got much more than they gave. Someday, it will be Joplin's turn to pay it forward and teach another community in crisis just how it's done.

The lesson of Joplin is clear, with teamwork and tenacity, the impossible is possible. By rebuilding Joplin stronger and better than ever, we will honor the memory and fulfill the legacy of those we lost.

Soon it will be too cold to pour concrete and lay sod. The line of pickups at McDonald's will be shorter, the motels not quite so full and as winter settles in, we may not build as much with bricks and mortar, but we can build something different, one to one.

They say that a lot of life goes on around the kitchen table. I think there's real truth in that, so take care of one another in the gray days of winter. Make a double batch of chili and share it with a neighbor. Take time to thank the teachers playing backstop for your kids. Remember those still grieving who may need a willing ear. Small acts of kindness make a big difference.

But before we know it, the days will grow longer, the nights warmer, flowers will bloom again, the trees we planted will send out new leaves and Joplin's forward progress will continue. So today, in the spirit of Thanksgiving, let us give thanks for one another, for the lessons and the mercy and for the lives filled with purpose and compassion and let each of us humbly seek God's blessing for the hard work that lies ahead. God Bless you Joplin forever.

Carol Stark and the Joplin Globe Served This Community Well

Seventh District Congressman Billy Long praised the work done by the Joplin Globe during the following statement placed in the May 17, 2012 Congressional Record.

MR. LONG. Mr. Speaker, I rise today to recognize Editor Carol Stark and her staff at *The Joplin Globe* for their steadfast coverage of the Joplin tornado disaster.

The Joplin community was dealt a devastating blow when it was struck by a deadly tornado on May 22, 2011.

During the entire aftermath of this catastrophe, Carol and her team did not waiver in providing up-to-date coverage to the nation. Amidst the chaos that included the destruction of half of the staff's homes and the death of a fellow staffer, *The Joplin Globe* carried on its work and managed to get the next day's newspaper out only an hour late.

Because of her unyielding dedication and leadership during these hard times, Carol is the recipient of the Local Media Association's Editor of the Year award. *The Joplin Globe* also received the Jesse Laventhol Prize for Deadline News Reporting by the American Society of News Editors on April 2, 2012 in Washington, DC for its coverage of the tornado.

Carol Stark

These are noteworthy accomplishments, and I am proud that they have been acknowledged for their efforts. Mr. Speaker, Carol Stark and her team at *The Joplin Globe* have served both our community and our Nation well amidst times of trial and it is an honor to recognize their dedication and work.

Thanks Be to This Ever-Present God

Pastor Kathy Redpath delivered the following sermon at Peace Lutheran Church, May 20, 2012, at the Praise on the Parking Lot service for the one-year anniversary of the tornado.

From the moment that funnel cloud touched down on the edge of Joplin and churned its way across the city there began a time to weep, a time to mourn.

This week, we mark the one-year anniversary of that day. I've heard people say things like "It's time to move on," or "we're not going to cry anymore over that." We're just going to move forward. Or we've had enough tears, let's just forget all that bad stuff and go back to life as it used to be. Don't we wish we could, just carry on as if it never happened.

But it did happen and because it happened, we are changed. We'll always find ourselves referring to before and after that tornado. We'll mark time by that day. We'll hear the date May 22, and into our minds will pop the Joplin tornado, and whether we like it or not, we will remember the events of that day.

Peace Lutheran Church Pastor Katharine Redpath blesses the church's new building prior to their first service in the building on Sunday, May 19, 2013. Redpath said 104 people attended the service, which happened almost exactly two years after the tornado. Photo by John Hacker

But there's something else that we can remember. We can remember that God is with us, that God never left us during that time. Through it all, God was here.

The storm was a product of the forces of the creation that God produced, and God doesn't usually step in to alter those forces. But that never means that God is absent from them.

From the moment that people began to crawl out from beneath the rubble, new stories came to light, and God was in them.

A family embracing family, neighbors helping neighbors. Strangers coming to the aid of strangers. God's presence was everywhere, in the acts of physical strength and raw courage and emotional connecting that took place up and down every street and in every neighborhood. From one side of the town to the other, God's spirit was here.

Through stories of love and care and concern, through acts of heroism and self-sacrifice and devoted energy, through donations of everything, from clothing and blankets to food and toiletries, and as a friend of mine said, enough bottled water to fill a lake. All these are evidence of God at work among you and in you. God was here.

And God remains at work a year later as volunteers continue to pour in, and donations continue to be sent and needs continue to be addressed. God is here. As recovery begins to overshadow loss, and laughing begins to replace weeping, and building up becomes more evident than the tearing down, God is here. And God promises a future, a future based on hope and peace.

In the waters of baptism and in the bread and wine of holy communion, we're reminded that God is with us for all season and for all times.

God promises peace. In that peace, we will remember what came before. But we also will be able to turn to face the future knowing that God is here, God was here, God will be here.

The congregation of Peace Lutheran Church continues to pray and discover where and how God is calling is to be engaged in mission to serve our community.

Whether we eventually rebuild right here on this site, or whether we are led to start over again in a new location, we don't know that yet. But we do know this; God will be with us wherever we are, because God never left us. Thanks be to this ever-present God.

the World Will Never Forget What You Achieved

Gov. Jay Nixon delivered the following remarks at the Joplin High School Graduation May 21, 2012 at Missouri Southern State University.

Thank you. Good evening.

Over the past year, the Joplin Schools have faced - and overcome - many daunting challenges. That was possible because of the vision, leadership and dedication of Superintendent C.J. Huff.

With unwavering courage and unshakable resolve, C.J. has led the Joplin Schools forward. He has been an inspiration to us all. I'm proud to have worked closely in partnership with C.J., and I'm even more proud to call him my friend.

Mr. President, ladies and gentlemen, please join me in thanking one of Missouri's - one of America's - finest leaders and educators, Superintendent C.J. Huff.

Exactly one year ago, I stood on this same stage to address the college graduates of Missouri Southern State University.

It was a time of optimism. A time to mark a major milestone. A time to look ahead toward the bright horizon, with full hearts and soaring hopes.

The next day changed everything.

The next day changed all of us.

But what a difference a year makes.

And tonight, we gather together - as we have so many times in the past year - to celebrate another Joplin milestone.

Joplin High School. Class of two thousand and twelve-Congratulations!

We are so proud of you.

All that you have achieved reflects your strength of character. hard work and high aspirations.

It also reflects the character of this community.

This is a community of optimists.

This is a community of believers.

This is a community of fighters.

This is a community that never gave up, never gave in and with hope in its heart and steel in its spine has come back stronger and better than ever.

From Day One, your faith and your fight have shown the world that the spirit of Joplin is unbreakable. Yes, Joplin lost many things in the storm, but never lost its heart or its soul.

Because the schools are the heart and soul of Joplin, as they are across our great state and our great nation. Our schools are a unifying force, a source of identity and pride. They are citadels of shared values, cherished hopes and common dreams. Public education is a bond not only between students and teachers. It is a bond between generations, between a community's leaders and the children who one day will carry on their unfinished work.

Joplin schools became the rallying point for this community.

With classes set to resume on August 17, there wasn't much time. But with each passing day, as the storms of spring gave way to the heat of summer, Joplin's army gained ground. And Joplin became a rallying point for a much larger community. A community of people

Surrounded by Gov. Jay Nixon and Joplin Superintendent of Schools C.J. Huff, President Barack Obama smiled as he took the stage during the Joplin High School Commencement Exercises for the Class of 2012 at the Missouri Southern State University Leggett & Platt Athletic Center on Monday, May 21, 2012, in Joplin, Missouri. President Barack Obama spoke at the event in commemoration of the one year anniversary of the city being struck by an EF-5 tornado. Photo by Shane Keyser

so inspired by your remarkable story. that they needed to be part of it.

They came by the thousands. from all faiths and all walks of life from Alaska to Florida. from Sweden to Japan.

Brick-by-brick and board-by-board ... Joplin rose from the rubble.

In Joplin, the sun rises every morning on a different place. and sets every evening on a better place.

And so, just 87 days after the most devastating tornado in our history, Joplin schools opened - just as Dr. Huff promised - on August 17.

That is the spirit of Joplin and each one of you is part of it.

This class, this school and this community will forever stand as a symbol of the best of our nation and the best in us.

Tonight, we look toward the bright horizon stretched before the Class of 2012.

With full hearts and soaring hopes, we celebrate the parents and grandparents, aunts and uncles, brothers and sisters, friends and neighbors who have loved and supported the Class of 2012 since they were in kindergarten.

The faith and values you have instilled in these young adults are the bedrock they will build their lives on. That foundation cannot be moved. We celebrate the faculty, staff and administration of Joplin High School.

In a year like no other, you put your personal needs aside and always put your students first. For your abiding compassion and devotion, we will be forever in your debt.

We celebrate each and every member of the Joplin community who gave so selflessly. worked so tirelessly, to ensure a bright future for your children.

They will carry on your unfinished work.

Most of all, we celebrate you - the Joplin High School Class of 2012.

The world will never forget what you achieved here.

You have been tried and tested, and are stronger for it, smarter, too.

You are now ready to take all that you've learned at Joplin High and use it to pursue your dreams - to become a doctor or a dancer, a soldier or a scientist, an engineer or an entrepreneur.

You have learned - perhaps too soon - that life is a fragile thread that binds us together. Never take a single moment for granted.

You know - because you have lived it - that from great adversity great blessings flow.

And with teamwork, tenacity and the grace of God, all things are possible.

Congratulations and God Bless.

Just a few days after the tornado struck, President Obama came to Joplin. As we walked the ravaged streets, he spoke with many of our families, folks who had lost everything.

He prayed with us, remembering the courage of those who gave their lives protecting others and asked the Lord to watch over us and guide us through the difficult days ahead.

The President pledged that our country would be with us and stay with us at every step as Joplin recovered and rebuilt.

And he has kept that commitment as a true partner and a true friend of Joplin.

Please join me in welcoming back to Joplin the President of the United States of America, Barack Obama.

Because You are from Joplin

President Barack Obama delivered the following remarks at the Joplin High School Graduation May 21, 2012 at Missouri Southern State University.

Thank you. (Applause.) Thank you, everybody. Please have a seat. A few people I want to acknowledge. First of all, you have an outstanding governor in Jay Nixon, and we are proud of all the work that he's done. I want to acknowledge Senator Claire McCaskill who is here. (Applause.) Representative Billy Long. (Applause.) Your mayor, Melodee Colbert Kean. (Applause.) Somebody who doesn't get a lot of attention but does amazing work all across the country, including here in Joplin, the head of FEMA, the administrator, Craig Fugate, who spent an awful lot of time here helping to rebuild. (Applause.)

Superintendent Huff. (Applause.) Principal Sachetta. (Applause.) To the faculty, the parents, the family, friends, the people of Joplin, and most of all the class of 2012. (Applause.) Congratulations on your graduation and thank you for allowing me the honor of playing a small part in this special day.

Official White House Photo

Now, the job of a commencement speaker primarily is to keep it short. Chloe, they've given me more than two minutes. (Laughter.) But the other job is to inspire. But as I look out at this class, and across this city, what's clear is that you're the source of inspiration today. To me. To this state. To this country. And to people all over the world.

Last year, the road that led you here took a turn that no one could've imagined. Just hours after the Class of 2011 walked across this stage, the most powerful tornado in six decades tore a path of devastation through Joplin that was nearly a mile wide and 13 long. In just 32 minutes, it took thousands of homes, and hundreds of businesses, and 161 of your neighbors, friends and family. It took a classmate Will Norton, who had just left this auditorium with a diploma in his hand. It took Lantz Hare, who should've received his diploma next year.

By now, I expect that most of you have probably relived those 32 minutes again and again. Where you were. What you saw. When you knew for sure that it was over. The first contact, the first phone call you had with somebody you loved, the first day that you woke up in a world that would never be the same.

And yet, the story of Joplin isn't just what happened that day. It's the story of what happened the next day. And the day after that. And all the days and weeks and months that followed. As your city manager, Mark Rohr, has said, the people here chose to define the tragedy "not by what happened to us, but by how we responded."

Class of 2012, that story is yours. It's part of you now. As others have mentioned, you've had to grow up quickly over the last year. You've learned at a younger age than most of us that we can't always predict what life has in store. No matter how we might try to avoid it, life surely can bring some heartache, and life involves struggle. And at some point, life will bring loss.

But here in Joplin, you've also learned that we have the power to grow from these experiences. We can define our lives not by what happens to us, but by how we respond. We can choose to carry on. We can choose to make a difference in the world. And in doing so, we can make true what's written in Scripture -- that "tribulation produces perseverance, and perseverance, character, and character, hope."

Of all that's come from this tragedy, let this be the central lesson that guides us, let it be the lesson that sustains you through whatever challenges lie ahead.

As you begin the next stage in your journey, wherever you're going, whatever you're doing, it's safe to say you will encounter greed and selfishness, and ignorance and cruelty, sometimes just bad luck. You'll meet people who try to build themselves up by tearing others down. You'll meet people who believe that looking after others is only for suckers.

But you're from Joplin. So you will remember, you will know, just how many people there are who see life differently; those who

President Obama mingles with Joplin High School graduates just before Monday night's commencement ceremony in Joplin. Photo by Rich Sugg

are guided by kindness and generosity and quiet service.

You'll remember that in a town of 50,000 people, nearly 50,000 more came in to help the weeks after the tornado -- perfect strangers who've never met you and didn't ask for anything in return.

One of them was Mark Carr, who drove 600 miles from Rocky Ford, Colorado with a couple of chainsaws and his three little children. One man traveled all the way from Japan, because he remembered that Americans were there for his country after last year's tsunami, and he wanted the chance, he said, "to pay it forward." There were AmeriCorps volunteers who have chosen to leave their homes and stay here in Joplin till the work is done.

And then there was the day that Mizzou's football team rolled into town with an 18-wheeler full of donated supplies. And of all places, they were assigned to help out on Kansas Avenue. (Laughter and applause.) I don't know who set that up. (Laughter.) And while they hauled away washing machines and refrigerators from the debris, they met a woman named Carol Mann, who had just lost the house she lived in for 18 years. And Carol didn't have a lot. She works part-time at McDonald's. She struggles with seizures, and she told the players that she had even lost the change purse that held her lunch money. So one of them, one of the players, went back to the house, dug through the rubble, and returned with the purse with $5 inside.

As Carol's sister said, "So much of the news that you hear is so negative. But these boys renewed my faith that there are so many good people in the world."

That's what you'll remember. Because you're from Joplin.

You will remember the half million dollar donation that came from Angelina Jolie and some up-and-coming actor named Brad Pitt. (Laughter.) But you'll also remember the $360 that was delivered by a nine-year-old boy who organized his own car wash. You'll remember the school supplies donated by your neighboring towns, but maybe you'll also remember the brand-new laptops that were sent from the United Arab Emirates -- a tiny country on the other side of the world.

When it came time for your prom, make-up artist Melissa Blayton organized an effort that collected over a 1,000 donated prom dresses, FedEx kicked in for the corsages, and Joplin's own Liz Easton, who had lost her home and her bakery in the tornado, made a hundred -- or 1,500 cupcakes for the occasion. They were good cupcakes. (Laughter.)

There are so many good people in the world. There is such a decency, a bigness of spirit, in this country of ours. And so, Class of 2012, you've got to remember that. Remember what people did here. And like that man who came all the way from Japan to Joplin, make sure in your own life that you pay it forward.

Now, just as you've learned the goodness of people, you've also learned the power of community. And you've heard from some of the other speakers how powerful that is. And as you take on the roles of co-worker and business owner -- neighbor, citizen -- you'll encounter all kinds of divisions between groups, divisions of race and religion and ideology. You'll meet people who like to disagree just for the sake of being disagreeable. (Laughter.) You'll meet people who prefer to play up their differences instead of focusing on what they have in common, where they can cooperate.

But you're from Joplin. So you will always know that it's always possible for a community to come together when it matters most. After all, a lot of you could've spent your senior year scattered throughout different schools, far from home. But Dr. Huff asked everybody to pitch in so that school started on time, right here in Joplin. He understood the power of this community, and he understood the power of place.

So these teachers worked extra hours; coaches put in extra time. That mall was turned into a classroom. The food court became a cafeteria, which maybe some of you thought was an improvement. (Laughter.) And, yes, the arrangements might have been a little noisy and a little improvised, but you hunkered down. You made it work together. You made it work together.

That's the power of community. Together, you decided that this city wasn't about to spend the next year arguing over every detail of the recovery effort. At the very first meeting, the first town meeting, every citizen was handed a Post-It note and asked to write down their goals and their hopes for Joplin's future. And more than a thousand notes covered an entire wall and became the blueprint that architects are following to this day. I'm thinking about trying this with Congress, give them some Post-It notes. (Laughter and applause.)

Together, the businesses that were destroyed in the tornado decided that they weren't about to walk away from the community that made their success possible -- even if it would've been easier, even if it would've been more profitable to go someplace else. And so today, more than half the stores that were damaged on the Range Line are up and running again. Eleven more are planning to join them. And every time a company reopens its doors, people cheer the cutting of a ribbon that bears the town's new slogan: "Remember, rejoice, and rebuild." That's community.

I've been told, Class of 2012, that before the tornado, many of you couldn't wait to leave here once high school was finally over. So Student Council President Julia Lewis -- where is Julia? She's out here somewhere. (Laughter.) She is too embarrassed to raise her hand. I'm quoting you, Julia. She said, "We never thought Joplin was anything special" -- now that's typical with teenagers. They don't think their parents are all that special either -- (laughter) -- "but seeing how we responded to something that tore our community apart has brought us together. Everyone has a lot more pride in our town." So it's no surprise, then, that many of you have decided to stick around and go to Missouri Southern or go to colleges or community colleges that aren't too far away from home.

That's the power of community. That's the power of shared effort and shared memory. Some of life's strongest bonds are the ones we forge when everything around us seems broken. And even though I expect that some of you will ultimately end up leaving Joplin, I'm pretty confident that Joplin will never leave you. The people who went through this with you, the people who you once thought of as simply neighbors or acquaintances, classmates -- the people in this auditorium tonight -- you're family now. They're your family.

And so, my deepest hope for all of you is that as you begin this new chapter in your life, you'll bring that spirit of Joplin to every place you travel, to everything you do. You can serve as a reminder that we're not meant to walk this road alone, that we're not expected to face down adversity by ourselves. We need God. We need each other. We are important to each other and we're stronger together than we are on our own.

And that's the spirit that has allowed all of you to rebuild this city, and that's the same spirit we need right now to help rebuild America. And you, Class of 2012, you're going to help lead this effort. You're the ones who will help build an economy where every child can count on a good education. (Applause.) You're the one that's going to make sure this country is a place where everybody who is willing to put in the effort can find a job that supports a family. (Applause.) You're the ones that will make sure we're a country that controls our own energy future, where we lead the world in science and technology and innovation. America only succeeds when we all pitch in and pull together, and I'm counting on you to be leaders in that effort, because you're from Joplin and you've already defied the odds.

Now, there are a lot of stories here in Joplin of unthinkable courage and resilience over the last year, but still there are some that stand out, especially on this day. And, by now, most of you know Joplin High's senior Quinton Anderson -- look, he is already looking embarrassed. Somebody is talking about him again. But, Quinton, I'm going to talk about you anyway, because in a lot of ways, Quinton's journey has been Joplin's journey.

When the tornado struck, Quinton was thrown across the street from his house. The young man who found Quinton couldn't imagine that Quinton would survive his injuries. Quinton woke up in a hospital bed three days later. And it was then that his sister Grace told him that both their parents had been lost in the storm.

So Quinton went on to face over five weeks of treatment, including emergency surgery. But he left that hospital determined to carry on, to live his life, to be there for his sister. And over the past year, he's been a football captain who cheered from the sidelines

Quinton Anderson (middle) who was nearly killed in the tornado that ravaged Joplin a year ago, blushes as President Barack Obama retells his story of recovery during commencement exercises Monday night for the graduating seniors at Joplin High School. Photo by Rich Sugg

when he couldn't play. He worked that much harder so he could be ready for baseball in the spring. He won a national scholarship as a finalist for the High School Football Rudy Awards. He plans to study molecular biology at Harding University this fall. (Applause.)

Quinton has said that his motto in life is "always take that extra step." And today, after a long and improbable journey for Quinton -- and for Joplin and for the entire class of 2012 -- that extra step is about to take you towards whatever future you hope for and whatever dreams you hold in your hearts.

Yes, you will encounter obstacles along the way. I guarantee you will face setbacks and you will face disappointments. But you're from Joplin and you're from America. And no matter how tough times get, you'll always be tougher. And no matter what life throws at you, you will be ready. You will not be defined by the difficulties you face, but by how you respond -- with grace and strength and a commitment to others.

Langston Hughes, poet, civil rights activist who knew some tough times, he was born here in Joplin. In a poem called "Youth," he wrote:

We have tomorrow
Bright before us
Like a flame.
Yesterday
A night-gone thing,
A sun-down name.
And dawn-today. Broad arc above the road we came.
We march.

To the people of Joplin and the Class of 2012, the road has been hard, and the day has been long. But we have tomorrow, so we march. We march together, and you're leading the way, because you're from Joplin. Congratulations. May God bless you. May God bless the Class of 2012. May God bless the United States of America. (Applause.)

a Building Where Students Can Chase Their Dreams (and Catch Them)

Secretary of Education Arne Duncan delivered the following remarks at the dedication of the new Joplin High School October 3, 2014.

Thank you for that kind introduction.

I visited Joplin not long after the tornado struck. And the devastation of the storm was seared throughout the community. But what you have accomplished here, together, is nothing short of amazing.

Both Joplin High School and Franklin Technology Center were destroyed. Makeshift classrooms, cafeterias, and recreational facilities had to be created within weeks. It was no surprise that after the tornado, student and staff absences went up. The number of students with chronic attendance problems climbed. Students' grades slipped. The demand for mental health services soared.

So, three years ago, it wasn't clear that this day and this celebration of progress would happen. But the commitment of parents, teachers, the remarkable leadership of Superintendent Huff, and the hard work of school staff for Joplin's children has been nothing short of extraordinary.

Teachers, counselors, coaches, and principals worked countless extra hours to help kids, while dealing with their own grief and

Secretary of Education speaks at the Joplin High School Dedication
October 3, 2014. Official White House Photo

sense of loss.

Despite the fact that Joplin's students and teachers had to move
schools a total of 18 times, 18 times, since the tornado, the on-time
graduation rate has actually risen almost ten percentage points in
Joplin since May 2011. The dropout rate has dropped more than 40
percent. That is a staggering accomplishment and it's all the more
remarkable because it was done without sacrificing rigor.

In fact, by the second semester of this school year, the number
of students at Joplin High enrolled in AP classes and dual credit
courses will have jumped by 40 percent since the fall of 2012, from
about 450 students to almost 650 students.

That progress is a tribute to the hard work, skill, and commitment
of teachers, principals, and, just as important, students themselves.

Collectively, the example you are setting is a powerful one—you
are leading the nation where we need to go. You are demonstrating
what is possible when a community pulls together to do the right

thing for children, even in the face of the most anguishing adversity.

No school, no rebuilding effort, can ever entirely end the grief or completely compensate for the devastation of May 22, 2011. Nothing can bring back the seven students and the middle school staff member lost on that terrible day, or the many members of the community who died. But you have honored their legacy by not just rebuilding the school system but by rebuilding it in a transformational way.

There is so much in life that we can't control. But we can choose how we decide to respond, over time, to tragedy and loss—and the new Joplin High and Franklin Technology Center is a wonderful testament to your unwavering commitment to progress.

You refused to let the tornado be the end of the story of Joplin. Parents, teachers, and school staff chose to pursue a bigger dream of what education should look like in Joplin. And the new Joplin High School and Franklin Technology Center establishes a great educational model for the rest of the world of a relevant and rigorous 21st century education.

Instead of just taking the insurance money to rebuild Joplin High as it was, you chose to reach higher.

Under the leadership of C.J. Huff, an advisory group of staff, students, parents, community members, business leaders, and education experts convened "dream" sessions to design the new school. You've created a visionary model that integrates, instead of separates, college and career preparation.

The career and technology focus of Franklin Technology Center is now integrated into the core college-prep curriculum of Joplin High School—and Franklin Technology Center itself is now part of Joplin High School.

Today, you have 34 career pathways for students to explore. But you also offer a dozen honors classes, a dozen AP classes, and 43 dual credit classes in both the core curriculum and the career and technical side. What a great way to reduce the cost of college for Joplin's hard-working families! What a great way to help every student find their passion and develop their unique strengths and talents!

Think about the opportunities you have created–a Joplin High student will now be able to graduate with both their diploma and an associate degree when they are only 18 years old.

The partnerships you have created with Missouri Southern State University and Crowder College are the kind of partnerships we need to duplicate at many more high schools across the nation.

The personalized learning experiences cultivated at JHS are our future. JHS's creation of blended learning classes, the switch to eBooks and mobile devices is helping to both transform and modernize JHS. You are striving to cultivate the 21st century skills that our students need to be college and career-ready–to be lifelong learners and problem solvers.

I am a huge fan of Superintendent Huff and I love what he says: "We're not teaching kids to chase their dreams; we're teaching them to catch them."

I look forward to watching both Joplin High School's evolution in this beautiful new building and the revolution of learning opportunities you are leading. I look forward to every student here catching their dreams. And I thank you for your collective courage, commitment, and creativity.

Thanks for believing in each other, caring about each other, and giving your community's children the combination of love, support, opportunity, and high expectations every child needs. The example you set for all of us in how you to live your values is powerful–and means more to me personally than you can ever know. Thank you!

You Are the Heart and Soul of America

Vice President Joe Biden was featured speaker at dedication ceremonies for the new Joplin High School October 3, 2014 and delivered the following remarks.

Governor, Mr. Mayor, students of Joplin High School, I tell you what, I'm happy to be here with you. You know, I was asked, I was asked why am I coming up to Joplin.

I'm here for the same reason I was at the Boston Marathon finish line. I'm here for the same reason that I was down at the Gulf oil spill. I'm here for the same reason (there are only places) where Americans have been truly, fundamentally devastated, had everything … that they thought their community was about questioned, ripped away from them.

I'm here because you are, you are the heart and soul of America.

You are an example of who we are as a people. We never bend, we never break, we never stop, and we always rebuild. That's why I'm here with you today. Governor, you govern a remarkable state made up of people with true grit and determination.

Every tornado venue I've visited you with afterwards, I've been amazed, amazed by the determination, the commitment, the

Official White House Photo

resilience, the unspeakable sense that nothing can defeat us. But most of all, by the way you all think in terms of community, not in terms of self.

Mr. Mayor, what a city. The rest of the region and here devastated by one of nature's most awesome furies: an E5 tornado. It's hard to imagine unless you've seen it, and impossible for those of us who have not been through it, to fully understand the devastation, physically, mentally, the devastation, the chaos that follows in its path.

Five hundred businesses destroyed, tens of thousands of cars tossed around like leaves in a fall windstorm. 161,000 (actually 161) brothers, sisters, mothers, fathers, sons, daughters, grandparents, lost.

C.J. asked for a moment of silence. I can tell you from experience – I lost a child and lost a wife – that every time there is an anniversary or a celebration that follows that, it brings it all back for the families of those who lost their loved ones.

Today is both celebration, but also, it's a vivid, vivid reminder of what happened. But as a community, you never stood down. You endured; you overcame. And look at you now.

You know, the book of Isaiah, chapter 40 verse 31, says "They that trust in the Lord shall renew their strength. They shall mount up

Vice President Joe Biden speaks at the Joplin High School dedication ceremony in Joplin, Missouri, October 3, 2014. Official White House Photo by David Lienemann

with eagle's wings. They that trust in the Lord." That's what you've done. You've come back, stronger than before, with a commitment and a passion to envision a new Joplin. A magnificent school, laptops instead of textbooks, hands-on learning opportunities like building robots, using, using your increase in high school graduation rate, increasing by nearly 10 percent, just since the tornado.

People moving into Joplin instead of out of Joplin, businesses moving back, and others coming. Why? Why would anyone who never lived in Joplin before decide to move to Joplin after what they saw?

What they saw is the character of this community. Anyone in America would want to be part of a community that has hung together like this one, that had the grit that this one has shown.

The whole nation, the whole world saw those terrible, terrible images in the aftermath of the tornado. But there's one image,

Official White House Photo

and I only saw it on television, there's one image that stood out in my mind. You didn't have televisions to watch it at the time. But it was the backyard of a devastated home, and a tree that was barely standing. Hanging in the branch of that tree was an America flag.

Alongside that flag was a quote from scripture. Jeremiah, chapter 29 verse 11. Alongside that flag it said, "For I know the plans I have for you, declares the lord, plans to prosper you and not harm you. Plans to give you hope and a future."

They say our toil on this earth is a toil of our own hands. You, the people of Joplin, you reestablished hope not just for the people of Joplin but for tens of thousands of people around the world who go through similar things like you went through and wonder, "How can we make it?"

And they remember this town in the middle of America, in Missouri, named Joplin, with no central, special asset other than its people, has rebuilt.

You underestimate the hope all of you give Americans who have been broken and devastated by crises in their lives, and you've guaranteed the future – we're looking at the future – you've guaranteed that it will remain your priority.

And folks, you've given an entirely new meaning to the word

"homecoming." An entirely new meaning. Because you know the word "homecoming" didn't start when public education came about at the end of the 1800s to mark those days when the football teams would play, etc.

"Homecoming" means, to me, a return and a reaffirmation of the basic values that make it all worthwhile with such incredible people, like all of you here.

"Homecoming" is about faith. It's about hope, it's about charity, it's about simply caring. That's what homecoming's about. And that's what I see here today.

And C.J., my guess is tonight, the Eagles of Joplin High School are going to fly very, very high.

And my guess is Arne Duncan, who was an academic all-America basketball player and played professional basketball, he says he wants to go see the gym. I was a runner-up at a state scoring championship in my home state in football; I want to go see the football field. And I'm just glad I'm not going to be on the other side of the line from the Joplin Eagles tonight when you take the field.

You know, the day will come, the day will come when students walking through these doors will have no personal memory of May 22, 2011. But they will always know the values of the community that raised them, the ballfields they played on, and the legacy of recovery.

And for the rest of them, and for the rest of their lives, they'll be able to say, "We are Joplin. We are Joplin strong." God bless you all, and may God protect our troops. C.J., I've got a V.P. hat for you in exchange.

a Day of Celebration and a Promise fulfilled

Gov. Jay Nixon delivered remarks at the opening ceremony for the new Mercy Hospital Joplin March 7, 2015. The new hospital replaced the former St. John's Regional Medical Center, which was destroyed by the deadly tornado that struck Joplin on May 22, 2011.

Thank you, Sister Roch. You and all of the Sisters of Mercy continue to be a source of inspiration for this community, and we thank you for all you do. It is indeed an honor, and a delight, to again be with the Mercy Joplin family as we celebrate, and dedicate, this center of healing.

Healing is a powerful blessing… and it always has been. The New Testament Gospels relate more than 25 miracles where Jesus healed those broken in body, mind or spirit.

Healing hands have long been a vital part of Joplin's character, and of its strength as a community, especially at Mercy. That has been true at each location where the staff of Mercy Joplin has served the people of this region, and it will be true here.

In those dark days of late May 2011, who could have dared dream – or even hope – of a day like today? Many of you here today, that's who…And especially, people like Lynn Britton… Gary Pulsipher… and Mike McCurry.

The dream to rebuild was helped immensely by friends from around the world – especially, as Lynn mentioned, through the generosity of the United Arab Emirates. We thank them for all they have done.

From the very beginning, Mercy was committed to rebuilding. But four years ago, on the morning of May 23, that was a task that seemed daunting… beyond comprehension. Yet you dreamed of this day – and then worked tirelessly to make it a reality.

Because you have the faith to know that "for God, all things are possible." When the hospital that stood for more than 40 years on McClelland Boulevard took a direct hit, it was the quick and courageous actions of staff that saved so many lives that day.

And in those dark days, you were not alone in responding to Joplin's many needs. Men and women from more than 400 law enforcement departments and emergency response agencies in Missouri and nearby states.

State resources from every department, including the National Guard, the Highway Patrol, SEMA, Health, Social Services and Revenue …and a flood of volunteers from across the country and around the world who would eventually number over 175,000, putting in more than 1.1 million hours of service.

And there has been a seemingly inexhaustible wellspring of resolve to energize the professionals of Mercy in continuing to meet the healthcare needs of this community.

You provided that care in a field hospital and emergency room established and set up by the Missouri National Guard, the Missouri Disaster Medical Team, SEMA and the Department of Health and Senior Services.

You provided that care in the modular hospital that took the place of the field hospital and in the temporary hospital that would

be the gateway to this magnificent place of healing and care.

With a vision that saw beyond the rubble to what could and would be... with a hope for a future that would see this city and this hospital rise again... and with a faith in each other and in God, you were equal to the challenge.

From May 22, 2011, through today, I have been proud to stand with the people of Joplin through the long process of rebuilding. I joined you at the Mercy prayer service for Joplin, just three weeks after the tornado. This extended family came together to pray, to remember, to mourn and, yes, to rejoice.

The themes that day touched on the tradition of service to Joplin, and the surrounding area... and how those traditions would continue in the face of an unprecedented challenge. Then there was the need to continue investing in human capital.

We all knew that for Mercy Joplin to succeed – and indeed, for Joplin's economy to come back – the pool of talented and highly skilled health care professionals who are the backbone of this region needed to be retained.

Mercy was committed to keeping this family together – and followed through on that commitment with the support that your staff needed... and that has helped make this blessed day a reality.

In the face of a challenge faced by few other communities in this nation, Joplin has persevered.

Together, you have made this city – and this hospital – symbols of courage and strength – and a symbol of the toughest people on God's green earth.

Today, we say another prayer of thanks… and ask for the continued blessings that have made Joplin a beacon of hope and inspiration for the whole world. My congratulations to the Mercy Joplin family… and to the people of Joplin… on this day of celebration – and on a promise fulfilled. Thank you, and God bless.

Randy Turner | John Hacker

in Memoriam

This monument, in Cunningham Park in Joplin, lists the 161 people killed in the May 22, 2011, tornado. Inside this monument is a time capsule containing a variety of items related to the storm and the people who died in it. Photo by John Hacker

José Alvarez

From JoplinMemorial.com

José O. Alvarez received his bachelor's degree in Anthropology from Colombia National University, master's degree in Hispanic Studies, and Ph.D. in Latin American Literature, from Florida International University.

He is a former editor of one of the first literary online magazine of University of Miami, and a pioneer in the application of educational online platforms like Blackboard, WebCT, and Moodle. He has a genuine enthusiasm and commitment on finding solutions to the digital divide problem.

He was a Professor with the Department of Modern Languages in Miami-Dade College, University of Miami, and Florida International University. Dr. Alvarez published five volumes of his students' short stories. Hirda

Dr. Alvarez was the author of the books "Cuentos de vida, muerte y resurrección," "Vivir del cuento", "Poética de la brevedad en Borges." He also created the first online Anthology of Latin American Literature, the first online Short Stories Anthology, movie reviews, literary reviews, and has participated in several short stories, anthologies, International Book Fairs, and lectures in several countries.

He was nominated "Faculty of the Year 1999" by the Federation of Black Greeks, the Interfraternity Council, and the Panhellenic Association, and Excellence in Teaching Award Instructional Advancement Center 2000 "of the University of Miami. José Alvarez was an assistant professor at Missouri Southern State University. He was teaching Spanish.

Bill and Sarah Anderson

From Ozark Funeral Home

William Austin "Bill" Anderson, 53, and Sarah Lee Anderson, 46, of Joplin, Missouri departed this life suddenly on Sunday evening, May 22, 2011 at their home from injuries sustained in the devastating Joplin tornado.

Sarah entered this life on

April 20, 1965 in Phoenix, Arizona to the late Todd Dean and Lois (Faux) Sherfy. At age 13, she moved with her family to Branson, Missouri. She graduated from Branson High School in 1983 and has resided in Joplin since 1985. She was employed by the Joplin School District as a secretary at South Middle School for the last 10 years.

On August 25, 1985 in Branson, Missouri, Bill and Sarah were united in marriage and to this union two children were born. They both enjoyed reading and were members of the 26th and Connecticut Church of Christ in Joplin.

They are survived by their two children, Grace and Quinton Anderson, both of the home. Bill is also survived by four siblings, Stuart Anderson, Neosho, Missouri, David Anderson, Tipton, Iowa, Marti Crawford, Granby, Missouri and Kay Anderson of Neosho, Missouri. Additional survivors for Sarah include her three siblings, John Sherfy of the state of Iowa, Sharon Sherfy of Branson, Missouri and Ellen Wiebelhaus of Waddell, Arizona. They are also survived by several nieces

and nephews, as well as a host of other family and friends.

Grace Aquino

From Mason-Woodard Mortuary

Grace Layug Aquino, age 46, Joplin, passed away May 22, 2011, at Harmony Heights Baptist Church, from injuries sustained in the catastrophic tornado. Grace was born on October 6, 1964 in Florida Blanca, Philippines, the daughter of Armando Layug and the late Elena Punzalan.

She has been a resident of Joplin for the past nine years. She received a bachelor's degree in business. She was a member of Harmony Heights Baptist Church. She worked as a hostess for China Pantry.

Grace unselfishly covered and protected her 12-year-old son during the tornado and as a result his life was spared.

She married Rizaldy Aquino on March 19, 1986 in the

Philippines, and he survives. Additional survivors include her son, Malachi Jacob Aquino, of the home; two daughters, Divine Aquino, Overland Park, Ks., and Eunice Aquino, Manhattan, Ks.; three brothers, Cezar Layug, of Germany, Noel Layug, and Eugene Layug, both of the Philippines.; her twin sister, Divina Villaruel, of the Philippines; sister-in-law Liberty Nicholas and husband Bernard and family, Seattle, Washington; great-aunts, Corazon Mangio and Ofelia Oakley; cousins, Leni and Robert Welch, Joplin, Lerma and Orlando Castaneda, Sacramento, Ca., Jerwin and Eden Signa, Joplin, Miranda and Perry Taylor, Joplin, Noreen Jean Smith, Ann & Robert Mathews, Joplin; many nieces and nephews; and her grand puppies, Orly and Klassy.

Cyrus Ash

From Parker Mortuary

Cyrus Edward (Ed) Ash, 87, Joplin, passed away May 22, 2011 from injuries sustained in a tornado. Born September 21, 1923 in Monett, Mo., he was a U.S. Navy veteran of World War II. He worked in the receiving department of Lozier, from the first day the company located in Joplin and remained over 20 years before retiring.

He was an avid Joplin Flea Market dealer and remained active there until age 83. He was a member of College Heights Christian Church. He was an expert billiards player and went fishing at Shoal Creek every evening to unwind.

On December 28, 1941, he married Emma Landreth in Joplin. She survives.

Additional survivors include two daughters, Brenda Nichols and husband Danny, Carl Junction, Shirley Elliott and husband Norman, New Hampshire; four grandchildren, Chad, Matt, Lisa and J.W.; five great-grandchildren; two sisters, Maxine Latimer and Evelyn Leedy, both of Wichita, Kansas.

Ed was preceded in death by two daughters, Helen Judith Ash in 1973, and Patricia Sue Miller in 2010 and three brothers, all of Kansas.

Robert Baker

From Mason-Woodard Mortuary

Robert W. Baker, 54, Joplin, Mo. passed away Sunday, May 22, 2011 from injuries sustained in the Joplin tornado.

Robert was born April 23, 1957 in Michigan to John W. and Katherine (Sanders) Baker. Robert worked at the parts desk for Cycle Connection.

He married Sandra Woodworth; she survives. Additional survivors include two daughters, Trisha Cortinas, Emperial, Missouri, and Brandy Baker, state of Texas; two brothers, Kenneth Baker, Alto, New Mexico and Daryl Baker, Joplin; two sisters, Shirley Randleman Joplin and Jackie Beatty, Blue Springs, Missouri and four grandchildren.

Bruce Baillie

From Midland Cremation Society

Bruce W. Baillie, 56, Joplin, was a page designer for the Joplin Globe and the father of a college-age daughter. Born in British Columbia, he worked for several Canadian newspapers before buying a bed-and-breakfast in Sedona, Ariz. He later worked for the Benton County (Arkansas) Daily Record and joined the Globe in 2003.

Bob Bateson

From Parker Mortuary

Robert E. "Rob" Bateson, Jr., 47, Joplin, has gone to be with His Lord and Savior as the result of injuries received in a tornado May 22, 2011. Born April 14, 1964 in Bowling Green, Ohio, he lived in Joplin most of his lifetime.

A licensed master plumber, he was both self-employed and did some contract work. For the past eight months he was employed at Modine. A Christian, he was a member of Central Christian Center in Joplin.

Survivors include his parents, Karen and Dan Mitchell, Joplin, Robert E. Bateson, Sr. and Donna, Sevierville, Tennessee.; three children, Eric Davis, Jamie Peavler and Mariah Bateson;

three grandchildren; five sisters, Diane Wood and Jack of Miami, Oklahoma, Teresa Worley, Neosho, Kim Kemp and Brian, Columbus, Ohio; Julie Hudson, Pineville, Ruth Buxton and Curt, Webb City; two brothers, James T. Brummett and Eric A. Brummett; paternal grandmother, Thelma Mitchell, Webb City; many aunts, uncles, cousins and extended family. Robert was loved by his family and he loved his family. Rob, we'll miss your beautiful smiling face and twinkling eyes. We love you so very much.

Dorthey Bell

Dorthey C. Bell, 88 Joplin, died as a result of injuries received in a tornado May 22, 2011.

She married Edwin M. Bell April 28, 1950, in Joplin. He died Sept. 29, 2000.

Survivors include three sons, David Bell, Joplin; Dan Bell, Plano, TX; Steve Bell, Fairfax, Virginia and five grandchildren: Frances Bell, Florida; Ian Bell, Houston, Texas; Lauren Bell, Plano, Texas; and Christopher

and Leanne Bell, Fairfax, Virginia.

Born October 15, 1922 in Barnsdall, Oklahoma, she had lived in Joplin for many years. She attended Joplin Junior College and graduated Pittsburg State Teachers College. Later she taught school and was a farm woman. She was a member of the Order of the Eastern Star and Central City Christian Church, and she was active in the Joplin Y. She enjoyed travel, birdwatching, reading, genealogy and water walking.

Barbara Boyd

Barbara Boyd, 87, Joplin, was a resident of Greenbrier Nursing Home. She worked more than 20 years in the burn unit of a Veterans Administration hospital in Richmond, Virginia. She liked to crochet and belonged to First Baptist Church in Joplin. She is survived by two sons, two daughters and six grandchildren.

Lathe Bradfield

From Parker Mortuary

Lathe Edward Bradfield passed away at St. John's Hospital Sunday, May 22, 2011 during the tornado that swept through Joplin. He was a husband, father, grandfather, brother, and uncle.

He was an avid fisherman in his youth and enjoyed all animals and children. He was Uncle Lathe to many and a stranger to none. He would often greet people with "hello friend," and he meant it.

He was proud of his service in the Army during WWII and was honorably discharged December 25, 1946. He was injured in the war and received a Purple Heart. He was a lifelong member of the Teamsters Union and Disabled American Veterans. He also belonged to the American Legion and the Veterans of Foreign War organizations.

He married Florence Ellen Clifton in Columbus, Kansas June 24, 1947. Lathe and Florence raised a family of two daughters and one son. They lived, laughed and cried together for 64 years. Lathe worked as an auto mechanic.

He spent a number of years at the old 408 Cab Company, at Joplin Police Station and retired from Fleming Foods where he worked as head mechanic for a number of years. He was sent to Indiana to a technical institute on repairing Thermo King units. He worked every day of his life and then would often come home and work on cars or build on his home. He would offer his help to anyone that needed it.

He is survived by his wife, Florence Ellen Clifton Bradfield; his daughter, Sharon Bradfield of the home, his daughter, Karen Bradfield and Ernie Blackford; his son Steven Bradfield and daughter-in-law Shelley Bradfield; his two grandchildren, Samantha Bradfield and Cole Bradfield, who were his pride and joy. We miss him dearly every day.

Lathe was the oldest of six brothers and two sisters. All survive him; Leroy and Earleen Bradfield, James and Joanne Burtrum, Bill and Mary Burtrum, Ray and Jolene Burtrum, Rex Burtrum, John Burtrum, Etta Morgan and Mary and Pauly Hembree, Cecil Weber, a cousin who grew up with Lathe and was always regarded as a brother.

Burnice Bresee

From Mason-Woodard Mortuary

Burnice M. Bresee, 91, Joplin, passed away Wednesday, June 22, 2011, at McCune-Brooks Hospital from complications with her health following the Joplin tornado. She was born Dec. 14, 1919, in Springfield, Missouri to Edward A. and Mary (Everly) Alexander.

She was a homemaker. Burnice was a member of Christ Point Church in Joplin.

She married Willie Bresee Sr. May 24, 1940, in Joplin. He preceded her in death November 10, 1980.

Survivors include two sons, Willie Bresee Jr. and wife, Pat, Carl Junction, and Homer Bresee and wife, Merna, Rockford, Illinois.; four daughters, Norma Jean Enlow and husband, Charles, Joplin, Bernice

Irene Smith and husband, Gene, Joplin, Margie Goetz and husband, Stanley, Joplin, and Teresa Thomas and husband, Ben, of Seneca; one daughter-in-law, Marsha Bresee, Joplin; one sister, Wilma Bresee, Galena, Kansas; 18 grandchildren; 34 great-grandchildren; and four great-great-grandchildren.

She was preceded in death by one son, Bobby Bresee April 24, 1991; one daughter, Donna Bresee Jan. 25, 1998; four brothers; and two grandchildren.

Ramonda Bridgeford

From Campbell-Biddlecome Funeral Home

Ramona Bridgeford passed into eternal rest May 22, 2011 from injuries sustained in the tornado that devastated Joplin.

Ramona Mae Pevey was born February 18, 1934 in Waseca, Minnesota, the daughter of Alvin Hugh and Violet Lilly (Sanders) Pevey. Ramona formerly taught pre-school in California.

She married Leo Russell Bridgeford Sr., July 15, 1952 in Yuma, Arizona and he preceded her in death in December 2001. Additional survivors include two sons, Leo Bridgeford Jr., Seneca and Robert "Bob" Bridgeford, Gravette, Arkansas, one daughter Brenda Lindo, Seneca.

Leo Brown

From Parker Mortuary

Leo E. Brown, 86, Joplin, passed away Sunday May 22, 2011 as a result of the tornado that hit St. John's Regional Medical Center, where he was a patient.

Leo was born April 18, 1925, the son of the late Wilburn and Mary Kingston Brown. He was a graduate of Joplin Senior High School Class of 1943. He graduated from Manhattan Bible College and Phillips University at Enid, Oklahoma. He was a retired clergyman of the Christian Church (Disciples of Christ) having served churches in Kansas, Missouri, Arkansas and Illinois.

He is survived by his wife, Katherine of the home; one daughter, Debra Brown, Spring-field, one son, Earl Brown of Fort Scott, Kansas; two grandchildren, Travis and Dixie; one great-grandchild, William; two brothers, Paul E. Brown, Joplin, Ivan Merle Brown of Eugene, Oregon. In addition to his parents, he was preceded in death by a brother, Carl W. Brown.

Hugh Buttram

From Lucas Funeral Home, Hurst, Texas

Hugh Odell Buttram, age 85, passed away Sunday, May 22, 2011, after sustaining injuries from the tornado that struck Joplin, Missouri that evening.

Odell, as he was known by friends and family, was born February 2, 1926 in Hillsboro, Texas. He was a veteran of WWII, serving as a chaplain's assistant in the Armed Forces.

He subsequently received his bachelor's degree from Southwestern Assemblies of God University in Waxahachie, Texas and did graduate studies in marketing at Texas Wesleyan College and Texas Christian University. He was an accomplished salesman receiving many significant sales awards over more than 50 years in the insurance business.

Odell was a devout Christian and lifelong member of Bethel Temple Assembly of God in Fort Worth, Texas. His family and friends are comforted that he is with the Lord and they will see him again. He was much loved and will be sorely missed.

Survivors: He is survived by his wife, Evelyn Buttram, Joplin; three daughters, Judith Rylee and husband Tom Rylee, Springfield; Lisa Satterfield and her husband Rev. Dallas Satterfield, Baxter Springs, Kansas, and Cathy Buttram, Joplin; two siblings, James Buttram and wife Lou, Sims Buttram and wife Fern; five grandchildren, Meredith Cunningham, Shannon Hachman, and husband, Chris Hachman, Paige Giarrizzo, and husband, David Glarrizzo, Morgan Satterfield, and Drew Satterfield; and one great-grandson, Dominic Ochoa.

Tami Campbell

From Hafemeister Funeral Home, Watertown, Wisconsin.

Tami L. Campbell, 28,

Joplin, passed away Sunday, May 22, 2011, as the result of the tornado in Joplin. An Angel on Earth is now an Angel in Heaven.

The former Tami Leigh Moldenhauer was born August 30, 1982, in Watertown, the daughter of Randy and Kathryn (Schuett) Moldenhauer. She attended St. Mark's Lutheran Grade School in Watertown and was a 2001 graduate of the Watertown High School.

On June 24, 2006, Tami married Steven Campbell at St. Mark's Evangelical Lutheran Church in Watertown. She was employed at Walmart in Joplin as a photo lab technician. Tami was a member of St. Mark's Evangelical Lutheran Church. She enjoyed photography and loved tigers. She was an avid collector of tigers in various arrays.

Tami is survived by her husband, Steven, Joplin; two sons, Jordan C. Campbell and Caleb J. Campbell, Joplin; a stepson, Austin M. Powell, Joplin; her parents, Randy and Kathryn Moldenhauer, Watertown; her maternal grandmother, Esther Schuett, Watertown; a sister, Angela (her son Christian) Moldenhauer, Watertown; a brother Jeffrey Moldenhauer, Watertown; her mother-in-law, Diana Mc-Lallen, Joplin; her father-in-law, Jim Campbell, Kansas City, as well as other relatives and friends.

Tami was preceded in death by her maternal grandfather, Clarence Schuett and her paternal grandparents, Roy and Elaine Moldenhauer.

Moises Carmona and Arriyinnah Carmona

Moises Carmona, 42, and his daughter, Arriyinnah, 8, of Joplin, passed away Sunday, May 22, 2011 from injuries sustained in the Joplin tornado.

Moises was born September 12, 1969 in Jabonera, Chihuahua, Mexico. He had lived in Joplin since 2001, moving here from Albuquerque, New Mexico. Moises was a heavy equipment operator with Anchor Stone Company east of Joplin. He was a member of Joplin Full Gospel Church.

Moises married Kari Patten October 24, 2001 in Albuquerque and she survives.

Additional survivors include two daughters, Marisela, and Adriennah "Audrey" Carmona, both of the home, three brothers, Abraham, Juan, and Pachino Carmona, all of Mexico, and six sisters, Manuela, Kick, Teo, Lula, Genoveva, and Lorenza, all of Mexico.

Arriyinnah Savannah Carmona, 8, was born March 1, 2003. She was a second-grade student at Royal Heights Elementary School.

In addition to her mother, and sisters, Arriy is survived by her maternal grandfather, Joe Garcia Padilla, Elgin Ill., and her maternal grandmother, Carol Ballard, Joplin.

Shante Caton

From Lakin Funeral Home

Shante Marie Caton, age 10, Joplin died Sunday, May 22, 2011 as a result of the tornado.

Shante Caton was born in Joplin April 05, 2001. She was the daughter of Moses Caton and Crystal Whitely. She was a student at Eastmorland School in Joplin.

Surviving are her mother and dad one sister: Keana Caton of the home, her maternal grandparents Felix and Aleta Whitely, Baxter Springs, Kansas and paternal grandmother Mary Caton, Joplin.

Trentan Caton

From Lakin Funeral Home

Trentan Maurice Steven Caton, 6, Joplin, died Monday, May 23, 2011 at Children's Mercy Hospital in Kansas City, as a result of the tornado.

Trentan Caton was born in Joplin on March 23, 2005. He was the son of Moses Caton and Crystal Whitely. He was a student at Eastmorland School in Joplin.

Surviving are his mother and dad, one sister: Keana Caton of the home, his maternal grandparents Felix and Aleta Whitely of Baxter Springs, Kansas and his paternal grandmother Mary Caton, Joplin.

Raymond Chew

From Campbell-Biddlecome Funeral Home

Rev. Raymond LeRoy Chew Sr., 66, Joplin, passed into eternal rest Sunday, May 22, 2011 from injuries sustained in the tornado that devastated Joplin.

Rev. Raymond LeRoy Chew Sr. was born July 30, 1944 in Joplin, the son of Rev. Dudley R. and Rev. Lenora D. (Riley) Chew.

Raymond was a veteran of the United States Marine Corps serving his country from 1961 to 1965. Raymond was a heavy equipment operator and had worked for Webb City Special Road District. He was a member of the Cornerstone Church in Carterville.

Raymond married Helen (Cauthren) Chew August 25, 1962 in Reno, Nevada and she survives.

Additional survivors include two sons, Raymond Chew II and wife Carla, Neosho, and Kevin Chew and wife Crystal, Seneca; one daughter Carol Gibby, Carterville, his mother Rev. Lenora D. Chew, Galena,

Kansas; five brothers, Dudley Ray Chew Jr., Sacramento, California, Pastor Frank R. Chew, Galena, Kansas, Terry U. Chew, state of Alabama, Jeff Chew, Joplin, and John Chew, Shelby, Montana; five sisters, Barbara Mullin, Joplin; Susan Edward, Sacramento, California; M. Jean Evans, Carterville; Kendra Seymore, Shelby, Montana; and Samantha Hawkins, Carl Junction; 11 grandchildren and two great-grandchildren.

Raymond was preceded in death by his father Rev. Dudley Ray Chew Sr.; two brothers, Sammy L. Chew and Danny M. Chew and one sister, Donna Kay Bedsual.

Clyde Coleman

From Derfelt Funeral Home

Clyde Coleman, 72, passed away May 22nd, 2011 in the tornado that struck Joplin.

He was born July 16, 1938 in Paxton, Nebraska to Austin D and Wanda Coleman. He graduated from Hayes County High in Hayes Center, NE in 1956 and married Carolene Yonker on Nov 4, 1956 in Dickens, NE. She survives at the home in Galena, Kansas.

He went to work for the Singer Sewing Machine Company in McCook, Nebraska. He managed stores in several locations in Nebraska before being transferred to Wichita, Kansas. In 1975 he made his final move to this area.

He owned and operated Coleman's Upholstery Shop in Galena, retiring in 2005. He then worked for USD 499 as a bus monitor and most recently a crossing guard. He was of the Catholic Faith. He was a member of the Joplin Elks Lodge #501 for 35 years.

He served on the Galena, Kansas City Council from 1997-1999. He also served on the Planning and Zoning Committee.

Among his interests were reading, gardening, storytelling, and community service.

He is also survived by two daughters, Melanie Tyler and Kelly (husband, Jack) Evans, Joplin, MO; five grandchildren, Heath Richmond Tyler (wife, January), Sarah Coleman Burkybile (husband, Travis), Megan Paris Tyler, Jared

Kingston Worley (wife, Kim) of Gardner, Kansas, Clinton Bradwell Worley (wife, Brittany) Joplin; six great-grandchildren, Quinton Tyler, Madison Worley, Phil Dean Burkybile, Joplin, MacKenly, Ellie and Molly Worley, Gardner, Kansas; four great-step-grandchildren, Alisa, Christian, and Jerrid Ireland, and Landon Tyler, Joplin; one brother, Vance Coleman, State of Nebraska, one sister Phillis Phyllips and son, Dwight, State of Nebraska. In addition to his parents, he was preceded in death by one brother, Walter Coleman.

Carolane Collins

From Grand Lake Funeral Home

Carolane Jean Collin, 62, Eagle Rock, passed away Sunday, May 22, 2011 in Joplin. Carolane was born May 9, 1949 in Southwest City to Otis and Mildred (Easter) Burton.

Carolane graduated from Jay High School in Jay, Oklahoma. She married Thomas in Joplin December 6, 1991. Carolane worked as a quality control technician for Eagle Picher Tech-

nologies for over 30 years before retiring. She was a member of Lighthouse Pentecostal Church in Eagle Rock, MO. She enjoyed cooking, spending time with family, canning, and antiques.

Carolane is survived by her husband Thomas of the home, one daughter; Shiela Merriman, Joplin, one stepson Nathan Collins, Fort Scott, Kansas, one brother; Don Burton of Disney, Oklahoma, one sister; Marilyn Turner, Greenwood, Arkansas, five grandchildren; Tasia Lyn Simms, Matthew Tyler Merriman, Tiffani Nicole Renne Merriman, Trevor Brandon Merriman, Jamie Collins, one great-grandchild; Aliviah Simms, several nieces, nephews, other relatives and friends.

Carolane is preceded in death by her parents and one brother James Burton.

Lois Comfort

From Simpson Funeral Home

Lois Ada Comfort, 66, Webb City, went to be with the Lord May 22, 2011, as a result of the tornado.

Lois was born January 27,

1945 in Doniphan, MO to Orison and Virda (Jones) McKinney. Lois was a member of the Emmanuel Baptist Church of Webb City.

She married Larry Comfort May 24, 1991, at Bethel Baptist Church, her death coming two days before their 20th anniversary. Larry survives of the home.

She worked for Eagle Picher for 30 years. Lois enjoyed working in the yard with her flowers and loved fishing at the river. Her first love was for God, her family and her many friends. Her greatest concern was to help those who could not help themselves. She was a wonderful wife, mother, grandmother, sister and friend who will be greatly missed.

Lois is also survived by her sons, Acel Little, Carl Junction; and Clayton Bickford and wife Shannon, Joplin; daughter, Katrina Feller and husband Rick, Joplin; brothers, Henry McKinney, Mansol McKinney and wife Kathy and Lindle McKinney; sisters, Thelma Brown, Norma Dudley and husband Bob, Faye Darnell and husband Cecil all of Doniphan; and five grandchildren, Kandice Gilliam, Kaycia Feller, Lauren Miller, Jordan Miller and Chad Miller.

Keenan Conger

From Simpson Funeral Home

Keenan Krise Conger, 49, Carl Junction, went to be with the Lord May 22, 2011, as a result of the tornado that went through Joplin.

Keenan was born April 12, 1962 in Detroit, Michigan to Aaron and Barbara (Tucker) Conger. During the tornado, Keenan gave his life trying to protect his dogs, Sissy and Sally, who survived the storm. Sissy and Sally gave Keenan great happiness. Also surviving the storm was Keenan's fiancée, Cheryl Hardin, whom he loved with all of his heart.

Keenan enjoyed working at a boat yard in his youth in Wyandotte, Michigan, but was disabled in his later years. Keenan worked all his life to gain knowledge and was always working on motorbikes and found happiness in his grandchildren and pets.

Keenan cared deeply for his family and friends.

Keenan is survived by his

mother, Barbara Jean Porter; one brother, Bryan Conger; and two sisters. Brenda Cook married to Michael Cook; niece, Brandy Morton, her two children, Jayzier and Jozelyn all of Carl Junction. Lisa Prater married to Jeff Prater; niece, Megan Prater her daughter Annalyse; and nephew, Jordan Prater all of Bronaugh.

Keenan's relatives in Michigan include Phil and Teresa Conger, and cousins Paul, Rebecca, Steve, and Jenny whom he thought the world of on his father's side and a great aunt and uncle on his mother's side, Lavaughn and Lloyd Wethington.

Keenan's adopted grandchildren, who gave Keenan the most happiness includes Jocelyn, Jacie, Brayden and their families, Cheryl's son and daughter and by Cheryl's mother who meant the world to him.

Keenan accepted Christ as his savior and was a member of the Pentecostal Church of God. No services will be held.

Jimmie Cookerly

James V. "Jim" Cookerly, 49, Joplin, passed away Tuesday, June 14, 2011 at 2:52 a.m. at Joplin Health and Rehabilitation Center.

Jim was born July 6, 1961 in Carthage, son of the late Eugene James Cookerly and Elizabeth Fay Smith Cookerly. He graduated from Grove High School and attended NEO Vo-Tech for two years before beginning his career in HVAC. He worked in Grove, Oklahoma City and Joplin. He lived in McDonald County for 12 years before moving to Joplin a year ago.

Survivors include his wife, MaryBeth Wilson Cookerly whom he married January 24, 1998 in Joplin; daughter, Amanda Werner and husband Brian, Seneca; son, Carl Cookerly, Grove, Oklahoma; grandchildren, Jake, Kyle, and Brianna; sisters, Karyl Conard and husband Robert, Wichita, Kansas, Debi Sparks, Joplin, April Parcher and husband Roy, Oklahoma City, Oklahoma, and Denise Kramme and husband Dave of Carl Junction, several nieces and nephews.

Edmon Cooper

Edmon A. Cooper, 88, Joplin, passed away Thursday, June 16, 2011 at Freeman West Hospital.

Edmon was born June 15, 1923 in Wheaton, son of the late Charles and May Cooper. He worked as a mechanic with farm equipment for Massey Ferguson from 1950 until 1988. He then went to work at Vollenweider Orchid in Exeter, which he did until retiring in 1995.

He was an Army veteran of World War II with the 96th Division.

In addition to his parents, he was preceded in death by his wife, Anna Cooper who died January 4, 2011, a daughter, Pamela Sue Murdock, brothers, Olen Cooper and Cecil Cooper, sisters, Elsie Phillips, Bernice Charles, and Blanche Lee.

Survivors include a son, Karl Cooper, Overland Park, Kansas; daughter, Vicky Weaver, Clarksville, Tennessee; 11 grandchildren, 13 great-grandchildren, one great-great-grandchild; and a brother, Glenn Cooper, Purdy.

Vickie Cooper

Vicki L. Cooper, 58, Joplin, passed away Sunday May 22, 2011 during the Joplin tornado.

Alice Cope

From Clark Funeral Home

Alice L. Hudson Cope, 79, Neosho, died Sunday, June 19, 2011, at Freeman West Hospital, after being in the Joplin tornado May 22.

She was born June 2, 1932, in Cassville. Alice had been a member of College Heights Christian Church in Joplin. She attended First Christian Church in Neosho before her long illness and was active in its annual apple pie baking program. She loved Bible studies and participated in them at the church and at Graystone Apartments.

She was a fine seamstress and made beautifully appliquéd dresses, drapes and stylish clothes. She was a voracious reader and enjoyed books on history and religion.

She graduated from Cassville High School and attended Southwest Missouri State College, now Missouri State University. After her children were grown, she returned to Springfield and completed a degree in archeology. She worked on an archeological dig in Israel.

Alice is survived by her son, Steve, and wife, Heather, Bella Vista, Arkansas; her daughter, Judy Cope and husband, Gary Rasmussen, Woodcliff, New Jersey; a sister, Dorothy Knoblauch, Joplin; three grandchildren, Stephanie Cope, Cara Cope and Alex Rasmussen; two great-grandchildren, Gavin James and Maddie Rose; and the father of her children, Stan Cope, and wife, Linda, Anacortes, Washington.

Teddy Copher

From Parker Mortuary

Teddy Ray Copher, 71, Joplin, passed away from injuries sustained in a tornado May 22, 2011. He has been a Joplin resident all of his life.

Born June 24, 1939 in Joplin,

he was the son of the late Benny F. Copher and Margaret Smith Copher. He was an employee of TAMKO as a Paper Hydro-Pulper Operator for 31 years.

He is survived by one son, Richard Ray Copher and his wife Angela, Joplin; one brother, Larry Copher and his wife Carolyn, Webb City; and six grandchildren.

In addition to his parents, he was preceded in death by one brother, Benny Copher Jr.

Malisa Crossley

From Mason-Woodard Mortuary

Malisa Ann Crossley, 36, Joplin, passed away May 22, 2011, at her home, from injuries sustained in the catastrophic tornado.

Malisa was born on January 29, 1975 in Joplin, the daughter of Jerald Lynn Gaston and Peggy "White" Gettler. She has been a lifelong resident of Joplin. She worked as a customer service representative at Walmart on 7th Street the past two years.

Malisa unselfishly covered and protected her nine-year-old

son during the tornado, and as a result, his life was spared. Malisa was a loving mother. She was always smiling, and she loved to make others smile. She will be greatly missed by all of her family and friends.

She is survived by her mother Peggy Gettler, Grand Prairie, Texas; two sons, Thomas Crossley, Joplin; and Chaz Martin of the home, one daughter, Shantal Crossley, Joplin; her fiancé Bryce Coleman; two sisters, Jennifer Gordon and husband David, Irving, Texas; Lindy Molina and husband Freddy, Irving, Texas; and her best friend, Angela Baumann, who was a sister to her.

She is also survived by aunts and uncles and nieces and nephews. Her father Jerald Lynn Gaston preceded her in death in 1980.

Adam Darnaby

From Derfelt Funeral Home

Adam Dewane Darnaby, 27, passed away Sunday May 22, 2011, as a result of the tornado that ravaged Joplin. Adam was born May 26, 1983 in Joplin. His parents were Ronald Wayne and Janet (Moore) Darnaby.

He was raised in the Galena-Riverton Kansas area. He earned an Associate of Electrical Technology Degree at Pittsburg State University. He was employed as an electrician at Jasper Products. He attended the House of Prayer and the Riverton Friends Church. He enjoyed fast cars, including racing and going 4-wheeling. He loved doing anything outdoors especially cat fishing.

Adam was married to Kaitlin E Kissee September 6, 2008 in Riverton, Kansas. She survives.

Additional survivors include his parents Ron and Janet Darnaby, Riverton; his maternal "little Grandma", Galena, Kansas; two brothers Matthew Darnaby, Joplin; and Aaron Darnaby, Riverton, Kansas; his father and mother-in-law, Ron and Debbie Kissee, Galena, Kansas; nieces and nephews, Kaleigh, Sanna, Dayton, Kaden, Madison, Courtney, Dawson, Bryson, Brandt, Victoria, Madelynn, Kaylee, and Carter.

He was preceded in death by grandparents, Carl R. Moore, Herbert and Hazel Darnaby.

Patricia Dawson

From joplinmemorial.com

Patricia Dawson, age 74, Joplin, died Sunday, May 22, 2011, at her home as a result of the tornado in Joplin.

Mrs. Dawson was born in Kansas City on January 01, 1937. She was the daughter of Jack and Ruth (McKinley) Sears. She was a homemaker and a member of the Temple Baptist Church in Springfield.

She is survived by three sons, Jerry Dawson, Springfield; John Dawson, Pierce City; and James Dawson, Saint Louis; three sisters, Jane Wimer, Joplin; Nancy Fox, Springfield; and Barbara Taylor, Buffalo; her former husband, Donald Dawson, Springfield; three grandchildren and one great-grandchild.

Michael Dennins

From Parker Mortuary

Michael Wayne Dennis, 52, Galena, Kansas passed away 11:57 p.m. Friday, June 10, 2011, at St. John's Medical Center, Springfield, from complications due to injuries he sustained in the May 22 Joplin tornado, while he was a patient at St. John's Regional Medical Center in Joplin.

Born April 7, 1959, in Parsons, Kansas, he was the son of the late Wayne Dennis and Shirley Cowley Dennis and lived in the Columbus and Baxter Springs, Kansas areas most of his lifetime. Michael was disabled. He graduated from Columbus Vo-Tech studying graphic arts. He enjoyed comic books and Play Station.

He was a resident of Emerald Pointe Health and Rehab Centre, Galena.

Survivors include his uncles and cousins.

Nancy Douthitt

From Parker Mortuary

Nancy Elizabeth Douthitt, 94, Joplin, passed away from injuries sustained in a tornado May 22, 2011.

Born September 5, 1916 in Newtonia, she was the daughter of the late Virgil A. Thornberry and Ether Virginia Hendrickson. She is a member of St. Paul's United Methodist Church, St. John's Prestige, and a former member of Surviving Spouses.

She married Curtis W. Douthitt January 12, 1937 and together they owned and operated Douthitt Grocery Store on 202 N. Gray, Joplin from 1947-1987.

Curtis preceded her in death November 27, 1989.

She is survived by one son, Robert (Bob) Douthitt and his wife Jean, Tulsa, Oklahoma; one brother, Walter Thornberry, Mount Vernon; one sister, Lenore Rhodes, Homer, Illinois, three grandchildren, James, Thomas and Cathleen; and eight great-grandchildren.

In addition to her parents, she is preceded in death by her daughter Barbara Douthitt and one sister, Genevieve Robinson.

Ellen Doyle

From Mason-Woodard Mortuary

Ellen Jeanette Doyle, 75, Joplin, passed away May 22, 2011, at her home, from injuries sustained in the catastrophic tornado.
Ellen was born November 29, 1935 in Carthage, the daughter of the late Raymond C. Kennell and the late Mary Virginia Pace. She has been a resident of the Joplin area her entire life.

She was a homemaker. She was a member of College Heights Christian Church. Ellen loved spending time with her family, going out to eat and shopping. She will be greatly missed by her family and friends.

She married Keith Doyle February 19, 1954 at Forest Park Baptist Church in Joplin. He preceded her in death September 2003.

Survivors include two daughters Susan Brookshire and special friend Mario Morales; Terri Branham and her husband Randy; five grandchildren, Jason Brookshire and his wife Stephanie, Lesa Branham, Stephanie Sargent and husband Jeremy, Jamie Fort and husband Matt;

five great-grandchildren, Tamerik Branham, Jasmine Sargent, Lilly Sargent, Kaden Fort and Jarett Fort; three brothers Jerry Kennell, Grandview; Bud Kennell and wife Dolly, Harbor City, California; and Johnnie Kennell, Kansas City; two sisters, Carol Davidson and husband Galen, Pittsburg, Kansas; and Linda Salman's husband Randy, Topeka, Kansas.

She was preceded in death by granddaughter Kelly Jo Brookshire, son-in-law John Brookshire and a sister, Nola Randall.

Faith Dunn

From Mason-Woodard Mortuary

Faith Constance Dunn, 71, Joplin, passed away Sunday, May 22, 2011 at her home from injuries sustained in the Joplin tornado.

Faith was born November 27, 1939 in St. Thomas, Ontario, Canada. She moved to Joplin in 1964 when she enrolled at Ozark Bible College. Following her graduation from Ozark, she was employed by the college for almost 20 years in the music department. She also taught sign language.

Faith was a member of the Park Plaza Christian Church. She was an avid horseman for many years and rode with two separate drill teams.

Faith is survived by one sister, Judy Dunn, rural Jasper, two nieces, and a nephew.

She was preceded in death by her parents, Fred and Connie Dunn, and a brother, Steve Dunn.

Amonda Eastwood

From Paul Thomas Funeral Home

Amonda Sue (Brashear) Eastwood, 49, Joplin, formerly of Miami and Commerce, passed away May 22, 2011 in Joplin.

Amonda was born May 6, 1962 in Miami, Oklahoma to Leonard and Sondra Sue (Turner) Brashear. She graduated from Commerce High School and received her registered nurse's license from Northeastern Oklahoma A&M College. She was employed by Freeman Hospital for several years.

Family: father: Leonard

Brashear, Picher, Oklahoma; mother Sondra and the late Clifford Crabtree of Miami, OK, one son Robert Hiram Eastwood, Miami, Oklahoma; two daughters Amber Helen Eastwood, Commerce, Oklahoma; Erika Lynn (Eastwood) Mitchell, Galveston, Texas; three sisters Leona Ceclie (Brashear) Lewin, Tulsa, Oklahoma; Peggy Sue (Brashear) Schneoring, Corpus Christi, Texas; Bonnie Ann (Brashear) Hall, Miami, Oklahoma; three grandchildren and a host of nieces and nephews.

church in Saginaw. He was a member of Saginaw Baptist Church.

He married Velta Hamilton May 13, 1993. She survives.

Additional survivors include five sons, Richard, Jr., Nick, Tony, Chris and Gary; five grandchildren; one great-grandchild; three stepchildren, Jason Hamilton, Brad Hamilton and Amber Sachetta; six stepgrandchildren; one sister, Betty De-Graffenried, Memphis; brothers, Donny and Ronnie, Memphis.

Richard Elmore

From Parker Mortuary

Richard Allen Elmore went to be with his Heavenly Father May 22, 2011. He was a resident of Greenbrier Health Center and was killed in the tornado.

Born in Memphis, Tennessee November 4, 1940, he was a foreman at Cole Steel in Tulsa for many years, retiring in 2003.

Richard loved to go to his

Randy England

Randy Edward England, 34, Granby, beloved husband, father, brother, uncle and friend, was born October 25, 1976 in Joplin. Randy left this world May 22, 2011, one of the many victims of Joplin's devastating tornado.

Randy leaves behind his wife of 14 years, Kelly Ann Barwick England; and their two wonderful children, Julie England, 12 and Justin England, 8.

Randy was preceded in death by his parents, Raymond and Ruby Greer England.

Additional survivors include three brothers, Ricky England, Joplin, Danny and Gary England, Neosho; three sisters, Tereasa Neal, Seneca, Sherry Johnson and Carolyn Jarmin, Neosho; as well as many nieces, nephews, great-nieces and great-nephews.

Born and raised in the Newton County area, Randy attended Seneca High School.

After leaving school, he joined the workforce, working for several years as a diesel mechanic and for the past seven years at La-Z-Boy in Neosho.

Randy loved his family, friends and life with a great passion. When he wasn't attending his children's activities or off on an adventure traveling or trading, he could be found at home with a group of family and friends barbecuing, watching movies, playing Rock Band, or reading.

Randy always had time to help a child or a friend. He was always working on a project vehicle, including a panel van that had belonged to his father.

Randy was a great organizer to plan fun trips with his family and friends, most recently, a deep-sea fishing trip to Texas. Randy had also taken up the game of golf and loved it. Randy will be missed by many.

Mark Farmer

Mark Farmer, 56, Joplin, worked at Joplin Workshops for more than 20 years. His friends and roommates, Rick Fox and Tripp Miller, died with him in the storm.

Ida Finley

From Clark Funeral Home

Ida M. Finley, 88, Joplin, passed away May 22, 2011, as a result of the tornado. Mrs. Finley was born May 12, 1923, in Logan County, West Virginia. She had worked at Continental Can in the warehouse for 31 years and moved to Missouri in July 2009 from Proctorville, Ohio.

She married James A. Finley July 8, 1942, at Huntington, West Virginia and he preceded her in death August 16, 2006.

She is survived by a son, Clinton R. Finley, Joplin; three grandchildren, Christina R. Finley, Arin Lunsford and Joseph Holtzman; a great-grandchild; and two great-great-grandchildren; a brother, William Raymond Cartmill, Hurricane, West Virginia and a sister, Nellie Mae Hutchison, Huntington, West Virginia.

In addition to her husband and parents, she is preceded in death by a son, Jan Robin Finley; a daughter, Marsha Kay Finley; and grandson, George Arthur Osborne.

Betty Jo Fisher

From Parker Mortuary

 Betty Jo Burrington Fisher, 86, Joplin, died Sunday, May 22, 2011, a casualty of the tornado. Born January 27, 1925 in Lubbock, Texas, she was the daughter of the late Henry McKinley and Mamie Hunter McKinley.

She was a long-time resident of Joplin where she owned and operated Betty's Beauty Shop for many years in her home. She was a member of Blendville Christian Church, a 4-H leader, a volunteer at St. John's and enjoyed square-dancing.

Her first husband, Roy Burrington, preceded her in death November 14, 1975. Her second husband, Jim Fisher, preceded her in death December 12, 2010.

Survivors include three daughters, Shelia Tasker and her husband, Larry, Janet Townsend, and her husband, Damond, and Sandy Blizzard, and her husband, Ron, all of Joplin; a son, Tom Fisher and wife, Patty, state of South Carolina; a brother, Harvey McKinley, Post Falls, Idaho; four sisters, Jean Love, Sahuarita, Arizona; June Boelsen, Spring, Texas; Jo Murdock, Lubbock, Texas; and Henrietta Wilson, Olvsmar, Florida; eight grandchildren; 10 great-grandchildren; and one great-great-grandchild.

She was preceded in death by a son, Jim Fisher Jr., and a brother, Payton McKinney.

Robert Fitzgerald

From Clark Funeral Home

Robert S. Fitzgerald died at his home in Joplin as a result of the tornado Sunday, May 22, 2011.

He was born in Granby to Shelby and Freda (Nunn) Fitzgerald December 22, 1949. Robert graduated from Granby High School and attended Crowder College and MSSU.

He was an army veteran from the Vietnam era and an avid St. Louis Cardinals fan. His great nephew, Tyler, plays ball for the local Food-4-Less team in Joplin, and his great-uncle, Robert was his greatest fan. He also loved putting on the "Santa Hat" and being Santa Claus to the nieces and nephews. He was a collector of music and loved to read. If you made friends with Robert, he was your friend for life.

Robert was a 10-year cancer survivor. He had battled cancer two different times.

Robert is survived by his wife of 33 years, Marti (Cupps) Fitzgerald.

Additional survivors include his brother, Max Fitzgerald and wife, Kathy, Lowell, Arkansas; sisters, Donna Fullerton, Granby; and Lana Deadmond, Branson; and Gordon and wife, Mary Jo Cupps, Branson; nephews Nathan Deadmond and wife, Michelle, Kansas City, Chad Deadmond, Branson, Brian Fitzgerald and wife, Christal, Sinking Springs, Pennsylvania; J. R. Fullerton, Granby; and Will Cupps (Amanda Daugherty), Joplin; nieces Melissa Cupps, Branson; and Serena Tinsley and husband, Kendon, Joplin; great-nephews Tyler Tinsley, Fletcher Cupps and Luke Fitzgerald; and great-niece Addison Cupps.

Robert worked over 27 years for Walmart and called them his "Walmart Family." Through his cancer battles, the "family" was wonderful and gave great support.

He was preceded in death by his parents; nephew, Ben Cupps; and his mother-in-law, Phyllis Cupps Darby.

Rick Fox

From Parker Mortuary

Rick E. Fox, 56, Joplin, passed away May 22, 2011 as a result of injuries sustained in the tornado.

Born October 20, 1954 in Joplin, he graduated from Eagle-Picher Training Center in 1975. Since 1976, he has worked at Joplin Workshops.

A Christian, he was a member of Calvary Baptist Church and attended First Presbyterian Church. Rick enjoyed all sports and was an accomplished bowler, participating on the Special Olympics Bowling Team.

His father, Richard E. Fox, preceded him in death on March 2, 2005.

Survivors include his mother, Doris Fox, Joplin; his aunt, Joann Chapman, Grand Prairie, Texas; cousins, Gary and Teri Selby, Steve and Kim Selby, John and Larrah Selby, Matt and Mike Selby, Jason and Chad Chapman, Aimee and Eric Golden, Stevie Selby, Mike and Paul Chapman, Dane and Katie Bell; very special friends Shirley and Sheila, with whom he enjoyed many vacations which enriched Rick's life. Numerous friends will also miss him.

Marsha Ann Frost

Marsha Ann Frost, 32, Joplin, passed away May 22, 2011 in the Joplin tornado. She was born July 10, 1978 at Lincoln, Arkansas, the daughter of Larry Joe and Ruth Esther Young Winkler. She was a member of the Christian Life Center in Joplin.

Marsha had been employed by Walmart in Bentonville, Arkansas.

Survivors include one son, Gabriel Frost of the home; her parents Larry Joe and R. Esther Winkler, Neosho; one brother Larry Winkler II, Neosho; two sisters, Bethany Burton, Joplin; and Christina Winkler, Neosho; paternal grandparents Willis and JoAnne Winkler, Lincoln, Arkansas; a maternal grandmother, Nedra Ann Johnson, Lincoln, Arkansas.

Sebastian Charles Frost

Sebastian Charles Frost, 10, Joplin, passed away May 22, 2011 in the Joplin tornado. He was born March 4, 2001 at Boonville, Missouri, the son of Marsha Winkler Frost.

Sebastian was a member of the Christian Life Center in Joplin. Survivors include one brother, Gabriel Frost of the home; his father Roger Frost, Moberly; maternal grandparents Larry and Esther Winkler, Neosho; maternal great-grandparents Willis and JoAnne Winkler, Lincoln, Arkansas; maternal great great-grandmother Nedra Ann Johnson, Lincoln, Arkansas; paternal grandparents Gary and Connie Whitehurse, Boonville; and paternal great-grandmother Betty Wells, Boonville.

Charles Gaudsmith

From Knell Mortuary

Charles Kenneth Gaudsmith, 21, Carthage, passed away Sunday, May 22, 2011 from injuries sustained in the Joplin tornado.

Charles Kenneth Gaudsmith was born November 7, 1989 in Glendale, California, the son of Russell Gaudsmith and Melisa Renee (Johnson) Gaudsmith. Charles and his family moved to Carthage in 1998 from California. He was a graduate of Carthage Senior High School Class of 2009 and was a cook for the south Carthage McDonald's. He was active in Carthage Tiger sports serving as a team member of the Carthage Tiger Football squad and the Tiger Wrestling team.

Survivors include a sister, Lashawnda (Travis) Cavener, Joplin; his father, Russell (Donna) Gaudsmith, Hemet, California; girlfriend Candice Harper, Carthage; three nieces, Cheyeanne, Kaylee, Alyssa; his grandparents, Jim (Jane) Johnson, Carthage, Mike Libby, Sunland, California.

Charles was preceded in death by his mother, Melisa, who was with him in the Joplin tornado; a brother, Jody Gaudsmith, and a grandmother, Gaye Libby.

Billie Joe Gideon

From Mason-Woodard Mortuary

Billie Jo Gideon, 77, Joplin, went to be with the Lord early Monday, May 23, 2011 at Freeman Hospital from injuries suffered during the devastating tornado that hit Joplin May 22, 2011.

Billie was born December 10, 1933 in Goodman, the daughter of Conley and Bernice (Johnson) Bellamy. She worked for 32 years at the Pentecostal Church of God Headquarters and Messenger Publishing. Billie attended the First Pentecostal Church of God which is now known as Crown of Life Chapel.

She was previously married to Delbert Gideon, he survives.

Additional survivors include three sons, Dennis Gideon, Sr. and his wife Blinda, Joplin; Danny Gideon and his wife Candy, Joplin; Scott Gideon and his wife Linda, Joplin, two daughters, Debbie Patterson, Joplin; and Betty Benfield and her husband Dale, Sr., Joplin; 10 brothers and sisters, 12 grandchildren and 24 great-grandchildren.

Billie was preceded in death by one sister.

Robert Griffin

From Greenlawn Funeral Home

Robert M. Griffin, 61, Battlefield, passed away Friday, June 3, 2011 in Christian Health Care West as a result of injuries from the Joplin tornado.

He is survived by his wife Kay Griffin, Battlefield; daughter, Bobbi Magana, Kansas City; three stepchildren, Lynn Scott, Kansas City; Todd Lisenby, Springfield; and Stacye Perriman and husband Tim, Willard; four grandchildren; and a host of family and friends.

Paul Haddock

Paul E. "Gene" Haddock, Sr., 62, Joplin, lost his life during the tragic tornado that hit Joplin May 22, 2011.

Paul was born at home in Spring City December 13, 1948, the son of Fred and Ada (Mullen) Haddock. He worked as a lead and set up welder for Lozier for 25 years before medical issues forced him to retire. Paul was well known around the Joplin YMCA where he had many friends.

He married Karen Hartje February 10, 1974 in Webb City. She survives.

Additional survivors include his three sons, Richard Haddock, Indianapolis, Indiana; David Haddock and fiancé Monica, Indianapolis and Christopher Haddock and his wife Faith, Neosho; three brothers, Bill Haddock, Kansas City; Bob Haddock, Kansas City; and Fred Haddock, Jr. Picher, Oklahoma., two grandchildren, Ayden Haddock and Collin Haddock.

Paul was preceded in death by his parents and by his son, Paul "Tiny" Haddock, Jr.

Johnna Hale

From the Kansas City Star

Johnna Hale, 49, a FAG Bearing Company employee, passed away Sunday, May 22, 2011.

Johnna Hale, 49, was calm as the tornado sirens blared over Joplin on May 22. She phoned her daughter; gathered water; corralled her dog, a border collie mix named Star; and hunkered down in the bathtub. But then Star bolted. Out the door, into the storm. And Hale followed.

She called her daughter again in those final, fraught moments — crying, frantic, scrambling — but the connection severed as the tornado bore down on the city. She was found nine days later in the rubble of a building where she took shelter. Star was there with her, in her arms.

Leola Hardin

From Mason-Woodard Mortuary

Leola L. (McCune) Hardin, 76, Joplin, passed away Wednesday, June 8, 2011, at Freeman Hospital from injuries sustained from the Joplin tornado. She was born December 23, 1934, in Jasper to Howard L. and Vera (Ferguson) McCune.

Leola worked as a packer for Bagcraft retiring in 2000. She made lap blankets for Hospice Compassus.

She married Kenneth Hardin February 14, 1954, in Jasper.

He preceded her in death in December 1999.

Survivors include two sons, Thomas Hardin, Joplin, and Kenneth Hardin and wife, Lori, Poplar Bluff; one daughter, Kathy Robbins and husband, Wade, Carthage, Indiana; one brother, Jim McCune, Carthage; one sister, Helen Carter, Carthage; and three grandchildren.

She was preceded in death by her parents and one brother, Roy McCune.

Lantz Hare

From Parker Mortuary

Caley Lantz Hare, 16, Joplin, passed away from injuries sustained in the Joplin tornado May 22, 2011.

Born September 2, 1994 in Coffeyville, Kansas, he had lived in Joplin since 1998 and attended Joplin Public Schools. He was a straight A student of the junior class of Joplin High School.

Lantz was an avid BMX bike rider. He rode at Autumn Ramp Park and loved spending time at The Bridge. He participated in Bible studies, was a member of the BMX Team, and volunteered at both The Bridge and Autumn Ramp Park. He attended Christ's Church of Joplin with fellow Bridge staff, members and close friends.

Survivors include his mother, Michelle Hare, Joplin; his father and stepmother, Walter Mike and Shannon Hare, Broken Arrow, Oklahoma; his brother, Matthew Hare, Joplin; two sisters Shaylee Albee, Colorado Springs, Colorado; Jayln Mattson, Broken Arrow; paternal grandmother, CeCelia Hare, Coffeyville, Kansas; maternal grandmother, Mary Lou Green, Coffeyville; maternal grandfather, Ron Green, Edna, Kansas; maternal grandmother, Teresa West, Findley, Ohio; several aunts, uncles and countless friends.

Lantz was preceded in death by paternal grandfather Caley Kitch and maternal grandfather Fritz Jehle.

Dorothy Hartman

From Knell Mortuary

Dorothy Viola Hartman

Dorothy Viola Hartman, 91, Joplin, passed away Sunday, May 22, 2011 from injuries sustained in the Joplin tornado.

Dorothy Viola Gray was born May 5, 1920 in Union, the daughter of John Thomas Gray, Sr. and Matilda Clementine (Clark) Gray. She was a homemaker and for many years was a member of the Bethel Methodist Church, south of Carthage. She married George Washington Hartman on October 4, 1940 in Carthage.

Survivors include her husband of 70 years, G.W. Hartman, Joplin; a daughter, Sherrie Hartman Messer, Oronogo; Jerry Messer, Oronogo; two granddaughters, Angela (Jeff) Howrey, Carthage; grandchildren, Tyler and Isabelle Howrey; Michelle (Kevin) Houser, granddaughter, Tiffanie (Matt) White; three great-great-grandchildren, Mathew, Ryan and Kenzye White; one brother, John T. (Neva) Gray, Carthage; two sisters, Lorraine Wright, Jeffer-

son City; and Marian (Chester) Hildgedick, Ashland; and several nieces and nephews.

She was preceded in death by her parents; three brothers, Earl, Curtis and Clifford; and two sisters, Laura and Pauline.

Dee Ann Hayward

From Derfelt Funeral Home

Dee Ann Hayward, 47, 302 E 22nd St, died Sunday evening, May 22, 2011 in the tornado that struck Joplin. Dee Ann was born August 25, 1963 in Glendora, California. Her parents were James Robert and Bernice Lee (Brady) Kelly. She had lived in Galena since 1977.

She graduated from Galena High School in 1981. She had worked the past four years for Hallmark Card Company maintaining card displays in area Walmart Stores. She was a member of Riverton Friends Church, Riverton, Kansas, where she had been a Sunday school teacher.

She had traveled to Brazil and Jamaica on different missionary journeys. She loved music and collected several recordings.

Dee Ann had a very kind heart, always looking for ways she could help people. She was married to Jim C. Hayward May 26, 1984 in Galena, Kansas. He survives.

Also surviving are two sons, Robert Glen Hayward and Caleb Grant Hayward, one daughter, Christina Gail Hayward, all of the home; her mother, Bernice Kelly, Seneca; two brothers, Michael Brady Kelly, Redding, California; and Kenneth J Kelly, Seneca; one sister Patricia Gail Penn, Nice, California; and her father-in-law, Jack Hayward, Baxter Springs, Kansas.

Her father preceded her in death.

Judy Head

No information was available on Judy Head, except that she was age 56 and from Joplin.

Kenneth Henson

From Paul Thomas Funeral Home

Kenneth James Henson of Miami, Oklahoma passed away Saturday May 28, 2011 at his home. He was 56.

Mr. Henson was born November 26, 1954 in Wichita, Kansas to Earnest Arwood and Zenia (Hudson) Henson, II. He had lived in Miami for many years, he was a master machinist.

He was preceded in death by his parents, four brothers and a sister Evelyn Porter.

Survivors include a son and his wife, James and Jamie Henson, Claremore, Oklahoma; and one grandchild Jadyn Dihel, Claremore, Oklahoma

Glenn and Lorie Holland

From Parker Mortuary

Glenn and Lorie Holland, Joplin, exchanged their earthly home for a better one

on the evening of May 22, 2011, having just returned from a week at Walt Disney World in Florida in celebration of their 15th wedding anniversary.

Glenn Wayne Holland was born June 21, 1951, in Joplin. He graduated from Memorial High School in 1969, and then later earned a bachelor's degree in business administration, a master's degree in health care management, and finally a bachelor's degree in computer information science. He was a retired Air Force major and a member of the Retired Officers Association, the National Rifle Association, the American Legion and the National Skeet Shooting Association. He was currently working at Leggett & Platt.

Lorie Marie Holland was born December 22, 1962, in Joplin. She graduated from Parkwood High School in 1981 and attended Southern Illinois University in Carbondale where she was a member of the Sigma Kappa Sorority. She was a drafter for several companies in St. Louis and Joplin, having most recently worked at Allgeier and Martin.

She loved scrapbooking,

was an avid Disney enthusiast, a seasonal worker at OCC, and election poll worker. She was training for the Boomtown Days half marathon. She was a member of First Presbyterian Church growing up and a member of the Mayflower Society.

Lorie and Glenn were married May 18, 1996 and were members of Central City Christian Church.

Glenn was preceded in death by his daughter Amy, grandparents Perry and Ruth Holland, and Wesley and Velma Tracy, and is survived by daughters Shannon Mills, Cibolo, Texas; and Rachel Alexander, Bryan, Texas; and grandchildren Ethan, Avery, Ryan, Taylor, Kyle. Glenn is also survived by his parents, Wayne and Mary Holland, Joplin, sister Dorothy Vaughan, Joplin, sister and brother-in-law Jenny and Rick Smith, Webb City, and numerous nephews and nieces.

Lorie was preceded in death by her grandparents, Paul and Edna Marti, and Dennis and Lois Lippoldt.

Lorie is survived by her mother and stepfather, Bonnie and William Mahood, Overland Park, Kansas; sister and brother-in-law, Kristie and Steve Tusinger, Joplin, niece and nephew, Abby Marie Tusinger and Zachary Tusinger, Joplin, father Victor Lippoldt, Joplin, stepbrother and wife, William and Michele Mahood, Overland Park, Kansas; and their children, Kristen and Kellen Mahood.

Charlotte Hopwood

Charlotte Hopwood, 84, Joplin, was killed in the May 22 Joplin tornado.

Rusty Howard, Harli Howard and Hayze Howard

From Mason-Woodard Mortuary

Russell T. "Rusty" Howard, 29, Harli Jayce Howard, 5, and Hayze Cole Howard, 19 months,

passed away in the catastrophic tornado May 22, 2011. Harli and Hayze were found securely in their daddy's arms.

Russell T. "Rusty" Howard was born on July 5, 1981 in Coffeyville, Kansas, the son of Harry Howard and Dianne Long Nunez. He was a graduate of Cherryvale High School, a member of the class of 2000.

He worked as an electrician for PCS Phosphates for the past five years and previously he worked for B.E.I. He was a member of St. Peter the Apostle Catholic Church. He was a member of the Kansas Army National Guard. He enjoyed fishing and riding motorcycles.

He married Edie Boss August 10, 2002, in Cherryvale, Kansas. He never met a stranger, and he would talk to anyone who would listen. He will be greatly missed by all who knew him.

Harli Jayce Howard was born February 6, 2006 in Joplin. She was known as the family chatter bug; she loved to talk almost as much as her daddy did. Her mother's favorite saying of Harli's was "Hi, Friend."

Hayze Cole Howard was born October 27, 2009 in Joplin. He was our sweet little baby boy and a force unto himself.

They are survived by their wife and mother, Edie (Boss) Howard, Joplin; parents and grandparents, Harry Howard, Grove, Oklahoma; and Dianne Long Nunez, Edna, Kansas; in-laws and grandparents, Marie and Mike Boss, McAlester, Oklahoma; brother and uncle, Jason Niemier, Cherryvale, Kansas; sister and aunt, Amanda Nunez; grandparents and great-grandparents, Marvin and Joyce Long, Cherryvale, Kansas; sister-in-law and aunt, Missy Niemier and cousins Cooper and Carson; brother-in-law and uncle Jeff Boss, sister-in-law and aunt Erin Boss; niece and cousin, Leila Boss.

Iona Hull

From Weng Funeral Home

Iona Lee Hull, 70, Carthage, passed away Sunday, May 22, 2011, in Joplin, as a result of the tornado.

Iona was born July 1, 1940, in Meade, Kansas to James and Violet (Waltye) Hinsdale. Iona was a homemaker. She was a member of the Joplin Full Gospel Church.

Survivors include: two daughters, Amanda Hull and Hannah Hull, of the home; one brother, Bill Hinsdale, Carthage; two sisters, Mary Norris, Carthage, and Corky Bassinger, Arkansas; nine grandchildren and 13 great-grandchildren.

She was preceded in death by her parents; two sons, Rick Hull and Bill Hull; one daughter, Tammy Patrick and one sister, Betsy.

Wendy Istas

From Mason-Woodard Mortuary

Wendy Ann Istas, 58, Joplin, went home to the Lord May 30, 2011, at KU Medical Center, as a result of injuries she sustained in the Joplin tornado.

Wendy was born April 26, 1953 in Peoria, Illinois, the daughter of the late James and Ardith (Pool) Wasson. She has been a resident of Joplin, for the past 21 years. She was a member of St. Paul's United Methodist Church.

She married Jason Istas September 1, 2001. Together they co-owned and operated J-W Solutions for the past 10 years. Wendy was an excellent accountant and Quick Books Specialist. She was an instructor of Quick Books for Franklin Technical School. Her clients quickly became her friends and greatly relied on her.

She was a director for Stained Glass Theatre and a member of its board. She enjoyed sewing, crafts and most of all, spending time with her grandchildren. Her kind nature and sense of humor will be missed by all.

She is survived by her husband, Jason Istas, Joplin; her children, Tracy Happs and husband Roy, Joplin, Beth Trenary and husband Jason, Rogers, Arkansas; Brian Gleason and wife Leslie, Blue Springs; and Ashley Istas, Joplin; three brothers Michael Wasson and wife Kathy, Estero, Florida; Stephen Wasson and wife Mary, Woodridge, Illinois; and James Wasson and wife Carol, Decatur, Indiana; and 10 grandchildren.

Jane Jaynes

From Parker Mortuary

Jane E. Jaynes, 86, Joplin, passed away from injuries sustained in a tornado May 22, 2011. She was born November 11, 1924 in Webb City. She is a member of Joplin Heights Baptist Church, and lived in this area for her lifetime.

She married Eugene C. Jaynes August 9, 1945 in Columbus, Kansas and together they owned and operated Gene's Dairy Jane at 26th and Main Street in Joplin from 1960-1985.

Eugene preceded her in death January 4, 1998.

She is survived by one son, Richard Jaynes and wife Debbie, Joplin; one daughter, Carole A. Waggoner and husband Ralph, Joplin; one brother, William Pierce, Alba; two sisters, Virginia Youst, Modesto, California; and Bobbi Holmes, Idaho.; four grandchildren, Jeff Jaynes, Christy Waggoner, Kelly Weaver, Chrisanna Jaynes; three great-grandchildren, Blake, Campbell and Owen.

In addition to her husband, she is preceded in death by her mother Josephine Pierce, her daughter Marilyn Jaynes, and four brothers, Fred Pierce, Andrew Pierce, Burt Pierce and Jack Pierce.

Melisa Johnson

From Knell Mortuary

Melisa Renee Johnson, 50, Carthage, passed away Sunday, May 22, 2011 from injuries sustained in the Joplin tornado.

Melisa Renee Johnson was born June 11, 1960 in Hollywood, California, the daughter of Jim Johnson and Marilyn Gaye (Myers) Johnson. Melisa was a graduate of Verdugo Hills High School, Sunland, California and was a homemaker.

Survivors include her daughter, Lashawnda (Travis) Cavener, Joplin; a brother, Joe Johnson, Sunland, California; stepfather, Mike Libby Sunland; three granddaughters, Cheyeanne, Kaylee, and Alyssa, Joplin; niece, Amber Failla, Springfield; nephew, Dennis Johnson, Carthage and aunt Joann Baugh, Carthage.

Melisa was preceded in death by two sons, Jody Gaudsmith and a son, Charley Gaudsmith, who died with her in the tornado; her mother, Gaye Myers Johnson Libby; her brother, Mickey Hunt; a sister, Debra Sprague; her grandparents Joe and Avis Myers, Cecil and Rose Johnson.

Cheryl Jones

Cheryl L. Jones, 39, Altamont, died Sunday, May 22, 2011, from injuries sustained from the tornado at St. John's Regional Medical Center in Joplin where she was a patient.

She was born at Parsons, Kansas to Lloyd D. and Mary L. (Uitts) Jones. She grew up at rural Altamont and attended Independence Bible School where she graduated in 1989. She worked as a telemetry technician at Via Christi St. Francis Hospital in Wichita for several years.

She enjoyed playing piano and writing in her journal.

She is survived by her son, Brendan Sean Hamilton, Sedgwick, Kansas; her father and stepmother, Lloyd and Ruth Jones, Altamont; one brother, Marvin Jones, Altamont; and one sister, Brenda Roark, Loveland, Ohio.

She was preceded in death by her mother in 2006.

Kathy Keling

Kathy Keling, 53, Joplin, died Sunday, May 22, 2011 in her home as a result of the Joplin tornado. Ms. Keling was born in Springfield March 7, 1958. She was the eldest daughter of Walter and Geneva (Garrison) Fischgrabe, Fair Grove.

She was an active member of Glendale Christian Church for many years and later Southland Christian Church, Springfield. More recently, she attended Alpine Christian Church, Riverdale, Utah.

She was a beautiful, nurturing caregiver to all of us. She gave us the best of herself. To say that we will miss her wouldn't give her justice. The love she showed us will remain inside us forever. She also loved the Lord and shared that with us daily.

She is survived and missed by her two children, Heather and Dustin and their spouses, Russ and Michele; beloved Nonny to five grandchildren, Nathan, Ocean, Hailey, Strayker and Jeremiah; big sister to Allen Fischgrabe, Trudy Pike and her husband Wayman, and Ann Fischgrabe; aunt to Tara Fischgrabe and dear friend to Debbie Larsen and Ray Keling.

James Kendrick

From Mason-Woodard Mortuary

James "David" Kendrick,

63, Joplin, passed away May 22, 2011 at the Elks Club during the tornado.

David was born in Joplin December 17, 1947 to Carl L. Kendrick and Olive "Billie" Reeves Kendrick, both deceased.

David is survived by two brothers: Clyde "Don" Kendrick (wife Colleen), Neosho and Toney Kendrick (wife Pam), Cocoa Beach, Florida. He was preceded in death by a brother, Carl Allen Kendrick (widow Anita). Also surviving are five sisters: Diana Porter, Carthage; Nita Lane (husband Vernon), Diamond; Mary Jane Eichelberger, Joplin; Sharon Prauser, Baxter Springs, Kansas; Suzanne Mael (husband Stanley), Colorado Springs, Colorado.

He is also survived by a daughter, Brandi Lawson, and a grandson Jonathan Matarazzo, Joplin.

David graduated from Duenweg High School in 1965. He served in the Army from 1968-1969 and was a Vietnam veteran.

He retired in 2010 after 40 years in the explosives industry, working for the former Atlas Powder and its successive own-ers. He enjoyed his retirement and spending time with friends and family.

David was interested in everything, but a special interest and the source of many stories were his experiences prospecting for gold in Alaska. He loved to fish and went on a spring fishing trip with the same group of fishermen for over 40 years.

He was an active Elks Club member and the Gold Prospecting Association of America. He also was a former member of the VFW group of fishermen for over 40 years.

He was an active member of the Elks Club and the Gold Prospecting Association of America. He also was a former member of the VFW.

Abe Khoury

From Parker Mortuary

Abraham H. (Abe) Khoury, 26, Joplin, went to be with his Lord and Savior Jesus Christ, Tuesday morning, May 31, 2011 at

University Hospital in Columbia from injuries sustained in the Joplin tornado.

Born December 7, 1984 in Stillwater, Oklahoma, he lived in Joplin most of his lifetime, attended Joplin public schools, and graduated from Joplin High School in 2004.

Currently, he was pursuing his degree in business and entrepreneurship at M.S.S.U. He also worked as a server at Outback Steakhouse in Joplin.

Abe was a Christian. He loved fishing, camping and the outdoors. He also loved to play Texas Hold-em and aspired to play professionally. He loved football, played in high school, and was a passionate K.C. Chiefs Fan.

Survivors include his mother, Teresa Worley, Joplin; his father, John Khoury, Gallatin, Tennessee; three brothers, Frank Carey, Joplin, Nicholas and Michael Khoury, Old Hickory, Tennessee.; a sister, Samantha Khoury, Old Hickory; a stepbrother, Zach Worley, Joplin; maternal grandparents, Dan and Karen Mitchell, Neosho; maternal grandparents, Robert and Donna Bateson, Sr., Sevier-

ville, Tennessee; paternal grandparents, Antoinette Khoury, Amman, Jordan; many aunts, uncles, cousins, nieces, nephews and countless friends.

Abe was preceded in death by a paternal grandfather, Ibrahim Khoury; an uncle, Robert Bateson, Jr., who also went to be the Lord after sustaining injuries in the same tornado, and an infant sister, Nadia Khoury.

Stanley Kirk

Stanley Dale Kirk, 62, Joplin, died Sunday, May 22, 2011, from injuries sustained in the tornado. He was born March 1, 1949, in Springfield to Elmer (Hap) Kirk and Evelyne (Tosh) Kirk.

Stanley worked 38 years at Rocketdyne, Teledyne, Sabreliner and Premier Turbines as an aircraft engine technician. He was member of the National Guard and United Aerospace Workers.

Stanley is survived by his wife, Janice Lynn, a daughter Jodelle Lynn Kirk of the home, a son, Bobby Wayne Giger, Jr., Joplin, two stepsons, Eric Shoenberger, Aurora; Rick Shoenberger; Siloam Springs, Arkansas; one stepdaughter, Kim Cumming, Neosho; and one brother, Kelly Kirk, Shawnee, Oklahoma.

Geneva Koler

From Clark Funeral Home

Geneva Eutsler Koler, 84, passed away at Greenbriar Nursing home in Joplin, Sunday, May 22, 2011, as a result of the Joplin tornado. She was born Aug. 17, 1926, in Galena, Mo., the daughter of Luther and Edna Eutsler. She was a lifelong area resident and had worked at La-Z-Boy in Neosho.

She is survived by two sons, Michael Koler, Dallas, Texas, and Patrick Koler, Yakima, Washington; two grandchildren, Sarah Ashbaugh and Aaron Koler, Yakima; five great-grandchildren, Yakima, four sisters, Lucille Moffett, Granby, Joan Eutsler, Neosho, Sharon Sanders, Neosho, and Lorene Myers, Fort Smith, Arkansas; two brothers, Richard Eutsler, Granby and Larry Eutsler, Granby.

In addition to her parents,

she was preceded in death by two brothers, Donald Eutsler and Herbert Eutsler.

Tedra Kuhn

From the Joplin Globe

Tedra Jewell Kuhn, 69, Joplin, was a homemaker who loved her family. She also enjoyed going to the casino, and she always had a smile on her face and cared for others before herself.

Survivors include two children, two grandchildren, and several great-grandchildren.

Donald Lansaw

From Thornhill-Dillon Mortuary

Mr. Donald Wayne Lansaw, Jr., 31, Joplin, departed this life suddenly Sunday, May 22, 2011 at his home from injuries sustained in the devastating Joplin tornado.

Don began his journey August 21, 1979 in Joplin, born to the union of Donald Wayne Lansaw, Sr. and Beth R. (Dinwiddie) Lansaw. He was raised in Seneca and was a 1998 graduate of Seneca High School. He furthered his education at Crowder College in Neosho. Don was a man of great work ethic. He owned and operated Lansaw Technologies and was a licensed Realtor with Charles Burt, both located in Joplin. He enjoyed spending time outdoors where his favorite activities were camping and float trips.

On July 2, 2005 in Webb City, he was united in marriage to Bethany Ann Krudwig and she survives of the home.

Additional survivors include his parents, Donald Wayne Lansaw, Sr., Joplin; and Beth Lansaw, Seneca; a brother, Zach Lansaw, Joplin; paternal grandmother, Mary Sargent, Carl Junction; his father and mother in-law, Jim and Donna Krudwig, Webb City; as well as a host of other family and close friends.

Illinois to James Lee Lievens and Darlene Kay (Kelso) Lievens.

Bruce moved to the Neosho area in 1975 from Illinois where he had worked in the family business of Circle L-Auctions Service as an auction clerk for over 30 years, He was an avid sports fan, loved being with his family and also buying and selling antiques.

He is survived by his parents James and Darlene Lievens, Neosho; two brothers, Bart Lievens, Seneca, Brett and wife Roxanne Lievens, Neosho; two sisters, Brenda Boyd and companion Mike Larson, Neosho; Betsy and Gabe Shorter, Neosho; 13 nieces and nephews, Marquise, LaKyne, Jake, Mark, Dakota, Garrett, Cara, Carinna, Trevor, Seth, Grace, Hollie and Katlyn; and his best friends Rick and Giselle Scott.

Bruce Lievens

From Clark Funeral Home

Bruce Allen Lievens, 48, Joplin, died Sunday, May 22, 2011, from injuries sustained in the Joplin tornado. He was born December 18, 1962, in Moline,

Billie Sue Huff Little

From Simpson Funeral Home

Billie Sue Huff Little, 65, Joplin went home to be with the Lord, Sunday, May 22, 2011 as a result of the tornado. Billie was born January 10, 1946 in Butler County, Missouri to Harry and Martha (Mitchell) Huff. She was a waitress.

Billie is survived by her daughter, Tammy Curtner and grandson, Donnie Reed both of Joplin along with other siblings. She will be missed by those who loved her.

Skyular Logsdon

Skyular Ignatius Logsdon, 16 months, Joplin, died Sunday, May 22, 2011, from injuries sustained in the Joplin tornado. He was born Jan. 19, 2010, in Joplin to Corderro I. Logsdon and Carol J. Tate.

He is survived by his parents; his paternal grandparents, Robin Logsdon and Michael Rickey, Joplin and John Logsdon and Alesha Feather, Goddard, Kansas; maternal grandparents, James Tate, Carl Junction, Milissa A. and Rusty, Carl Junction; paternal great-grandparents, Sue Crow Slaughter and husband,

Ralph, Grove, Oklahoma; Frank Reynolds, Rutledge, Georgia; maternal great-grandparents, Debbie and Lee Cummins, Carl Junction, Nancy Reynolds, Joplin, Carol Tate, Joplin; maternal great-great-grandmother, Joyce McGuirk, Sarcoxie; numerous aunts, uncles and cousins.

Mary Lovell

From Mason-Woodard Mortuary

Mary Lois Lovell, 65, Joplin, passed away Sunday, May 22, 2011 in the tornado that devastated Joplin.

Mary was born September 30, 1945 in Joplin the daughter of the late Emmett and Alice (Cook) O'Connell. She worked for the Carl Junction School District as a cafeteria cook for many years before retiring.

Mary married Burton Lovell May 4, 1963 in Joplin; he survives.

Additional survivors include two sons, Rick Lovell and his wife Joanna, Carthage; Emmett Lovell, Carl Junction; one daughter, Michelle Lovell, Carl Junction, two brothers, George Himes and his wife Dollie, Joplin; Charles Himes, Springfield; four sisters, Faye Hance, Michigan City, Indiana; Helen Rigs and her husband Bob, Webb City; Janie Wood and husband Jay, Webb City and Twyla Murphy, Joplin, three grandchildren, Amanda, Josh and Rebecca, and one great-grandchild expected in June or July.

She was preceded in death by her parents, two twin brothers, Emmett Lee and Jackie Lee O'Connell and two sisters, Dolly Bigbee and Joyce Vance.

Chris Lucas

From Luginbuel Funeral Home

Christopher Don Lucas, 27, a former Vinita resident, died Sunday May 22, 2011 in Joplin. He was born November 24, 1983 in Claremore to Terry Don Lucas and Pamela Jean Parker.

Chris attended Vinita Schools, then joined the United States Navy in August 2003, and was honorably discharged in July of 2009. He was assistant manager of Range Line Pizza Hut in Joplin.

The family includes his two daughters, Chloe Alexandra Lucas and Emily Kay Lucas; father Terry Don Lucas and wife Angel; mother Pamela Jean Praytor and husband Michael; grandparents, Mary J. and Bill K. Parker, Alice F. and Bobby D. Lucas; his girlfriend Brooke E. Praytor and their unborn child; brothers and sisters, Jacqueline Rene Bass, Terri Jo Bass and her fiancée` D. C. Williams, Tiffanie Faye Wickliff, Terri Dawn Breger, Joshua Aaron Lucas, Jacob Ryan Lucas, Jeremy Kyle Lucas, Cody Lee Lucas, Cody Michael Praytor; the mother of his children Andrea Monique Lucas; numerous nieces, nephews, aunts, uncles, cousins and many friends.

Preceding him in death were his great-grandparents Alfred and Julia "Babe" Woolman

Patricia Mann

From the Joplin Globe

Patricia Mann, 64, Joplin, worked for Rouse Heating and Air Conditioning for 25 years. She loved animals and enjoyed reading, particularly mystery novels.

Survivors include a brother.

Rachel Markham

From the Kansas City Star

When Katy O'Keefe awoke and was pulled from the rubble of her home in the 2500 block of Murphy Avenue, she had no idea where her cousin Rachel Markham was.

The two had taken shelter in a closet to wait for the tornado to pass, but it wouldn't be until days later that O'Keefe and her cousin — Markham's brother Bobby — would locate Markham's five-month-pregnant body at a morgue.

"She was so excited about the baby," said Rachel's grandmother, Eleanor Markham, who lives in Escondido, California. "I just have to believe there's somewhere they're safe and together."

Eleanor said Rachel's friends and family gathered to remember her at a karaoke lounge in Escondido that she used to frequent. They sang songs to Rachel, celebrating her life.

"Everybody loved Rachel," Eleanor Markham said. "She would light up a room when she walked into it."

Rachel Markham, 33, was a hostess at the Red Onion Cafe.

Nancy Martin

Nancy Ann Martin, 52, Neosho, died Sunday, May 22, 2011, in Miami, Oklahoma from injuries sustained in the Joplin tornado. She was born June 19, 1958, in Lebanon, MO to Marion Kyle Grinage and Betty M. (Paulson) Grinage.

Nancy was a lifelong Neosho resident and a Neosho High School graduate. She worked at the New Vision Group home as a caregiver.

She is survived by her two sons, Anthony Kyle Owen and Brandon Shane Martin, Neosho; one granddaughter Khristeena Ann Marie Owen, Goodman; a brother Michael Grinage, Kansas City; a sister Linda Dettmer and husband Jim, Joplin; and four nephews, David Dewitt and wife Rinatta, Mesa, Arizona; Tyler Dewitt, Neosho; Daniel Dewitt, Neosho; and Christopher Dettmer, Colorado.

Janice McKee

Janice Kay McKee, Wyandotte, Oklahoma, 60, passed away Wednesday, June 15, 2011 at Select Specialty Hospital in Springfield. She was born December 6, 1950 in Webb City to Charles and Grace (Cleveland) Yeager. She married Gary McKee, Sr., on May 15, 1968 in Carl Junction.

Janice was survived by her mother, Grace Lawton, Webb City; husband Gary, of the home., one son; Gary McKee, Jr., and spouse Jennifer, Wyandotte, Oklahoma; one brother; Gerald W. Yeager, Quapaw, Oklahoma; one sister; Joyce Goodpasture, Carl Junction; and one granddaughter; ShaKetha Lei McKee, Commerce, Oklahoma.

She was preceded in death by her father, Charles, and one grandson: Kacee Lynn Star McKee.

Jesse McKee

From Clark Funeral Home

Jesse Len McKee., 44, Neosho, died Sunday, May 22, 2011, from injuries sustained in the Joplin tornado. He was born May 17, 1967 in St. Louis to Lee Roy McKee and Irma (Rayfield) McKee.

Jay and Susan Johnston were married June 15, 1991 in Ellington. They moved to Neosho in 1998. He served in the United States Air Force. Jay was a self-employed master electrician and a member of the Set Free Ministries in Wyandotte, OK. He was an avid fisherman, hunter and loved playing music.

He is survived by his wife Susan McKee; his parents Irma Hampton, Seneca; his children, Jessica McKee, Justin McKee and Zachary McKee, all of the home; two sisters, Judith Peters, Sumerland, Florida; and Janet McKee, Webb City; two stepbrothers, Robert Hampton, St. Louis; and David Hampton, St. Louis; stepsister Tina Klesterman, St. Clarks.

James and Mary McKeel

From Parker Mortuary

James Edward McKeel, 69, Joplin, passed away Sunday, May 22, 2011 at his home as a result of injuries sustained in the tornado.

Jim was born October 22, 1941 in Warsaw, Illinois, son of the late Marvin and Ollie McKeel. He was a baker for over 30 years for several companies in the Joplin area. He enjoyed life and was always trying to make people smile. He loved to entertain and cook for his family.

He was preceded in death by his first wife, Donna Marie McKeel in 1999. Jim was with his current wife, Mary McKeel, during the tornado, she also passed away.

Survivors include sons, Jimmy McKeel, Asbury; and Kenny McKeel, Lebanon; daughters, Jamey McKeel, Duenweg, and Regina McNamara, Webb City; grandchildren, Darin Keen, Ashley Hoskins, Dylan Ward, Amber Ward, Brandi Whitehead, Jesseca McNamara, Samantha Mc-Namara; great-grandchildren, James Micheal Keen, Brandon Hoskins, Bailyn Mercer, Zachary Whitehead, and Austin Whitehead.

No information about Mary McKeel was included in the obituary.

LaDonna Mcpurdy

From Forbes-Hoffman Funeral Home

LaDonna S. (Journot) McPurdy, 68, Joplin, formerly of Parsons, Kansas, went home to be with her Lord at 4:57 p.m., Tuesday, May 31, 2011, at Freeman West Hospital in Joplin from injuries sustained in the tornado.

She was born October 6, 1942, in Parsons, Kansas, to Frank and Myrtle (Johnston) Journot. She grew up in Parsons where she attended St. Mary's Elementary School and was a graduate of Labette County Community High School in Altamont.

Following high school graduation, she attended Fort Scott

Community College where she earned a degree in cosmetology. Later in life, she attended Independence Community College where she earned a cosmetology teaching certificate and had taught classes at Vatterott College in Joplin. She was a lifelong hair stylist in Parsons before moving to Carl Junction in 2005.

She was a member of St. Mary's Catholic Church in Joplin. She enjoyed painting, ceramics, gardening, fishing, camping and traveling. She especially enjoyed spending time with her family and friends.

She and Richard McPurdy were married in 1983 in Miami, Oklahoma. He survives of the home.

Additional survivors include: one son – Dale Gough Parsons, Kansas, four daughters - Karla March Weir, Kansas; Lisa Dhooghe, Diamond; Debra Shields, Parsons, Kansas; Julie Ramsey, Carl Junction; stepson – John McPurdy, Kings Mountain, North Carolina; 27 grandchildren, 28 great-grandchildren, one sister – Christine Jones Valley View, Texas and an aunt – Ann Pontious, Parsons, Kansas.

She was preceded in death by her parents and one brother, Eugene Quirin.

Randy Mell

From Simpson Funeral Home

Randall Elvin Mell, 49, Webb City, passed away Sunday, May 22, 2011 as a result of the tornado. Randy was born November 15, 1961 in Joplin to Elvin E. and Peggy (Musgrave) Mell.

He was a longtime custodian and helped in maintaining Jasper County Courthouse in Carthage. Randy was a former member of Emmanuel Baptist Church in Webb City for many years and currently attended Open Door Baptist Church in Carthage.

When he wasn't working, Randy enjoyed going to watch productions at Stained Glass Theatre, Webb City High School, Ozark Christian College and MSSU, where he was also a lionbacker season ticket holder. He loved to attend Webb City High School sporting events at every chance and enjoyed their music and drama programs.

Randy was courteous and kind and a wholesome man who will be greatly missed by those who knew him.

He is survived by his parents, Elvin and Peggy Mell of the home, his sister, Carole D. White, Mission, Kansas and several cousins.

Angelina Menapace

From Parker Mortuary

Angelina Ann Menapace was born September 18, 1958 to Leo Louis and Julia Ann Menapace in Joplin. She passed on from this earthly life to her heavenly home Sunday, May 22, 2011 at age 52 from a devastating tornado that hit Joplin.

Angelina worked as office manager of Behavior Management and Associates for 12 years. She truly enjoyed her job there and felt as if she were part of each of their families.

Angelina raised two children, Kebra Renee and Kevin Erik Menapace. Her pride and joy were her two granddaughters, Jazmine Reann and Alexis Darlene Menapac.

Some of Angelina's favorite things were cooking, shopping at consignment stores, spending time with her granddaughters and playing with her Boston terrier, Frank Duke.

One of Angelina's favorite times was the holidays. She would always prepare plenty of extra food while teasing each of her nieces and nephews, and often playing practical jokes on them. We never got through a Thanksgiving or Christmas season without her famous turkey dressing.

Angelina is survived by one sister, June V. Boyer, Joplin; two brothers, Frank L. Armstrong, Huntsville, Alabama; and Leo L. Menapace Jr., Joplin; two children, Kebra R. Menapace and Kevin E. Menapace; two granddaughters Jazmine R. Menapace and Alexis D. Menapace, as well as several cousins, nieces and nephews.

She was preceded in death by her parents Leo L. and Julia A. Menapace; sister, Katherine M. Pence and brother Steven A. Menapace.

Ronald Meyer

From Mason-Woodard Mortuary

Ronald D. Meyer, 64, Joplin, passed away May 22, 2011, at his home, from injuries sustained in the catastrophic tornado.

Ronald was born August 5, 1946 in Metropolis, Illinois, the son of the late Nelville Meyer and Adele Elizabeth Bourm. He moved to Joplin in 2008 from Murfreesboro, Tennessee.

He worked as a night auditor for hotels until he became the full-time caregiver of his brother George. Ronald was an Air Force veteran serving in the Vietnam War.

He is survived by his three brothers, Roger Meyer, Joplin, George Meyer, Joplin and Billy Meyer, Maryland: and one sister, Brenda Meyer, Metropolis, Illinois.

Tripp Miller

From Parker Mortuary

Tripp Miller passed away Monday morning, May 23, 2011, after sustaining severe injuries from the tornado that hit Joplin Sunday afternoon.

Tripp was the son of Patricia Gray Miller and Ray Donald Miller, Jr., Joplin and was born at St. John's Hospital in Joplin July 20, 1961. He graduated from Collegeview State School in 1982.

After graduating, Tripp began working at the Sheltered Workshop in Carthage for two years and then joined the work force at Joplin Workshop, Inc. and worked there for the last 27 years.

He was a lifelong member of the First Presbyterian Church in Joplin and regularly attended his God's Fellowship Sunday School class. Some of Tripp's many loves in his full life were living with his childhood friends, Rick Fox and Mark Farmer, at their home at 2302 Iowa; his special friends, Penny Morehouse, at Joplin Regional Center and James Newman, case worker of connections case management and Tripp's support staff of Community Support Services; bowling weekly with friends at 4th Street Bowl; meeting with friends at 1st Presbyterian Church; his title of "Number 1 Uncle" to his five nieces and four nephews; traveling to see his brother and sisters; going to Mizzou football games with his family where he was a very proud member of the University of Missouri Alumni Association; and rooting, as a lifelong fan, for his St. Louis Cardinals and then calling his dad to let him know the results of the game.

Tripp loved sports. He was an enthusiastic fan of local high school sports teams, particularly the Parkwood Bears and Joplin Eagles. He was a participant in Special Olympics since his school days.

He excelled at bowling and in his early years, swimming. He won his last of many gold medals at the State Special Olympics in the fall of 2010 at 4th Street Bowl in Joplin by bowling the best game of his life.

Tripp was a happy, gentle, kind, and loving man. He didn't know a stranger. He was your friend for life even if he just met you and was always so glad to see you. He touched the lives of so many people, and we were all better people having him in our life. His family will miss him ter-ribly every moment of every day.

Tripp is survived by his sisters, Melinda Miller Crowe and her husband, Lawrence Kerdolff Crowe, Overland Park, Kansas; Rebecca Miller Gurley and her husband, Curtis Raymond Gurley, Farmington, New Mexico; and Mary Elizabeth Williams, Galena, Kansas; brother, Thomas Gray Miller and his wife Patti O'Sullivan Miller, St. Louis; nephews, Lawrence Kerdolff (Kert) Crowe, Jr., Nathan Miller Crowe, Jackson Miller Gurley, Davis Cummins Gurley; nieces Laura Elizabeth Crowe, Elizabeth Leigh Williams, Riley Grace Miller, Molly Ann Miller and Madison Rose Miller; uncles William R. Gray and family, New Berlin, Wisconsin; Thomas R. Gray and family of Columbia, aunt Patricia Miller Righthouse, Broken Arrow, Oklahoma and many additional cousins and relatives.

Lorna Miller

From the Joplin Globe

Lorna "Kay" Miller, 72, Joplin, lived most of her life in Kansas and was retired from the food service industry where she worked as a waitress, grocery store clerk, and school cafeteria cook. She enjoyed sewing, reading and birdwatching, and she loved nature and cats. Survivors include one daughter and two grandchildren.

Suzanne Mock

From the Joplin Globe

Suzanne Mock, 39, Forsyth, is survived by her husband, Thomas Mock, her son, Thomas J. Mock, and her daughters, Amber Mock and Amanda Mock. She also had two grandchildren.

Doris Montgomery

Doris Marie Menhusen Montgomery, 83, Joplin, passed away at her residence from injuries sustained in the tornado Sunday, May 22, 2011. Born April 22, 1928 in Glen Elder, Kan., she was the daughter of the late Harold Finley and Doris Mae Shane Finley and graduated from high school in Glen Elder.

She attended Kansas State University, from which she received her teaching certification. Marie was a teacher in Kansas for several years. She lived in Joplin for 20 years, before moving to be near her children in Tonganoxie for 13 years. She returned to live in Joplin with her local children two years ago. She attended Christ's Community United Methodist Church.

Her first husband, Gordon Menhusen, to whom she was married for 48 years, preceded her in death. Her second husband, Richard Montgomery, also preceded her in death.

Survivors include three daughters, Jeanie Morris and Cathy Menhusen, Joplin; Debbie Gravatt and husband Bob, Tonganoxie, Kansas; one son, Gary Menhusen and wife Patricia, Tonganoxie; stepchildren, Dick and Pat Montgomery, Kansas City; Bill and Pat Montgomery, Tonganoxie; and Judy Forbach, Lawrence, Kansas; one brother, Vernon Finley and wife Mary, Hiawatha, Kansas.; nine grandchildren; 12 great-grandchildren and nine great-great-grandchildren; many nieces and nephews.

Edie Moore

From Thornhill-Dillon Mortuary

Edith "Edie" L. Moore, 48, passed away May 22, 2011 due to injuries sustained in the Joplin Tornado. She was born in Columbus, Kansas July 18, 1962 to Herman William Froelich and Edith Emma (Henderson) Froelich who preceded her in death.

Edie was raised in Columbus and then moved to Joplin where she had lived for the last several years. She is survived by her son, Bowen Daniel Greninger, Joplin; daughter, Emily Diane DeGraff, Joplin; and a brother, Herman Wayne Froelich, Parsons, Kansas.

Edie was a dedicated mother to both her children and loved her cats that she adopted.

Estrellita Moore

From Mason-Woodard Mortuary

Estrellita M. Moore, 64, Joplin, passed away May 22, 2011 from injuries sustained in the catastrophic tornado. She was born December 4, 1946 in Angeles City, Philippines, the daughter of the late Faustino and Felisa (Mercado) Manansala.

She was a hairdresser for J.C. Penney. She was a Catholic and attended St. Mary's Catholic Church.

Estrellita loved going to the casino.

Sally Moulton

From the Mascoutah, Ill. Herald

Helping others find shelter from the approaching tornado in Joplin May 22nd, may have cost a former Mascoutah resident her life.

Killed in the storm was Sally Ann (Harris) Moulton, 58, who graduated from Mascoutah High School in 1971.

Before moving to Joplin, Moulton worked at MarKa Nursing Home here, and is remembered by friends as "a very nice lady."

Her brother, Rick Harris, was a member of the Mascoutah Police Department.

In Joplin, Moulton was a member of a theater group that had been performing "I Remember Mama," at Stained Glass Theater, on the afternoon of the tornado. Moulton was playing the part of Aunt Jenny in the production. According to family members, the theater is just a block away from St. John's Hospital, which took a direct hit from the giant storm.

Nadine Mulkey

From Clark Funeral Home

Georgia 'Nadine' Mulkey, 91, Joplin, died June 1, 2011 at Spring River Christian Village from injuries sustained in the May 22 tornado. Nadine was born April 9, 1920 in Pierce City, the daughter of George Morris and Myra Burton Morris.

She was a lifelong area resident and had worked in the food service of the schools and Sale Memorial Hospital, now Freeman Neosho. She was a member of the First Baptist Church in Neosho.

Nadine married John Mulkey April 9, 1939 at Cassville and he preceded her in death January 30, 1997.

She is survived by four children, Myra Koeneke, Joplin; William 'Bill' Mulkey, Joplin; Barbara Krambeck, Denver, Colorado and John W. Mulkey, Carthage; five grandchildren and six great grandchildren.

In addition to her parents and husband, she is preceded in death by two sisters, Claudia Kuklenski and Goldie Miller.

Edmund Mullaney

From the Springfield News-Leader

Edmund Vincent Mullaney was born March 24, 1929, in Adrian, Michigan, the son of Edward Vincent Mullaney and Marie (Clancy) Mullaney. He was a veteran of the United States Marine Corps. He was a member of Our Lady of the Lake Catholic Church and was a member of the Knights of Columbus. He had been a resident of the area for the past 10 years.

He is survived by his wife, Marilyn Mullaney, Hollister; his sister, Julie Forester and husband Stephen, Oxford, Connecticut; and brother, Robert Mullaney, Huntington, Connecticut.

He was preceded in death by his parents.

Sharyl Nelson

From Mason-Woodard Mortuary

Sharyl Anyssa Nelsen, Webb City, passed away in the catastrophic tornado May 22, 2011.

Sharyl was born November 11, 1976 in Brownsville, Texas. She was working as a sales representative for the AT&T store on Range Line when the tornado struck. Sharyl was able to help a family out of harm's way moments before the tornado struck the building.

Sharyl was a loving mother and wife, a caring daughter and sister, and a nurturing person whose heart and arms were open to everyone who was blessed to have known her.

Sharyl is survived by her loving husband, Chad Nelsen, her beautiful children, Matilyn Jade Perry (14), and Aaron Cain Nelsen (10), her stepdaughter Ashley Nelsen Baker, her parents Yolanda Reed and Ernest San Miguel, her stepfather Terrel Reed, her sisters Cynthia Hopkins and Sandra Mendoza, her brother Ernie San Miguel, and her stepbrother Tim Reed.

She is preceded in death by her grandparents Enrique and Cecilia Ybarra and Pedro and Josefina San Miguel, and her stepsister Tamara Reed.

Will Norton

From Parker Mortuary

William Richard Norton, known by friends and family as Will, went home to heaven Sunday evening, May 22, 2011.

Will was born and raised in Joplin where he did so much more than just attend Joplin High School.

The tragedy of the Joplin tornado has left behind his parents Mark and Trish Norton of Joplin, his sister Sara Norton, grandparents Richard and Laveda Norton, aunts and uncles Tracey and Jeff Presslor, Jane and Chuck Haver, Connie Allen, and Ralph Worster II, along with many loving cousins.

Will was preceded in death by his grandparents Ralph Worster, Lora Worster-Kaffenberger, and Leo Kaffenberger.

Those who were blessed to know Will watched him live a full and joyful life in his short 18 years. Very few of us can say we've accomplished half of the things this young man has done or touched a community with a heart such as his. Will has left an endless legacy to the people influenced by his numerous YouTube videos, tweets, and outstanding contributions to those in need.

To recognize the enormity of those lives he touched, he had over 2 million upload views on his Willdabeast YouTube account (which can be found at http://www.YouTube.com/Will), over 6,000 followers on Twitter, and over 800 friends on his personal Facebook page, not to mention the 50,000 people across the world who have been praying for him since the storm through the Help Find Will Norton Facebook community page.

Will has always noticed the small things in life as an excited and optimistic dreamer. With such a creative mind, we've witnessed his many clever videos as he partnered with YouTube with the ability to reach thousands. One of his videos mentioned the 50 things he had done as of three years ago.

We can add multiple highlights to this list including graduating high school on the very day of this tragedy. To name a few, Will loved traveling, and one of his favorite places was Africa, where he got to see the great wildebeest migration. He played on a state-level tennis team and became a private pilot this year. He traveled to Washington DC with his state-winning US Constitution Team where he rallied outside of the White House after Bin Laden was killed.

Will was an avid volunteer and loved the Joplin Humane Society. He was accepted to Chapman University for Film

Production, which was his lifelong dream. Will's faith in his savior was evident in his everyday life and powerfully so, as he quoted scripture in the arms of his earthly father before being taken to his heavenly father that day.

Dennis Osborn

From Campbell-Biddlecome Funeral Home

Dennis M. Osborn, 34, Seneca, passed into eternal rest May 22, 2011 from injuries sustained from the tornado that devastated Joplin.

Dennis Melvin Osborn was born June 3, 1976 in Savannah, Illinois, the son of Richard Joel and Helen Azenith (Rothenbeuhler) Osborn. Dennis had worked for Jasper Foods and was a member of the 203rd National Guard.

Dennis married Steffannie Michelle (Hufferd) Osborn, April 15, 2000 in Joplin and she survives. Additional survivors include one son, Matthew Osborn, Seneca; one daughter, Aundree Osborn, Joplin, his mother Helen Osborn, Seneca;

three brothers, Rick Osborn, state of Illinois, Ron Shafer, Seneca; and Todd Shafer, state of Illinois; four sisters, Dianne Denson, Seneca, Brenda S, state of ILL, Peggy Jackson, state of Texas; and Roxanne Smith, Seneca.

Dennis was preceded in death by his father Richard Osborn in November of 2000.

Charles Oster

From Clark Funeral Home

Charles E. Oster was born July 30, 1933 in Roads, the son of Raymond Oster and Velma Rosebud Hampton Oster. He entered into rest May 22, 2011 as a result of the tornado.

Charles was a lifelong area resident and served in the U.S. Army during the Korean Conflict. He was semi-retired, working for Share Corp, Milwaukee, Wisconsin in sales. Charles was a member of the First Christian Church in Webb City and served as a deacon.

Shirley Parker

From Bath-Naylor Funeral Home

Shirley Ann Parker, 68, Joplin, died Sunday, May 22, 2011 in the tornado that devastated Joplin. She was born February 11, 1943 in Sterling, Kansas the daughter of Kenneth and Rosemary (Greene) Stange.

She was married to Ronnie G. Parker and later divorced. Shirley was a mammography technician at Loveless Health Care System in Albuquerque, New Mexico for many years, she retired in 2008.

Survivors include a son, Greg Parker and fiancée Jennifer Willey, Pittsburg, a daughter Stephanie Woods and husband Joseph, Joplin, MO, along with six grandchildren Jessawynne Parker, Shelby Ann Woods, Alexis Kathryn Woods, Mitchell William Woods, Daniel Thomas Willey and Connor Peyton Willey.

She was preceded in death by her parents and a brother Robert Dee Stange.

Nichole Pearish

From Mason-Woodard Mortuary

Nichole Sherie Pearish, 23, Joplin, passed away 3:21 p.m. Saturday, June 4, 2011 at the University of Missouri Medical Center in Columbia, from injuries sustained in the Joplin tornado.

Nichole was born July 24, 1987 in Joplin and lived in the Joplin area most of her life. She was a 2006 graduate of Sarcoxie High School and was active in FFA. She was employed as a Customer Service Supervisor with Aegis Communications. Nichole was a member of the First Baptist Church of Sarcoxie and was a member of the Route 66 Cloggers.

Joyce Perry

Mary Joyce Perry, 76, Joplin, passed away Sunday May 22, 2011, from injuries sustained in the tornado.

Joyce was born November 16, 1934 in Joplin, the daughter of John and Vivian Thurman. She was a lifelong resident of

Joplin and a graduate of Joplin High School.

In October 1953, she married Warren E. Perry in Joplin. He preceded her in death October 31, 1983. She was a secretary for Prudential Insurance and KODE TV and then owner of It Figures in Joplin. She presently worked for C.J. Uniform Shop in Joplin. She was a member of Epsilan Sigma Alpha and AARP. She enjoyed spending her time with her grandchildren.

She is survived her daughter, Debbie McMurry and husband Doug, Pittsburg, Kansas; her son, Dan Perry, St. Louis; grandsons, Eric Smith, Carl Junction; and Ryan Smith, St. Charles; great-grandson, Cooper Smith; great-granddaughter Catie Smith, Carl Junction; and a sister, Jean Goff, Joplin.

She was preceded in death by her husband and parents.

Ben Peterson

James Benjamin John "Ben" Peterson, 27, Joplin, passed away Sunday, May 22, 2011 due to injuries sustained in the tornado.

Ben was born September 20, 1983 in Joplin and graduated from Joplin High School in 2003. He was currently working at the McDonalds on Main Street with the night shift.

Survivors include a mother, Leilani Halvorsen, Joplin; stepfather Tom Halvorsen, Joplin; sister, Myra Boatright, Joplin; grandmother, Margaret Heuer, Skokie, Illinois; nephews, Austin and Job; nieces, Quin and Laci.

He was preceded in death by his father, James E. Benham.

Anna Pettek

Anna Pettek, 91, a Greenbriar resident, passed away Sunday, May 22, 2011.

Jay Petty

From Clark Funeral Home

John Henry (Jay) Petty, Jr., 37, Joplin, died Sunday, May 22, 2011, from injuries sustained in the Joplin tornado. He was born April 3, 1974, in Hoopston, IL to John

Henry Petty, Sr. and Linda Sue (Watson) Petty.

Jay moved to the Neosho area five years ago and worked at Jasper Products in Joplin for the past five years. He spent two years serving in the Army Rangers. He loved God, his country and spending time with his family. He also loved to hunt, fish and play the guitar and had a band, Iris Road.

He is survived by his parents John Henry, Sr. and Linda Sue Petty, Gray Ridge; his fiancé, Lisa Hartman, Neosho; two daughters, Hannah Petty, Dexter; Hayli Petty, Dexter; his fiancé's children, Leif Larson and Jedidiah Larson, both of the home; two brothers, Dallas Petty, Malden; Nicholas Petty, Gray Ridge; and one sister, Alisha Hagy, Essex.

Marie Piquard

From Mason-Woodard Mortuary

Hallie "Marie" Cook Piquard, 78, Joplin, passed away Sunday May 22, 2011

from injuries sustained in the catastrophic tornado.

Marie was born October 20, 1932 in Lufkin, Texas to Arthur and Nobbil (Mossingelle) Agleton. She worked as a deputy collector for Jasper County, and with CFI for eight years. She was a member of the Harmony Heights Baptist Church. She enjoyed bowling and southern gospel music.

She married Elbert "Dick" Cook December 3, 1960 in Texas, he preceded her in death December 8, 2000. She then married Lloyd Piquard May 3, 2003, he survives.

Additional survivors include two sons, Lloyd Piquard Jr. and wife Donna, Neodesha, Kansas; Chris Piquard and wife Pamela, Joplin; three daughters, Bonita Harrison and her husband Gary, Carthage, Debbie Poole and her husband Karl of Jena, Louisiana and Susan Tatum and her husband Mike, Joplin; 13 grandchildren and 24 great grandchildren; one niece and two nephews.

She was preceded in death by one brother, Gene Agleton, in 2011, one daughter Carolyn Piquard and one grandson, Joshua Harrison.

Natalia Puebla

From Ulmer Funeral Home

Natalia Puebla, 17, Carthage passed away Sunday, May 22, 2011. She was born on July 26, 1993 in Joplin. Natalia was the daughter of Carey and Latina Puebla. She was an Ozark Christian College student and had just completed her first year. Natalia was loved by her piano students, church family and college friends. She was a member of Joplin Full Gospel Church.

Natalia is survived by her parents, two brothers, Joshua and Jacob, Springfield, and one sister Angela (Elliott) Pinkham, Webb City; four nieces Kaylene, Kristin, Kelly, and Kara, Uncle Jesse and Pam, Carthage.

Natalia is preceded by paternal grandparents, Jesus Puebla and Marjorie Scoville. She is also survived by two aunts, Shelly Simon of Davenport, Iowa and Ramona Lacy, Farmington, IL.

Loretta Randall

From Clark Funeral Home

Loretta Lea Randall, 54, Webb City, died May 23, 2011, from complications of the May 22, 2011, tornado. Loretta was born August 13, 1956, in Neosho and was a lifelong area resident.

She currently taught at the SEK Learning Center in Girard, Kansas. She was a member of First Christian Church in Webb City; a member of the Cardigan Welsh Corgi; National Education Association of Teachers, Smoke-Free Webb City and MSSU Alumni Association.

Loretta married Kyle Randall August 1, 1986, in Joplin and he survives.

She is also survived by a daughter, Krista Lee Rubottom Stark and husband, Jason, Webb City; two grandchildren, Reannon Lea Stark and James Stark; her mother, Janet Oster, Joplin; two brothers, Carey Oster, Carl Junction; and Tim Oster, Joplin; and one sister, Cheryl Davis, Independence, Kansas.

She was preceded in death by her father, Charles Oster, who perished in the tornado, and a brother, Mark Oster.

Troy Ramey

Troy Ramey, 39, was originally from Trinity, Texas.

He is survived by his parents, Tom and Vicki Ramey, Trinity, two sisters, Melanie Watanabe, Beaumont, Texas, and Jennifer Ramey, Houston, and four children, Allison Leech, Tommy Ramey, Trey Ramey and Tigh Ramey.

Shelly Ramsey

Shelly Marie Ramsey, 42, Neosho, died Sunday, May 22, 2011 from injuries sustained in the Joplin tornado.

Shelly was born September 26, 1968 in Ft. Scott, Kansas and grew up in the Ft. Scott area. She moved to southwest Missouri in 1991 from Fort Scott and currently worked at Jay Hatfield Mobility in Joplin.

Her children were her priority, and she was a very giving person, always having a smile and positive attitude.

She is survived by her son, Blake Ramsey and daughter, Mikayla Ramsey, both of Neosho; her father, Jerry Gray and wife, Kathy, Fort Scott; her mother, Shorty Cooper and husband, Dan, Richards; maternal grandmother, Marilyn Fowler, Fort Scott; two brothers, Scott Brillhart and Eric Gray, Fort Scott; two nephews, Johnathon and Austin; two nieces, Aura Lee and Morgan and the father of her children, Thad Ramsey and wife, Michele, Neosho.

Loretta Randall

Loretta Lea Randall, 54, Webb City, died May 23, 2011, from complications of the May 22, 2011, tornado.

Loretta was born August 13, 1956, in Neosho and was a lifelong area resident. She taught at SEK Learning Center in Girard, Kansas. She was a member of First Christian Church in Webb City; a member of the Cardigan Welsh Corgi; National Education Association of Teachers, Smoke-Free Webb City and MSSU

Alumni Association.

Loretta married Kyle Randall August 1, 1986, in Joplin and he survives.

She is also survived by a daughter, Krista Lee Rubottom Stark and husband, Jason, Webb City; two grandchildren, Reannon Lea Stark and James Stark; her mother, Janet Oster, Joplin; two brothers, Carey Oster, Carl Junction and Tim Oster, Joplin; and one sister, Cheryl Davis, Independence, Kansas.

She was preceded in death by her father, Charles Oster, who perished in the tornado, and a brother, Mark Oster.

Cheryl Rantz

From Clark Funeral Home

Cheryl E. Rantz, 62, Carl Junction, died May 30, 2011 at Cox South in Springfield from complications of the May 22 Joplin tornado.

Cheryl was born September 14, 1948 in Carthage and was a lifelong area resident. She worked as a tax preparer for H and R Block and was a member of the Nazarene Church. She is survived by a daughter, Kim-

berly Phillips, Springfield; two grandchildren, Steven McReynolds and Mabel Phillips; one brother, David Spruce, Carthage and two sisters, Judy Baugh, Carthage and Karen Gregory, Altus, Oklahoma.

She is preceded in death by her parents, Edward and Dorothy Spruce; her husband, George Rantz and brother, Gary Spruce.

Darlene Ray

From Derfelt Funeral Home

Darlene Kay (Hall) Ray, 63, a former employee of King Louie Manufacturing, Baxter Springs, Kansas, passed away Wednesday, June 1, 2011 at Kindred Hospital, Kansas City following an illness.

She was born August 18, 1947 in Joplin, Missouri. Her parents were George and Oleta Hall. She was a lifetime resident of Galena.

She graduated from Galena High School in 1965. She had previously worked as a seamstress at King Louie Manufacturing, Baxter Springs, KS. She enjoyed going to Bordertown Casino to play bingo.

She was married to Wesley G. Ray on October 29, 1974 in Miami, Oklahoma. He survives.

Additional survivors include one son, Steven Wade Ray, Galena, Kansas; one brother, Tom Hall, Joplin; and one sister, Barbara Fields, Galena, Kansas.

One sister, Phyllis Strickland, preceded her in death.

Tom Reid

From Bath-Naylor Funeral Home

Virgil "Tom" Reid 77, Columbus, Kansas died 5:45pm Sunday May 22, 2011 at Joplin during the tornado tragedy.

Virgil was born May 14, 1934 in Hallowell, Kansas, the son of Charles Marion "Shorty" and Melba Trucilla (Hutchens) Reid. He was a lifelong resident of the area and a graduate of Columbus High School. He was a veteran of the Army.

In 1959, he married Barbara Napier; they later divorced. On May 22, 1992 Tom married Jesse Williams in Miami, OK; she survives at the home.

Tom worked in construction all his life and started SEK Construction with Ivan Crossland.

He was affiliated with Maxwell Bridge Company in Columbus, Kansas. Tom retired after working 50 years in construction in 2000. Tom was a member of the Hallowell Word of Life Church in Hallowell, Kansas, enjoyed gardening, pecans, coin collecting, elephant collecting, cooking, dominos with his friends and family and finding recipes on the internet.

Survivors include his wife, children Tom D. Reid and wife Rhonda, Columbus, Kansas; Cindy Davis, Columbus; Robert Cox, Columbus; Rhonda Norris and husband Mike, Owasso, Oklahoma; and Jeri Lyons and husband Erving of Parsons, Kansas; an aunt Martha Back of Hallowell, Kansas; special friends Don and Susan Gurnee, Hallowell, who he enjoyed dominos with; grandchildren Brian Reid and wife Jennifer, Hope Von Soosten, Alexander Cox and wife Heather, Samantha Cox, Cassie Norris, MacGyver Norris, Elyjah Lyons and Aliyah Lyons; and great-grandchildren Madalyne, Monica and Copper Dean Reid.

He was preceded in death by his parents and brother Richard Reid.

Johnnie Richey

From Parker Mortuary

Johnnie Ray Richey, 52, Joplin, passed away Sunday, May 22, 2011 as a result of injuries sustained in the tornado.

Johnnie was born October 7, 1958 in Webb City, son of the late Ernie "Cork" Richey, and Joyce Mosher Richey, Joplin. Johnnie graduated from Webb City High School and attended MSSU. He has worked for Allgeier Martin and Associates for over 30 years and was currently a project engineer. He was an active member of the Joplin Elks Lodge #501 where he was a trustee.

He enjoyed volunteering his time with the youth at both Carl Richard locations and worked with Habitat for Humanity. He attended St. James United Methodist Church.

In addition to his mother, Johnnie is survived by a son, SSgt. Adam Richey and wife Raygen, Jacksonville, North Carolina; a grandson, Griffin Ray Richey; sister, Kerri Simms and husband Don, Farmington;

nieces and nephews, Kelsey Smith, Fayetteville, Arkansas, Tara Simms, Farmington, Justin Simms, Jordan Simms, and Jesse Simms, Festus; several aunts and uncles and cousins, and his faithful canine companion Sugar.

Vicki Robertson

From Parker Mortuary

Vicki Patrice Robertson, 66, Joplin, passed away Sunday, May 22, 2011 as a result of injuries sustained in the tornado.

Vicki was born October 8, 1944 in Joplin, daughter of the late Clifford and Clancy Scott.

Survivors include her children Mike Johnson, Danny Robertson, Joe Robertson, Dannielle Robertson, and Ardis Robertson.

Cayla Robinson

From Mason-Woodard Mortuary

Cayla Ann Selsor Robinson, 64, Joplin, passed away early Saturday June 4, 2011 from injuries suffered in the devastating tornado that came through Joplin May 22, 2011.

Cayla was born October 31, 1946 in Joplin, the daughter of Charles and Colleen (Conner) Selsor. She was a lifetime area resident and was a stay-at-home mom caring for her family. Cayla attended Frisco Church in Webb City, Mo. and later attended Forest Park Baptist Church in Joplin.

She is survived by three daughters, Nicole Shultz and her husband Joey, Joplin, Pam Spencer, Carthage; Donna Fisher, Springfield; one son, Jerry Michael Fisher, Carthage; one sister, Marcy Hays, Webb City; one brother, Cary Selsor, Webb City; eight grandchildren and one great-grandchild, Karlee Laramore, with another on the way.

She was preceded in death by her mother, Colleen and two sons, Billy and Matthew Fisher.

Keith Robinson

From Mason-Woodard Mortuary

Keith Derek Robinson, 50, Joplin, passed away May 22, 2011, from injuries sustained in the Joplin tornado, at Greenbriar Nursing Home.

Keith was born August 1, 1960 in Joplin, the son of Charles and Betty (Love) Robinson-Gray. He has been a lifetime Joplin resident. He worked as a CNA for Greenbriar Nursing Home, prior to that he worked 18 years for Freeman Hospital.

Keith had a wonderful way with his patients. He would motivate them to do their rehabilitation in a stern but kind and respectful manner. He was responsible for many patients being able to recover and even walk again. He thoroughly enjoyed watching old movies.

He is survived by his mother, Betty Robinson-Gray, Joplin; one sister, Mary Katherine "KK" Robinson, Joplin; one brother, Charles Robinson, Jr.; nephews, Jeremy and Justin Robinson and Dylan Rapp, Joplin; three uncles, J.D. Love, Joplin, Jerry Love, Jr. and wife Elaine, Joplin, and Robert Love, Farmington; and many, many cousins and friends.

He was preceded in death by his father, Charles D. Robinson; his stepdad William O. Gray; his grandparents, Jerry and Katherine Love, and an uncle, Raymond Love and two aunts Vera Jenkins and Helen Derrick.

Margaret Row

Margaret Ellen Row, 50, Joplin, formerly of Fredonia, Kansas, died Monday, June 6, 2011 at St. John's Hospital in Springfield as the result of injuries sustained in the May 22, 2011 Joplin tornado.

She was born March 31, 1961 in Fredonia, the daughter of Billie (Palmer) Row Kidd and the late William A. Row. Margaret was a 1979 graduate of Fredonia High School. She attended college at Labette Community College in Parsons, Kansas, and obtained her RN nursing degree.

Margaret worked at Mercy Hospital in Independence, Kansas and St. John's Hospital in Joplin for many years. Most recently she was employed as a hospice nurse in Joplin. She took pleasure in collecting clowns and piggy banks and enjoyed traveling.

Margaret is survived by her mother Billie Kidd, Fredonia, Kansas; three brothers, William (Bill) and Karla Row, Cassville; Bob and Cathy Row, Fredonia, Kansas; Jack and Renee Row, Golden City; one sister Rose Mary and Greg Rhodes of London, Arkansas.

She is also survived by several nieces and nephews, as well as great nieces and nephews.

Margaret's father, grandparents, aunts and uncles preceded her in death.

Virginia Salmon

Virginia Mae Salmon, 80, passed away Sunday, May 22, 2011, at her home in Duquesne, from injuries sustained in the tornado that devastated Joplin.

Virginia was born June 21, 1930, in Wichita, Kansas to John Raymond and Opal Louise (Cravens) Templeton and attended high school in Porterville, California.

She married Raymond Jesse Salmon May 7, 1949, in Las Vegas, Nevada. He preceded her in death October 17, 2002. She lived in California for 34 years, moving to Joplin in 1973 with her husband and family.

She was a homemaker and loved spending time with her family. She had a wonderful sense of humor and enjoyed telling stories about her childhood. She loved to shop, especially for others, and was a big fan of country and gospel music. She was disliked by no one and will be missed by all.

Rest in peace, Mom, and thank you, God, for allowing her to be with us for almost 81 years.

Virginia is survived by one daughter, Shelley Russow and fiancé Bud Ochsenbein, Joplin; four sons, Gary Salmon and wife Mary Jane, Joplin; Gayle Salmon, Boise, Idaho; and Leta Salmon, Cleveland, Oklahoma; Stacey Salmon and wife Cindy, Joplin; and Scott Salmon and fiancé Bev Stepp, Seligman; two sisters, Margaret Young, Joplin; and Roberta Miller, Yuma, Arizona; three brothers, Charles Templeton and wife Phyllis, Lakeland, Florida; Frank Templeton and wife Linda, Tigard, Oregon; and Jim Templeton and wife Juanita, of Seres, California; 15 grandchildren; 28 great-grandchildren; five great-great-grandchildren; many nieces and nephews; as well as many other family members and friends.

In addition to her husband and parents, she was preceded in death by two sisters, Juanita Baggs and Jenny Mayfield.

Grace Sanders

Grace Marie Sanders passed from this life 3:08 p.m. Monday, June 20, 2011, at St. John's Intensive Care Unit in Springfield from complications following surgery.

Grace was born to Elmer and Francis Dummit April 11, 1929, in Buhl, Idaho.

Following a tragic car accident, Grace and her sister, Elouis, now deceased, were adopted at the age of 7, by their aunt and uncle Hupperfelt, of Miami, Oklahoma in October 1936.

Grace married Robert Dale Sanders, Carthage, November 21, 1946, and they enjoyed nearly 65 years of marriage together. Bob remains at the couple's home in Carthage.

Grace was recovering from surgery at St. John's Hospital in Joplin, on Sunday, May 22nd and was located on the west end of the upper floor when the EF5 tornado struck, destroying her room and the entire end of the floor on which she was seeking cover.

She survived the tornado, but sustained multiple injuries requiring 18 stitches at the triage at Memorial Hall. She, along with 39 other patients from Joplin, was transported to Springfield, for further care. She was discharged and returned home but required further surgery June 17 and died Monday from various complications. Her husband and a nephew were present with her at the time of her passing.

Grace was employed for many years at Joplin Stockyards as a bookkeeper and was always a gracious and welcoming person. She will be most dearly missed by all who loved her and respected her.

Thomas Sarino

From the Joplin Globe and Kansas City Star

Thomas Sarino, 75, Joplin, lived alone. His family, including several children and grandchildren, live in the Philippines. He had worked for Warner Brother Inc.'s finance department in New York before moving to Joplin in 1995 to work in finance for Loma Linda Golf Resort. He was retired.

Toni Sawyer

From Cheney Witt Memorial Chapel

Tonja Lee "Toni" Sawyer, 41, Fort Scott, died Sunday, May 22, 2011, as a result of the Joplin tornado. She was born December 17, 1969, in Olympia, Washington, the daughter of Larry Goldsby and Sandra Gamache Goldsby.

Toni married Chad Sawyer January 3, 2011. She was employed by Taco Bell in Fort Scott. She enjoyed painting, collecting antiques and writing poems and short stories as well as listening to the rain and sitting around a bonfire. Toni loved animals and often took in strays. She attended the Apostolic Pentecostal Church.

Survivors include her husband, Chad Sawyer, Fort Scott; her children, Dashedin Goldsby, Fort Scott, Jarred Goldsby,

Shelton, Washington; Makyah Goldsby and Samara Hernandez, Fort Scott. Also surviving is her father, Larry Goldsby, Shelton, Washington; two brothers, Ron Larson, Matlock, Washington and Gerald Goldsby, Olympia, Washington; two sisters, Julie Goldsby and Dottie Goldsby, Shelton, Washington; and a granddaughter, Icysis Goldsby.

She was preceded in death by her mother, and infant son, Jed Goldsby and a sister, Crissy Goldsby.

Frances Scates

From Bennett-Wormington Funeral Home

Frances Ann (Worm) Scates, 71, Joplin, formerly of Monett, passed away May 22, 2011 at her home. She was a victim of the recent tornado. She was born July 14, 1940 in Freistatt to Earnest and Nora (Jackel) Worm.

Frances was a member of St. John's Lutheran Church in Freistatt.

Frances is survived by two sons: Brian Scates, Bentonville, Arkansas; and Bruce Scates, Joplin; three daughters: Bridgit

Ferrell, Stella; Brenda Seward, Stella; and Brandi Parker, Monett; one brother: Martin Worm, Verona; one sister: Marcel Mitchell, Springfield; 11 grandchildren and six great-grandchildren.

Gladys Seay

Gladys J. Seay, Welch, Oklahoma, 83, passed away Sunday, May 22, 2011 at St. John's Regional Medical Center, Joplin, during the recent tornado.

Gladys was born January 30, 1928 in Miami, Oklahoma to William Jefferson and Myrtle Florence (Morris) Seay. She was a graduate of Miami High School.

Daniel Shirley

From the Joplin Globe

Daniel Wayne Shirley, 48, Joplin, traveled all over the United States and Canada as a salesman with a carnival. He moved to Goodman one year ago and had been living at Greenbriar Nursing Home in Joplin since February. He enjoyed metal detector hunting, fishing, and collecting knives and guns. He was a member of First Baptist Church of Pineville.

Gene Smith

Gene Smith, 71, Joplin, passed away Sunday, May 22, 2011 from injuries sustained in the Joplin tornado. Gene was born November 24, 1939 in Webb City. He had lived in the Joplin-Webb City area all his life.

Gene was employed with Union Pacific Railroad for 24 years. He was a U.S. Army veteran and served 29 years with the National Guard and Naval Reserves. Gene was a member of Webb City Church of the Nazarene. He was also a member of Joplin Eagles Lodge, and the Greater Joplin U.S. Bowling Congress. He loved Webb City Football and the St. Louis Cardinals.

Gene married Donna Gunlock August 10, 1973 in Webb City and she survives.

Additional survivors include one son, Jeff Smith, Joplin, one daughter, Robin Shember and husband James, Webb City, and two grandsons, Nick and John Shember.

Judy Smith

Judy Lee Smith, 71, Joplin, passed away Thursday, May 26, 2011 at Cassville Healthcare and Rehabilitation.

Judy was born May 30, 1939 in Webb City, the daughter of Lloyd and Fern (Cromer) Brown Carter.

Judy spent most of her life in Joplin and owned and operated Second Hand Rose Consignment Store. She was a member of St. Paul United Methodist Church and graduated from Joplin High School with the class of 1957. She enjoyed reading, watching movies, playing Trivial Pursuit and bridge as well as shopping.

Judy is survived by two daughters, Nikki Oliver, Joplin and Jill Walkinshaw, Kansas City; four grandchildren, Jamie, Sally, Amon and Jesse; three great-grandchildren, Robbie, Eric and Havaah; one brother, Cokher Carter and wife Claudia, Joplin; one sister, Garlanda Davis, St. Louis; one aunt, Emma

Edie, Bowerston, Ohio; five nieces and nephews; and a lifelong friend, Linda Cupp, Joplin.

Judy was preceded in death by her parents.

Nicholaus Smith

From the Joplin Globe

Nicholaus Smith, 23, Joplin, worked for Ozark Technical Ceramics. He moved to Joplin in February from his hometown of St. Louis. He and his brother, Chris, were interested in music and video production and were preparing to open their own entertainment business as well as a hot dog stand. He had also recently become engaged. His friends called him "Chill."

Shyrell Smith

Shyrell was born January 13, 1943 and passed away Sunday, May 22, 2011.

Shyrell was last known to be living in Fredonia, Kansas.

She graduated from Altoona Rural High School in 1961. She graduated from Phillips University, College of the Bible,

Enid, Oklahoma, in 1965 with a degree in religion. In 1968, she received a Bachelor of Science Degree in Nursing from the University of Kansas. Shyrell received an advanced degree in Education Specialist and Human Resource Development in 2003 at Pittsburg State University. She was working as a nurse at Freeman East.

Lois Sparks

From Mason-Woodard Mortuary

Lois L. Sparks, 92, Joplin, went to be with her Lord and Savior Sunday May 22, 2011, from injuries sustained in the Joplin tornado.

Lois was born June 8, 1918 in Wichita, Kansas, the daughter of Mable and Will Schnoor.

She married Wallace Sparks April 26, 1936 in Wichita; they were married for 71 years. He preceded her in death February 14, 2007. She was member of the Eastern Star and a devout member of the Baptist Church, attending both Harmony Heights Baptist Church and later Eastview Baptist Church, working many years in childhood evangelism.

She is survived by her son, Ralph Sparks and wife Charlene, Joplin; four grandchildren, Jerry and Nanda Sparks, Joplin, Travis and Cassie Sparks, Joplin, Jodi and Kevin Austin, Springfield, and Ron Sparks, Tulsa, Oklahoma; and eight great-grandchildren.

Steven Stephens

From Parker Mortuary

Steven J. Haack Stephens, 28, passed away Sunday, May 22, 2011 as a result of injuries sustained in the tornado.

Steven was born March 17, 1983 in Holdreg, Nebraska, son of Tracy Haack, Geneva, Nebraska and Tina Salsbury Davis, Savannah. He was a construction worker and a Baptist.

He was preceded in death by a daughter, Aspen Haack Stephens, sister-in-law, Meranda Stephens, grandmothers, Linda Salbury and Shirley Clevenger.

Survivors include his wife,

Tasha Stephens, Troy, Kansas; children, Dayton Stephens, Alexander Haack Stephens, Alaris Haack Stephens; father, Fred Piska, Wichita, Kansas; sister, Kali Haack, Savannah; grandfather, Mike Salsbury, Rockaway Beach; mother-in-law, Terrie Stephens; father-in-law, Rusty Stephens; aunts, Nora Campbell, Robin Sisk; nephews, Juan DeDios, Zeke Soldanels, niece, Lyrik Stout; uncles, Steve Salsbury, Michael Salsbury; many other family members.

Betty Stogsdill

From Parker Mortuary

Betty J. Stogsdill, 83, Joplin, passed away Wednesday, June 8, 2011 at Cox South Hospital in Springfield as a result of injuries sustained in the Joplin tornado.

Betty was born April 10, 1928 in Joplin, daughter of the late George Toops and Gertrude Shelton Toops. She graduated from Carl Junction High School and attended Joplin Junior College before receiving her bachelor's degree from DePaul University in Chicago. She also received a master's degree from

Northwestern University, and a second master's from University of Chicago.

She was a high school teacher for many years in Chicago. She moved to Joplin in 1994 and was a substitute teacher for the Joplin School District for many years before retiring. She was a member of Forest Park Baptist Church, Joplin Woman's Club and was active in several Joplin bridge clubs. She loved the arts and theater.

In addition to her parents, Betty was preceded in death by her husband, Ralph Stogsdill who died April 30, 2004; sisters, Cora Kope, Ruth Haliday, Alice Marley, and Leatha Tiberghien.

Survivors include a sister, Wanetta King and husband David, Joplin, several nieces and nephews.

Ralph Stover

From Paul Thomas Funeral Home

Ralph Gilbert Stover, 85, passed away Friday, June 3, 2011 at the Miami Hospital after being in St. John's Hospital during the Joplin tornado.

Ralph was born July 16, 1925 to Louisa (Porter) and Chauncey Stover in Columbus, Kansas. Ralph married Betty Hudson August 25, 1946 in Treece, Kansas. She survives of the home.

Ralph worked in the floor covering business since 1954. He started Stover's Floor Covering in 1970 and retired in 2001. However, he continued to go to the store to "supervise" each morning.

He was a member of First United Methodist Church. He loved woodworking and gardening.

The family would like to give special thanks to Nurse Bekki Johnson at St John's Hospital and Nurse Kathy Hicks at Miami Hospital for the special care they gave him. Also, to John Seay for his help carrying our dad to safety after the tornado.

Ralph is survived by his wife, Betty; one son and his wife, Rodney and Becky Stover, Miami; two daughters, Virginia Foster, Jenks and Belinda and husband Rod Pfeiffer, Pryor, Oklahoma; nine grandchildren, Lesley Whitewater, Greg Stover, Dusty Stover, Brian Foster, Rusty Stover, Levi Pfeiffer, Jason Scott,

Kim Harmon and Ashlee Stover; and eight great-grandchildren and many nieces and nephews.

He was preceded in death by his parents and four brothers.

Gregan Sweet

Gregan Douglas Sweet, 59, Joplin, passed away from injuries sustained in the tornado May 22, 2011.

Born Jan. 6, 1952, in Joplin, he was the son of the late Nathan and Evelyn Johnson Sweet. He was a member of Citywide Christian Fellowship in Joplin and worked as a carpenter in residential building for many years of his life. He also did prison ministry with the Bill Glass Team. He was a member of Citywide Christian Fellowship in Joplin. He also did prison ministry with the Bill Glass Team.

He married Vickie L. Fort July 7, 1977, in Joplin; she survives.

Other survivors include a daughter, Laramie Sweet, of the home; a son, Paul Sweet, Tulsa, Oklahoma; one brother, Byran Sweet and his wife, Kuemok, Gladstone; one stepbrother, Terry Jackson, Dallas, Texas; and three stepsisters, Janet Fletcher, Neosho; Nancy Woodley, Neosho; and Cathy Jackson, Dallas. Gregan is also survived by his special brother and sister in Christ, Brett Fowler and his sister, Laurie Fowler.

Jeff Taylor

Jeff Taylor, 31, Kansas City, died Friday, June 3, 2011, as a result of injuries sustained while assisting in the rescue efforts in Joplin.

Born March 7, 1980, in Cameron to Patricia (Steelman) Bestgen and Steve Taylor, Jeff graduated from Harrisonville High School in 1998 and attended Missouri Southern State University, receiving his POST Certificate in 2001. He began his law enforcement career in Webb City, and then served on Platte County Sheriff Department, before his current post with Riverside Department of Public Safety where he held the positions of Firefighter, SWAT, Master Patrol

Officer, K9 Officer, and Field Training Officer.

Jeff was nominated and awarded Officer of the Year from Riverside DPS in 2008.

On August 7, 1999, Jeff married his college sweetheart, Kelly Hawkins, in St. James. Jeff loved to golf, coached his son's soccer team, played softball with his friends from Riverside DPS, and always put his family first.

Jeff was preceded in death by his sister, Jodi Lynn Gitthens; a niece, Trinity Faith Roberts; and a grandfather, Jefferson Steelman.

Survivors include his wife Kelly and sons, Caden and Cameron of Kansas City; parents, Steve and Rose Taylor, New Bloomfield; mother, Patricia Bestgen, Osborn; sister, Staci Roberts, Overland Park, Kansas; two brothers, Zach and Nick Bestgen, Osborn; grandparents, Gerald and Phyllis Taylor Cameron; Ernest and Phyllis Denny Maysville; Betty Jean Jacobsen, Roeland Park, Kan.; as well as many aunts, uncles, nieces, nephews and cousins.

Kayleigh Teal

From Paul Thomas Funeral Home

Kayleigh Savannah Teal, Seneca, 16, went to be with Jesus May 22, 2011 in Joplin.

Kayleigh was born March 22, 1995 in Bamburg, Germany to Robert Eugene Teal and Karen Sue (Stanton) Long. She attended Bluejacket and Welch Schools early and was attending Seneca High School where she loved mixed choir. Kayleigh was employed as a waitress in the Joplin Pizza Hut and was of the Christian Faith.

She is survived by her father Robert and wife Karen Louise Teal, Pittsburg, Kansas; mother Karen Sue Long and stepfather Shaun Higginbothan, Seneca; three brothers Rowdy Teal, Pittsburg; Trey Saltsman, Seneca; and Jordan Ray Bicknell, Pittsburg; four sisters Shandra Renee Bicknell, Pittsburg, Brandi Sue Moore, Pittsburg, Tayler Higginbothan, Seneca and Dakoata Higginbothan, Seneca and paternal grandparents William and Judy Fromm, Oklahoma City, Oklahoma; and Richard Teal, Bluejacket, Oklahoma, maternal grandmother Betty Stanton (Davis) and paternal great grandmother Margaret Ann Teal, Chetopa, Kansas.

Heather Terry

Heather Leigh Terry, 36, Joplin, died May 22, 2011 from injuries sustained in the May 22, 2011, tornado.

Heather was born February 16, 1975 in Aurora, attended Aurora Schools and was a lifelong area resident. She worked at La Barge in Joplin.

Heather married Michael Duane Terry March 20, 2010 at Miami, Oklahoma and he survives.

Additional survivors include her mother, Vicky Baum, Joplin; her father, Rex Baum, Carterville; her sister, Erin Baum-Smith, Joplin; two nieces, Bayleigh Smith and Ashleigh Smith and her maternal grandmother, Juanita Channel, Granby.

John Thomas

From Bath-Naylor Funeral Home

John L. Thomas Jr. 40, Joplin, died 5:30 p.m. Sunday May 22, 2011 in the tragic tornado that hit Joplin.

John was born April 27, 1971 in Wichita, Kansas, the son of John L. Thomas Sr. and Kathie S. Campbell; he was a lifelong resident of the area and attended area schools.

On December 1, 1990, he married Lori Stevens in Frontenac, Kansas; they later divorced.

On April 27, 2002 he married Carin Neely in Riverton, Kansas; they later divorced.

John worked for Jasper Products in Joplin; he was of the Christian Faith; enjoyed golfing, gambling, fishing, hunting, football, playing catch and was known to love work.

Survivors include his parents, children Caleb W. Thomas, Girard, Kansas; Kevin W. Neely, Joplin; Adam L. Thomas, Girard, Kansas; and Joel B. Thomas, Boston, Massachusetts; step-mother Chris Thomas; maternal grandmother Juanita Campbell, Pittsburg, Kansas and numerous aunts, uncles and cousins.

He was preceded in death by a brother Christopher D. Thomas, maternal grandfather Herman Campbell, paternal grandparents Lewin A. and Twilla I. Thomas.

Sandra Thomas

From Ulmer Funeral Home

Sandra Thomas, 55, Carthage passed away Sunday, May 22, 2011. She was born July 30, 1955 in Berryville, Arkansas. She was the daughter of Alvin and Betty Thomas.

Sandra was an employee of Justin Boots for the past 20 years. She was a 1974 Carthage High School graduate.

Sandra was a member of Joplin Full Gospel Church where she volunteered in the nursery. Sandra is survived by her parents and one sister Latina Puebla.

Zach Treadwell

From Parker Mortuary

Zachary Delbert Treadwell, 9, Joplin, passed away Sunday, May 22, 2011 as a result of injuries sustained in the tornado.

Zach was born August 10, 2001 in Joplin and was a third-grade student at Emerson Elementary School. He loved to be outdoors, playing soccer was a passion, and fishing. He was described as "all boy" with the dirt and scrapes that come with that. He was a big fan of Pokemon, loved to sing, and had a mature sense of humor, always telling elaborate stories, or a joke.

Zach was preceded in death by grandparents, Manuel Berumen and Gerald Treadwell.

Survivors include his mother, Crystal Cogdill; brother, David Arreola'Berumen; sister, Whitley Treadwell; father, Jeffery Treadwell all of Joplin; grandparents, Rose Cast, Pittsburg, California, Glenda and Grady Carmical, Diamond; great-grandparents,

Lupe Berumen, Pittsburg, California; several uncles and aunts including Jessica Torres, Pittsburg.

Margaret Tutt

From Parker Mortuary

Margaret Ann Tutt, 92, passed away May 22, 2011 at her home in Joplin. She was born November 24, 1918 in Belvidere, Kansas. Her husband, Jack H. Tutt died on April 8, 1973.

She is survived by her daughter, Mary Ann Christman and son-in-law, David Christman; two grandchildren Mary C. Sgroi and husband Fred, Prairie Village, Kansas; Dr. Jim Christman and wife Debbie, Joplin; two great-grandchildren, Annie and Katie Sgroi; two great-step-grandchildren, James Brown and wife, Lauren, Sandy Brummitt and husband Justin; five great-great-step-grandchildren; one brother, Col. William T. Unger of Sunrise, Florida.

Margaret Ann was a volunteer worker with the Blind Association, Meals on Wheels, Crosslines and Friends of the Library.

Michael Tyndall

Michael Eugene Tyndall, 33, Joplin, was a victim of the recent storms. Michael was born in Joplin March 11, 1978 and was a graduate of Joplin High School Class of 1997. He was an equipment operator in construction.

Michael was preceded in death by his father, Dennis J. Tyndall Sr.; maternal grandparents, Victor and Mary DeCastro; paternal grandparents, Westin Fenton and Josephine Tyndall; and one sister, Victoria Lois.

He is survived by three children, Kaylee and Carson Tyndall, Sarcoxie, and Arron Tyndall, Joplin; his mother and stepfather, Margie and Ronnie King, Duenweg; grandparents Ronald and Charlotte King, Duenweg; two brothers, Dennis Tyndall, Joplin, and Phillip King, Cassville; one sister, Amanda Sheehan, Neosho; and numerous aunts, uncles, nieces, and nephews.

Dee Vanderhoofven

From Parker Mortuary

Darian "Dee" Vanderhoofven, 44, left behind her mortal life Sunday, May 22, 2011, in the rubble of her home caused by the tornado that evening.

Dee was born June 28, 1966, to Gaylord "Charley" Weaver and Annette Denny Weaver in Dillon, Montana.

Darian moved to Joplin in 2004, and met her future husband, David A. Vanderhoofven. Dee and David were married February 11, 2010 at Jack and Nancy Dawson's log chapel in Webb City. It was a wish come true for Dee.

Her second wish, to be a mom, was fulfilled on March 28, 2010, with the birth of her son, Joshua Dean Vanderhoofven, at Freeman Hospital in Joplin. Tragically, Joshua accompanied his mother in death on May 22, 2011. Darian's third wish was unable to be honored.

Dee was passionate about organ, eye and tissue donation and served as the Joplin Regional Manager for the Heartland Lion's Eye Bank. She strongly encouraged family and friends to become designated donors and she had also wished to donate.

However, the tragic circumstances of her death prevented that from occurring.

Darian was an accomplished cook and loved to entertain, host a party or bake a theme cake for someone special. Dee collected art glass media. She was an animal lover and took in strays. Dee held a deep belief in her Lord and Savior, Jesus, and was a member of Wildwood Baptist Church in Joplin. She was an open, easygoing person who enjoyed making people laugh.

Dee loved to visit, work in her garden or reminisce. Darian's path in life crossed so very many others, and she was loved by many. She will be greatly missed by all of us. Aunt Dee was held in especially high regard by the children of her siblings, and she had favored status in all their lives. They have been extremely sorrowed by her loss.

They are Braedon and Jesse Day, Tucson, Arizona., Jason Weaver, Laramie, Wyoming; Kaili Holloway and Megan

Weaver, Casper, Wyoming; Kaden and Braylon Weaver, Kingman, Arizona; and James Weaver, Racine.

Darian is also survived by her husband, David A. Vanderhoofven, and two stepchildren, Megan and Brian Vanderhoofven, Joplin; her father, Gaylord "Charley" Weaver and his wife, Linda, Springdale, Arkansas.; her father and mother-in-law, David S. and Marilynn Vanderhoofven, Arvada, Colorado.; her sister, Genelle Day and husband John, Tucson; her brothers, Patrick Weaver and wife Amanda, Kingman, Howard "Dean" Weaver, Butte, Montana., and Dan Weaver and his wife, Cindy, of Racine; her stepbrother, Jeff Neal and his wife, Stephanie, and their children, Blake, Taylor and Tanner Neal, of Springdale, Arkansas.; brother and sister-in-law Philip and Sue Vanderhoofven, Kailuah, Hawaii.; John and Abby Vanderhoofven, El Paso, Texas; and Nathan Vanderhoofven, Arvada, Colorado; and sister-in-law Daneen Weaver, Casper.

Josh Vanderhoofven

From Parker Mortuary

Joshua Dean Vanderhoofven, 14 months, departed his worldly walk Sunday, May 22, 2011, in the arms of his mother, as a result of that evening's tornado in Joplin.

Joshua was born at Freeman Hospital in Joplin March 28, 2010, to Darian Dee Vanderhoofven and David A. Vanderhoofven.

Joshua was a gift from God to both his parents. He was nearly always happy and smiling. He enjoyed watching Sponge Bob with his father and playing in his bounce swing. He had a voracious appetite. Joshua had just started to walk and liked to explore his home. He was the apple of his mother's eye and he will be missed by all of his family.

Joshua is survived by his father, David, of the home; and his grandparents, David S. and Marilynn Vanderhoofven, of Aurora, Colo.; Gaylord "Charley" Weaver and Linda Weaver, of Springdale, Ark. He was dearly loved by all of his mother Darian's survivors as well.

Miguel Vasquez-Castillo

From the Joplin Globe

Miguel Vasquez-Castillo, 29, Joplin, was born in Mexico, where most of his family still lives. He was one of four children and described as the "life of the party" by Monica Lopez, who worked with him at the El Vaquero restaurant in Joplin. His girlfriend, Maria Alvarez-Torres, also died in the tornado.

Dean Wells

From Simpson Funeral Home

M. "Dean" Wells, 59, Webb City, passed away Sunday, May 22, 2011 at Home Depot.

Dean was born August 31, 1951 at Ft. Carson, Colorado to parents Paul and Jean (Hall) Wells. He served his country in the U.S. Army.

Dean married Margaret Sue Simons May 23, 1969 in Boulder, Colorado, his death coming one day before their 42nd anniversary. Sue survives of the home.

Dean was a member of the First Christian Church of Webb City where he sang with his church group every Tuesday at area nursing homes or with ill members of the church and community. He loved music and was very adept at whistling. He recorded records of his whistling and often sung and whistled for his church. Dean was a Department Head at Home Depot where he saved several lives May 22, 2011 and ultimately lost his life in the process.

Anyone who knew him knew this was his style of living, helping others first.

Dean is also survived by his daughters, DeAnne Mancini and husband John, Tucson, Arizona; and Paulla Wells, Hot Springs, Arkansas; his mother, Jean Wells, Tucson, four grandchildren, Ashley Gietz, Staten Island, New York; Anthony and Laura Larkin, Hot Springs and Dillon Gietz, Tucson; and a great grandson Maximus Michael Jaslow.

Tiera Whitley

Tiera Nicole Whitley, 20, Fort Scott, Kansas, died Sunday May 22, 2011 as the result of the Joplin tornado.

She was born September 20, 1990 at Overland Park, Kansas, the daughter of Jerry and Mary Johnston Whitley. She attended Prescott, Kansas Elementary School and graduated from Jayhawk Linn High School in 2009.

Tiera was a talented artist and photographer and enjoyed fishing and woodworking. She was employed as a shift manager at Taco Bell in Fort Scott. She was preceded in death by her maternal grandfather, Forrest "Bud" Johnston.

She is survived by mother and father, Mary and Jerry Whitley, Prescott, a sister Shelby Whitley, a brother Joseph Whitley, Prescott, maternal grandmother Ladean Kempinger and husband Karl, paternal grandparents, Eldred and Carol Whitley, and maternal great grandmother Virginia Dozier,

and eternal friend Ashley Stark. Tiera was her entire family's pride and joy.

Douglas Williams

From White Funeral Home

Douglas Earl Williams, 52, Purdy, passed away Friday, June 3, 2011 at Cox South Hospital in Springfield from injuries sustained in the Joplin Tornado.

Mr. Williams, son of Dozier and Mattie (Ross) Williams, was born October 28, 1958 in Nacogdoches, Texas. Douglas was raised in the Nacogdoches area and moved to Purdy in 2005.

He was united in marriage to Leah Nance February 13, 2007 in Cassville. Together they enjoyed raising horses, and Douglas loved spending time in his garden with his dog, Tuff.

Survivors include his wife, Leah Williams, Purdy; one daughter, Randi Williams and her companion, Jeff Freeman, Purdy; four stepdaughters, Marilyn, Katie, Jackie, and Kat Hughes, Purdy; two brothers, Rex Williams, and his wife, Lisa, Garrison, Texas, and Donald Ray Williams and his wife,

Bernadette, Garrison; two sisters, Jeannie Williams, Nacogdoches, Texas, and Bonita Finley, and her husband, David, Hutchins, Texas; a mother-in-law, Leona Nance, Berryville, Arkansas; two brothers-in-law, Monty Nance, Eagle Rock, and Mark Nance, Oak Grove, Arkansas; three sisters-in-law, Deborah Hammons, Newberry Park, California, Carla Dearing, of Gentry, Arkansas, and Samantha Minton, of Cassville; and numerous nieces and nephews.

Regina Williams

From Knell Mortuary

Regina Mae Bloxham Williams, 55, Joplin, passed away Sunday, May 22, 2011 from injuries sustained in the Joplin tornado.

Regina Mae Kirkpatrick was born August 9, 1955 in Reno, Nevada, the daughter of George F. Kirkpatrick and Pauline (Porter) Kirkpatrick. She was a graduate of Hugg High School, Reno, Nevada and attended the University of Nevada for three years.

She married Leslie Lynn Williams October 2, 2009; he survives.

Regina worked for AT&T as a customer service representative. She moved from Nevada to Ozark in 1992, then to Carthage and to Joplin in 2002. She was a member of the AT&T Pioneers.

Survivors include her husband, Leslie Williams; three daughters, Jennifer (Chad) Bybee, Strafford; Catrina Bloxham, Joplin and Miranda Lynn Williams, Lebanon; two sons, Kirk Bloxham, Joplin, and James Paul Williams, Springfield; one sister, Candace Harrison, Las Vegas, Nevada; her mother, Pauline Kirkpatrick, Joplin; two grandchildren and Edgar Allen Bloxham, Sacramento, California. She was preceded in death by her father, George Kirkpatrick.

Zach Williams

From Bradford Funeral Home

Zachary Allen Williams was born June 19, 1998 at Fort Leonard Wood Memorial Community

Hospital in Fort Leonard Wood, to Franklin Eugene Williams and Tammy Renee Clark Niederhelman. He lost his life in the tornado at Joplin Sunday, May 22, 2011 making his age 12 years 11 months and 3 days.

Zach was a student at East Middle School in Joplin where he attended seventh grade. He attended the Calvary Baptist Church in Joplin. Zach was a happy person who would strike up a conversation with anyone. He enjoyed hot wheel cars, Legos, riding his bike, and spending time with his friends. He was looking forward to his summer vacation, so he could spend more time with family and read more of his favorite books. He is preceded in death by his great grandpas, Howard Jackson and R.L. Clark, great-great-grandfather Pearl Jaco, great-grandmother Maxine Clark, great-great grandmother Gladys Jaco.

Zach is survived by his mother Tammy Niederhelman and husband Tony, Joplin; his father Frank Williams and wife Valerie, Mayesville, North Carolina, brother Andy Williams, Mayesville, North Carolina,

grandparents Earnest and Kathy Clark, Summersville; grandparents Jim and Kathleen Williams, Summersville; Helen and Frank Jones, Terre Haute, Indiana; great-grandmother Lillie Jackson, Summersville; uncles and aunts, Chad and Billie Clark and children, Austin and Brittani and future son-in-law Levi, Neosho; Jim Williams, Tulsa, Oklahoma; Warren Williams and wife Vicki, St. Louis, Missouri, Cindy Heller, Springfield; several great-uncles and aunts, cousins and friends.

Charles Writer

Charles William Writer, 74, Purdy, passed away Sunday, May 22, 2011, in the Joplin tornado.

He was born October 29, 1936, in Barry County, the son of Herbert and Georgia M. (Pryor) Writer. On February 20, 1954, he was united in marriage to Peggy Hyde (now Peggy Dalton), and to this union one son and one daughter were born.

On December 1, 1978, in Miami, Oklahoma, he married Gerda (Ehrmann) Henderson who survives.

Also surviving are four sons, Rick Writer and his wife, Peggy, Butterfield; Jim Henderson and his wife, Linda, Monett; John Henderson and his wife, Terri, Exeter; Kenny Henderson and his wife, Misty, Collinsville, Oklahoma; four daughters, Rena Kennedy and her husband, Gary, Lampe; Beverly Bacon and her husband, Joe, Cassville; Debbie Henderson and Marty Wolf, Butterfield; and Brenda Fryman and her husband, Rob, Eureka; one brother, Eugene Writer and his wife, Mava, Cassville; two sisters, Yvonne Stumpff and her husband, Max, Cassville; and Linda Mitchell and her husband, Richard, Washburn; 18 grandchildren and 22 great grandchildren.

Preceding him in death were his parents and a grandson, Chris Henderson.

Charles received his education at Sparks and Victory rural schools and Cassville and Southwest High Schools. From April 1, 1954, until December 18, 1964, he served in the United States Navy.

After his discharge from the Navy, he worked several years for Pryor Motor Company. He then owned and operated the DX Gas Station, High Point Trucking Company and a transport truck leasing company, retiring around ten years ago. Most of his life was spent cattle farming, which he loved. He also enjoyed his horses.

About the Authors

Randy Turner was an eighth grade English teacher at Joplin East Middle School and was a reporter and editor at southwest Missouri newspapers. He has authored 12 non-fiction books, including The Buck Starts Here: Harry S. Truman and the City of Lamar; Lost Angels: The Murders of Rowan Ford and Doug Ringler, Silver Lining in a Funnel Cloud: Greed, Corruption and the Joplin Tornado and Let Teachers Teach, and three novels, Small Town News, Devil's Messenger and No Child Left Alive. Turner is the editor of the Turner Report and Inside Joplin blogs.

John Hacker is the former managing editor of The Carthage Press and has covered Missouri and Kansas news for three decades. A graduate of Missouri Southern State University, Hacker has won numerous awards for reporting and photography. He currently freelances for Carthage News Online and The Joplin Globe.

Made in the USA
Middletown, DE
09 October 2023

40493230R00295